LIQUID LIFE

Fig. 1. Hieronymus Bosch, *Ship of Fools* (1490–1500)

The Center for Transformative Media, Parsons School of Design, is a transdisciplinary media research initiative bridging design and the social sciences, and dedicated to the exploration of the transformative potential of emerging technologies upon the foundational practices of everyday life across a range of settings.

First published in 2019 by CTM Documents Initiative,
an imprint of punctum books, Earth, Milky Way.
https://punctumbooks.com

ISBN-13: 978-1-950192-17-5 (print)
ISBN-13: 978-1-950192-18-2 (ePDF)

DOI: 10.21983/P3.0246.1.00

LCCN: 2019935887
Library of Congress Cataloging Data is available from the Library of Congress

Book design: Vincent W.J. van Gerven Oei
Cover image and the figures in Chapter 09 'Liquid Apparatus' are by Simone Ferrancina based on original laboratory footage of Bütschli droplets taken by Rachel Armstrong at The Centre for Fundamental Living Technology in Odense, Denmark, 2010. All drawings in Chapter 11 'Liquid Notations: A Common Language of Transitions' are by Simone Ferracina, Newcastle University, United Kingdom, 2017. Photograph on pp. 508–9 by Rachel Armstrong of headlamp light scattered from mineral surfaces at the Smallcleugh mine in Nenthead, taken during the Cthonic workshop onsite field study on 20 July 2017. Photograph on pp. 514–15 by Rachel Armstrong, from the *Being (In)human* performance, advertised as *Unquiet Earth: From Victoria Tunnel to Quantum Tunnelling* that took place in the Victoria Tunnel, Newcastle-upon-Tyne on 17 November 2018.

HIC SVNT MONSTRA

Rachel Armstrong

Liquid Life
On Non-Linear Materiality

with contributions by
Simone Ferracina & Rolf Hughes

Contents

I. CONTEMPLATION

II. DETERMINISM UNBOUND

III. HYPERCOMPLEXITY

IV. MAKING

V. BEING

VI. TRANSITIONING

*This drop, what will come of it?
Will it be a plant fiber, the light
and silky down that one would not
take for a living being, but which
already is nothing less than the
first-born hair of a young goddess,
the sensitive and loving hair that
is so well named Venus' hair fern?
This has nothing to do with fables,
this is natural history. This hair
of two natures (plant and animal) into which the drop of water
thickens, it truly is the eldest child
of life.* (Debré 1998, 169)

Exquisite Matter

We are life; the most exquisite condensations of sentient matter/energy in the universe. While most of the cosmic substance is dark; we shine. Unstable and theatrical, we are temporary bodies, existing as whirlpools, transformers and shape-shifters in relation to our surroundings. Although the physical effects of the living matter we're made from seem inconsequential, when compared with the material events that constitute our expanding cosmos, our rare experiences confer a quality of 'being' that is unique. This is neither a perceptual position, nor a question of material performance, but a value-loaded, unfathomably complex choreography of events, states of existence and encounters, from which we can never fully disentangle ourselves. An inescapably subjective experience, the definitions of life lie beyond the reach of the tools of science to fully rationalise, or explain. Despite our yearning to 'solve' these riddles, life continues to surprise us.

Author's Note

I am fascinated by the way creatures work and live together. My earliest recollections are in the back yard, with a series of empty jam jars, collecting all kinds of creepy-crawlies and observing how they responded to change—whether a helpful handful of soil, or a thimble of water could help them live peacefully together with adversaries, like spiders and wasps. These naive experiments failed spectacularly and each evening, my mother would sigh deeply, as she emptied out my drowned worlds over the fence.

As I grew, my curiosity for life's character never left me. Since synthetic biology, which proposes to design and engineer with nature, was not on the curriculum at university, I studied medicine instead. During a sabbatical in India, I worked in a leprosy colony with a hand surgeon who performed tendon transfers that would restore movement to important muscles by sacrificing the function of not so important ones. Through the rehabilitation process, I saw how someone's quality of living could be transformed through simple modifications. This exceeded their anatomical reconfiguration and extended to their social and environmental reintegration, so people once excluded from a community through their illness, could now live joyfully, bring in an income and raise a family.

I began to see how our accounts of the living world shaped our relationship with it. Modern science has contributed to many positive narratives that direct our cultural discourses, values and practices, but at the same time, it has also led to unhelpful truisms. While I had read Richard Dawkins under the table in biology lessons at school, by the time I was working on hospital wards, the whole notion of biological determinism that underpinned the idea of the 'selfish gene' was deeply problematic. It endorsed the idea of social inequality as a biological 'fitness', which trapped people in cycles of poor health and despair. Repositioning actors differently within established hierarchies of order — such as replacing men with women, or one race with another, and vice versa — was also not enough to bring about real change, as these inversions simply reasserted the same kinds of inequality they proposed to address through a different set of actors. To empower alternative futures, different technical platforms and alternative ways of interpreting findings are needed, so we can find ways of thriving together and defeat the incredible odds against our survival at the start of the Sixth Great Extinction.

Searching for testable narratives to underpin new stories of life, I wanted to find an experimental field that was very poorly inhabited by the humanities and awkwardly articulated by the sciences. The prebiotic context of lifelike events presented an ideal opportunity, as they operate without the cultural and historical tropes that frame biological narratives, where lifelike chemical assemblages made from programmable* materials such as droplets, clays, crystals and nucleotides, can perform in ways that are not already framed by expectations of species, gender, function, form or aesthetics.

In 2008, I began to work with dynamic droplets in an *origin of life* context. The droplets, or protocells, were model systems for early cells that did not possess any DNA. Exhibiting strikingly lifelike features, such as being able to move around their environment and interact with each other, they also provided a platform through which a theory and practice of protolife based in material phenomena, could be developed and tested. However, the conceptual framing of these models of early non-biological life were already framed by the logic and atomistic construction principles of machines. For example, dynamic oil droplets were conceived as 'soft robots', which meant that all outcomes were interpreted according to a mechanistic worldview, referring to the agency of chemical assemblages as actuators, their material

---

*   In this sense, 'programmable' infers a degree of agency and decision-making acting within the material system, which is typical of natural computing.

expressions as manufacturing processes and their organisational abilities as (computer) programs (PACE Report 2008).

Liquid life started as a provocation and approach towards an alternative view of life than the *bête machine*. Originally it took the form of a 'cytoplasmic manifesto' (Gyimah 2009), which opposed notions of genetic determination by looking to the 'fluid' character of the body of a cell, by shifting the perspective on cellular control from gene to metabolism (De Lorenzo 2015). This is achieved by thinking through, and with, the characteristics of liquids, as well as bodies that are capable of flowing such as gases, amorphous solids and creatures. 'Liquid' also indicates more than a phase state, or an incompressible fluid that takes up the shape of its container, and references a metaphorical and technological platform that draws on the potentiality of dynamic, nonlinear systems. The ongoing extension of this research is centred on the Living Architecture project, which draws on the principles of liquid life to investigate a possible framework for approaching the construction of lifelike systems beyond established preconceptions of biological 'Just So Stories' (Gould and Lewontin 1979). I am coordinator of this project which is funded by the Horizon 2020 Research and Innovation Programme under EU Grant Agreement no. 686585, and brings together experts from the universities of Newcastle, UK; the West of England (UWE Bristol); Trento, Italy; the Spanish National Research Council in Madrid; LIQUIFER Systems Group, Vienna, Austria; and Explora, Venice, Italy and runs from April 2016 to April 2019. Envisioned as a freestanding, next-generation, selectively programmable bioreactor composed of integrated building blocks (microbial fuel cell, algae bioreactor and a genetically modified processor), which are developed as standardised building segments, or bricks, the project explores how metabolic agents that are carried by liquid flows can be orchestrated by advanced electronics and (bio)technologies to perform useful domestic 'work' such as making electricity, clean water, removing pollution and producing specific substances like inorganic phosphate.

This book is, therefore, an accumulation of thoughts, studies, propositions, experimental texts and transdisciplinary experiments that embody the story of liquid life. The aim is to establish a set of principles from which the design, engineering and construction of our living spaces may be brought to functionality, although a detailed study in relationship to architectural projects is not provided and will be the subject for further publications. Constituting an experimental platform that resists a linear narrative by fluidly interweaving quotes with personal observations, experiments, and creative writing, *Liquid Life: On Non-linear Materiality* comprises a *liquid manifesto* that stands 'against' the mechanical metaphor of the *bête machine*. Within its substance, it documents how native liquid technologies can support human development in ways that respect the innate liveliness, ingenuity, and fertility of our planet.

Preface

> Every epoch not only dreams the next, but dreaming impels
> it towards wakefulness. It bears its end within itself, and
> reveals it … by ruse. (Benjamin 1997, 176)

If we lived in a liquid world, the concept of a 'machine' would
make no sense. Liquid life explores an alternative organisational
infrastructure and experimental technological platform than
the machine, through which the living realm can be imagined,
observed and engaged. It sets the scene for an ecological approach to design and engineering our living spaces, whereby
the platforms for thinking and making increase the liveliness
of the living realm. Resisting the persuasive logic of Descartes'
Treatise of Man, where conceptual models of humans are made
up of separate elements, the body and (rational) soul that exist
independently of one another, it seeks an alternative integrative
synthesis between them.

> Cartesian dualism breaks man up into two complete sub-
> stances, joined to another no one knows how: on the one
> hand, the body which is only geometric extension; on the
> other, the soul which is only thought — an angel inhabit-
> ing a machine and directing it by means of the pineal gland
> (Maritain 1944, 179)

By removing any element of mentality, Descartes prepared the
way for mechanistically-functioning, 'brute' geometrical bodies*, to be better described by the *new physics,* while the character of the soul was outlined only its barest details. A mysterious substance where 'the animal spirits' flowed from the pineal
gland through a network of vessels (neurons) like fine air, it was

---

* In a letter to Richard Bentley, Isaac Newton uses the term 'brute' to refer to
an (inert) body (Newton 2017).

thought to be responsible for higher qualities of existence, like rational thought, which are distributed across the whole body's system of organs. While Descartes did not suggest a formal relationship between the body and soul, Gert-Jan Lokhorst describes Descartes as 'an interactionist who thought that there are causal interactions between events in the body and events in the soul ...' (Lokhorst 2005). This brilliantly simple act of dualism created the foundations of modernity where matter is without innate agency and therefore requires animation through external agencies such as energy, or computer programs.

> People — who themselves are in fact a process — are afraid of whatever is impermanent and always changing, which is why they have invented something that doesn't exist — invariability, and recognised that whatever is eternal and unchanging is perfect. (Tokarczuk 2010, 110)

Simultaneously a metaphor and technological apparatus of fluid forces, in this book the term 'liquid' is used both literally and metaphorically to denote a testable philosophy capable of producing new kinds of encounters and artefacts (Stengers 2000). Its 'new' materialist discourse embraces those aspects of the living realm that are relevant to an ecological era, which cannot be accounted for by the *bête machine,* and include the 'soul substance'. Although this conception of soul is not a literal derivation from Descartes' model, where the soul was gaseous*, it is compatible with the Aristotlean-Thomistic conception — as the substantial form of the human body which penetrates all living matter — and shares allegiances with Rosi Braidotti's notion of the posthuman†, since it is not an exclusively human agency.

---

*   Descartes' theories are actually inconsistent with contemporary anatomical theories of the brain, which established that the brain cavities, or ventricles, 'are filled with liquid rather than [an] air-like substance' (Lokhorst 2005).

†   Braidotti considers life as a monistic expression of a universe of matter, not as the property of individuals and points to a zoe-centric worldview that decentres bios as the measure of all things (Braidotti 2013, 61).

This book is a monster: an uncategorisiable treatise and transdisciplinary synthesis of text, quotations, provocations, images, conceptual slippages, voices, ideas, writing styles, events, poetry and narratives. As its arguments unfold, its loose body plan responds to its context — where sections support, contradict and hybridise with each other. An orchestrated cacophony, it is an ecological project — a *Babel in the making* — that, despite all its inherent conflicts and paradoxes, seeks to maintain its diplomatic coherence.

The compositional strategy of this book possesses a liquid character. Intermingling quotes within the body of discourse and observations, it emphasises conventions of thought and their contradictions, pertaining instead to an active investigation of the nature of lively matter by embracing its; scientific understanding; incorporation within creatures; associated technical developments; experimentation with nascent apparatuses; as well as the regenerative processes of decomposition. Through these juxtapositions, interminglings and fusions, new kinds of agencies begin to appear, where — for example — portraits of creatures with liquid and monstrous character, generate a counterpoint to the modern view of the *bête machine,* rendering it strange and unsuitable for a third-millennium notion of the living realm. Angels (see section 01.5) also act as vectors of liquid life, establishing a language with the potential for 'angelfication' (Lokhorst 2005; Maritain 1944, 179) that resists the reduction of its constituent concepts into a series of finite explanations.

In keeping with an alternative philosophy of the living realm, the parts of this book embody an alternative *life cycle* of events:

CONTEMPLATION This section constitutes an elemental pause, where the terms, key concepts and conditions used in this study are established that re-problematise the character of living matter.

DETERMINISM UNBOUND Enlightenment concepts; the world of machines, the hard question of matter and complexity, are outlined and juxtaposed against a third millennial understanding of the material realm including the concepts of quantum physics, non-linear phenomena and astronomical observations. These juxtapositions infer the existence of strange substances such as dark matter/energy, which cannot be readily described by the laws of classical physics and raise further questions about what kinds of discourses are 'missing' from our understanding of the living world.

HYPERCOMPLEXITY Through a study of states of existence that go beyond determinism, a portrait of life that is difficult to completely reduce, or solve, within a mechanistic discourse is presented, and juxtaposed with the notion of life as flâneur and the possibility of liquid creatures.

MAKING The possibilities for working with liquids as materials and technologies are explored.

BEING This chapter establishes the conditions for alternative ideas, languages and grammar that engage with the concepts of and encounters with liquid life. The Bütschli system is introduced as a liquid apparatus through which these proposals can be tested and directly engaged. Juxtaposed with quotations that speak to a range of known and imaginary phenomena, this section explores the transdimensionality and peculiarity of the living realm.

TRANSITIONING In this section, transdisciplinary practices engage with the concepts and experiences of liquid life. Rolf Hughes constructs an 'angelology' of language through the transformative invocations of prose poetry, while Simone Ferracina explores how graphical notations can help shape our concepts of metabolism, upcycling and designing with fluids.

REGENERATION Through a technique of composting, new encounters with liquid life are generated, where content is (re)worked and reconstituted from the present exploration.

Setting out to provoke change in thinking and dreaming by opening up hidden landscapes (real and imaginary) that may be accessed in uncertain times, this book creates an expanded portfolio for navigating unfathomable terrains and conjuring forth alternative futures than are possible through the Anthropocene's omnipresent paradigms. No formal conclusion to the experiments and explorations is proposed, which, by implication, would be a conversational dead end. Nor is there an attempt to fully resolve the strangeness of our existence with a distilled set of principles through which we may create life on our own terms. Rather, this 'monster' provides an alternative framework for observing the living realm than the *bête machine,* which through its (re)examination, sorting, ordering and valuing, aims to provoke new conversations about the nature of living matter and how we may imagine, construct and inhabit our living spaces at a time of ecocide.

Protean Prose

The following section is a starting point for an exploration of liquid life, where fourteen quotes by major voices in the study of life sciences depict different concepts of 'life'. These evolving and sometimes incongruous perspectives are viewed through the contemporary theories and technological developments that frame them — from the rejection of magical or divine influences, to mechanical principles of organisation, or extraterrestrial sources of 'information'. The (monstrous) contradictions exposed in this study, provide an initial embryology of thought, reaching into the core of our contemporary view of life and attesting that its nature remains very much unresolved.

Fourteen Portraits of Life

1   Ironically, the idea that life requires an explanation is a relatively new one. To the ancients, life simply was; it was a given; a first principle, in terms of which other things were to be explained. Life vanished as an explanatory principle with the rise of mechanics, when Newton showed that the mysteries of the stars and planets yielded to a few simple rules in which life played no part, when Laplace could proudly say 'Je n'ai pas besoin de cet hypothèse'; when the successive mysteries of nature seemed to yield to understanding based on inanimate nature alone: only then was it clear that life itself was something that had to be explained. — Robert Rosen (Rosen 1991, 11)

During the Enlightenment, the rise of secular atomism prompted investigators to provide a material explanation for the phenomenon of life. Through their rationalisation, the characteristics of living things needed to be accounted for by the properties of 'brute' (Bennett 2010b, 64) matter, without recourse to a vitalising agency. Although the concept of spontaneous generation was rejected, where non-living matter like dust could give rise to creatures like fleas, or dead flesh to maggots, Louis Pasteur demonstrated that life could not be accounted for by the forces of 'brute' matter alone. Concluding that vital agencies were involved in the making of living things, his experiments established a new rigour for the investigation of previously invisible forces (microbes) at work.

2   I took my drop of water from the immensity of creation, and I took it filled with that fecund jelly, that is, to use the language of science, full of the elements needed for the development of lower creatures. And then I waited, and I observed, and I asked questions of it, and I asked it to repeat the original act of creation for me; what a sight it

would be! But it is silent! It has been silent for several years, ever since I began these experiments. Yes! And it is because I have kept away from it, and am keeping away from it to this moment, the only thing that it has not been given to man to produce, I have kept away from it the germs that are floating in the air, I have kept away from it life, for life is the germ and the germ is life. — Louis Pasteur (quoted in Debré 1998, 169)

In the first part of the twentieth century, John Haldane conceived one of the most important scenarios about the origin of life on Earth, which offered a material explanation for chemical evolution that occured in Earth's early seas. Proposing that a hot dilute soup of inorganic substrates was capable of producing organic molecules, he freed the actions of matter from the need for vital forces (Tirard 2011).

3 Until about 150 years ago it was generally believed that living beings were constantly arising out of dead matter. Maggots were supposed to be generated spontaneously in decaying meat. In 1668 [Francesco] Redi showed that this did not happen provided insects* were carefully excluded. And in 1860 [Louis] Pasteur extended the proof to the bacteria which he had shown were the cause of putrefaction. It seemed fairly clear that all the living beings known to us originate from other living beings. At the same time [Charles] Darwin gave a new emotional interest to the problem. It had appeared unimportant that a few worms should originate from mud. But if man was descended from worms such spontaneous generation acquired a new significance. The origin of life on the earth would have been as casual an affair as the evolution of monkeys into man. Even if the latter stages of man's history were due to natural causes,

* The reference to insects is on account of their propensity to lay tiny eggs in organic matter, which then hatch and may be interpreted as 'proof' of spontaneous generation.

pride clung to a supernatural, or at least surprising, mode of origin for his ultimate ancestors. So it was with a sigh of relief that a good many men, whom Darwin's arguments had convinced, accepted the conclusion of Pasteur that life can originate only from life. It was possible either to suppose that life had been supernaturally created on earth some millions of years ago, or that it had been brought to earth by a meteorite or by micro-organisms floating through interstellar space. But a large number, perhaps the majority, of biologists, believed, in spite of Pasteur, that at some time in the remote past life had originated on earth from dead matter as the result of natural processes. — J.B.S. Haldane (Haldane 1929)

Contemporary explanations regarding how inert matter becomes animated, is framed by the discovery of deoxyribose nucleic acid (DNA), which provides organisational 'information'. Situated within the nucleus of all cells, the processes of life governed by this polymer are equated with computing algorithms, which instruct the operations of machines. The rise of modern computers coincided with the rise of molecular biology, which consolidated a fundamentally mechanistic approach to the nature of life, and even shared many terms of reference such as virus, code and program. This is situated in a deterministic universe, thrives on the existence of stable things, and only generates change through random errors occurring spontaneously in cellular information.

In the beginning was simplicity … Darwin's 'survival of the fittest' is really a special case of a more general law of survival of the stable. The universe is populated by stable things. A stable thing is a collection of atoms that is permanent enough, or common enough to deserve a name … — Richard Dawkins (Dawkins 2006, 15)

While mechanisms require self-similarity to perform their functions, molecular imaging techniques such as crystallography demonstrated that the precision of the *code of life* was not perfect — or omnipotent — and naturally produced variety within the limits of the system, effectively establishing life's operations were probabilistic, rather than deterministic.

5 All the work of the crystallographers serves only to demonstrate that there is only variety everywhere where they suppose uniformity … that in nature there is nothing absolute, nothing perfectly regular. — Georges-Louis Leclerc, Comte de Buffon (de Buffon 1783–1788, 433)

Increasingly, scientific investigation links living things to their environment that contextualises them in ways that exceed mechanistic explanation.

6 Living systems are units of interactions, they exist in an ambience. From a purely biological point of view they cannot be understood independently of that part of the ambience with which they interact: the niche; nor can the niche be defined independently of the living system that specifies it. — Humberto Maturana and Francisco Varela (Maturana and Varela 1928, 9)

Studies of gene expression reveal that the cell milieu does not slavishly carry out its programs but is actively enabled and modulated by a range of systems that include epigenetic processes and environmental contexts.

7 … life is defined as a material system that can acquire, store, process, and use information to organize its activities. In this broad view, the essence of life is information, but information is not synonymous with life. To be alive, a system must not only hold information but process and use it. It is the active use of information, and not the passive storage, that constitutes life. — Freeman Dyson (Dyson 2001)

Explanations for such fluid relationships are attributed to the properties of gelatinous matrixes such as protoplasm, nucleoplasm, cytoplasm and ectoplasm, which house 'metabolic' cellular systems capable of translating between internal imperatives and external circumstances.

8 Life is the mode of existence of albuminous bodies, and this mode of existence essentially consists in the constant self-renewal of the chemical constituents of these bodies. — Friedrich Engels (Engels 1947)

Expressions of living matter are thought to emerge from liquid environments, where a sophisticated and increasingly complex understanding of chemistry renders the synthesis of biological systems possible through a practice of *synthetic biology.*

9 The elementary phenomenon of life is the contact between an alimentary liquid and a cell. For the essential phenomenon of life is nutrition, and in order to be assimilated all the elements of an organism must be brought into a state of solution. Hence the study of life may be best begun by the study of those physico-chemical phenomena which result from the contact of two different liquids. Biology is thus but a branch of the physico-chemistry of liquids; it includes the study of electrolytic and colloidal solutions, and of the molecular forces brought into play by solution, osmosis, diffusion, cohesion and crystallisation. — Stéphane Leduc (Leduc 1911)

Accounts for the liveliness of matter, still cannot be completely resolved as a function of the individual properties and atoms and molecules by *looking downward for answers.* The continued pursuit of such an approach challenges the usefulness of the idea of 'life' at all.

10 Evolutionary biologists will sometimes suggest that origins is a subject different than the evolutionary history of life, but in so doing they reveal themselves as closet vitalists who assume that life is different than nonlife ... origins is merely one stage of the grand history of replicators, which have elaborated themselves over time from simple strings of nucleic acids to complex strings of nucleic acids surrounded by the diversity of biological bags that we see today... as with all science, such questions should be bounded by naturalism, to avoid the temptation to slide into the supernatural just because the natural is often frustrating. — Andrew Ellington (Ellington 2012)

In reaching the limits of classical science, ensuing nihilism returns investigations into living systems back to a pre-Enlightenment context, where it seems pointless to even consider their nature.

11 Life has always been there; it has always propagated itself in the shape of living organisms, from cells and from individuals composed of cells. Man used to speculate on the origin of matter, but gave that up when experience taught him that matter is indestructible and can only be transformed. For similar reasons, we never inquire into the origin of the energy of motion. And we may become accustomed to the idea that life is eternal, and hence that it is useless to inquire into its origin. — Svante August Arrhenius (Arrenhius 1908, 218)

While the character of life cannot be explained through the collective action of individual molecules alone, an appreciation of the dynamic ecology of matter/energy relationships, generates new questions and modes of investigation that produce recognisably lifelike phenomena.

12 ... we are literally inhabited by highly motile remnants of an ancient bacterial type that have become, in every sense, a part of ourselves. These thriving partial beings represent the physical basis of anima: soul, life, locomotion; an advocation of materialism in the crassest sense of the word. Put it this way: a purified chemical is prepared from brain and added to another purified chemical. These two chemicals — two different kinds of motile proteins — together crawl away, they locomote. They move all by themselves. Biochemists and cell biologists can show us the minimal common denominator of movement, locomotion. Anima. Soul. These moving proteins I interpret as the remains of the swimming bacteria incorporated by beings who became our ancestors as they became us. — Lynn Margulis (quoted in Brockman 2011)

Our capacity to manipulate and synthesise living agents from first principles and recruit them in a technological capacity increasingly relies on a better understanding of the flux of matter and context in which 'beings' exist. The Central Dogma whereby genetic codes alone, establish the fate of an organism, is giving way to alternative theories about how biological outcomes are shaped, specifically through the process of metabolism.

13 ... by looking at the genes we should know everything in biology, and by just modifying them one could re-program the behaviour of living systems at our ease. It is like bacteria were computers making computers, and just by replacing the program one could make them do things that they normally do not do. The interpretative frame that places all emphasis on genes has dominated much of the biological research agenda of recent decades and has been recently boosted by the ease of cheap DNA sequencing. But is such a focus on genes and DNA the ultimate way to go? After many years of trying to genetically re-program environmental bacteria for release as agents of in situ bioremediation of toxic pollutants, my candid answer is: no. And the one reason is that one cannot just play with DNA while ignoring chemistry and metabolism, let alone some principles of chemical engineering … This calls for a novel view (and possibly a fresh research agenda) in which metabolism has the leading role in the chain of biological command, opposite to the standard direction of the information flow in the canonical Central Dogma. — Victor de Lorenzo (de Lorenzo 2015)

Despite all that has been deduced and established through many advances in molecular science, and even with an in-depth knowledge of its ingredients, life still has not been built from scratch. Even the most sophisticated machines today are not autonomously self-producing agents, but workhorses for other agencies. The inability to recapitulate this aspect of life suggests that either assembling an organism from its components is unfeasibly hard, or that the ideas used to frame this process are fundamentally wrong.

14 … life on the Earth may be a miracle, or a freak, or an alien infection … in the fifties [it was anticipated that] … the answer to the origins of life would appear in some footnote to the answer to the question of how organisms work. Something much more will be needed. Something odd. — Alexander Graham Cairns-Smith (Cairns-Smith 1985, 8)

All but Blind

What I cannot create, I do not understand. — Richard Feynman (Caltech Archives 1988)

Our inability to assemble an organism from its basic ingredients, implies that our understanding of ecosystems and the living world is also incomplete. As tipping points in the order of the living world are reached, a better, more inclusive, understanding of life's nature is critical to the ongoing survival of our species and, indeed, the biosphere. These forces do not just involve the natural realm but also extend to the laboratory environment and technosphere, where synthetic life and man-made environmental networks are already part of the living world. Creating life from scratch would mark an incredible advance in human knowledge, which would be accompanied by a form of power that is comparable with the invention of the atomic bomb. More than a scientific endeavour, this colossal ethical and moral proposal could change everything we know about this planet — and the worlds beyond it.

It's organism(s) that die, not life. — Gilles Deleuze (Deleuze 1995, 143)

Our current way of addressing the greatest challenges we face this century are based on universal and deterministic ideals. While this approach may have suited the challenges that typified the Industrial Revolution (new materials and energy sources, efficient modes of production, effective transport etc.) they are poorly suited to this ecological era. Alternative, multiple, inclusive frameworks are needed, and the first step towards this process is to establish an alternative to the *bête machine*.

Part I

CONTEMPLATION

PAUSE

Highlighting how the living world is poorly
served by mechanistic metaphors that deal
with inert substances, this chapter outlines
liquid life's key concepts, terminology, and
principles that inform the characterisations
depicted in sections 01.12, 01.13 and 01.14,
which re-problematise the potency of the
material realm.

Air

> The air is a single, moving fluid that stretches from the
> heavens to the earth. The higher you go in the air, the less
> there is of it, but it never actually ends. About halfway from
> the earth to the moon — say, a hundred thousand miles
> aloft — one molecule of the air may meet another only
> every week or so, and the solar wind is as likely to send that
> molecule into interplanetary space as back down toward the
> earth. Still, there is just a touch of the air even way up there.
> (Logan 2012, 7)

The ground is our interface with the core of the world, which
exerts a gravitational pull on gaseous molecules that constantly
tug upwards into the vacuum of space. In this rarefied realm,
our bodies appear to be made up of hierarchies of solid parts,
while the air that surrounds us seems as *nothingness*. If we shut
our eyes and enter the realm of the senses, the sun warms our
faces and the mischievous air pulls our clothing, as if to raise us
aloft. The ancient desire of flight succumbs to this world of flow,
which does not wish us bound to the ground but compels us to
be free, like wraiths, and rise with the air currents.

01.2

Water

> If there is magic on this planet, it is contained in water.
> (Eiseley 1973, 15)

Residing at the boundary between water and other media, our construction of reality is shaped by encounters between our naked senses and the impacts of physics and chemistry on water. Our bodies have learned to carry and contain inner seas. Although this oxide of hydrogen is a versatile and common molecule on Earth, it is also abundant in space accounting for around 10% of interstellar matter, or space 'dust', which takes the form of ice. Arising from the primordial clouds of gas that produced the Sun and other stars, it forms in warm, dense regions of space where complex, ionic chemical reactions between hydrogen and oxygen occur. Although the liquid phase of water is relatively rare in the cosmos, it is relatively abundant on our planet, occupying 70% of its surface and its origin is enigmatic. Our already 'wet', water-containing planet acquired even more of the stuff during the cometary collisions that characterised the Hadean epoch to form our first seas around 4.6 million years ago. In liquid form, it is a universal solvent with paradoxical properties that are associated with the emergence of 'life', which is characterised by constant flux and leaky bodies.

> I could see a turbulent stream flowing down between the hills. I could see trees set deep into the ground like huge, one-legged creatures. The stillness of what I could see was only the surface to what lay underneath. Under the bark of the trees I could see rivulets of water, streams of sap flowing up and down the trunk. Under the roof of the house I could see the bodies of people asleep, and their stillness, too, was only superficial — their hearts were beating gently, their blood was rippling in their veins. (Tokarczuk 2003, 1)

44

Earth

> The body of a soil is a sky where seeds and worms and ions fly. (Logan 2007, 171)

Around 3 percent of the Earth's surface is made up of a thin layer of organic matter, which ranges from a few centimetres to several metres deep, and is folded into much more durable inorganic substances such as sand and clay. These soil amalgams are 'living hypermaterials', with complex metabolisms that actively process and organise their substrates, as a continuous, self-producing system. They also host many diverse communities of soil-dwelling creatures. Our own human bodies resonate with the character of this 'humus', which references the ancient belief that we sprang from the earth.

> People born where the soil is light and sandy are small, with fair, dry, skin. At first glance they seem rather weak and lacking in energy, but they're like the sand — dogged and able to hold on to life just as pine trees hold on to the sand in which they grow. (Tokarczuk 2003, 190)

The varied composition of our soils betrays our 'geostory', a non-human narrative fabric, which is woven through tectonic plates, meteorite impacts, and ice ages (Latour 2013). Permeated by liquid life, these giant bodies orchestrate many acts of 'biochemical burning', or metabolism, without need for a central organising system such as DNA, or even a brain. Collectively, soil's myriad processes orchestrate an unbroken cycle of continuous exchanges that link the living and the dead. Through its expanded and active relationship with death, the metabolic decoherence of a discrete body is neither a passive process, nor a final destination. Soils provide a place for this 'energetic pause' of living matter, where constituent molecular systems are released from the constraints of one set of metabolic relationships and, through an active process, are reincorporated into others. Soils may even be thought of as regenerative 'hyperorganisms', whose continual flow and assimilation of resources maintains the cycles of life on this planet, and have done so for the last 3.5 billion years.

Invisible Realms

> ... at first the muon was thought to be the Youkawa meson
> mediating nuclear forces. When it was proved, that the
> muon is insensitive to the strong force, it was not concluded
> that 'muons do not exist' but 'muons are not mesons'.
> This reminds us of the imaginary case treated by [Saul]
> Kripke where cats are found to be demons. One should
> not conclude 'that there turned out to be no cats, but that
> cats have turned out not to be animals'. (Corsi, Chiara and
> Ghirardi 1993, 270)

Animism holds that all things, living and non-living, have a
spirit and soul. Before the Enlightenment, these occult forces
were thought to govern the natural world, under the guidance
of an 'invisible hand' that was arbitrated by angelic and demonic
activities (Vivenza 2005). These concepts are so deep-rooted in
our cultural imagination that even during the scientific revolution, the demon as trickster concept was used widely to characterise the unreliable nature of reality. During the seventeenth
century, the effects of nature's mysterious agents started to be
named, explained, and actualised, as a tangle of invisible rays.
Most of these intangible forces could only be inferred, rather
than evidenced, until the nineteenth century when advanced
imaging techniques such as photography were developed, which
could convert them into readable, physical traces. Ephemeral
phenomena that could not be recorded in this manner continued to be attributed to unreliable senses and weakened minds.
By the twentieth century, the mysterious effects of angels and
demons were replaced by metaphors that generated vivid conceptual models of how material processes work. While many of
these models could account for the nature of matter through
mathematical formulae and simple causes and effects, others
could not decipher the peculiar nature of certain (quantum) effects. Cats are still a favourite metaphor, which have taken the

place of demons, since as contradictory creatures,[1] they embody the uncertain realms beyond the laws of classical science.

---

1   Erwin Schrödinger's famous thought experiment involves considering the effects of a sample of radioactive material on a cat locked inside a window-less box, which is at the same time, alive and dead.

Monsters

> Monsters exist, but they are too few in number to be truly dangerous; more dangerous are the common men, the functionaries ready to believe and to act without asking questions. (Levi 1986)

To explore the potential of liquid life is to make monsters. At the heart of evolution, without monsters, there is no change. Only stasis.

> I have beheld the birth of life. I have seen the beginning of motion. My pulses throb even to the point of bursting. I long to fly, to swim, to bark, to bellow, to howl. Would that I had wings, a carapace, a shell — that I could breathe out smoke, wield a trunk — make my body writhe, divide myself everywhere — be in everything — emanate with all the odours — develop myself like the plants — flow like water — vibrate like sound — shine like light — assume all forms — penetrate each atom — descend to the very bottom of matter — be matter itself! (Flaubert 2005, 190)

Monsters are only monstrous when an ethics is absented.

01.6

Angels and Demons

> ... we can't see other people's Angels, only our own.
> (Rimbaud 2004a, 161)

Angels, and their demonic counterpoints, are transitional beings whose substance is relative, since they are incorporeal and immaterial when encountered by mortals, but embodied and substantial when compared with God (St. John of Damascus 2017). Thomas Aquinas considered angels to be a range of intermediate beings that governed natural law and helped divine forces regulate the universe. In Jewish, Christian and Islamic folklore they play a symbolic role, relaying messages between Heaven and Earth (Stiles 1996, 9), where their wings represent freedom from the material world through flight. They are advisors, conveyers of partial knowledge from enlightened realms and revealers of visions (Stiles 1996, 9) that communicate through many levels of meaning with indeterminate, and even dubious status.

> Genesis [the] 'origin book' ... is the first book and it tells
> the origin of everything (but it does not tell of the creation
> of angels). The apparent omission raise[s] troubling
> implications: it either call[s] into question the completeness
> of the biblical text, or allow[s] for the possibility that there
> exist certain creatures which ha[ve] not been made by God.
> (Sowerby 1983, 19)

While cats stand in for paradoxes and thought experiments in physics — angels and demons are used throughout this book as ethical vehicles for liquid life, which highlight the role of moral agency and decision-making, within the uncertain terrains that characterise the living world. Although modern science has provided many insights into our knowledge of the planet, its account of 'life' is incomplete. While we can name the elemental building blocks of the organic realm — carbon, hydrogen, nitrogen, sulphur, phosphorous — this information still cannot be used to build life from scratch. In search of a better understanding of life's processes, liquid life draws upon those realms that exist beyond the established portfolio of scientific methods that comprise the Modern Synthesis (see section 04.2). Its aim is to develop an ecological engagement with the natural realm, so that its animating forces can be better characterised and engaged through experiment. Both angel and monster, this book conveys ethical questions between knowledge disciplines about our understanding of 'life', and juxtaposes science with uncertainty, so that alternative realms and bodies may be called into being.[2]

It seems ironic that human experiences known by artists
and saints and yogis in different cultures over the millennia,
and repeated over and over again in quite different
situations, are dismissed as superstition and illusion, but an
elementary particle that only exists as a nanosecond impulse
on a screen seen only by a handful of high priests at CERN
at a cost greater than the construction bill for the Great
Pyramids is considered to be 'scientifically real'. Elementary
particles are no more real than angels or garden dwarves;
they are … 'brought forth'. Elementary particles are
brought forth by linear or ring accelerators, just as angels or
bodhisattvas are brought forth by meditation. Physics … is a
language. (Thompson 1991, 20)

2   In a (hyper)complex reality, we can coherently be many simultaneous things without contradiction: a woman, employee, daughter, mother, citizen, angel, and monster.

01.7

Language of Angels

> A new angelology of words is needed so that we may once again have faith in them. Without the inherence of the angel in the word — and angel means originally 'emissary', 'message bearer' — how can we utter anything but personal opinions, things made up in our subjective minds? ... We need to recall the angel aspect of the word, recognizing words as independent carriers of soul between people. We need to recall that we do not just make words up or learn them in school, or ever have them fully under control. Words, like angels, are powers that have invisible power over us. They are personal presences, which have whole mythologies: genders, genealogies (etymologies concerning origins and creations), histories, and vogues; and their own guarding, blaspheming, creating, and annihilating effects. For words are persons. This aspect of the word transcends their nominalistic definitions and contexts and evoked in our souls a universal resonance. (Hillman 1991, 28–29)

John Dee and Edward Kelley claimed to have spoken with angels during scrying sessions in 1581, where they acquired knowledge of a language, which bore similarities to calculation tables, with its own alphabet, grammar, and syntax that was documented in manuscripts and workbooks. They asserted this Enochian[3] code, or keys, could reveal the language of angels and so, communicate with other dimensions of reality (Harkness 2008, 5).

Metaphorically allied with angels and transitional beings that enchant our habitats and render our world more liveable, liquid life invokes its own angelology to better describe and engage with the many varied aspects of the living world.

---

3   John Dee asserted that the Biblical Patriarch Enoch was the last human to speak in the language of angels and so coined the term 'Enochian' (Harkness 2008, 147).

… you have to look at everything that changes and moves, that doesn't fit into a shape, that fluctuates and disappears: the surface of the sea, the dances of the sun's corona, earthquakes, the continental drift, snows melting, and glaciers moving, rivers flowing to the sea, seeds germinating, the wind that sculpts mountains, a foetus developing in its mother's belly, wrinkles near the eyes, a body decaying in the grave, wines maturing, or mushrooms growing after a rain. (Tokarczuk 2010, 110)

Although existing lifeforms may already be read as liquid bodies such as venous and arterial circulations, or cerebrospinal system, they are inevitably framed within the conventions of the *bête machine*. This Enlightenment metaphor frames the characteristics of life as being appropriate for discourses of efficiency, geometric perfection, hierarchies, and determinism. To circumvent these biases, an apparatus for producing direct encounters of liquid bodies is needed. The Bütschli system (see section 09.1) is introduced in this context, as an apparatus that provides a counterpoint to established mechanistic narratives. Operating through the activities of dynamic droplets, it generates direct encounters with a polysemic 'language of angels' (see chapter 09). Arising from the intersecting fields of olive oil and strong (3M)[4] alkali, it generates a semiotic system that conjures dynamic material expressions from liquid states through the actions of matter at far-from-equilibrium states (Armstrong 2015). These *computations*[5] acquire specific value in conversation with observers and how they are read, is established through juxta-

---

4 M refers to the 'molar' strength of a solution where one 'mole' of matter (M), equates to the atomic mass of a compound in grams, which is dissolved in one litre of solvent (usually water). In this specific case, the atomic mass of sodium hydroxide is 40, so one mole is 40g and for a 3M solution, 120g of the compound is dissolved in a litre of water.
5 Computation in this sense is not a symbolic operation but an actual, material event made up of iterations of events. It alludes to the kind of platform that Alan Turing was concerned with, in understanding how nature computes.

positions of diverse hermeneutic conventions — such as science, poetry, and design. Revealing a generative 'angelology' of material expressions and associated terms, these Bütschli 'angels' provide an apparatus, or lens, through which the creativity of liquid life can be examined, experimentally engaged, and reviewed without recourse to the framework of the *bête machine*.

Angels and Ethics

> Every reference to angels is incidental to some other topic.
> They are not treated in themselves. God's revelation never
> aims at informing us regarding the nature of angels. When
> they are mentioned, it is always in order to inform us
> further about God, what he does, and how he does it. Since
> details about angels are not significant for that purpose, they
> tend to be omitted. (Erickson 1983, 434)

The indeterminate status of angels means they are difficult to
characterise and so embody an ethical dimension that asks us
to embrace their protean identities and multiple forms, so that
we may begin to apprehend the alternative forms of knowledge
they convey. Such beings are compatible with Donna Haraway's
notion of Chthulucene, and in this book angels personify the
'ongoing generative and destructive forces that characterise the
natural worlding and reworlding of the planet' (Haraway 2016).
Many kinds of angels have been described throughout the millennia. The Sumerian bee goddess, flourished in the Mesopotamian civilisation of Sumer between 5300 and 3500 BCE, alongside the first known (bird-)winged figures such as lions and
humans, which are thought to be the inspiration and archetype
for biblical angels. Bees in particular, have been regarded as pur-
veyors of order since ancient times. Their hives have inspired
the organisation of many Mediterranean temples attended by
the oracular *melissae,* who induced ecstatic trances by drinking
fermented honey, or mead. The pillars of faith in Islam state that
an angel, created from light, accompanies each raindrop, while
in Estonian folklore,[6] birds move as angels from the Earth to
the heavens taking the souls of the deceased with them. Such a
diversity of beliefs is framed by a range of spiritual perspectives
that describe various relationships with the natural realm that

6   The cosmos turns around a central world tree in Estonian folklore, of which
    the Milky Way (linnutee or birds' way in Estonian) is a branch.

differently incorporate the presence of angels into their communities. As new understanding arises, the messages that angels convey also change along with their nature.

> ... angels [are a] prism through which to study broader changes in contemporary society. (Sowerby 2016, 4)

During the European Middle Ages, the relationships between angels and demons were formalised into Christian doctrines and their cultural significance significantly increased between the eighth and twelfth centuries. Angels in particular, provided the vehicle through which the ethical principles upon which societies came together could be discussed. As most people did not travel (Sowerby 2016, 2), the concepts associated with angels were shaped by local customs, superstitions, obsessions, and fables where 'the wealth of disparate narratives involving angels led men and women of all sorts to expect their own interactions with these spirits' (Keck 1998, 209). Such angelology helped make sense of people's actions, their outlook, and provided narratives about how societies were organised. Angelology was more than a set of doctrines and practices, it also inspired ways of living and inhabiting the world, and in the eighth and ninth centuries the church began to mount resistance to the direct worship of angels as a form of resistance to paganism by reducing the diversity of angels. While the calling upon angels with names other than Raphael, Gabriel and Michael was condemned (Keck 1998, 174), it was not possible to eradicate the public appetite for them. During the twelfth and thirteenth centuries, their absence from the book of Genesis stimulated scholastic debate, rational argument, philosophy, logic, and reason. These new pedagogical systems benefited the wider social and economic communities of medieval Europe in their rapid transition towards an urbanising, profit economy (Keck 1998, 81). In the transition towards the industrial revolution cultural utilitarianism through secularism, 'brute' materialism and rationalisation of material events banished ethical and moral debate. Instead, the principle of 'survival of the fittest' stood in for notions of fairness within society

(Irons 1901). With competition and inequality at the heart of modern 'progress', a truth-bearing language to counter the anti-vitalist concepts of the *bête machine* is still needed to restore a sense of human 'purpose' in the world.

> All of these stories are a lure to proposing the Chthulucene as a needed third story, a third netbag for collecting up what is crucial for ongoing, for staying with the trouble. The chthonic ones are not confined to a vanished past. They are a buzzing, stinging, sucking swarm now, and human beings are not in a separate compost pile. We are humus, not Homo, not anthropos; we are compost, not posthuman. (Haraway 2016)

By embracing the concept of angels, liquid life upholds an ethical view of the organising principles of the living world and the way it is, or should be inhabited, as a counterpoint to the Anthropocene. In our transitioning towards an ecological era, liquid life upholds the diversity in our approaches towards an understanding of the innate strangeness of the natural realm, its complex epistemologies of 'being' (Latour 1993), and our relationship with them through its discourses with angels.

01.9

Angels and Ecocide

> The angel would like to stay, awaken the dead, and make
> whole what has been smashed. But a storm is blowing
> from Paradise; it has got caught in his wings with such
> violence that the angel can no longer close them. The storm
> irresistibly propels him into the future to which his back is
> turned, while the pile of debris before him grows skyward.
> This storm is what we call progress. (Benjamin 1969, 257–58)

Despite our best efforts to resist the atrocious environmental
legacy of intensive global industrialisation, we are losing our
connection with those agents that mediate exchanges between
the living and non-living realms. The Anthropocene, which embodies this worldview through the logic and practices of machines, is driving angels from the complexity of living realm, resulting in catastrophic losses in biodiversity, which carries clear
messages of impending disaster in the Sixth Great Extinction.

To mitigate what we can of the present ecocide and establish
alternative approaches that may secure our ongoingness, conceptual frameworks, and metaphors that embrace vitality are
urgently needed. Most pressingly, if we are to break away from
the enduring habits that have scarred the surface of our planet,
it is imperative that the stranglehold of the machine metaphor
upon all aspects of 'life' must be broken.

Seeking to renew our relationship with the natural world,
liquid life draws on the irreducibility and strangeness of fluids,
which conjure forth the vital forces that flow through the world's
metabolic networks. Within our guts, cells and environments,
hubs of vitality nurture its presence. Like the wind, we cannot
see it, but we know it is here by the effects it exerts on other
things and how it makes us feel. Through the countless, irreducible acts of 'being', liquid life (re)introduces the 'soul substance'
into the contemporary discourse of 'life'.

Bête Machine

> [T]he appeal to mechanism on behalf of biology was in its
> origin an appeal of the well-attested self-consistent physical
> concepts as expressing the basis of all natural phenomena.
> But at present there is no such system of concepts.
> (Whitehead 1925, 128)

René Descartes replaced the ancient, spiritual view of the living
world (Dickinson 1911, 2–8) with an extreme model of humanity, where the rational soul (mind) and body were made up of
qualitatively different substances. While people were capable of
rational thought and therefore, had souls (which departed when
the body machinery no longer worked), non-human life did not
and was regarded as a mere *bête machine* governed by the laws
of mechanics. Observed sensibilities were not considered to extend to anything more sophisticated than reflexes and instinct
(Newman 2001). This view enabled science to begin invasive
studies, where the living bodies of animals and human cadavers could be dissected without concern for religious, or ethical
dilemmas, since the 'appearance' of pain was thought to be no
more than an unconscious reflex (Admin 2013). The machine
metaphor proved such a successful approach to understanding
the living world that Julian Offray de la Mettrie took this to its
logical extreme, referring to the human creature as as soulless,
self-winding automaton — *'L'homme machine'*.

Brilliantly, the concept of machine not only describes atomism's worldview; it embodies its ideas. Its principles and operations can be tested and reinforced by mechanical technologies.
The demonstrable and (potentially) perfectible success of machines is not only inspiring; its self-reinforcing procedural simplicity is peerless.

Like atomism, machines are built from fundamental parts
and are structurally assembled according to mechanical principles, which are derived from classical physics. Its components
are inert, lifeless, and unchanging, so it has to be powered by ex-

ternal forces (fossil fuels, electricity, computer programs, etc.), which tip it away from equilibrium and command it into action. Lumbering from molecule to molecule, and joint to joint, the *bête machine* (the material apparatus of life) has no innate agency and is blind to its environmental context. Organised within a hierarchy of inert geometric objects, it embodies a 'brute' mechanical view of reality. Through our quest to incorporate their benefits into our lives, machines have become so sophisticated they are more than workhorses for industrial processes. Through personalised gadgets and robots, they have become our companions, acquiring this status through our projections of their worth on to them. Validated through our ability to incorporate its logic into our daily lives, the machine worldview with its automata (alluding to self-movement), robots (workhorses) and cyborgs (hybrids of human/animal/machine), pervades everything we do. Indeed, we have reached the point where we believe that we are little more than 'survival machines' guided by 'informatic' selfish replicators (Dawkins 2006, 24–25).

> … a human society based simply on the gene's law of universal ruthless selfishness would be a very nasty society in which to live. But unfortunately, however much we may deplore something, it does not stop it being true … if you wish … to build a society in which individuals cooperate generously and unselfishly towards a common good, you can expect little help from biological nature. Let us try to teach generosity and altruism, because we are born selfish. Let us understand what our selfish genes are up to, because we may then at least have the chance to upset their designs, something that no other species has ever aspired to. (Dawkins 2006, 3)

Reaching to the status conferred on ancient gods, their ubiquity and potency is deployed at the scale and power of natural forces, like the atomic bombs that razed Hiroshima and Nagasaki in August 1945 during the final stages of World War II. Mechanical systems also provide substitutes for natural phenomena, like the Moonlight Towers of Austin, Texas (Oppenheimer 2014), which floodlit the city with artificial night light, not only replacing the moon, but also 'improving' upon its performance, or the Norwegian Rjukan sun, which consists of three giant mirrors that extend daylight for the town. The influence of machines on our existence is so profound that they even epitomise the human project — specifically, the *anthropos,* which is built upon a particular kind of power and forms of privilege that elevate humanity over other life forms (Braidotti 2013, 65–66). In this way, the machine embodies and articulates the Enlightenment project of objectivity and progress, extending its reach and impacts through colonisation and the global marketplace.

While the mechanistic principles of the *bête machine* have contributed significantly to the modern understanding of the natural world, they do not speak perfectly for the extraordinary phenomenon of the living realm. In many ways, 'life' is a counterpoint to machines: while it obeys the laws of physics, it cannot be predicted by them; it is probabilistic, while machines are deterministic systems; life expresses its far-from-equilibrium states through its (hyper)complex materiality, while through their rigid embodiment, machines transform the external inputs of energy that tip them away from relative equilibrium into simple, predictable, unchanging chains of causes and effects; the living realm is deeply correlated with its surroundings, yet machines are not sensitive to their environmental contexts. These fundamental incompatibilities present a situation where characteristic and important phenomena associated with living things, cannot be discussed or explored through the logic of the *bête machine* and are therefore excluded from relevant (ethical) debates.

Even when non-human matter is imagined through its biomolecular components, the observed behaviour of the whole is 'other' than the sum of these parts. Whatever it is that emerges through the 'brute' body of the *bête machine,* its irreducible, sensible, and irrepressible presence allies much more closely with Descartes notion of the soul than with an unthinking, unfeeling assemblage that awaits instruction by an external agency. More than a mechanism, the agency of living matter squeezes through the gaps of our capacity to 'reduce' its nature into a set of simple causes and effects — declaring itself 'liquid'.

Entropy

> ... the whole organic world constitutes a single great
> individual, vague and badly co-ordinated it is true, but none
> the less a continuing whole with inter-dependent parts: if
> some accident were to remove all the green plants, or all
> the bacteria, the rest of life would be unable to exist. This
> individuality, however, is an extremely imperfect one — the
> internal harmony and the subordination of the parts to
> the whole is almost infinitely less than in the body of a
> metazoan, and is thus very wasteful; instead of one part
> distributing its surplus among the other parts and living
> peaceably itself on what is left, the transference of food from
> one unit to another is usually attended with the total or
> partial destruction of one of its units. (Huxley 1912, 125)

Our planet formed around 4.6 billion years ago from collisions
between colossal gas and dust clouds that clumped together to
form our solar system. Since its inception, it has been permeated with instability and change. As our world cooled, convection cells in its molten iron core formed and cast magnetic fields
around the planet, which established the dynamic material
conditions in which life could emerge. Today, the boundaries
between these bodies continue to move and subduct as tectonic
crusts, while the planet's magnetosphere dances in the Sun's
strange ionised winds. In this sheltered yet turbulent realm, a
transition from inert matter to life became possible. Arising
from such a vivacious place, it is little wonder, then, that since
ancient times, the dynamic character of the planet has been considered a 'living' being, whose nature varies according to differing perspectives.

Plato's organicist view proposed the planet possessed both
soul and intelligence, while the hylozoism of pre-Socratics regarded all matter to some degree was 'alive' and Plotinus understood that all beings were interconnected. Such concepts can be
traced through to the modern era in various schools of thought

such as, Thomas Aquinas's natural theology, Ralph Waldo Emerson and Henry David Thoreau's nature writing, Rachel Carson's Silent Spring and the eco-activism of the late 20th century (Ruse 2013).

While starkly contrasting with the mechanistic approach of the scientific revolution that operated according to predictable laws, notions of a 'living world' became incorporated into the perspectives of 'systems' sciences.

> The experiment is not traditional, reductionist, discipline-oriented science, but a new, more holistic level of ecosystem science that has been called 'biospherics.' (Odum 1993, 878)

Specifically, James Lovelock and Lynn Margulis championed the Gaia hypothesis, which regards Earth as a self-regulating 'organism', and imagined these principles could be applied through climatological, biogeochemical, and bacterial mechanisms to produce Earth-like environments in off-world settlements and spaceships (Anker 2014). While cybernetics and systems science generated a framework that provided more fluidity in the relationships between 'components' (or 'living' beings) than the mechanistic model of the living world, from a material perspective, life itself also did not seem to comply with the classical laws of physics. According to Erwin Schrödinger, it characteristically avoided the inevitable decay towards thermodynamic equilibrium — or inertia:

> An organism's astonishing gift of concentrating a 'stream of order' on itself and thus escaping the decay into atomic chaos — of 'drinking orderliness' from a suitable environment — seems to be connected with the presence of 'aperiodic solids', the chromosome molecules, which doubtless represent the highest degree of well-ordered atomic association we know — much higher than the ordinary periodic crystal — in virtue of the individual role every atom and every radical is playing here. To put it briefly, we witness the event that existing order displays the

power of maintaining itself and of producing orderly events. (Schrödinger 2012, 77)

Ernst Mayr observed that biology is unique among the sciences, as certain principles of physics cannot be applied to biology, nor do biological principles apply to the inanimate world (Mayr 2004, 21).

> A chemical compound once formed would persist for ever, if no alteration took place in surrounding conditions. But to the student of Life the aspect of nature is reversed. Here, incessant, and, so far as we know, spontaneous change is the rule, rest the exception — the anomaly to be accounted for. Living things have no inertia and tend to no equilibrium. (Huxley 1870, 75)

Despite their protean nature, living systems remain stable within chaotic environments by shedding heat, which actually results in a minuscule increase in overall cosmic entropy and so, comply with the second law. From a highly localised perspective, however life *appears* to contravene this principle, as its it operates through highly local, specific molecular, and quantum effects, which maintain their relevance to particular microniches.

> … there are places where matter creates itself, coming into being on its own out of nothing. They are always just small chunks of reality, not essential to the whole, and as a result they are no threat to the balance of the world. (Tokarczuk 2010, 203)

Ilya Prigogine described the material systems that possess these characteristics as 'dissipative structures' (Prigogine 1997, 27), which are paradoxical objects/assemblages that arise from the persistent flow of matter through a space (see section 08.9). Dissipative structures remain stable by dispersing energy into their surroundings, becoming increasingly structured during the process of *'dissipative adaptation'* (England 2015; Wang 2014) (see section 08.10). Such dissipation-driven adaptation of matter is not unique to life but applies to all forms of dissipative structures in the physical world, from the formation of volcanoes to the crystallisation of snowflakes. The most primordial forms do not self-replicate, but spontaneously arise from collisions at energetically charged interfaces between lively matter/energy fields. While these fields persist, dissipative structures continue to be produced. Physical constraints on the system keep the performance of these bodies in check. Should these limits be loosened, they can reconfigure and adapt rapidly to altering circumstances. While not all dissipative structures are alive, all living things are dissipative systems, where organisational stability is produced by continual activity and flow, with all constituent substances (not just genes) actively participating in life's flux. Some of these agents persist by using all possible diversionary material strategies within their reach and, therefore, evade the direct pathway towards thermodynamic equilibrium — a form of material inertia, or death. Dissipative systems are also compatible with notions of niche construction, where agents exhibit a reciprocal relationship with their surroundings through energy-shedding activities that include, but are not limited to, metabolic exchanges. In turn, these events have a feedback effect in the system, producing anisotropy and therefore enabling the production of increasingly complex (or hypercomplex) structures, which further resist the energetic descent towards thermodynamic equilibrium. While such physical principles alone do not inevitably result in biology, their countering of entropic forces through dissipative adaptation constitutes the very process of living, and is the start of a transition from lively matter towards life (Ball 2017b).

> A thousand incidents arise, which seem to be cut off
> from those which precede them, and to be disconnected
> from those which follow. Discontinuous though they
> appear, however, in point of fact they stand out against the
> continuity of a background on which they are designed, and
> to which indeed they owe the intervals that separate them;

they are the beats of the drum which break forth here and there in the symphony. Our attention fixes on them because they interest it more, but each of them is borne by the fluid mass of our whole physical existence. Each is only the best illuminated point of a moving zone which comprises all that we feel or think or will — all, in short, that we are at any given moment. It is this entire zone which in reality makes up our state. Now, states thus defined cannot be regarded as distinct elements. They continue each other in an endless flow. (Bergson 1922, 3)

The driving forces of these operations may be envisaged as dynamic fields of activity and quantum phenomena that are capable of odd material behaviours. These are largely factored out of classical scientific narratives, which are based on the average behaviours of large numbers of atoms whereas life's processes produce their effects at the (sub)microscopic scale, with many fewer atoms in play.

> ... physics doesn't make a distinction between life and not-life. But biology does. (Eck 2016)

Alfred North Whitehead proposed a fluid view of the living realm where 'actual occasions' are the 'final real things of which the world is made up ... drops of experience, complex and interdependent' (Whitehead 1979, 18) and 'the flux of things is one ultimate generalisation around which we must weave our philosophical system' (Whitehead 1979, 208). Such plastic models of the material realm draw attention to protean and fluid phenomena, which is not a solution to uncertainty, but an attitude of iterative engagement with events that are context-sensitive and framed by chemical laws. The operational framework for these processes must therefore be updated continually, so that the conditions for the next iterations of decisions may be appropriately shaped.

As systems dissipate energy, they drift in an irreversible direction and by doing so become 'exceptional,' ... not perfect or ideal. 'A bird is not a global optimum for flying ... It's just much better at flying than rocks or worms.' (Eck 2016)

How matter at far-from-equilibrium shapes life's complex modes of embodiment may be experimentally observed, explored, and tested by applying the principles of liquid life through identifying a portfolio of native materials, apparatuses, and prototypes, some of which will be explored in this book (see chapters 08 and 09).

Liquid Bodies

> The onion has many skins. A multitude of skins. Peeled, it
> renews itself; chopped, it brings tears; only during peeling
> does it speak the truth. (Grass 2008, 4)

Liquids are non-bodies, as they are constantly changing and
therefore possess no formal boundaries. Possessing their own
logic these protean structures assert their identity through their
environmental context. They are pluripotent, not amorphous,
being forged by oscillations and iterations of material expressions. Arising from interfaces, they persist through local connections and networks, which have the capacity to internalise
other bodies as manifolds within their substance. Such multiple entanglements invoke marginal relations between multiple
agencies that exceed the classical logic of objects, being capable of many acts of transformation. Although their behaviour
may be approximated by classical laws, like the liquid parcels
described by Lagrangian hydrodynamics, they resist complete
reduction into this framework.

Giving rise to the very acts of life, such as the capacity to
heal, adapt, self-repair and empathise, the diversionary tactics
of liquid bodies de-simplify the process of embodiment through
their visceral entanglements. While they are strange, they are
not the invention of fanciful imaginations but exist outside of
the current frames of reference in which our global industrial
culture is steeped. Aspects of their existence stray into the unconventional and liminal realms of auras, quantum physics, and
ectoplasms, which invite poetic engagement.

> ... every creature is contained within certain limits of its
> own nature, and inasmuch as those invisible operations,
> which cannot be circumscribed by place and bounds, yet
> are closed in by the property of their own substance ...
> (Ambrose 2009)

Liquid bodies also challenge the idea that embodiment is 'just' a question of anatomy and physiology. Intersecting with each other across multiple interfaces, they generate a bounded spectrum of events, structures, and inter/intra-relationships. Inseparable from their context. Offering alternative ways of thinking and experimenting with the conventions of making and being embodied, they possess the capacity to surprise us.

Liquid bodies are political agents, which redefine boundaries and conditions for existence in the context of dynamic, unruly environments. Radically transformed, monstrous, coherent, raw — and selectively permeated by their nurturing media, they embody alternative ways of 'being'. While the choreographies that shape their iterations invite us to articulate the fuzziness, paradoxes, and uncertainties of the living realm, they remain instantly recognisable like — tornado, cirrus, soil, embryo, biofilm. Challenging the structure of our grammar beyond the causality implied in the links between nouns (objects) and verbs (process), they invite us to invent monsters that defy all existing forms of categorisation taking us beyond the conventions of grouping and relational thinking. Making possible a new kind of corporeality by relating one body to another, liquid bodies produce contradictions of morphology and existence, which invite alternative readings of how the world is sorted, ordered, agentised, and valued.

Liquid Consciousness

> If animals were soulless, they were just machines. Therefore they didn't feel pain—they only acted as if they did. (Admin 2013)

With the senses deemed untrustworthy, the *bête machine* denies non-humans the capacity to perceive, or interpret reality, and are deemed to behave like blind automata awaiting cogent instruction. Since rational thought is entangled with Descartes' conception of the soul, liquid life's innate agency raises questions about the quality of decision-making and capacity for self-awareness of liquid bodies, providing a model for non-human thought (see section 05.9).

Provoking an expanded notion of consciousness that is situated at interfaces, 'liquid consciousness' is sensitive to the environment, responding to the flows between lively fields of matter/energy, which comprise a primitive mode of self-observation. Since action and matter are intrinsically coupled in a liquid body, there no need for an internal model of the world to instruct it, so it does not anticipate the nature of reality *a priori*.

> The main problem with *#emergence* as a metaphysical idea is that it's too atomist at the outset. It denies that consciousness is the very process of self-individuation, as one awakes from dormancy. (Fuller 2018)

Always discovering its context, liquid consciousness constantly reveals a world that is tinged with mystery. With persistence, it begins to differentiate between the mundane — where molecular species hurtle towards stability — and the extraordinary diversions of molecular assemblages at far-from-equilibrium states, which enable it to persist awhile. Becoming increasingly sophisticated, pervasive liquid bodies develop an indulgent palette of natural resources, food sources, waste materials, energy fields, and act on opportunistic events. Neither fully defined by any specific locale nor set of material resources, they are permeable to their particular circumstances and constantly capable of change.

> ... there's certainly intelligence there, of a kind ... they know what they're doing. Look at it this way. Granted that they do have intelligence; then that would leave us with only one important superiority — sight. We can see, and they can't. Take away our vision, and the superiority is gone. Worse than that — our position becomes inferior to theirs because they are adapted to a sightless existence, and we are not. (Wyndham 2000)

Without a predetermined, idealised form towards which to aspire, 'liquid consciousness' becomes optimised to its surroundings. Depending on the complexity of bodies, the richness of their environments, specific events, and sustained experiences, the character of thought is contingently shaped by its contexts. Some liquid bodies lose the capacity to respond to light because they live in darkness, others are primarily informed by ambient vibrations by which they navigate the world, while a few, like web-building spiders, extrude their mind maps into structural forms that penetrate their world (see section 07.14).

> So the octopus thinks: 'All right. I'm going to make an intelligence test for humans, because they show a little bit of promise, in a very few ways.' And the first question the octopus comes up with is this: How many color patterns can your severed arm produce in one second? (Williams 2011)

While theirs is not a human version of existence, their responsive apparatuses of liquid bodies forge appropriate agency within their habitats, which empowers them to act independently of humans, or other observers, and become co-authors in the unfolding narratives of their 'living' world.

Liquid Life

Liquid life is a paradoxical, planetary-scale material condition, with no fixed shape, but a characteristic readiness to flow and therefore takes on the shape of any container. Forged by the persistent instabilities of an uncertain realm, it is unevenly distributed but spatially continuous and is what remains when logical explanations can no longer account for the experiences that we recognise as 'being alive'.

Liquid life is not a homogeneous *life force,* but a kind of 'metabolic weather' — a dynamic substrate, or hyperbody, that permeates the atmosphere, liquid environments, soils, and Earth's crust. 'Metabolic weather' refers to complex physical, chemical, and even biological outcomes that are provoked when fields of matter at far-from-equilibrium states collide. It is a vector of infection, an expression of recalcitrant materiality and a principle of ecopoiesis, which underpins the process of 'living' events. These arise from energy gradients, density currents, katabatic flows, vortices, dust clouds, pollution, and the myriad expressions of matter that detail our (earthy, liquid, gaseous) terrains (see section 05.23). Since our unique planetary conditions are the generative source of this unique material phenomenon, as long as they remain, life is 'effectively' immortal.

Liquid life is also a worldview — a phantasmagoria of effects, disobedient substances, evasive strategies, dalliances, skirmishes, flirtations, addictions, quantum phenomena, unexpected twists, sudden turns, furtive exchanges, sly manoeuvres, blind alleys, and exuberant digressions. It discusses a mode of existence that is constantly changing, not as the cumulative outcomes of 'error', but as a highly choreographed and continuous spectrum of events that arise from the physical interactions of matter at far-from-equilibrium and their associated cascades of events.

Few men are gifted with the capacity of seeing; there are
fewer still who possess the power of expression ... the
external world is reborn ... natural and more than natural,

beautiful and more than beautiful, strange and endowed
with an impulsive life like the soul of its creator. The
phantasmagoria has been distilled from nature. (Baudelaire
1995, 12)

Steeped in the fluid conditions of hypercomplexity and hyper-
object-ness, liquid life exceeds our ability to observe, or compre-
hend it in its totality, owing to its massively distributed nature.
Typically, we recognise its epiphenomena as discrete beings,
which draw sustenance from the immense continuum of unevenly distributed, planetary scale, metabolic events that underpin its myriad forms of expression. At far-from-equilibrium
states it ambles through transitional molecular states and enter-
tains rebellious quantum phenomena, which evade permanent
commitments to form or function. Seeking strategies of disobedience through meandering pathways, it moves in directions
that evade thermodynamic efficiency and equilibrium's death
drive. Neither purposeless, nor goal oriented, it contemplates
the spectacle of 'living', revelling in its indulgences and resisting
the efficiencies of material transaction that coerce it towards inertia. Culturally speaking, this resistance shares resonances with
Charles Baudelaire's flâneur, who resists the path towards con-
sumer transaction within the 'arcades' of experience (Benjamin
1997, 79–80). Such diversions forge the very processes of life.

The crowd is his element, as the air is that of birds and water
of fishes. His passion and his profession are to become
one flesh with the crowd. For the perfect flâneur, for the
passionate spectator, it is an immense joy to set up house
in the heart of the multitude, amid the ebb and flow of
movement, in the midst of the fugitive and the infinite. To
be away from home and yet to feel oneself everywhere at
home; to see the world, to be at the centre of the world, and
yet to remain hidden from the world — impartial natures
which the tongue can but clumsily define. The spectator
is a prince who everywhere rejoices in his incognito. The
lover of life makes the whole world his family, just like

the lover of the fair sex who builds up his family from all the beautiful women that he has ever found, or that are or are not — to be found; or the lover of pictures who lives in a magical society of dreams painted on canvas. Thus the lover of universal life enters into the crowd as though it were an immense reservoir of electrical energy. Or we might liken him to a mirror as vast as the crowd itself; or to a kaleidoscope gifted with consciousness, responding to each one of its movements and reproducing the multiplicity of life and the flickering grace of all the elements of life. (Baudelaire 1995, 9)

Liquid life creates a platform for thinking with and through fluids, where the defining characteristic of our planet is acknowledged within the concept of life itself. Such expanded perspectives also engage with alternative power and identity relationships that move towards inclusive, horizontal interrelations, which are consistent with an ecological era. Proposing to distribute agency more equally within an expanded notion of immanent spaces, liquid life dilutes, decentres, and reduces the environmental impact of the *anthropos* in the construction of industrial processes (Steinberg and Peters 2015). It also raises critical questions about notions of society that embrace all humans and even includes species that have become so intrinsic to our biology they are integral to our being. For example, bacterial commensals (bacterial microbiome), symbionts (pets) and even 'living' fossils (mitochondrial bodies, viral, and bacterial gene sequences in 'junk' DNA) are fundamental to our existence, their diffusion within our flesh conferring us with unique character. As members of our 'fluid' communities, their rights and (potential) responsibilities are emphasised, as are notions of agency and modes of conversation. Such considerations invite alternative notions of personhood, currently potentially extended to chimpanzees, dolphins (Revkin 2013), machines (Prodhan 2016), land, rivers (Rousseau 2016) and planet (Vidal 2011). These recognitions may also extend to building coalitions (Bastian 2006) for (environmental) peace and include plants (ancient trees) (Martin 2000), insects (bees and other pollinators), soil organisms (mycorrhiza) and other creatures upon which our immediate existence depends. Although such notions could potentially extend indefinitely to embrace every being on the planet, from a 'lived' perspective, the appropriate limits and relevance are bestowed by community members through shared ethical concerns and values, which are at the heart of ecological change.

While liquid life is effectively immortal, its epiphenomena are not. At some point, beings reach thermodynamic equilibrium, where their deceased matter lies quiescently, patiently waiting for its reanimation through compost where it is assimilated back into the cycles of life and death.

This book does not set out to resolve the questions it provokes, but to stimulate conversation and debate about fundamental issues that enable the development and interrogation of an alternative technological platform than the machine, with an associated ethics that is appropriate for issues that characterise the third millennium.

Part II

DETERMINISM
UNBOUND

THE WORLD OF MACHINES

This chapter sets the concept of liquid life as an alternative to mechanistic thinking and its principles of certainty, which frame the discourses implicit in René Descartes' concept of the *bête machine*. In this way, it problematises the modern story of life and how we work with, relate to, and give an account of it.

Introduction

Einstein wrote, 'If the moon would be asked why it follows
its eternal path around the earth, he may answer that he
is gifted with self-consciousness and that his decision was
made once and for all.' We smile, because we know that
his path abides by Newton's Laws. Einstein asks that we
should also smile when you believe that you act on your
own initiative. Our initiative is simply an illusion, because
there is no reason that determinism — which is found in
nature — would stop in front of the human brain. In other
words, man is an automaton. He may believe that he's free,
but he is not free. It would be like we're in a movie. We
don't know who was killed, we don't know who's the killer,
but somebody knows it — the person who made the movie.
In some sense, every action, every part of our life, of the
life of the universe, is already determined by the initial
conditions as they were present in the big bang. Therefore,
the pleasure of being invited to this beautiful ceremony,
and my friendship with Professor Ruffini, would have been
included in the information at the big bang. But that seems
very strange, and I could never accept this view. (Prigogine,
not dated)

The modern story of life is recounted as a set of linear material
causalities. They are related to each other through lines of vertical descent and ancestral lineages from a hypothetical common
progenitor being — the *last universal common ancestor* (LUCA)
(LePage 2016). Life's hypothetical prototype appeared around
3.8 billion years ago to produce the major divisions on the phylogenetic tree of life: bacteria, archaea, and eukaryotes.[1] From

---

1   Viruses are debatably part of the phylogenetic tree of life. While they have
    been traditionally considered 'degenerate' cells without the full apparatus
    for self-replication, recent discoveries of 'giant viruses' challenge this theory
    (Ludmir and Enquist 2009).

these primitive origins, a biodiverse range of creatures began to blossom and wither, like branches on trees, from an initial set of around 355 genes.[2]

Liquid life is not a reversible phenomenon and is inextricably coupled with the vector of time (Prigogine 1997). Life does not only unfold through vertical pathways in a forward direction, it also unfurls sideways through space-time, continually permeating slippery spaces. This is not merely via the transmission of life's forces through the structuring of bodies, but also by the propagation of its reactive fields — its potent intersections provoke the events that form beings, memories, relationships, traumas, conversations, dreams, and hopes for the future.

Liquid life arises from the process of living that deals in multiples, paradoxes, and occupies the fuzzy edges of existence. It does not stand fast as an object, but dissolves into a spectrum of unfolding phenomena such as eating, breathing, sleeping, thinking, loving, metabolising, being, moving, growing, healing, hurting, dreaming, denying, aspiring, and observing. It perpetually evades those conditions in which it may fossilise into a permanent form, without hope of reprieve.

Life's 3.5 billion years of unbroken legacy is currently under threat, as its vital global infrastructures are in a state of decline. We are witnessing dramatic losses in biodiversity — more than ten times the accepted background rate. Of course, this is not the first time the planet has faced a viability crisis. At the time of biogenesis, life on earth is likely to have been extinguished many times during an epoch of relentless asteroid bombardment that characterised the Hadean era. Geological records also indicate that, since its inception, life has been almost wiped out five times

---

2   Recent phylogenetic analyses of ubiquitous and presumed-to-be vertically inherited 'core' genes, suggest that there might in fact be only two primary domains of life, Bacteria and Archaea, with the eukaryotes having emerged from within the latter (Williams and Embley 2014). This lends greater weight to the deep origins of the 'partial digestions' of creatures at the early stages of evolution, which are raised by Lynn Margulis (Margulis and Sagan 1995) and emphasised by Donna Haraway (Haraway 2015), as counter narratives to genetic hierarchies and forms of biological organisation.

in the last half a billion years (Ceballos et al. 2015). While these previous catastrophes have been wrought by natural disaster, uniquely, we are currently facing catastrophic human-initiated environmental damage that is precipitated by global industrial development. The tragedy of the Anthropocene is that the ensuing Sixth Great Extinction is not just wrought upon existing creatures, but also upon the elemental systems that expedite planetary viability.

Although every civilisation exploits its environment in some way, the intensity and scale of the wounds inflicted by the Industrial Era are preventing the capacity of ecosystems to repair themselves. The 'great stone book of nature' (Anstead 1863) is etched with indelible fossils, as our seas are turn into plastic soups, and concrete rocks lie as prehistoric bones under our urban skylines. The kinds of reducing gases that once choked the skies of the Hadean period now clog our atmosphere, while intensive farming practices are turning our soils to dust. Threatening the viability of our planet, these changes herald a cultural 'Ecocene', or Ecological Era, which seeks a new relationship with nature capable of countering the ongoing massive destruction of our natural environment.

Laplace's Demon: On Determinism

> We ought then to regard the present state of the universe
> as the effect of its anterior state and as the cause of the one
> which is to follow. Given for one instant an intelligence
> which comprehends all the forces by which nature is
> animated and the respective positions of the beings which
> compose it — an intelligence sufficiently vast to submit these
> data to analysis — it would embrace in the same formula
> both the movements of the largest bodies in the universe
> and those of the lightest atom; for it, nothing would be
> uncertain and the futures, as the past, would be present to
> its eyes. (Laplace 1902, 4).

Although the Enlightenment addressed life's paradoxes through
the lens of rational thought, this did not render them entirely
knowable through a detailed understanding their components.
In 1814, Pierre-Simon Laplace used a thought experiment to assert this fundamental concept, which was originally conceived
by Gottfried Leibniz. Imagining a scientist who could see all
the events of all times present to the mind of God, who became
known as 'Laplace's Demon', he proposed that all the past and
future possible states of the universe could be calculated by such
a superintelligent being. With such knowledge, no place for law-
lessness or arbitrary events would remain, providing the present
state of the universe and the positions, velocities, and forces
on all particles acting on it at one time, were already known
(Laplace 1902, 4).

Laplace's Demon was endorsed by Roger Joseph Boscovich's *Theoria philosophiae naturalis,* which documented practical findings on the principles of causality and continuity (Van
Strien 2014, 27; Koznjak 2015, 51) but today, the provocation is
disregarded. Not only does it assume the classical laws of physics apply at all times, which flies in the face of quantum physics,
but the amount of information needed to make these calculations is also impossibly vast. No matter how much data is gath-

ered for the demon, the stochastic processes that give rise to events which shape 'open', or 'probable' futures — like the evolutionary processes that take place in the natural world — simply cannot be predicted from their initial conditions. Today's understanding of reality is fundamentally probabilistic, while its (real and imagined) paradoxes are framed by the pre-modern notion of *demons*.

Of What Are Machines Made?

> Machines embody the atomic world, which is without a
> rational soul or innate capacity for reason and intellect.
> The objects that make up mechanical systems stand in
> for atoms, which are composed of different combinations
> of fundamental particles. These organisational principles
> can be embodied and recapitulated through the machine
> metaphor, namely, '… material things with fixed sets of
> properties … which exist independently of the activities
> they engage in …' (Nicholson 2018, 3)

Machines are stable systems that exist within the ancient
framework of atomism, which was championed by Leucippus,
Democritus, Epicurus and Lucretius that shapes the modern
worldview, where reality is made up of infinite combinations
of fundamental 'uncuttable' parts known as 'atoms' (Berryman
2016). While atoms are constantly moving, and colliding into
each other, machines begin at a ground state of relative thermodynamic equilibrium. Machines like a clock or an orrery, are apparatuses that perform a discrete choreography of objects which
reveal the nature of the world, but before they can perform this
useful work, they first need to be first tipped off balance by an
external energy source. Championed by Galileo, who proposed
that the *book of nature* was waiting to be decoded through the
language of mathematics, this shift in representation began to
specify reality in terms of geometrically described object relations, which took the form of patterns and trajectories.

> Mathematics, rightly viewed, possesses not only truth,
> but supreme beauty — a beauty cold and austere, like that
> of a sculpture, without appeal to any part of our weaker
> nature, without the gorgeous trappings of painting or
> music, yet sublimely pure, and capable of a stern perfection
> such as only the greatest art can show. The true spirit of
> delight, the exaltation, the sense of being more than a

man, which is the touchstone of the highest excellence, is to be found in mathematics as surely as in poetry. What is best in mathematics deserves not merely to be learnt as a task, but to be assimilated as a part of daily thought, and brought again and again before the mind with ever-renewed encouragement. (Russell 1920, 73–74)

Verifiable through observation, experiment, and measurement, the new empirical reality could be described by equations, which were instrumental in determining how events would unfold. In this way, objects too could be sorted, ordered, and ultimately controlled as microcosms of the universe.

> … mathematics [is] a language and scientific modelling [a] process of writing a story … that should have meaning, not just rules. In considering complexity it is not only impossible to expunge the natural referent, but their natural semantic qualities must be retained in order to cross the bridge back into mathematical formalism in a valid way. (Edson, Henning, and Sankaran 2017, 82)

Eugene Wigner discusses the 'unreasonable effectiveness' of mathematics to describe reality (Wigner 1960), which is taken to an extreme by Mark Tegmark, who proposes that mathematics itself is reality and the whole of our universe is a giant mathematical object (Tegmark 2014). However, mathematics remains an abstraction of reality and evolves as concepts change, questions seek new territories and number theory evolves. Even the cultural biases and prejudices of mathematics are embodied in its algorithmic expressions, giving lie to Descartes' assumption that it is uncontaminated by our unreliable senses.

> It is not possible for algorithms to remain immune from the human values of their creators. If a non-diverse workforce is creating them, they are more prone to be implanted with unexamined, undiscussed, often unconscious assumptions and biases about things such as race, gender and class.

What if the workforce designing those algorithms is male-dominated? This is the first major problem: the lack of female scientists and, even worse, the lack of true intersectional thinking behind the creation of algorithms. (Bartoletti 2017)

Slippages between actuality and modes of representation are particularly noticeable when mathematical rules are used to denote subjective encounters. For example, in 'affective' computing, feelings such as grief, love, and hate are signified, rather than experienced. While mathematical formulae and their derivative computer algorithms have provided incredible insights into the material realm, the associated discourses, tools, apparatuses, and languages value a particular kind of 'reality' that poorly deals with subjectivity, or ephemeral experiences. While the resultant notion of reality is verifiable, it has difficulty appreciating quality of experience, since not everything of value can be meaningfully delineated, or measured.

The universe is made of stories, not atoms. (Rukeyser 1968, 111)

To circumvent this difficulty, algorithms, and data, which are regarded as the virtual equivalent of atoms (Negroponte 1996) are used to generate elicit complex experiences (Hoel 2017), however, outcomes are inevitably inexact. Rather than relating content to a specific context and appropriately transforming it, which is typical of (living) agents of 'thought', the descriptors of higher forms of order such as emotions (love, intelligence, etc.) are built upon 'neutral' channels that relay information impartially (Shannon and Weaver 1949). Nicholas Negroponte (1996) observed, 'while today's computers can exhibit an uncanny grasp of airline reservations (a subject almost beyond logic), they absolutely cannot display the common sense exhibited by a three- or four-year-old child. They cannot tell the difference between a dog and a cat' (Negroponte 1996, 156). Moreover, while people change over time, machine learning unfortunately doesn't work that way (Wachter 2018) and the slippages between artificial and human thinking can produce odd effects. When 'bits and bytes' (Negroponte 1996) are equated and substituted for one another, a form of cognitive dissonance occurs which is known as the 'uncanny valley' (Kuwamura et al. 2015; MacDorman and Chattopadhyay 2016). Currently these conjunctions are largely limited to simulacra of specific bodies — e.g., companion robots, humanoids. While conversations between human and artificial intelligences continue to remain relatively simple, it is becoming difficult to discern chatbots from real human subjects (University of Reading 2014). Ongoing research into the linking of the digital and material realms through bio-digital interfaces raises questions about new conjunctions and dissonances are possible.

> The bot, known as Tay, was designed to become 'smarter' as more users interacted with it. Instead, it quickly learned to parrot a slew of anti-Semitic and other hateful invective that human Twitter users fed the program, forcing Microsoft Corp to [apologise and] shut it down … ("Microsoft 'Deeply Sorry' for Racist and Sexist Tweets by AI Chatbot" 2016)

Such limitations are being addressed by major breakthroughs in machine learning using various forms of convolutional neural networks that have enabled computers to accurately classify images based on their object representations. These principles are being applied in self-driving vehicles, with the potential to transform the whole transportation sector (Tollefsen 2017).

> Looking further ahead, there are no fundamental limits to what can be achieved: there is no physical law precluding particles from being organized in ways that perform even more advanced computations than the arrangements of particles in human brains … (Hawking et al. 2014)

As thought is folded into the *bête machine,* we are obliged to observe the way the world works through a mechanistic lens, which becomes a self-fulfilling prophecy; irrefutably, we are machines (Fuller 2011).

> ... [machines that think] ... [complete] a naturalistic understanding of the universe, exorcising occult souls, spirits, and ghosts in the machine. Just as Darwin made it possible for a thoughtful observer of the natural world to do without creationism, Turing and others made it possible for a thoughtful observer of the cognitive world to do without spiritualism. (Pinker 2015)

Detailing the *Bête Machine*

The process of improvement was cumulative. Ways of
increasing stability and of decreasing rivals' stability became
more elaborate and more efficient. Some of them may even
have 'discovered' to break up molecules of rival varieties
chemically and to use the building blocks so released
for making their own copies. These proto-carnivores
simultaneously obtained food and removed competing
rivals. Other replicators perhaps discovered hot to protect
themselves, either chemically, or by building a physical wall
of protein around themselves. This may have been how the
first living cells appeared. Replicators began not merely to
exist, but to construct for themselves containers, vehicles
for their continued existence. The replicators that survived
were the ones that built survival machines for themselves
to live in. The first survival machines probably consisted of
nothing more than a protective coat. But making a living
got steadily harder as new rivals arose with matter and more
effective survival machines. Survival machines got bigger
and more elaborate, and the process was cumulative and
progressive. (Dawkins 2006, 24–25)

Cells are the fundamental units of the *bête machine,* which are
governed by 'selfish genes' (Dawkins 2006). These units are
hierarchically ordered into increasingly sophisticated arrange-
ments of tissues, organs, bodies, populations, and ecosystems
through an evolutionary process that is most compatible with
an incremental, gradualist view of change. Combinations of
'selfish' molecules, however, are so abstracted from our everyday
experiences of living things that — to better relate to them — our
discourses about the *bête machine* are vitalised by essences
(metaphysics) and functions (teleology), which are ascribed
anatomical and physiological narratives.

... when the sapid and slippery morsel — which is and is gone like a flash of gustatory summer lightning — glides along the palate, few people imagine that they are swallowing a piece of machinery (and going machinery too) greatly more complicated than a watch. (Huxley 1884, 47)

These modern approaches are founded on the ancient idea of Aristotle's hylomorphism, which proposes that 'being' is the condensation of matter and form (Conti 2001). Even then, this is not sufficient to account for the unique capacity for life to produce more of itself. The transfer of form and character between generations through 'genes' bears striking resemblance to the pangenesis theory. Championed by Hippocrates and Democritus, the homunculus, the 'little man' inside a sperm, mysteriously develops once it is in a fertile soil, or egg — to produce a mature (self-similar) being. However, modern genetic theories replace the homunculus with encoded DNA. Georges-Louis Leclerc, Comte de Buffon, who pioneered the idea of biological change taking place over long timescales, and Charles Darwin, who coined the idea of descent with modification, supported this homuncular notion of vertical inheritance, where every parental organism carries tiny heritable particles within them. Darwin proposed that specific characteristics could be acquired through atomic-sized 'gemmules' formed by cells that were concentrated in the reproductive system (Zirkle 1935). However, this mechanism alone could not account for increasing diversity, but tended towards homogenisation, where differences between creatures would be diluted and 'averaged' out. This disparity between theory and observation was finally resolved by introducing the theory of Mendelian inheritance, which involved a very structured shuffling of traits during cell division to produce asymmetric phenotypes.

In the late twentieth century, molecular science established that the DNA responsible for cellular identity did not self-govern, but was regulated and even modified by other systems. The implications of these findings meant that the operational codes of living things could not be entirely predetermined, but were customisable and even (re)programmable using advanced biotechnological toolsets. While the powerful tool for editing genomes *Clustered Regularly Interspaced Short Palindromic Repeats* (CRISPR; pronounced 'crisper'), allowed the cell's genome to be cut and edited at highly specific locations (Ledford 2015), life's processes remained vulnerable to influences beyond the genetic code.

No single definition, or list of characteristics encoded by genes, exists that universally defines life. While classical descriptions describe a list of characteristic functions, namely: *homeostasis,* the internal (physiological) regulation of the organism; *respiration,* the production of energy for cellular systems; *reproduction,* the copying of the biological system with differing fidelity that results in heritable change and ultimately the open-ended development of life; *sensitivity,* the response to changes in the external environment; *growth,* a higher rate of anabolic than catabolic activity that results in an increase in structural organisation over time; *movement,* locomotive activity such as bending towards a light source or running; *excretion,* the removal of metabolic waste; and *nutrition,* fuelling metabolic activity — some creatures do not fulfil all these criteria but are clearly alive, like the sterile mule, which is a cross between a male donkey (jack) and a female horse (mare). While widespread variations in opinion exist, a commonly used definition in scientific literature is Jack Szostak's notion of a 'self-sustained chemical system capable of undergoing Darwinian evolution' (Szostak 2012). In practice, working definitions of life are used as evaluative toolsets to experimentally 'convert abstract concepts into entities' (Gould 1981, 56). Many of these are molecular models where DNA stands in for 'life'. One study that was based on more than 100 tabulated definitions revealed nine groups of terms that indicated (self-)reproduction and evolution (variation) were the minimal set of characteristics needed for an entity to be considered 'alive'. The phrase, *'self-reproduction with variations'* (Trifonov 2011) was therefore recognised as the preferred terminology for a concise, inclusive definition, and 'useful' working definition of life.

When taking an experimental approach to the nature of 'life', an appropriate evaluation toolset is also needed, some of which have been inspired by Alan Turing's 'imitation game', as a 'Turing test' for living things (Cronin et al. 2006). Turing's original approach addressed the conundrum of intelligence, which evaded a clear definition or empirical solution (Turing 1950) by incorporating the experience of human participants as part of the decision-making system. Similarly, life is not an absolute, but something that is constructed and evaluated through an existing value system. While Turing's technique does not guarantee reproducible views, it is a valuable way of approaching unfathomably complex systems and enables researchers to shape better questions about the performance of the system under interrogation, which may ultimately, lead to insights that were not available at the start of the experiment (Armstrong 2015, 29).

Since life cannot be defined descriptively in absolute terms, some investigators prefer to refute the utility of definitions, regarding them as beyond the remit of scientific investigation. Viewing life as a physiochemical world, which could be approached through the logic of (bio)chemistry Claude Bernard claimed that

> there is no need to define life in physiology ... [such attempts are] ... stamped with sterility ... It is enough to agree on the word life to employ it: but above all it is necessary for us to know that it is illusory and chimerical and contrary to the very spirit of science to seek an absolute definition of it. We ought to concern ourselves only with establishing its characteristics and arranging them in their natural order of rank. (Bernard 1974, 19)

A similar approach is currently adopted by molecular biologists such as Andrew Ellington.

> If we haven't figured out what life is by now, there is little hope that we will figure out a definitive definition in the near term, and there is no research program that I can

imagine, at any price, that will provide such a definition. (Kaufman 2012, 38)

While classical science needs to precisely establish the terms of its investigations, it is nonetheless possible to meaningfully work with life's processes without having a universally accepted definition of what is being observed. Even while the molecular science of genetics is still being deciphered, synthetic biology deploys life's processes in ways that are addressing some of the world's most challenging problems, such as offering ecologically beneficial alternatives to fossil fuels and returning 'excess' carbon dioxide to the metabolically active realm (Gill 2010).

> The change for biology came in the 1970s, when biotechnology began to deliver synthetic tools. At first, biologists cut and pasted single genes, rearranging what was naturally available. Then, in the early 1980s, synthetic biologists moved away from nature, synthesizing entire genes, artificial genetic systems with extra nucleotides and proteins with more than 20 kinds of amino acid. To do more than tinker with natural biological parts, however, a synthetic grand challenge must be at the frontier of the possible. If it is, it forces scientists to solve new problems. Should their design strategies be flawed, they will fail in ways that cannot be ignored. Thus, synthesis drives discovery and technological innovation in ways that observation and analysis cannot. (Benner 2010)

Today's mechanistic view of synthetic biology employs the genome to stand in for the synthesis of objects-to-be. In this manufacturing system, cell function can be changed by writing the programs of life using nucleotide bases and modular units called 'biobricks' (Knight 2003). CRISPR enables this editing function to be carried out with precision, so that life's processes are not only 'programmable', but can also be artificially assembled. These rigorous systems are also being used to establish what constitutes 'life' by experimentally establishing the minimal requirements for a functional cell. Present approaches involve stripping away from what already exists, like an anatomy dissection rather than assembling a living thing from a toolkit of fundamental building blocks. Examining systems at the threshold of life, such Minimal Life experiments were actualised through the extraordinary 'biohack' of the *Mycoplasma mycoides* bacterium by J. Craig Venter's research group. The synthetic organism, which is the first species to have computers as parents, was dubbed 'Synthia' by the press in 2010. Marking a significant technical step in artificially 'cranking out' genomes like a factory system for the code of life, it rebooted these synthetic codes into 'ghost cell' chasses (the organic equivalent to the homuncular soils, or egg matrix) (Gibson et al. 2010). Synthia now has a life of its own and has replicated over a billion times.

Biotechnological breakthroughs continue to produce new tools and methods to interrogate the nature of life and test the outcomes. J. Craig Venter's group have already improved upon their landmark development by producing Syn 3.0, a minimal cell that is simpler than any natural one. Much faster growing than Synthia, it possesses an even smaller number of genes (only 473 genes in Syn 3.0 compared with 516 genes in Syn 2.0 and 525 in *M. genitalium*). While a third of these vital genes remain unknown, the progression of this minimal cell approach promises new insights into fundamental biological principles. The ultimate goal of these research projects is to develop a cell so simple that every gene can be completely understood according to its molecular and biological function (Service 2016). Such intentions rest upon long-standing controversial assumptions, such as the relationship between genotype (code) and phenotype (what aspects of the cell's capabilities are expressed in the living organism). Venter's continued successes clearly demonstrate that the nature of life can be equated with advanced, programmable machines — but are based on certain preconditions. The synthesised cell is not autonomous but requires a donor life support system that is provided by cytoplasm from the bacterium *M. capricolum,* which has had its DNA removed. Moreover, the purpose of the 149 unknown genes in Syn 3.0 remains mysterious. Some products appear to produce molecules that stick out from the surface of the cell, while others are transport systems that shuttle substances in and out of the cell. This introduces a degree of uncertainty within the manufacture of unspecified synthetic cell products and which poses an investment risk for funding bodies interested in commercial applications of these genetic codes, even when the whole system is highly controlled (Yong 2016).

While Venter's quest centres on biological coding as the source for deterministic instruction for cell-machines, other experimenters are searching for even more minimal definitions that may invoke other kinds of less tightly determined modes of control, while introducing far fewer mysteries into the experimental method. Tibor Gánti's 'principles of life' for building an artificial cell are applied in the Chemoton experimental criteria (Gánti 2003) which defines the fundamental components of life as — metabolism, compartment, and information. Used as the investigatory framework for contemporary origins of life experiments this model enables the lifelike behaviours of chemical systems to be investigated in many ways by, for example, lacing their matrices with biomolecules (Armstrong 2015, 36).

We start with things that are not alive. So, protein by itself is not alive, DNA by itself is not alive — but somehow, when you put these things together, under the right conditions, you get life. Nobody knows how that is, and so that's what we're trying to figure out. I guess you'd say we are exploring the boundary between living and non-living ... building an artificial cell with biological parts and studying the origins of life are two separate fields ... [we are] trying to build a cellular Turing test. All living things communicate chemically, so we're trying to build an artificial cell that can speak the same chemical language as a natural cell, and then we want to ask whether natural cells understand that ours are artificial, or do they think that they are talking to other natural friends, a natural neighbor? So can we trick E. coli, for example, into thinking it's talking to another E. coli? If

97

we keep getting better and better at this, then perhaps they will become indistinguishable, not only to a bacterium, but to us. (Eng 2013)

Homeostasis

> The living body, though it has need of the surrounding
> environment, is nevertheless relatively independent
> of it. This independence which the organism has of its
> external environment, derives from the fact that in the
> living being, the tissues are in fact withdrawn from direct
> external influences and are protected by a veritable internal
> environment which is constituted, in particular, by the
> fluids circulating in the body. (Schultz 2003, 4)

The mechanical model of life requires environmental stability in order to coordinate the multitudinous functions that organisms typically perform and therefore resists change. Claude Bernard established the concept of a stable *milieu intérieur,* as a precondition for dealing with external change, which was later called 'homeostasis' by Walter Bradford Cannon, as 'the condition for free life'.

> The highly developed living being is an open system having
> many relations to its surroundings … The coordinated
> physiological reactions which maintain most of the steady
> states in the body are so complex, and so peculiar to the
> living organism, that it has been suggested … that a specific
> designation for these states be employed — homeostasis.
> (Cannon 1929, 400)

Internal constancy enables the *bête machine* to resist fluctuations in the environment and therefore avoids the potentially destructive effects of change in the living system. Organic bodies however, do not demand absolute stability, but can operate within variable limits of performance. Channelling the flow of matter/energy through its internal systems, '[t]he organs and tissues which regulate the internal environment … are constantly taking up and giving off material of many sorts, and their 'structure' is nothing by the appearance taken by this flow of material through them' (Haldane 1917, 90).

Microvariations exist within all organisms. For example, core body temperature is higher than at the periphery, yet oxygen-carrying cells still need to function effectively within these limits. In other words, homeostasis establishes the range of conditions within which living systems can be constantly tipped off balance and constantly move away from a physiological condition of stasis (or equilibrium). They are able to continually perform the processes of life, by constantly re-equilibrating their surroundings for example, to alter nutrient concentrations and waste products.

The concept of homeostasis therefore depends on whether a deterministic machine, or a probabilistic organic body is invoked. While the bête machine seeks environmental independence and internal stability, the processes of organic homeostasis are open, highly changeable dynamic conditions that are bounded by chemicophysical limits. However, when life and machines become ontologically interchangeable, the expectations of the different kinds of systems are confused. For example, the notion of a 'closed loop' ecological system as a homeostatic system that can indefinitely recycle resources simply does not work in practice as an organic system. With time, a 'closed' organic system will grind to a thermodynamic halt owing to inevitable (dissipative) matter/energy losses.

> The essence of mechanical explanation, in fact, is to regard the future and the past as calculable functions of the present, and thus to claim that all is given. On this hypothesis, past, present and future would be open at a glance to a superhuman intellect capable of making the calculation ... But duration is something very different from this ... We perceive duration as a stream against which we cannot go. It is the foundation of our being, and, as we feel, the very substance of the world in which we live. It is of no use to hold up before our eyes the dazzling prospect of a universal mathematic; we cannot sacrifice experience to

the requirements of a system. That is why we reject radical mechanism. (Bergson 1922, 29)

02.6

Ship of Theseus

> We cannot speak of a machine 'theory' of the organism, but
> at most of a machine fiction. (von Bertalanffy 1933, 38)

Life's continual ability to enter into material negotiation with
multiple systems and update itself accordingly, is a defining
quality that cannot be easily articulated by mechanistic models.
Mechanical operations can be framed so that machines *appear*
to be capable of adapting and evolving according to the paradox posed by the Ship of Theseus. During an annual journey
from Athens to Delos, the vessel underwent constant repairs, so
that its original parts were completely replaced. Although the
outward appearance of the ship is preserved, its materials are
entirely different, which raises questions about the authenticity
of the returning vessel. Depending on the perspective of the observer, this may be decided according to preferred value systems
that may for example exalt preserved function over the origin of
the components (Nicholson 2018, 21).

As a counterpoint to this conundrum, it is worth considering
whether the Aegean Sea, upon which Theseus' vessel sails, is the
same or different during the voyage. Liquid bodies are expected
to constantly reconfigure themselves while maintaining a coherent character. The paradox of the Thesian ship is therefore
imposed on a system by a mechanistic framework, rather than
arising as the conundrum of an evolving materiality.

Cats and Computers

Cats travel between worlds. Prowling the edge of the visible realm, they walk a shadowy line between darkness and light. They exude the kind of strangeness that only unearthly wisdom might possess. Infamous for their fluid bodies, cats can squeeze through small gaps, and land like snow.

Cats and computers are often found together. Computer hard drives are cat-magnets with added benefits that are capable of reaching temperatures of 50 degrees Celsius, while also promising endless amusement. Their depressible keyboards activate alluring images that lurk behind warm screens. While relationships in a cat-and-computer-containing household are deeply entangled, most people would not confuse one with the other. Cats and computers are easily distinguishable through their discrete characteristics using classical taxonomic systems such as Aristotle's *systema naturae*,[3] which identify claws, tail, eyes, ears, and fur — or screen, keyboard, and power supply.

Through the lens of the *bête machine,* the warm furry cat shares the mechanical ontology of the cold, hard laptop, and there are strikingly few differences between them. Each is made up of fundamental components (atoms/cells), consumes energy, each has a 'mouse', produces waste (heat/organic matter), moves, and ultimately breaks down or 'dies'. The most striking difference between them is that following death, the creature cannot be resurrected by reorganising their non-functioning parts, while the machine can. From a mechanical viewpoint, the organic world possesses a theoretically preventable deficiency and therefore, is an inferior mode of existence.

3   Aristotle's approach influenced Carolus Linnaeus in the construction of his Latin-based classification system, which grouped natural phenomena into the animal, vegetable, and mineral realms. This taxonomic system, which is characterised by universal naming conventions and the consistent use of binomial nomenclature to sort things into taxa according to their type, has become the foundation for modern scientific classification.

While metaphors are neither true nor false, they may be appropriate to greater or lesser extents. Conflating ontologically distinct entities through their use has real consequences, as they start to 'become' each other. In this way, the *bête machine* becomes an existential trap that prevents us from using alternative perspectives than industrialisation to address the pressing issues of planetary-scale ecocide. By using its mechanisms more efficiently, through reducing, reusing, and recycling its resources, we are convinced that *somehow,* our living world will be spontaneously restored.

THE HARD QUESTION OF MATTER

This chapter establishes a contemporary portrait of the material realm. Moving from a classical worldview through to quantum and nonlinear accounts, it investigates the unknowns and seeds of material rebellion that inform the physical principles of liquid life.

Origin of Atoms

> What makes the atom more real [than a ghost] is that it has
> more allies, and these allies stretch well beyond humans.
> Experiments testify to the atom's existence; instruments
> stabilize it and make it indirectly visible; generations of
> children learn of it and pass the word along: Brownian
> motion shows that particles of water are moved by it. The
> ghost, by contrast, has only a paltry number of allies bearing
> witness to its reality. But the atom's allies may one day desert
> it too. (Harman 2004, 16)

Atoms were formed during an extremely rapid expansion of the
universe during the Big Bang, when it went from 'nothing' to
'relative' infinity around 13.8 billion years ago. In the first three
minutes, when temperatures cooled from 100 nonillion Kelvin
to one billion Kelvin, the lightest elements were born as protons and neutrons formed deuterium, a stable isotope of hydrogen. Clouds of this primitive matter condensed and collapsed
to form the first cosmic bodies in the non-luminous early universe, which swallowed up the high-energy ultraviolet light produced by the earliest galaxies and stars.

> Physicists have brilliantly reverse-engineered the
> algorithms — or the source code — of the universe, but left
> out their concrete implementation. (Mørch 2017)

Around 150 million to one billion years after the Big Bang, supermassive black holes had sufficiently expanded to take over
the reionisation process. As they interacted with other forms
of matter and radiation the universe became luminous (Yeager
2017). Around five billion years after cosmogenesis the current
expansion of the universe was initiated, and matter started to
condense under the space-time warping influence of gravity
(Creighton 2015b), which were countered by dark energy's in-
flationary influences (Choi 2017). 4.6 billion years ago, our Sun

was formed from a giant, spinning cloud of gas and dust, and at 4.5 billion years, it was encircled by a cloud of hot debris, which cooled and combined into clumps. Congealing into increasingly larger clots, this moulten matter formed planetesimals and planets that frequently collided and vaporised each other.

Out of this primordial fluidity, atoms congealed to produce the dissipative systems that shape our dynamic planet.

Structure of Atoms

> ... it was thought that atoms were rather like the planets
> orbiting the sun, with electrons (particles of negative
> electricity) orbiting around a central nucleus, which carried
> positive electricity. The attraction between the positive and
> negative electricity was supposed to keep the electrons in
> their orbits in the same way that the gravitational attraction
> between the sun and planets keeps the planets in their
> orbits. The trouble with this was that the laws of mechanics
> and electricity, before quantum mechanics, predicated that
> the electrons would lose energy and so spiral inward until
> they collided with the nucleus. (Hawking 1995, 65–66)

The quest to characterise atoms at the start of the twentieth
century, set the scene for new ways of thinking about the material realm. Through this inquiry, experimental evidence that
supported non-classical concepts amassed and matter became
stranger.

In 1900, Max Planck set out to establish how to create maxi-
mum light from light bulbs with minimal energy, but won-
dered why his black body experiment did not appear to obey
his predictions, which were based on the idea of 'continuous
matter' that behaves like waves. Looking to Boltzmann's statistical interpretation of the second law of thermodynamics, which
suggested that electromagnetic energy could only be emitted
in quantised form — i.e., emitted as discrete particles, as an
act of despair, he established the foundations for the theory of
quantum physics (Kragh 2000). Other theoretical models also
emerged during this period such as Niels Bohr's atomic model,
where atoms are made of electrons that circumscribe quantised
orbits around a nucleus.

To observe the fundamental particles from which atoms are
composed, giant instruments as big as cathedrals were built to
accelerate the nuclei of hydrogen atoms to the speed of light in
giant underground tunnels. Torn apart at the moment of colli-

sion with lead (or other hydrogen) nuclei fragments, the curved trajectories and tight spirals they leave behind can be used by physicists to calculate the momentum of a particle, and so deduce its identity. This new science of 'quantum' physics began to reveal the strange characteristics of infinitesimally small realms, which suggest that matter is not made of solid blocks, but are mostly empty space (De Jesus 2016). Requiring its own 'quantum mathematics', e.g., 'mirror symmetry' (Dijkgraaf 2017), the realm is divided in into two kingdoms which includes bosons, which tend to behave collectively, and fermions, which are individualists that enable reactive chemistry by refusing to occupy the same quantum states (Wilczek 2017). Quantum effects reach beyond the nanoscale and are capable of 'spooky' remote entanglements (Einstein, Podolsky and Rosen 1935) and improbable forms of 'tunnelling' that shortcut through previously insurmountable energetic barriers (Razavy 2003, 462). In fact, the strange laws of quantum physics, now appear to apply to things of all sizes such as, birds, plants, black holes, and maybe even people (Vedral 2015).

Darkness

> … our separateness and isolation are an illusion. We're all made of the same thing — the blown-out pieces of matter formed in the fires of dead stars. (Crouch 2016, 245)

Albert Einstein's special relativity theory changed the classical physical law that stated matter could not be created or destroyed. His simple and elegant equation described the relationship between matter and energy as $(E = mc^2)$,[1] where mass was reversibly considered as a super-concentrated form of energy that could be released from atoms. Although his equation was not used directly to set off the nuclear fission chain reactions of the 1945 Hiroshima and Nagasaki atomic bombs — it came to epitomise the pinnacle of all Enlightenment knowledge, where humanity could command the fundamental forces of nature in the most absolute manner.

With the rise of quantum science, humanity's attention to the nature of the world turned from inwards and downwards (Kauffman 2008, 17) to outwards and upwards into the cosmos. Through the new gaze of radio telescopes and particle detectors, it is apparent that our cosmos is mostly a vacuum that comprises 95% dark matter and energy, which does not obey our universal laws. Our understanding of the whole of reality is based solely on our knowledge of the 'luminous' matter that makes up only 5% of its substance. This 'darkness' is made up of dark energy and dark matter, which have little in common — other than their nature is elusive.

> According to the Planck mission team, and based on the standard model of cosmology, the total mass–energy of the known universe contains 4.9% ordinary matter, 68.3% dark energy and 26.8% dark matter. This is a non-luminous

---

1   Where E = the total energy in the system, m = the atomic mass of an atom and, c = the speed of light.

hypothetical substance, first proposed by Jan Oort in 1932, as a way of accounting for missing mass in the universe. Its characteristics are inferred from the gravitational effects on visible matter, radiation, and the large-scale structure of the universe. It cannot be seen directly with telescopes, as it does not respond to the presence of light, although it may emit its own unique kind of gamma ray. This may be a fundamental property of an as yet uncharacterized type of subatomic particle, whose discovery is one of the major efforts in particle physics today. So, while there is more dark matter than normal matter in the universe, the most abundant substance is actually dark energy, which may be an innate property of space. (Armstrong 2016, 36)

Dark stars were first proposed by William Thomson (who would become Lord Kelvin), as a way of accounting for dark regions in the sky, where a theoretical form of matter could account for the uneven distribution of cosmic bodies. Henri Poincaré indicated that, theoretically, much more of this 'dark matter' than Kelvin supposed should be expected (Bucklin 2017). By studying the Coma galaxy cluster, Fritz Zwicky produced the first evidence for dark matter by deducing that it did not contain enough visible matter to hold it together. Vera Rubin and Kent Ford also calculated that about ten times as much dark matter than luminous matter was needed to account for the characteristics of spiral galaxies (Scoles 2016). Today, the nature of the dark matter particle remains elusive and it is not even clear that there is just one kind of agent at work.

The most widely accepted theory about dark matter is that it largely works to hold the matter in space together. It accounts for galaxies clumping together despite appearing to lack sufficient visible matter to do so. It is made of weakly interacting particles that move about slowly under the influence of gravity but cannot account for all associated phenomena. Justin Khoury and Lasha Berezhani suggest this may be due to a phase change, where most of the time dark matter behaves like conventional cold dark matter, but under other circumstances becomes a superfluid, with zero viscosity. Then again, Erik Verlinde suggests that dark matter may not exist at all, its apparent effects being caused by interactions between dark energy and matter, which generate curved space-time (Wolchover 2016).

Dark energy is *even more elusive* than dark matter, having been deduced by comparing theoretical and actual cosmological observations. Unchanged by time it acts in some way to counter gravity. While there are also no convincing theories about what it might actually be, its existence accounts for why the expansion of the universe appears to be accelerating.

A more recent theory by James Farnes at Oxford University's e-Research Centre proposes that dark matter and energy can be unified into a fluid that comprises a sea of negative masses, which repels all adjacent matter. All positive mass surf upon this dark substance, which does not thin out over time, as it is continually produced and therefore, does not become diluted as the universe expands (Farnes 2018).

Our understanding of the cosmos is framed by our knowledge of the small amount of luminous matter with which we are familiar, which means our understanding of the cosmos is likely to be incomplete. It is possible that, as our understanding of dark and quantum realms advances, we will discover that matter is even more extraordinary than we have assumed.

Not-matter

> One of our joys was to go into our workroom at night; we
> then perceived on all sides the feeble luminous silhouettes
> of the bottles or capsules containing our products. It was
> really a lovely sight and one always new to us. The glowing
> tubes looked like faint, fairy lights. (Curie and Curie 1923,
> 187)

The peculiar realm of radiation was discovered by accident. In
1896, Antoine Henri Becquerel, who was intrigued by the capacity of some materials to glow when exposed to sunlight, was
hoping to demonstrate a link between these minerals and a new
type of electromagnetic radiation discovered by Wilhelm Rönt-
gen, called X-rays. Although he set up an experiment overcast
conditions prevented him from studying the fluorescing material (uranyl sulphate) and he placed it in a drawer, so he could
observe its behaviour on a sunny day. On returning to the unex-
posed plate, he discovered strong, clear images, which indicated
that the uranium had emitted radiation without recourse to an
external source. Later, Marie and Pierre Curie discovered that
both radium and polonium could also emit such rays. This invisible radiation, or 'radioactivity', was further characterised as a
complex phenomenon by Ernest Rutherford, who split its beams
into alpha, beta, and gamma particles, which could be classified
according to their ability to penetrate matter. Niels Bohr theoretically demonstrated these rays originated from the emission
of charged particles, which jumped between the orbits of atomic
nuclei, when they were excited by collisions with other agents.
The further characterisation of radiation has not lessened its
strangeness, which enjoys an odd relationship to matter, since it
interacts with matter, is created by matter, can create matter and
is emitted by matter, but it is just too ephemeral to 'be' matter
(Armstrong 2016, 36).

  With the discovery of a stranger invisible, massless, almost
volumeless material world, the once indivisible atom became

the backdrop against which these subatomic agents could be observed. With further developments in radiation science, charge-carrying explanations were sought for the properties of matter, which identified other kinds of phenomena. Some of which were surprising, like neutrinos, which do not play a major role in the structure of atoms (Lincoln 2017) and not only provided new accounts of atomic identity, but also firmly established quantum physics as a new field of science.

Spooky Reality

> The hard problem of matter is distinct from other problems of interpretation in physics. Current physics presents puzzles, such as: How can matter be both particle-like and wave-like? What is quantum wavefunction collapse? Are continuous fields or discrete individuals more fundamental? But these are all questions of how to properly conceive of the structure of reality. The hard problem of matter would arise even if we had answers to all such questions about structure. No matter what structure we are talking about, from the most bizarre and unusual to the perfectly intuitive, there will be a question of how it is non-structurally implemented. (Mørch 2017)

The first steps towards the standard model that is currently used to understand the anatomy of atoms were established by Sheldon Gashow in the 1960s, when he grouped discoveries in quantum field theory into quarks (up, down, charm, strange, top, bottom); leptons (electron, electron neutrino, muon, muon neutrino, tau, tau neutrino), gauge bosons (gluon, photon, Z-boson, W-boson) and the Higgs boson (Glashow 1961). Like Mendeleev's periodic table, which further advanced the understanding of the combinatorial properties of the atomic realm by formulating the 'periodic law' according to eight base types, Gashow's system is a deductive and predictive instrument, not only establishing the characteristics of known particles, but also predicting the existence of as yet undiscovered ones. For example, since gravity exists, it is counterintuitive that subatomic particles are massless. The light Higgs boson, or other interactions between particles may confer this missing mass and therefore renders the standard model complete. Further concepts like string theory and supersymmetry also aim to fill in these gaps between knowledge and experiment. String theory proposes that fundamental particles are different manifestations of one basic object: a 'string'. These are one-dimensional point structures with no internal organisation that become different particles through the way they oscillate in space-time. So, in one direction, we see an electron, and in another, a photon or a quark. String theory predicts that a type of connection, called supersymmetry, exists between particle types despite their almost oppositional character — for example, fermions and bosons and is almost magical in its oddness. Notably, it anticipates the lightest supersymmetric particle that is stable and electrically neutral, which interacts weakly with the particles of the standard model, has exactly the characteristics of dark matter.

It is still not known how these massless specks establish a connection with gravity. While the nature of matter is still being pieced together, the quantum realm is fundamentally counterintuitive and produces strange phenomena. For example, time crystals have been demonstrated, which spontaneously break time translation symmetry and create the possibility of regularly repeating motion without the need for extra energy from external sources (Yao et al. 2017). Other odd nanoparticles called 'magnetic skyrmions' behave in ways similar to the atomic 'knots' proposed by Lord Kelvin in his model of atomic structure. This followed on from the work of Hermann Helmholtz in the late nineteenth century, who observed that vortices exert forces on each other and their cores act as a line-like filament that can become knotted with others in ways that could not be undone. Inspired by the coupling potential of these fundamental structures, Lord Kelvin proposed an atomic model where atoms were structured like liquids as knots of swirling vortices in the aether (Zyga 2017). Imagine a bath half filled with water, with not one, but lots of plugholes. Now envision how the surface of the water looks as those plugs are pulled. This is how Lord Kelvin imagined the structure of atoms. Unusually, 'magnetic skyrmions' can be observed experimentally (Hou et. al. 2017), which means they may at some point be manipulated to test new theories such as 'knotting' them into various types of stable configurations by twisting a magnetic field (Zyga 2017).

While initial studies of quantum phenomena were assumed to be confined to imperceptibly small and cold realms, by the late twentieth century these assumptions were challenged through the identification of exotic materials at the macroscale. For example, semi-metals can produce a current when heat and a magnetic field are applied simultaneously (Gooth et al. 2017); their properties cannot be accounted for by classical physics. Perhaps even more striking are findings in the developing field of quantum biology, where physics meets the life sciences and 'biology emerges from chemistry, which in turn emerges from how atoms and molecules interact in the microscopic realms ruled by quantum probabilities' (Byrne 2013). While classical quantum experiments take place in the laboratory at temperatures close to absolute zero, biology can process quantum information at room temperature and stabilise coherent quantum states in extremely complex systems for extended periods.

> It turns out that organic systems with tailor-made molecules are highly tunable. The trick is to not lose the input data. (Byrne 2013)

For the observed events to take place, they must disobey a fundamental concept known as decoherence, where quantum effects are averaged out at the macroscale. By demonstrating that quantum phenomena can be effective in these unlikely situations, this means that even at relatively hot temperatures typical of living systems (Al-Khalili and McFadden 2014), the individual properties of matter may be — at least in part — contributing to the 'weird' nature of matter and life. Schrödinger drew his inferences on the nature of life,[2] from the experimental research conducted by Max Delbrück during the 1930s, where organic molecules overcame energy barriers to enable the chemistry of life, which was established by quantum interactions between the subatomic and atomic interactions of organisms (Byrne 2013). Yet, it is still not known what prevents biological systems from

---

2   Specifically, Schrödinger observed that discrete systems are capable of 'negative entropy' that enables system reordering and resistance to entropic decay (Schrödinger 2012, 70).

becoming what Schrödinger called 'quantum jellyfish', which refers to the anticipated blurriness and featurelessness when many overlapping boundaries exist, which are characteristic of quantum fields.

> … nearly every result produce[d] is about the probability
> of this or that … happening — with usually a great many
> alternatives. The idea that they be not alternatives but
> all really happen simultaneously seems lunatic … just
> impossible … if the laws of nature took this form for …
> a quarter of an hour, we should find our surroundings
> rapidly turning into a quagmire, or sort of a featureless jelly,
> or plasma, all contours becoming blurred, we ourselves
> probably becoming jelly fish. (Schrödinger 1995, 19)

Nevertheless, the biological domain does not demonstrate the typical paradoxes associated with information processing in quantum physics (Byrne 2013). The practical implications of these findings are far from reaching a consensus view. This is hardly surprising, as the more that is discovered about the quantum realm, the stranger it seems. To establish a relationship with this realm means that decisions about the kind of information that is useful to us have to be made that can challenge our assumptions. Françoise Chatelin cautions that the mathematical philosophical framework underpinning quantum science is also capable of distorting interpretations of experimental findings because the effects of other forces and agencies involved get smaller as objects get larger. Also, unlike classical physics, the sample sizes are also very small and therefore deal with exceptional behaviour, rather than the averaging effects of huge numbers of molecules (Chatelin 2012).

> After the experimental discovery of Quantum Mechanics,
> the strange wave/particle behaviour at the subatomic
> level was taken by Bohr (1927) as a fiat from Nature. Bohr
> posited the 'complementarity' principle which states that
> quantum-mechanical results can only be described in

classical but contradictory terms. Therefore a description in space-time precludes any classically causal description, and if classical causality is maintained then the uncertainty principles (Heisenberg) emerges. In other words, sub-atomic randomness is only the result of looking at things through the lenses of classical causality. The radically dualistic perspective of Bohr accepts as a gift the two contradictory messages sent by Nature. This paradoxical picture fits perfectly in the organic logic ... which stems from hyper computation. But it was a constant source of discomfort for the majority of his peers. Therefore Bohr's view was abandoned for the most easy-to grasp theory of entanglements, which puts randomness at its foundation. (Chatelin 2012, 558–59)

Nevertheless, researchers are beginning to develop experimental approaches that enable us to test our understanding of our idiosyncratic universe in a constant state of flux.

Maxwell's Demon

> ... atoms do not swerve a little and initiate the kind of
> motion which in turn shatters the laws of fate, but leave
> effect to follow cause inexorably forever, where does that
> freewill come from that exists in every creature the world
> over? (Lucretius 2007, 43)

Lucretius introduced the concept of the 'clinamen' to discuss the
disobedience of the material realm to the laws of physics. He
believed that this unpredictable swerve of atoms accounted for
the free will of all living things.

James Clerk Maxwell proposed a thought experiment that
aimed to contravene the second law of physics, which states that
the entropy in a closed system (a box) cannot decrease (Maxwell
1872). Imagining gas at a particular temperature (or pressure) in
a sealed environment, he proposed that within this space some
molecules were hotter (moving faster) and some cooler (moving slower) than others. Guarding a membrane-like partition
with a small trapdoor (a pore-like system) inside the box, was
an imaginary intelligent being (later called a 'demon' by Lord
Kelvin) that could perform 'work' without expending energy, by
deciding which side of the membrane the gas molecules ended
up on. By sorting the mixed gas molecules into an ordered state
with lower entropy the demon could contravene the second law
of physics (Kelvin 1879).

> The word 'demon,' which originally in Greek meant a
> supernatural being, has never been properly used as
> signifying a real or ideal personification of malignity.
> Clerk Maxwell's 'demon' is a creature of imagination
> having certain perfectly well-defined powers of action,
> purely mechanical in their character, invented to help us
> to understand the 'Dissipation of Energy' in nature. He is a
> being with no preternatural qualities, and differs from real
> living animals only in extreme smallness and agility. He can

at pleasure stop, or strike, or push, or pull any single atom of matter, and so moderate its natural course of motion. Endowed ideally with arms and hands and fingers — two hands and ten fingers suffice — he can do as much for atoms as a pianoforte player can do for the keys of the piano — just a little more, he can push or pull each atom in any direction. He cannot create or annul energy; but just as a living animal does, he can store up limited quantities of energy, and reproduce them at will. By operating selectively on individual atoms he can reverse the natural dissipation of energy ... (Kelvin 1879, 144)

Both Maxwell and Kelvin concluded that the presence of an intelligent agent in a disordered system could encapsulate life's thermodynamic disobedience, but in 1929, Hungarian physicist Leo Szilard demonstrated that the demon had to exert energy to sort the molecules into hot or cold groupings, which would not actually violate the second law (Edwards 2010). Maxwell's demon therefore gives the appearance of violating the second law, without actually contravening it, which is exactly what life manages to do.

Time's Arrow

> An organism does not have a temporal trajectory; it is itself
> a temporal trajectory. (Nicholson 2018, 22)

In classical physics, time is a reversible phenomenon. It deals
with space and the statistical analyses of large numbers outlined
by Ludwig Boltzmann, where random events cancel out any behaviours that may appear to contradict the second law of thermodynamics. This banishes time to the realm of phenomenology (Boltzmann 1964).

In the natural realm, time is a material process that operates
at small scales in highly localised situations and produces its effects on a paucity of molecules, where statistical analyses cannot
iron out any irregularities. In this contrary space, lively matter
has the capacity to retain or increase its order. Tim Maudlin observes that standard geometry, which is algebraic and designed
for making directionless spaces, considers time to be an arte-
fact of space. In this case, either nothing alters, or events can
be reversed (Musser 2017). Drawing on Henri Bergson's concept
of 'pure duration', Ilya Prigogine developed a concept of 'third
time' in physics, where qualitative local changes melt into and
permeate one another, without precise outlines. This provided
a new model for examining space-time, where time was 'pure
heterogeneity' (Bergson 2010, 104), rather than a series of successive (linear) occurrences. *Third time* is therefore characterised by irreversibility, which provides a source of creativity for
the living realm and exists in space-time rather than standard
geometric space.

> Irreversibility can no longer be identified with a mere
> appearance that would disappear if we had perfect
> knowledge. Instead, it leads to coherence, to effects that
> encompass billions and billions of particles. Figuratively
> speaking, matter at equilibrium, with no arrow of time

is 'blind,' but with the arrow of time, it begins to 'see'.
(Prigogine 1997, 3)

Symmetry Breaking

> According to Archemanes the world was created as a
> result of the synergy of two primal forces. He understood
> these powerful forces to be eternal and universal. Their
> synergy would best be described as never-ending
> consumption — one devours the other, ceaselessly — and
> the existence of the world is dependent on this. (Tokarczuk
> 2003, 99)

All natural forces and elementary particles are assumed to
have been identical just before the Big Bang. For the universe to
have any character, this fundamental symmetry had to be broken, which is an active phenomenon caused by countless small
matter/energy fluctuations acting on a system that tip it into an
irreversible cascade of events and is at the heart of all meaningful dynamic events.

First, the colour force between quarks broke away from the
electroweak interaction. Then, hadrons developed very different masses from leptons. Next, electroweak forces split into
two — electromagnetism and the weak force (or weak nuclear
force). Out of these moments of asymmetry, an ocean of particle
types blossomed, which gave rise to our present reality.

Liquid life is an asymmetric phenomenon (Coleman 1975),
where like no longer breeds like, but moves towards a condition
of heterogenesis — where, under the influence of time's irreversible arrow, nothing can be exactly self-similar, so variation in
living systems is the norm, not the exception.

03.9

Invisible Realms

> Aethers were invented for the planets to swim in, to constitute electric atmospheres and magnetic effluvia, to convey sensations from one part of our bodies to another, and so on, until all space had been filled three or four times over with aethers. ... The only aether which has survived is that which was invented by Huygens to explain the propagation of light. (Maxwell 1878)

Perhaps the hardest of all questions for science to answer is not the nature of matter, but of space. If atomism is correct, then it is possible to measure and detect 'something', but it is paradoxical to characterise nothing. Nothing must be filled with *something,* which can then be negated and considered 'nothing'. Such existential conundrums produce material and conceptual blind spots, which they ask us to imagine concepts beyond our knowledge, experience, or ability to verify them and open up a realm of unnamed mysteries, forces, and unexplained phenomena, which cannot be verified directly through our senses, or even by scientific instruments.

While we cannot directly perceive the invisible realm, its effects can sometimes be indirectly encountered like feeling a breeze upon your face, or watching a dust devil dancing. At other times, invisible realms must be deduced where there is no other available explanation, such as dark energy and matter, which seem to be simultaneously holding the universe together and pushing it apart. The invisible realm remains problematic, as to be accounted for, it must be correctly theorised and conjured into existence. Failure to do this means that our knowledge of reality is incomplete, and what we do not know is banished to the realms of speculation, mythology, or wishful thinking.

From the time of Aristotle, nature was said to 'abhor' a vacuum, while Parmenides opposed the concept of 'creatio ex nihilo', since the idea of nothingness by definition did not exist. Up until the fourteenth century, the narratives of 'nothing' were attributed to supernatural forces, which sprang from demonic, divine, and unknown influences, that were thought to hold reality together (Barrow 2002, 71–72). These mysterious invisible forces also shaped our world and even extended beyond the reach of the cosmos. From an experimental perspective, scholars such as Al-Farabi began to make vacuums using pumps and closed containers, which provoked a range of theories accounting for the contradictory nature of these spaces and how they could 'actually' hold the universe together. For example, Walter Burley proposed that voids could exist momentarily but were prevented from collapse by celestial forces. Enlightenment perspectives took a mathematical view of the paradox of matter and space, where Descartes proposed that the single essential property of matter was its 'extension' of volumetric space (Descartes 1985). This separated bodies at a distance and implied the existence of a continuous medium between them. The idea of invisible rays and uncharacterised forces inevitably led to disagreements about their nature. Isaac Newton and Gottfried Wilhelm Leibniz differed in their views about the way gravity influenced bodies, Leibniz regarding Newton's view of remote interactions as akin to 'occultism' (Clarke and Leibniz 1998).

Soon, the idea of force fields and geometric frameworks began to fill up these invisible realms and everything moved through a universe filled with an ocean of ubiquitous (uncharacterised) ethereal fluid. Collectively, these forces were discussed as transmission media or aethers. These space-filling substances and fields were necessary for the action of bodies, forces, and light to act upon. However, most of these ideas could not be empirically validated. For example, the 'odic' force, which was proposed by Baron Carl von Reichenbach as a vital substance that permeated crystals, magnets, and living things, could be detected through the senses. Reichenbach believed that some people were more predisposed to these forces than others and could be seen as a field gliding spectacularly along magnets and crystals in total darkness by sensitive individuals.

While many 'invisible forces' were debunked, numerous paradoxes of the invisible realms remain. Isaac Newton's laws of gravity — a cornerstone of physics — remain mysterious, since the hypothetical fundamental gravity-carrying particle, or graviton, has not been identified. Others, such as the luminiferous aether proposed by Christiaan Huygens that could be traversed by light, steadily gained credibility and led to the discovery of electromagnetic phenomena.

It is possible that the fundamental assumptions of atomism leave blind spots in our conception of reality, and may even prevent our complete characterisation of the cosmos. For example, the influence and relevance of dark energy and matter currently exceeds the capacity of our philosophical and experimental apparatuses to ascertain. While this should not preclude investigation of the phenomena, our discoveries are anticipating a particular set of observations that place them within an existing understanding of reality. Alternative ways of conceiving the world are vital for exploring the spandrels of opportunity that exist beyond the limits of a geometrically organised universe, and may help us gain a more complete understanding of the nature of the cosmos.

> Physical knowledge has advanced much since 1905, notably by the arrival of quantum mechanics, and the situation [about the scientific plausibility of aether] has again changed. If one examines the question in the light of present-day knowledge, one finds that the aether is no longer ruled out by relativity, and good reasons can now be advanced for postulating an aether ... We can now see that we may very well have an aether, subject to quantum mechanics and conformable to relativity, provided we are willing to consider a perfect vacuum as an idealized state, not attainable in practice. From the experimental point of view there does not seem to be any objection to this. We must make some profound alterations to the theoretical idea of the vacuum ... Thus, with the new theory of electrodynamics we are rather forced to have an aether. (Dirac 1951)

In an age of quantum theory, the notion of 'aether' has become outdated and replaced by more theoretical models and terminology to invoke the character of the void. Even stranger forms of aether than classical physics proposed are explored through the idea of 'quanta', or packets of matter. The quantum realm, however, does not assume that space is empty, but already 'occupied' by a quantum vacuum. While the term may superficially imply another kind of nothingness, its nature is, unsurprisingly, contradictory. For starters, a quantum vacuum is a very different kind of 'absence' than the classical void, as it is not truly empty, but filled with space-time, which has curvature, structure, and is teeming with potential particles, pairs of virtual matter and antimatter units, which are being simultaneously created and destroyed in massive numbers on a quantum scale. This peculiar vacuum also contains 'quantum foam', which is made up of many types of electromagnetic fields that permeate space-time, where each domain gives rise to specific subatomic particles — for example, electron fields produce electrons. Quantum foam is imagined as a ubiquitous medium that underpins the propagation of electromagnetic waves by incorporating the transitioning of photons into electrons and positrons[3] — even within the space between galaxies. Since these characterising events are so incredibly small they do not significantly interact with us at the macroscale, so in everyday terms, they can effectively be ignored.

> ... 'empty space' is not what we think it is — it is a soup of a lot of things that average out to zero. Like thermodynamic equilibrium, i.e. 'no net flow' is nowhere near the same as 'no flow' at all! (De Jesus 2016)

Other theories that characterise the nature of 'space' manage to evade the tricky subject of matter altogether. For example, Albert Einstein's approach to gravity proposes that it is a smooth force

3   This is an example of radiation (photons) becoming matter (electrons and positrons)

and curvature of space-time that is induced by mass and energy. Therefore, an object's mass/energy warps space-time — similar to how a rubber sheet is deformed by a heavy body (Creighton 2015b). In this way, Einstein evades the need to discuss the 'hard question' of the nature of the material realm.

Theory of Everything

> It would be very difficult to construct a complete unified theory of everything all at one go. So instead we have made progress by finding partial theories. These describe a limited range of happenings and neglect other effects, or approximate them by certain numbers. In chemistry, for example, we can calculate the interactions of atoms without knowing the internal structure of the nucleus of an atom. Ultimately, however, one would hope to find a complete, consistent, unified theory that would include all these particle theories as approximation. The quest for such a theory is known as 'the unification of physics'. (Hawking 2007, 111)

Quantum theory and general relativity are different worldviews, so there is a schism in theoretical physics, which could be healed by a unifying Theory of Everything (TOE). In approaching this quest Paul Dirac developed an equation that decipher the behaviour of an atom moving at relativistic speed, which combined quantum theory and special relativity. However, the outcome posed a significant problem, in that the equation had a positive and a negative solution, which anticipated the existence of antimatter.

> From our theoretical picture, we should expect an ordinary electron, with positive energy, to be able to drop into a hole and fill up this hole, the energy being liberated in the form of electromagnetic radiation. This would mean a process in which an electron and a positron annihilate one another. The converse process, namely the creation of an electron and a positron from electromagnetic radiation, should also be able to take place. Such processes appear to have been found experimentally, and are at present being more closely investigated by experimenters. (Dirac 1933)

Such investigations raise profound implications about the conventions we use to understand the universe. For example, attempts to produce a quantum theory of time that brings together the theory of relativity with the quantum realm, suggest that space-time might arise as a side effect of entangled 'quantum bits' (*qubits*) that are situated on the temporal boundaries of the universe (Cowen 2015). Other theories, like 'bootstrapping', which was pioneered by Alexander Polyakov in the 1970s, search for geometric frameworks that can accommodate universal principles within quantum field theory by searching for identical behaviours in diverse materials, where 'correlation functions' can be computed. These correlations happen at phase transitions (such as heating iron to the point where it loses its magnetism), where molecules suddenly all exhibit the same behaviours. Such 'conformal symmetries' constrain the variables within matter, so that all possible quantum field theories can potentially be unified to generate a quantum TOE. This framework has implications not only for dark matter, but also for space-time and the quantum origin of gravity (Wolchover 2017a).

> There's no telling what insights such a theory would yield. Physicists struggling to marry Einstein with quantum mechanics have already made one startling discovery. In 1971, Russian physicist Yakov Zel'dovich guessed that black holes aren't truly black, but instead combine with quantum-mechanical fluctuations to emit photons and other particles. Stephen Hawking proved the idea three years later, and these emissions are now called Hawking radiation. All fledgling theories of quantum gravity also make a more general and even weirder prediction: the structure of space and time is very different from the gentle curves predicted by general relativity. The American physicist John Wheeler realized in the 1950s that if you look at things on a scale of about 10–35 metres, quantum fluctuations become powerful enough to play tricks with the geometry of the Universe. Space and time break down into 'fuzziness' or 'foaminess'. A spaceship that size could find itself negotiating virtual black

holes, or getting sucked into one wormhole after another and tossed back and forth in time and space. (Brooks 1999, 28)

With such determination to combine the best of both worlds, physicists could be creating a contrary model of reality like the 'Tycho Brahe solution', which attempted to reconcile the ancient Ptolemaic system and Copernican cosmology by imagining the Earth at the centre of the universe while all the other planets orbited the sun (Ouellette 2017). It is possible that the range of contradictory findings that characterise the observations of quantum science may simply mean that our current models of the universe are profoundly mistaken.

> ... if you believe that the universe is not arbitrary, but is governed by definite laws, you ultimately have to combine the partial theories into a complete unified theory that will describe everything in the universe. But there is a fundamental paradox in the search for such a complete unified theory. The ideas about scientific theories outlined ... assume we are rational beings who are free to observe the universe, as we want and to draw logical deductions from what we see. In such a scheme it is reasonable to suppose that we might progress ever closer toward the laws that govern our universe. Yet if there really is a complete unified theory, it would also presumably determine our actions. And so the theory itself would determine the outcome for our search for it! And why should it determine that we come to the right conclusions from the evidence? Might it not equally well determine that we draw the wrong conclusion? Or no conclusion at all? (Hawking 1995, 14)

Provided they are not slammed into competition, the accumulation of differing perspectives on the nature of reality enriches our understanding of it. Since our understanding of matter is incomplete, the pursuit of unifying theories may not be sensible, let alone possible. However, the contradictions that arise from such a pursuit can offer more complex and nuanced modes of understanding than any one theory alone. Perhaps, as we dwell among the uncertainties, mysteries, and incompleteness of the universe, closer attention to its contradictions to observe what emerges from these uncertain terrains. For example, what does it mean that we best understand the imperceptibly small aspects of reality through the gargantuan scale such as the Large Hadron Collider and how does this relate to human experience? Does quantum entanglement play any role within dissipative structures and, if so, how might this change our understanding of life? To address such questions, our concepts, language, and narratives need to be sufficiently rich to deal with our constantly emerging understanding of reality.

'Pataphysics

> To understand 'pataphysics is to fail to understand
> 'pataphysics. To define it is merely to indicate a possible
> meaning, which will always be the opposite of another
> equally possible meaning, which, when diurnally
> interpolated with the first meaning, will point towards a
> third meaning which will in turn elude definition because
> of the fourth element that is missing. What we see of
> 'pataphysics in the so-called real world is what has been
> created to provide the evidence of 'pataphysics. It seems to
> connect with the paradoxes and uncertainties of quantum
> mechanics, yet it does so through a very different kind of
> mathematics, a purely imaginary science. (Hugill 2012, 2)

Alfred Jarry's imaginary science of exceptions resists definitions. 'Pataphysics is intent upon seeking imaginary solutions to
real or non-real phenomena, and is remarkable for its purpose-
lessness and unfathomability. Nevertheless, it is a coherent set of
ideas and experiments that embrace the specific and irreducible
aspects of reality to establish where contradictory and exceptional solutions may be found, such as sailing in a sieve, building
a time machine and mathematically calculating the surface area
of God (Jarry 1997).

> It will already be apparent that definitions of 'pataphysics
> are to be treated with caution. This is because the very
> notion of a 'definition,' which is a cluster of words that
> gives the specific sense of a terms that holds true in all
> (or as nearly all as makes no different) situations, is itself
> unpataphysical. (Hugill 2012, 3)

'Pataphysics opens up a space for liquid life by enabling the
impossible, invisible, imaginary, and contradictory qualities
of the living realm to be acknowledged — not as truths but as

paradoxes — and to hold spaces open for experiment that would otherwise be closed by logic and empiricism.

Speck

> A vigorous speck. An imperceptible ort of life.
> Against the odds.
> The chances of life forming by random processes alone
> based on the possibility of the random synthesis of a small
> protein are said to be less than one in ten to the power
> of forty thousand. In other words, the odds against life
> happening by accident are greater than it occurring once in
> thirteen billion years — the age of the universe.
> Life should not exist.
> And yet, a dot of life.
> Here (.) (Armstrong, forthcoming 2020)

Against all probability life exists and when it is encountered, it springs from an appropriately lively material condition. The questions missing from the classical worldview of 'life' pertain to its native vital materiality, which is a material condition that permeates matter at far-from-equilibrium states and is capable of being incorporated into existing and new assemblages of participatory matter. 'Vital materialist' Jane Bennett proposes that the 'life-principle that animates matter, exists only when in a relationship with matter, but is not itself of a material nature' (Bennett 2010b, 47–48). In providing examples of vital materiality from the inanimate world — where 'glove, pollen, (unblemished dead) rat, cap, stick … comman[d] attention in their own right, as existents in excess of their association with human meaning, habits or projects …' (Bennett 2010b, 4) — she responds to the oddness of a 'lively' material composition. Bennett's desire to reunify inert matter with a vital essence, (re)transposes this liveliness into an ephemeral realm, which beyond its compelling description is nonetheless complicit with the logic of the *bête machine*.

   Appreciating that matter itself is a fundamentally strange actor that appears disobedient to classical laws (see sections 09.9 and 08.10), does not mean that anything goes. Rather, a non-classical set of principles also govern 'actual' material agency. Observations made throughout the twentieth century indicate that innate vitality is bestowed upon the material realm without invoking spiritual infusions through the laws of quantum physics, the passage of 'third time' and 'dissipative adaptation'. Since energy flows freely through agentised matter in unidirectional time, it can also dynamically alter its program, which raises questions about the origins of 'mind'. These operations are not self-contained, but are fundamentally open and directly coupled to the environment. Moreover, the molecular interactions that comprise these material expressions, such as dissipative structures, are shaped by the transformations encoded by their spatial configuration, elemental character, laws of physics, chemistry, and, also, by their context. Furthermore, these behaviours and transformations have also been independently shown to become even more complex — whether they are directly observed, or not (Prigogine 1997).

> We now know that irreversibility leads to a host of novel phenomena, such as vortex formation, chemical oscillations, and laser light, all illustrating the essential constructive role of the arrow of time … The claim that the arrow of time is 'only phenomenological,' or subjective, is therefore absurd. We are actually the children of the arrow of time, of evolutions, not its progenitors. (Prigogine 1997, 3)

To engage with such lively entities is not to subdue, but to engage and provoke them. Given that the material realm is stranger than our classical laws attest, and the 'emergent' properties arise from agents that cannot be meaningfully reduced into their components, then it is possible that, as yet uncharacterised, forces or events may also be in play. Such perspectives do not negate the soul substance that is necessary for 'life' but through its irreducibility and inseparability from matter, as a unique and fundamental material property of the (luminous) cosmos.

138

The role of the observer was a necessary concept in the introduction of irreversibility, or the flow of time, into quantum theory. But once it is shown that instability breaks time symmetry, the observer is no longer essential. In solving the time paradox, we also solve the quantum paradox and obtain a new, realistic formulation of quantum theory. This does not mean a return to classical deterministic orthodoxy; on the contrary, we go beyond the certitudes associated with the traditional laws of quantum theory and emphasize the fundamental role of probabilities. (Prigogine 1997, 5)

COMPLEXITIES

This chapter highlights the fluidic, mutable nature of living systems by outlining the challenges faced by the *bête machine* when explaining, or imitating, the irreducibly complex processes of life.

Making Life

> Complexity gives the lie to the motto which was so
> often used in order to claim that everything is clear, at
> least in principle. 'This is the same thing that we already
> understand, just more complicated.' This was precisely
> Jacques Monod's claim: the study of bacteria had produced
> the secrets of life; the royal road, the only scientifically
> relevant one, had been opened. For the mouse or the
> elephant, or man, it would be the same questions, the same
> road. (Stengers and Lissack 2004, 92)

Mechanistic models of the living realm suppose that life can be built once all the fundamental parts of an organism are identified and fully connected together. In other words, the only difference between life and non-life, is the *bête machine*'s organisational complexity.

For more than 150 years, scientific experiments aimed towards producing sufficient complexity within systems of organic, as well as mechanical and artificial parts, has failed to work (Hanczyc 2008; Hanczyc 2011), as the living and mechanical realms are not materially equivalent. The machine's 'brute', unagentised ontology, belongs to a deterministic world at relative equilibrium (brute matter), while organic life occupies far-from-equilibrium states (agentised matter) that are situated in a world of flux (Mayr 2004). The theorised challenges in life's artificial construction, exceed those of reaching sufficiently advanced levels of higher-order complexity to generate life. Living systems arise from persistent hubs of activity, which perform multitudinous operations that are structured by patterns and repetitions, yet descriptions of this process do not comprise a buildable strategy for compiling 'life'.

> Can the emergence of real new properties in complex
> systems really be explained? If the sciences of complexity
> offer important new insights, theories, and methodologies

for dealing with complex, higher-order phenomena (as we think they do), and if the traditional view of explanation cannot account for the explanatory strategies we find here, we should look for other accounts of scientific explanation. Perhaps the very idea of scientific explanation as a strictly deductive argument should be reinterpreted and explanations seen in a more dynamic and context-dependent setting, eventually themselves being emergent structures, 'emergent explanations'. (Baas and Emmeche 1997)

'Living' matter is innately agentised, sensitive to environmental conditions and capable of behaving unpredictably. Although various approaches, such as Gantí's Chemoton model and the Maturana–Varela notion of autopoietic systems, are used to explore its characteristic phenomena, a mature portfolio of accessible apparatuses capable of working with matter at far-from-equilibrium states, is still far from mature.

... *in silico* and *in vitro* investigations are paving the way to a novel research arena that appears to be both very rich (thanks to its intrinsic interdisciplinary character) and promising (because only via synthetic/constructive approaches is it possible to enquire about the features of simple, early cells). This approach also stimulates more theoretical considerations with respect to intriguing questions, such as 'What is life?' and further supports abiogenesis as the theoretical framework for understanding the emergence of living systems on Earth. (Stano and Mavelli 2015)

As an experimental discipline, building life from its fundamental ingredients remains as challenging as nailing jellies to walls.

Life as Fundamental Change

The process of inheritance is unaffected by the processes
that introduce an adaptive bias to form, and by the process
of development. Organisms do not inherit what would
be advantageous for them to inherit, instead, for better
or worse, they get the traits their parents donate to them
at conception. Novel evolutionary characteristics (i.e.,
mutations) are unbiased by the adaptive demands of the
organisms in which they first occur. They are said to occur
at random. Neither of the processes of inheritance or
development introduced evolutionary changes to biological
form. The structure of the inherited material is completely
unaffected by the downstream developmental processes
that turn programs into organisms. What arises anew in
development cannot be genuinely inherited. As neither
inheritance, nor development, nor mutation is adaptively
biased, there must be another, wholly independent process
that introduces adaptive change. Adaptive evolutionary
change is the sole province of natural selection. (Huneman
and Walsh 2017, 2–3)

Life's persistence through its self-replication, or reproduction, is
at the crux of the modern story of life, which is characterised by
the Modern Synthesis that centres on genes. Originating in the
early twentieth century, it combines the Mendelian theory of inheritance with the neo-Darwinian theory of population change
in evolutionary dynamics (Huneman and Walsh 2017).

According to the Modern Synthesis, genes act on inert organic matter, which has no innate agency. Since genes, which are
also 'just' molecules,[1] are bequest a special status in their ability
to act, they perform the role of the molecular 'brain' of the cell,

---

1   While crystals have historically been considered 'primordial seeds' of life,
    molecular biology regularly confers chemical structures with agency and
    even 'personifies' them with attributes such as selfishness (Dawkins 2006).

or the soul in the *bête machine*. Their potency is particularly persuasive, since our molecular evidencing systems are developed to further endorse their centrality. Every explanation of the living world in the Modern Synthesis is reduced back to the action of genes, or more recently, their networks. Deviance from the assumed standard of self-similarity of genetic reproduction are caused by genetic 'errors' — rather than other active organising systems working in parallel with them — that result in 'modification by descent'. Regarding variation as a second-order narrative, the Modern Synthesis views these unconventionalities as carrying narratives of functional adaptation and identity, which provide 'Darwinian selection [with the] genetic variation to work on' (Dawkins 2006, 320). Remaining silent until a time of evolutionary need, they are then expressed wherever difference — not sameness — is the key to survival.

> … a transparent worm-like creature [is] moving uncomfortabl[y] on the surface of an exploded rock. It has recently ingested a woodlouse. Although the worm's meal is fully enveloped within its simple gut, the ingested crustacean's shell has protected it from digestion. The worm is at risk of being split open by the woodlouse, which kicks out against its soft, suffocating intestines. Perhaps an unlikely truce can be struck between them. While the louse continues to struggle in its transparent organic bag, a gelatinous swarm of cells surrounds the coupled bodies — anticipating that one of these battling systems will fail. The amorphous mass pulses as tiny particles moving through its very simple spaces, or veins. Its approach is marked by a trail of translucent slime that exteriorises and records its primitive thinking … In its own manner and at its own speed, the formless blob attempts to swallow whole the conjoined creatures. (Armstrong 2018a, 87)

Bacteria, which are among the most abundant organisms on Earth (Nature Reviews Microbiology 2011) reproduce by different means than 'higher' organisms. Asexually dividing by 'binary fission', a bacterial cell prepares for the synthesis of two daughters by enlarging to twice its starting size before it divides. In preparation for fission, a complex system of proteins, which make up the cell division machinery, condenses at the division site. Genetic material is then copied and partitioned to opposite ends of the cell through a complex choreography of structures, which avoids damaging the DNA during the process. The sequence of events starts at the site called the 'origin' and appears to be tightly regulated by the cell apparatus, which orchestrates DNA replication, segregation, division site location, cell envelope invagination and new cell wall synthesis. As the cell divides, the cytoplasm splits and a new cell wall is produced around the daughter cells, which are (functionally) identical to the progenitor and are clones of each other.

> Although the tiniest bacterial cells are incredibly small, weighing less than 10^{-12} grams, each is in effect a veritable micro-miniaturized factory containing thousands of exquisitely designed pieces of intricate molecular machinery, made up altogether of one hundred thousand million atoms, far more complicated than any machinery built by man and absolutely without parallel in the nonliving world. (Denton 1986, 250)

Even for such a seemingly straightforward process, the choreography of events is incredibly complex. If each cell is to remain viable and competitive within the bacterial community, division must occur at the right time, in the right place, and bestow each offspring with a full set of essential organelles and genetic material (a circular chromosome). In a dynamic environment, successful organisms also need to respond quickly to altering circumstances. The adaptive plasticity of cells poses problems for the Modern Synthesis, which places genetic mutations at the heart of adaptive change, that take place randomly through 'error'. However, adaptive changes are not produced at random but in response to specific change, and modifications can confer

147

advantages at their first appearance.[2] Organisms can also preferentially increase copies of genes in areas of the genome where modifications could be beneficial — a hypothesis called 'adaptive mutation' (Cepelewicz 2017).

In bacteria, the whole cell[3] (rather than just its genetic information) can be regarded as the fundamental unit of propagation, particularly since its offspring are self-similar. The advent of multicellularity complicates the biological notion of the 'self' in replication, or reproduction, as it tends towards *differential specialisation.* With only a few cells becoming *gametes,* genetic codes become the unchanging masterplan whose differential expressions leads to various cell types, which are functions of their (invisible) interiority, rather than expressions of the whole creature (phenotype).

Owing to cellular specialism, the lifecycles of multicellular organisms become much more complex. Needing to generate various tissues and organs, their developmental process is regulated by a complex choreography of events in which genes play an important part, but do not determine every event. The choreography between the biological 'self' (genes) and these 'other' factors (metabolism, environment, infection, epigenetics, culture) is highly complex. Of particular interest is how structural complexity is generated in multicellular creatures, since many different species show significant genetic homologies with others — from bananas to fruit flies, mice, and humans — which over evolutionary time, are highly conserved, and raise questions about exactly what causes them to be so very different (see section 05.6). Within the various forms of embodiment that make up the developing biological 'self', differential states of existence capable of performing different functions are expressed,

2   According to the Modern Synthesis, adaptation is an etiological concept, that is, it refers to a trait that has occurred in the past (Huneman and Walsh 2017, 9).

3   While the Modern Synthesis places genes as the central organising agents in evolutionary narratives, the role of whole organisms must also be acknowledged in the processes of change namely, development, adaptation, and evolution itself (Huneman and Walsh 2017, 10).

whereby an egg does not directly reproduce another egg and a chicken does not lay another chicken (see section 06.1). Or, as Stephane Leduc notes, 'the substance of the child is other than that of the ovum, and the substance of the adult is not that of the child' (Leduc 1911, 3).

HeLa cells complicate the concept of multicellular agency even further, since they are the progeny of an immortal cell line of cervical cancer cells taken on February 8 1951 from Henrietta Lacks, a patient who died of cancer on October 4 1951. Characterised only by their genes, rather than the being as a whole, these beings-in-themselves thrive independently from the anatomical conventions that frame other human beings. Although they have not been legally granted personhood, HeLa raises critical questions about what it means to be 'human' and 'alive'.

While the Modern Synthesis implies that genes are discrete codes and rule-makers, advances in molecular biology reveal there is no consensus on what a gene actually is. Nor do they act entirely by their own agency, but are influenced by networks of other molecular actors (Keller and Harel 2007).

"… This molecule can't dance without a team of choreographers", that [means] "it comes alive only when numerous proteins pull its 'strings'". (Pennisi 2003)

This alternative decision-making agency speaks to a dynamic, amorphous realm of metabolism, which is located within the cytoplasm and leaks out into the environment beyond the cell boundary. The formlessness and fluidity of metabolic reactions provides a permissive matrix in which genes, gene systems, and gene networks, become connected to each other within dynamic in a sea of 'invisible' exchanges.

The onset of synthetic biology opens a different perspective by leaving aside the question about the evolutionary origin of biological phenomena and focusing instead on the relational logic and the material properties of the corresponding components that make biological system work as they do. Once a functional challenge arises, the solution space for the problem is not homogeneous but it has attractors that can be accessed either through random exploration (as evolution does) or rational design (as engineers do). Although these two paths (i.e., evolution and engineering) are essentially different, they can lead to solutions to specific mechanistic bottlenecks that frequently coincide or converge-and one can easily help to understand and improve the other. Alas, productive discussions on these matters are often contaminated by ideological preconceptions that prevent adoption of the engineering metaphor to understand and ultimately reshape living systems-as ambitioned by synthetic biology. (de Lorenzo 2018)

The fundamental creativity, heterogeneity, and plasticity of biological systems challenges the central doctrine of Neo-Darwinism, which states that every cell in a multicellular organism is identical. Recent findings of a study into the genetic causes of abdominal aortic aneurysms discovered that blood and tissue samples were not genetically identical (Gottlieb et al. 2009). This finding was anticipated by Kevin Kelly in 2006 in *The Edge,* where he proposed that biological information is not stable, but contextual.

… the DNA in your body (and in the bodies of all living organisms) varies from part to part. I make this prediction based on something we know about biology, which is that nature abhors uniformity. Nowhere else in nature do we see identity maintained to such exactness. Nowhere else is there such fixity. I do not expect intra-soma variation to diverge very much … if my belief is true, it would matter where in your body a sample of your DNA is taken. And it would also matter when your DNA is sampled, as this variation could change over time. (Kelly 2006, 207–8)

Value systems come into play when translating dynamic cell functions into mechanistic programs, as their established range of concepts eliminate a spectrum of robust material processes, such as development, which are necessary for resilient and versatile forms of life. The terminologies used to indicate the character of these phenomena portray them as flaws, errors, modifications, mutations, adaptations, and variations — deviancies from 'the norm', where interspecies hybridisations, such as the breeding between polar and grizzly bears observed in the Northwest Territories of Canada, are reported through (unintentionally) value-loaded accounts.

> 'Polar bears would most likely prefer to mate with other polar bears and grizzlies with other grizzlies, rather than with an odd-looking hybrid' ... (Roach 2006)

> The breakdown of species barriers may start with atypical mating preferences of select individuals; however, the story we present can be traced to a single female polar bear who, along with three of her known F1 offspring, has been killed. (Pongracz et al. 2017, 151)

Such terminology not only spotlights human preferences for biological 'order' within the natural realm but also obfuscates the underlying principle of organic life: that material transformation is at the heart of the living realm, rather than being a deviant side effect of pre-determined processes. This fundamental material creativity is expressed in all complex life forms, which are likely to have evolved independently at least 25 times, in groups as diverse as animals, fungi, plants, slime moulds, and seaweeds (Sebé-Pedrós et al. 2013; McGowan 2014). Even within a single lifespan, multicellular organisms may also undergo multiple transitions in their development (like the instar stages of development of insects) and even integrate other organisms into their lifecycles. The intoxicating exchange between bee and orchid during the pollination process captured Marcel Proust's imagination, where unorthodox modes of sexuality working together through completely different (and extravagant) life forms, could ensure the diverse and effusive propagation of life.

> Like so many creatures of the animal and vegetable
> kingdoms, like the plant that would produce vanilla, but
> which, because, in it, the male organ is divided by a septum
> from the female organ, remains sterile unless humming
> birds or certain small bees transport the pollen from one
> to the other, or unless man fertilizes them artificially ...
> their sexual needs depend on the coincidence of too many
> conditions, too difficult to encounter. (Proust 2003, 30–31)

Reproductive tactics are not always consistent with 'efficient', or conservative, reproductive solutions, but are frequently promiscuous, materially indulgent, and highly risky. In fact, the material choreography of reproduction seems to be designed to be as challenging as possible.

According to the doctrine of the *selfish gene,* life should be *stable* and change very little over the course of evolution, but this is clearly not the case. Donald Williamson suspects that the variety of body forms that were produced in a geological period of morphological variation, the Cambrian Era, were potentially much more plastic and fluid in their ability to fuse with other beings than modern biology is today willing to acknowledge (Williamson 2006a). In other words, these primitive bodies formed strategic 'error-generating' communities.

> About 600 million years ago, shortly before the Cambrian,
> animals with tissues (metazoans) made their first
> appearance ... All Cambrian animals were marine and, like
> most modern marine animals, they shed their eggs and
> sperm into the water where fertilization took place. Eggs
> of one species frequently encountered sperm of another,
> and there were only poorly developed mechanisms to
> prevent hybridization. Early animals had small genomes,
> leaving plenty of spare gene capacity. These factors led to
> many fruitful hybridizations, which resulted in concurrent

chimeras. Not only did the original metazoans hybridize but the new animals resulting from these hybridizations also hybridized, and this produced the explosion in animal form … (Williamson 2006b, 188)

While genetic studies do not support Williamson's specific idea that modern larvae evolved by *hybridogenesis* (Oransky 2011), his view is worth mentioning as a tool for considering the story of life through deep time, when the developmental plasticity of bodies may not have been the same as today.

> … the great majority of novelties which define the taxa are not led up to via the adaptive continuums that might have endowed selection with causal directive agency. Unfortunately, very few are prepared to follow the logical implication of this absence: namely, that the origin of the basic Types of nature must have been determined or directed by causal factors other than gradual cumulative selection. (Denton 2016, 42)

Those life forms that have very distinct modes of existence and development, which depend on radical transitions and transformations like embryos and larvae, continue to challenge the Modern Synthesis by drawing attention to the possibility of multiple loci of organisation within the biological 'self", which organisationally adapt and evolves.

> … though the oyster seems the type of dull animal vegetation in its adult condition, it passes through a vagabond, if not stormy youth, between the time in which it is sheltered by the parental roof, and that in which it 'ranges itself' as a grave and sedentary member of the oyster community. (Huxley 1884, 47)

They also raise important questions about which aspects of their being are conserved during these radical material reorganisations such as during birth and metamorphosis. Slippages in

153

these modes of existence are more than the sequential expression of individual genes, but highly orchestrated modes of restructuring that must simultaneously manage physical change and existential continuity, which is characteristic of dissipative systems (see section 08.10).

> What is this egg? … First there is a speck which moves about, a thread growing and taking colour, flesh being formed, a beak, wing-tips, eyes, feet coming into view, a yellowish substance which unwinds and turns into intestines — and you have a living creature. This creature stirs, moves about, makes a noise. I can hear it cheeping through the shell — it takes on a downy covering, it can see. The weight of its wagging head keeps on banging the beak against the inert wall of its prison. Now the wall is breached and the bird emerges, walks, flies, feels pain, runs away, comes back again, suffers, loves, desires, enjoys, it experiences all your affections and does all the things you do. And will you maintain, with Descartes, that it is an imitating machine pure and simple? (Diderot 1976, 158)

In the process of resisting entropy's call, life's effusive strategies, exquisite choreographies, paradoxical relationships, and material indulgences, present many challenges for the Modern Synthesis, by indulgently exploring the many strategies for existence beyond the restrictions of the (genetic) *bête machine*.

Life — the ultimate flâneur.

Complexity, Cybernetics and Complicating Things

> Entelechy is born in the negative spaces of the machine
> model of nature, in the 'gaps' in the 'chain of strictly
> physico-chemical or mechanical events'. (Bennett 2010b, 50)

The nature of life's dynamic character has been considered since ancient times through a broad range of philosophical frameworks, many of which are animistic and so, refuse the logic of the *bête machine.* Heraclitus compared life to a flame, while Aristotle proposed that 'entelechy', a vital substance that was neither truly material nor spiritual (Bennett 2010, 71), was responsible for the operations of living things.

Within these discourses, the flow of matter and liquids are pervasive themes, which are used to discuss the nature of life and are potentially testable. While some of the properties of liquids can be simulated using mechanisms, their full range of non-linear characteristics cannot be exactly replicated even if attempts to do so provide an enchanting spectacle.

Dating from the eighteenth century, the Silver Swan is an automaton that entranced Mark Twain. Driven by three separate clockwork mechanisms, the ornate bird swims upon a stream of twisted glass and moves gracefully to the sound of music. Periodically it catches a golden fish from out of the stream and has done so for around 250 years (Kennedy 2017; Bowes Museum 2017).

> I watched the Silver Swan, which had a living grace about
> his movement and a living intelligence in his eyes, watched
> him swimming about as comfortably and unconcernedly as
> if he had been born in a morass instead of a jeweller's shop.
> (Kennedy 2017)

Advances in mechanics made possible the development of cybernetic apparatuses, which differ from classical machines by their methods of control, information exchange, and feedback systems (von Bertalanffy 1950). By performing repeated cycles of work, cybernetic apparatuses provide mechanical models for life's fundamental flows and processes that are iteratively updated by information flowing into the apparatus (von Bertalanaffy 1968, 18–19). Largely achieving their effects through the repetitions of inert-bodied machines, which are recursively dependent on each other, they transduce work back into the system to maintain a 'steady state', or mechanical 'homeostasis'. Applying systems science to cybernetics, Ludwig von Bertalanffy championed a new 'natural philosophy' through his General Systems Theory (GST), which modernised Heraclitus' view that life is in constant flux, which could be tested through the flowing interactions and connectedness of cybernetic apparatuses (von Bertalanffy 1950). Such concepts prompted the search for self-maintaining machines, such as Ross Ashby's 'homeostat', which was designed as an 'artificial brain'.

> I have been trying to develope [*sic*] further principles
> for my machine to illustrate stability, + to develope [*sic*]
> ultrastability. (quoted in British Library 2016)

While the fields of GST and cybernetics created a new scientific language, in essence they upheld 'a model of centralization, a real acting-out of it' (Ballantyne 2007, 26). Without an ontological shift in the organisation of a physical system, i.e., an evolutionary development, cybernetics actually strengthens the idea that the difference between non-life and life is merely down to its degree of material complexity. By possessing a richer language than classical machines, however, GST and cybernetics invoke testable notions of change and adaptation.

Since life is more than persistent iterations of recursive systems, which feedback on themselves but is also capable of spontaneous, material, and organisational transformation — before an artificial system is capable of radical 'developmental' change, it must first attain systemic and material non-linearity.

Autopoiesis

Humberto Maturana and Francisco Varela introduced the concept of autopoiesis into machines, as self-producing, self-maintaining systems. Made up from a network of components and
processes of production, they could continuously regenerate
themselves through their interactions and transformations, to
maintain and produce the network of processes that sustained
them. This integrated 'knot' of exchanges constituted a 'unified'
entity whose elements specified the topological domain of its
'machine' network.

> Professor Humberto Maturana, with his colleague Francisco
> Varela, have undertaken the construction of a systematic
> theoretical biology which attempts to define living systems
> not as they are objects of observation and description,
> nor even as interacting systems, but as self-contained
> unities whose only reference is to themselves ... they are
> autonomous, self-referring and self-constructing closed
> systems — in short, autopoietic systems in their terms.
> (Maturana and Varela 1928, v)

When open to their environment and able to receive external
energy and matter, autopoietic systems perform softer, semipermeable, more agile, and persistent notions of work, and agency
than are possible through classical mechanical systems.

> *Autopoietic* structures have definite boundaries, such as a
> semipermeable membrane, but the boundaries are open and
> connect the system with almost unimaginable complexity to
> the world around it. (Briggs and Peat 1989, 154)

'Open' exchanges between the interior and exterior spaces are
not *exactly* circular, but possess 'circularity'. This is a cyclical
concept that is not sealed in an unending loop of precision but
allows the corkscrewing of energy and matter into and out of the

system through iterations of events. In this lifelike model of exchange, the idea of object permanence is decentred, as the whole system is constantly remaking, or reasserting, itself through its iterations.

> It makes no sense to identify an organism over time with the materials that compose it, given that these are constantly being replenished by the whole. (Nicholson 2018, 23)

When a body is infiltrated by its surroundings, it must manage active change — from self-maintenance, to active growth and (re)production. In classical mechanics, such alterations in baseline conditions are disruptive events with the potential to destabilise the established hierarchies of order that govern the machine's actions and may threaten catastrophic system failure. In contrast, life's agile iterations are heteropoietic and at times of stability generate 'self-similar' iterations of work. Niles Eldredge and Stephen Jay Gould observed that for most of evolutionary history, these iterations expressed through the morphology of species, is remarkably stable and reaches a condition of 'stasis'.

> 'Nothing will come of nothing.' Cordelia's dilemma arises in science when an important (and often pre-dominant) signal from nature isn't seen or reported at all because scientists read the pattern as 'no data', literally as nothing at all. This odd status of 'hidden in plain sight' had been the fate of stasis in fossil morphospecies until punctuated equilibrium gave this primary signal some theoretical space for existence. Apparent silence — the overt nothing that actually records the strongest something — can embody the deepest and most vital meaning of all. (Gould 2007, 38)

At times of stress however, living systems are capable of radical shifts in order, which prevent system collapse, and may rapidly confer organisms with the ability to adapt to new conditions. Such abrupt transformations are evidenced in the fossil record as 'punctuated equilibrium', where certain new characteristics like shells, bones, and eyes, appear over relatively short evolutionary time periods.

> Evolution is a theory of organic change, but it does not imply, as many people assume, that ceaseless flux is the irreducible state of nature and that structure is but a temporary incarnation of the moment. Change is more often a rapid transition between stable states than a continuous transformation at slow and steady rates. We live in a world of structure and legitimate distinction. Species are the units of nature's morphology. (Gould 1979, 18)

In a truly open autopoietic system, it might be reasonable to anticipate spontaneous and sudden advances in the configuration of 'autopoietic machines', albeit over protracted periods of apparent stability. With such an eventuality, the ontological differences between mechanism and 'life' would disappear.

04.5

RepRap: Self-replicating Machines

> The general struggle for existence of animate beings is not
> a struggle for raw materials — these, for organisms, are air,
> water and soil, all abundantly available — nor for energy
> which exists in plenty in any body in the form of heat, but
> a struggle for [negative] entropy, which becomes available
> through the transition of energy from the hot sun to the
> cold earth. (Boltzmann 1974, 24)

Attempts to produce self-replicating machines focus on the
specific (re)placement of components using external 'intelligence' and agency, which has been impossible to complete to
date. Adrian Bowyer initiated the RepRap (*Rep*licating *Rap*id-
protoyper) project in 2004, which is an open-source, 3D printing apparatus that prototypes plastic objects and also explores
the possibility of self-replicating machines. It prints the plastic
components for a kit that can be assembled into a new machine,
which account for about 70% of the necessary parts — printing
the electronic circuity remains particularly problematic (Jones
et al. 2011; Giaimo 2019).

Current RepRap machine kits are not self-compiling. They
operate a recursive assembly process on pre-given materials,
which is hardly autonomous, and kits come with instructions so
that gaps in the 'autopoietic' process of 'self'-production, must
be completed by (external) human input. Even when it becomes
possible to self-print all the components of a 3D printer, RepRap
still relies on a maker community to evolve its design. Com-
pare this with a plant, for example, that is able to turn elemental
materials into complex, constantly changing, structural systems.
The present generation of self-replicating machines therefore do
not address the infrastructural conditions in which the entire
spectrum of their vital operations takes place and instead, rely
on existing human production systems for their completion.
Ontologically speaking, these machines not differ from factory-
made machines, other than through the degree of automation

used in the assembly process. While rapid prototyping changes the distribution of economic and social power among people using these tools, it has little effect on the degree of autonomy within the machine itself.

Natural Selection

> To suppose that the eye with all its inimitable contrivances
> for adjusting the focus to different distances, for admitting
> different amounts of light, and for the correction of
> spherical and chromatic aberration, could have been formed
> by natural selection, seems, I confess, absurd in the highest
> degree ... The difficulty of believing that a perfect and
> complex eye could be formed by natural selection, though
> insuperable by our imagination, should not be considered
> subversive of the theory. (Darwin 2010, 82)

Charles Darwin's theory of 'natural selection' proposed that the 'fitness' of an organism was reflected in its reproductive success that was passed on through heritable traits. These in turn helped certain types of organisms survive and become more common in a specific population over time — ultimately to produce new species (Paradis 2007, 113). While he gave the principles of his theory, Darwin did not propose a physical process that explained how the actual 'means of modification by descent' worked.

Without these details, early critics such as Samuel Butler, accused him of advocating truisms — where 'survivors survive' — as a way of avoiding giving real causes and effects (Butler 2008, 351), while George Henry Lewes argued that by referring to 'chance' in his explanations, Darwin demonstrated that could not explain the effects he proposed.

> Mr. Darwin seems to imply that the external conditions
> which cause a variation are to be distinguished from the
> conditions which accumulate and perfect such variation,
> that is to say, he implies a radical difference between the
> process of variation and the process of selection. This I have
> already said does not seem to me acceptable; the selection
> I conceive to be simply the variation which has survived.
> (Lewes 1878, 109)

With the advent of the Modern Synthesis, DNA was identified as the agent of heredity and evolutionary change, although not all biologists agree on the principles that govern these processes and natural selection has become a semantic stage upon which technical paradigms related to biological theories continually clash in a wider, and often undeclared, political arena.

> In the traditions of 'Western' science and politics—the tradition of racist, male-dominant capitalism; the tradition of progress; the tradition of the appropriation of nature as resource for the productions of culture; the tradition of reproduction of the self from the reflections of the other— the relation between organism and machine has been a border war. The stakes in the border war have been the territories of production, reproduction, and imagination. (Haraway 1991)

Those that embrace a Neo-Darwinist, deterministic reality like Richard Dawkins, regard natural selection as governed by 'real' interiorised genetic 'means', to produce specific outcomes, which may be further modified through environmental and social events (Dawkins 2006).

> Neo-Darwinism is an attempt to reconcile Mendelian genetics, which says that organisms do not change with time, with Darwinism, which claims they do. (Brockman 1995, 133)

Others that take a more contingent and therefore probabilistic view of natural selection, like Richard Lewontin and Stephen Jay Gould, look to the myriad forces that shape evolution through the processes of living (Gould and Lewontin 1979). These are so varied and contingent that their effects have many more de-grees of freedom and are produced by networks of distributed processes, which enable organisms to dynamically respond to change, even while overarching organisational principles (ge-netics, laws of physics and chemistry) are at work.

163

... organisms must be analyzed as integrated wholes, with baupläne[4] so constrained by phyletic heritage, pathways of development, and general architecture that the constraints themselves become more interesting and more important in delimiting pathways of change than the selective force that may mediate change when it occurs. (Gould and Lewontin 1979)

The association of *natural selection,* with Herbert Spencer's adage 'survival of the fittest', bestows it with a politics, where the most ruthless and uncaring organisms may be regarded as 'fittest', since through proactive aggression, they are more likely to survive.

The total amount of suffering per year in the natural world is beyond all decent contemplation. During the minute that it takes me to compose this sentence, thousands of animals are being eaten alive, many others are running for their lives, whimpering with fear, others are slowly being devoured from within by rasping parasites, thousands of all kinds are dying of starvation, thirst, and disease. It must be so. If there ever is a time of plenty, this very fact will automatically lead to an increase in the population until the natural state of starvation and misery is restored. In a universe of electrons and selfish genes, blind physical forces and genetic replication, some people are going to get hurt, other people are going to get lucky, and you won't find any rhyme or reason in it, nor any justice. The universe that we observe has precisely the properties we should expect if there is, at bottom, no design, no purpose, no evil, no good, nothing but pitiless indifference. (Dawkins 2001, 155)

When used in a Neo-Darwinist context, natural selection also negates the agency of organisms beyond the level of organisa-

4 *Baupläne,* or ground plans, is a biological term for a set of morphological features that are common to many members of a phylum of animals.

tion of their molecular hierarchies, which do not directly account for the sophisticated aspects of behaviour (see section 04.7), such as empathy for other beings. While non-humans are frequently treated as if they lack social order, or codes of conduct, certain creatures like capuchin monkeys (Markey 2003) are demonstrably capable of making ethical decisions. Negating the capacity for creatures to act altruistically against their own interests George Price argues there is a 'rational' selfish genetic theory underpinning such 'irrational' actions, since close family members 'benefit' from the sacrifice made by a genetically related individual (Reigner 2016). These accounts assert biological 'fate' as a final cause through with a creature's agency can be denied as: they do not address morality, neither do they engage with a whole spectrum of complex behaviours, nor can they provide a framework that indicates what *ought* to be done, when faced with a given set of circumstances.

> Our culture has the genetics and the nature theory. You
> come into the world loaded with genes and are influenced
> by nature, or you come into the world, are influenced by
> the environment, and are the result of parents, family,
> social class and education. These theories don't speak
> to the individuality or uniqueness that you feel is you.
> (NurrieStearns 2017)

With the politics of enablement at the core of its ethics, liquid life seeks empowering narratives that return autonomy to all beings through the innate agency of matter at far-from-equilibrium states. By constantly negotiating its relationship with genetics, which is part of its wider community of collaborating agents, liquid beings resist the material programs and mechanisms of power that strive to supress them (Foucault 1998).

165

Causal Emergence

> Romeo wants Juliet as the filings want the magnet; and if no
> obstacles intervene he moves towards her by as straight a
> line as they. But Romeo and Juliet, if a wall be built between
> them, do not remain idiotically pressing their faces against
> its opposite sides like the magnet and the filings ... Romeo
> soon finds a circuitous way, by scaling the wall or otherwise,
> of touching Juliet's lips directly. (James 1890, 8)

At far-from-equilibrium states, bodies are not governed by the
simple interactions between individual atoms, nor through a
chain of command initiated by nucleotide programs but ally
with the operations emerging within intersecting agentised
fields, whose mutual attractions are expressed as 'causal entropy'
(Wissner-Gross and Freer 2013). When these active fields link
together, massive exchanges between populations of molecules
take place, which are also dynamically interacting with their
local surroundings. Consequently, the resultant phenomena
frequently exceed causal explanations at higher levels. In these
instances, higher-scale events that arise from the constitutive
fields of interaction begin to shape real events observed at the
macro-scale. This 'causal emergence' challenges existing ideas
about the nature of laws, powers of scale and how they relate.
This is not only a more efficient way to model complex phenomena, but also constitutes a real force. It is not a cipher for true
causes but embodies the actual agents responsible for high-level
system behaviours. While at first, it appears counterintuitive
that higher-level organisation is more predictable than even the
most detailed micro-scale description of systems (Hoel 2017), it
is likely to underpin the behaviour of many kinds of emergent
phenomena such as superconductivity, murmurations, crystals,
and waves, which establish the natural scales that correspond
with each other and generate real consequences such as tsuna-
mis, weather, complex behaviours, and the formation of planets
(Wolchover 2017b).

Non-linearity

> Where chaos begins, classical science stops. For as long
> as the world has had physicists inquiring into the laws of
> nature, it has suffered a special ignorance about disorder
> in the atmosphere, in the turbulent sea, in the fluctuations
> of wildlife populations, in the oscillations of the heart and
> brain. The irregular side of nature, the discontinuous and
> erratic side — these have been puzzles to science, or worse,
> monstrosities. (Gleick 1997, 3)

A glimpse of dynamical chaos was first provided by Henri Poincaré when he entered a competition held in 1890 by Oscar II, the
King of Sweden. One of the challenges was to demonstrate that
Newton's solar system equations were dynamically stable, but his
incomplete solution to the classical 'three-body problem' indicated that a range of factors could alter the movement of the solar
system in ways that defied calculation. These first clues indicated
that astonishing chaotic behaviour was possible in the deterministic solar system and enormous incalculable changes could
be produced by tiny variations, whose behaviour was shaped
by their initial conditions but still obeyed fundamental physical laws. Demonstrating that accurate long-term predictions of
chaotic systems were impossible (Peterson 1993), Poincaré later
suggested such phenomena were likely to be common in other
fields of study such as meteorology. Chaotic systems are also able
to produce recognisable patterns with striking characteristics
that include; responding to their context, producing persistently
repeating patterns, reaching equilibrium states, or undergoing
unpredictable changes that are not proportional to their inputs.
None of these systems can be decomposed into parts, then subsequently reassembled back into their original state.

> … the theory of nonlinear systems is like a theory of non-
> elephants … It's impossible to build a theory of nonlinear

systems, because arbitrary things can satisfy that definition.
(Hardesty 2010)

With the advent of modern computers in the mid-twentieth century, researchers such as Edward Lorenz began to experiment with the equations of complex dynamic systems in ways that were previously impossible. Lorenz's 'toy model' of atmospheric convection produced a solution with characteristic 'butterfly wings'. Lorenz argued that this *strange attractor* suggested why it is hard to predict the weather — as it was sensitive to initial conditions. Characteristically, the patterns never settled down to equilibrium, or entered a predictable, 'periodic' state (Lorenz 1963). The wing-like trajectories of this model system inspired the aphorism of the 'butterfly effect' — where tiny disturbances produced by the flutter of the insect's wings could be chaotically amplified to ultimately cause a tornado.

> Determinism was equated with predictability before Lorenz. After Lorenz, we came to see that determinism might give you short-term predictability, but in the long run, things could be unpredictable. That's what we associate with the word 'chaos'. (Dizikes 2011)

Working for IBM, Benoit Mandelbrot was one of the first to use computer graphics to demonstrate how visual complexity could be produced from simple mathematical rules. He codified and popularised them as 'fractal' images, which could be taken up into a variety of subjects such as the emerging field of mathematical biology.

> Clouds are not spheres … Mountains are not cones. Lightning does not travel in a straight line. The new geometry mirrors a universe that is rough, not rounded, scabrous, not smooth. It is a geometry of the pitted, pocked, and broken up, the twisted, tangled, and intertwined. The understanding of nature's complexity awaited a suspicion that the complexity was not just random, not just an

accident. It required a faith that the interesting feature of a lightning bolt's path … was not its direction, but rather the distribution of zigs and zags. Mandelbrot's work made a claim about the world, and the claim was that such odd shapes carry meaning. The pits and tangles are more than blemishes distorting the classic shapes of Euclidean geometry. They are often the keys to the essence of a thing. (Gleick 1997, 94)

The theory and practice of non-linear systems provides entry into paradoxical spaces and material states where qualitatively new outcomes are possible. In the field of 'mechanical meta-materials', non-linear degrees of freedom that arise in suitably designed microstructures are programmed to perform specific mechanical tasks. The aim is to create a new class of controllable, dynamical, and active materials that combine unconventional physical properties such as swelling and non-linear elasticity, with substrates like *metagels,* which are structured hydrogels that respond to osmotic shock (Florijn, Coulais and van Hecke 2014). An appropriate conceptual and operation framework is therefore needed to anticipate and fully engage the potential of these fields. Precedents already exist within the realm of fluids, such as Rayleigh–Bénard cells and the Bütschli system, which behave according to the laws of chaotic systems but, through their specific materiality, also possess the seeds of technological disruption.

04.9

From Hard to Soft Machines

When Stephane Leduc first coined the term 'synthetic biology', the difference between lively chemistry and biological systems was regarded as 'a gradual chemical elaboration, which culminates in those high compounds which, under surrounding influences, manifest those complex changes called vital' (Leduc 1911, 116). Even today, the question of life is regarded as a challenge for combinatorial chemistry. However, 'brute' matter that lacks innate agency is simply unable to account for material 'decisions' about *becoming*. Concepts that engage with a (new) materialist discourse must encapsulate the capacity for the material realm to act autonomously in making decisions about what it might become, without recourse to the influence of external agencies such as divine forces, or genetic 'intelligence'.

One of the hypotheses Denis Diderot makes in in *D'Alembert's Dream,* is that not only can matter think, but that all of matter is sensible:

> Just as a drop of mercury fuses itself with another drop of mercury, so a sensitive and living molecule fuses itself with a sensible and living molecule ... At first there were two drops—after the contact there is only one ... Before the assimilation there were two molecules; after the assimilation there is now only one ... The sensibility becomes common to the common mass ... And, indeed, why not? ... In my thinking about the length of an animal fibre, I can distinguish as many parts as I like, but the fibre will remain a unity ... yes ... a unity. The contact between two homogeneous molecules, perfectly homogeneous, creates the continuity ... and it's an example of the greatest union, cohesion, combination, and identity one could imagine ... Yes, philosopher, if these molecules are elementary and simple ... but what if they are aggregates, if they are compounds? ... The combining will still take place no less than before and the resulting identity and continuity ...

and then the usual actions and reactions … It's certain that contact between two living molecules is something different from the contiguity of two inert masses … (Diderot 1976, 167)

This possibility is examined in a thought experiment, where a marble statue is ground into powder then mixed into the earth. Plants spring from this soil which are eaten by animals and then, by a woman, where this matter is organised in the womb to produce a human life. The inanimate statue therefore becomes a person (Diderot 1976, 150–53) — a process that Diderot calls 'animalisation'. This journey however, is not an isolated set of transformations but invokes extended fields of potentiality that are more extensive than an ort of matter, like metabolisms, and so, animalisation does not simply work on discrete objects alone but is an account that describes a much more extensive process. For life to be constructed from fundamental units requires more than material complexity but also the right context in which transformation can take place. The specific context that is required, is something that is not easily reducible, but odd (Cairns-Smith 1985, 8).

… just adding complexity to the system in an unprincipled way [is] likely to lead to 'black tar' rather than any interesting higher-order behavior — the addition of complexity must be done with care. This leads to an as yet unanswered question: Are there principles to guide us in adding complexity at the right places in the system, or are we essentially left to experiment by trial and error? (Taylor et al. 2016, 413)

Robert Rosen notes that there is no syntactic way across the complexity bridge (Rosen 1991). This could mean that our current knowledge of what we call 'emergence' is incomplete, or that we cannot generate sufficient complexity for the construction of 'life' to succeed. While complexity, and even those recipes that provoke it can be recognised, they cannot be 'built' into a

171

system through assembling their parts into specific configurations alone and something 'irreducible' has to happen for the system to become autonomously agentised. While massive increases in 'information' flow through physical systems could potentially 'solve' this issue, the nature of this information cannot be general — such as applying a huge amount of heat — it must be ordered and specific, so that it can develop particular relationships — material, energetic, temporospatial — with the host at specific scales of operation. Alternatively, the fundamental premise that life is an incredibly complex machine, which can be assembled from molecular parts, may require radical rethinking.

> In the history of science and philosophy there is hardly a less happy expression than that of the bête machine of Descartes. No concept leads to such a distorted view of the problem underlying it, or so greatly falsifies its proper meaning. It might even be said that, in spite of its heuristic success, the notion of the machine has had a destructive effect on the development of biological theory. It has entangled the investigator even today with scholastic artificial problems, and at the same time as prevented the clear discernment of the essential problem of organic nature. Only the displacement of the machine theory ... will put an end to the paralysis of biological thinking for which this Cartesian expression has been responsible. (Bertalanffy 1933, 36–37).

A revival of material discourses is needed in view of the present unfolding environmental catastrophe. To advance the theory and practice of building, this must take place in conjunction with alternative narratives, models, and prototypes, to living systems, where 'the difference between the living and the non-living can become an object of practices instead of definitions ... It is no longer a question of a unitary logic, but rather of the creation of new types of artefacts' (Stengers 2000, 88).

The expanded language, associated metaphors, and conceptual toolsets offered by new materialism and the semiotics of soft machines, reject notions of instrumentalised 'brute' matter and instead, respond to a livelier, agentised non-human realm in constant flux, which implies the devolution of human agency. This is not to say that people are debased, but that 'if matter itself is lively, then not only is the difference between subjects and objects minimized, but the status of the shared materiality of all things is elevated' (Bennett 2010a, 12–13). Advances in the life sciences are providing new apparatuses that challenge traditional perspectives of materials, where 'conversations' with lively matter can be shaped by altering genes (Caputo 2016), culturing living tissues (Sandhana 2004) or changing the environments in which responsive (living) materials are placed (Anthill Social 2009). This enlivened realm shifts invokes an age of 'living' technology (Armstrong 2015, 31–33), and cyborgs (Haraway 1991), which resist the conventions applied to brute obedience (Bennett 2010a, vii) and move towards a participatory realm of 'thingly power' (Bennett 2010a, xiii). Here, the boundaries that separate life from matter, organic from inorganic, human from non-human, man from god, are 'not necessarily the most important ones to honor' (Coole 2010, 47). Such 'vital' agency invokes the poetics of 'soft' machines, whose components (or agents) are loosely coupled and form horizontally organised power structures through groupings (or assemblages) that de-territorialise and re-territorialise within the logic of 'desiring-production' (Ballantyne 2007, 18–38; Deleuze and Guattari 1979; Deleuze and Guattari 1983). Such 'machines' are not actual apparatuses, but philosophical instruments for (mostly) thinking through how these concepts may be actualised. New materialist perspectives also hybridise with the concepts of speculative realism (Morton 2010), Actor–Network Theory (Latour 1996), and feminist theory, to address a range of issues, including hierarchies, the nature of relationality, and the relationships between nature, society, humans, and other agencies that constitute the living planet. Collectively these perspectives propose the existence of dynamic, emerging, and constantly negotiated ecological relationships across and between unlike bodies that evolve co-constitutive relationships, or anatomies, such as wasp orchids[5] and thynnine wasps (Deleuze and Guattari 1983, 284); while 'oceanic' ontologies (Steinberg and Peters 2015) and hyperobjects (Morton 2013) also generate discursive platforms for exploring massive material flows and irreducible complexity. The orientation of soft machines however, remains ontologically consistent with Descartes' dualistic corpus and soul substance — albeit with softer and fuzzier boundaries. Jane Bennett, for example, summons Hans Driesch's interpretation of Aristotle's entelechy (Driesch 1929, 1–113), and Henri Bergson's 'vital' principle (Bergson 1922, 44) to place emphasis on ephemeral essences as external operative agencies in new materialist discourses; while supreme consciousnesses are implied in James Lovelock and Lynn Margulis' invocation of Gaia — 'a tough bitch and is not at all threatened by humans' (Brockman 2011) — as sources of agency and metaphor for planetary systems (Lovelock 1979). The challenge in adopting such terminology is how to practically apply the proposed ideas without rearticulating them within the context of the *bête machine*.

The most successful collaborations that emerge from these alternative transdisciplinary practices are not simply theoretical, but also synthetic (bringing concepts together), which involve 'making', or prototyping possibilities to functionality. Isabelle Stengers proposes a constructivist platform that promotes experimental modes of collaboration that may apply to ongoing developments in the characterisation of life, such as coupling and causality in complex systems, which resist easy instrumentalisation (Stengers 2000, 87). These may be brought into proximity with cultural developments. In this 'ecology of practices' (Stengers 2005), the aim is not to address the state of knowledge and making right now, but to generate new kinds of methods and discursive prototypes that may underpin alternative approaches to building life in the laboratory. By producing prototypes of the collaborative work, they may be subject to iterative

---

5   Part of the wasp orchid has evolved to closely resemble female thynnine wasps, so when males try to mate with these structures, they deposit pollen, which pollinates the flowers (Ballantyne 2007, 23)

interrogation, and as they are developed, may be capable of responding to and incorporating new findings.

> Each branch of science at its commencement employs only the simpler methods of observation. It is purely descriptive. The next step is to separate the different parts of the object studied — to dissect and analyze. The science has now become analytical. The final stage is to reproduce the substances, the forms, and the phenomena, which have been the subject of investigation. The science has at last become synthetical. Up to the present time, biology has made use only of the first two methods, the descriptive and the analytical. The analytical method is at grave disadvantage in all biological investigations, since it is impossible to separate and analyze the elementary phenomena of life. The function of an organ ceases when it is isolated from the organism of which it forms a part. This is the chief cause of our lack of progress in the analysis of life. (Leduc 1911, 5)

While the empirical aspects of lively agents can be framed by the machine metaphor, their 'invisible' (irreducible) potencies cannot. By changing the framework through which the complex actions of living systems operate, liquid life raises the status and influence of non-human actors — such as the bacteria that Margulis indicated were Gaia's agents of change (Margulis and Sagan 1995), so that a broader recognition of Earth's liveliness can be acknowledged, engaged, and valued.

Part III

HYPERCOMPLEXITY

BEYOND DETERMINISM

This chapter examines the physical and material properties of liquid at far-from-equilibrium states and the strange phenomena they emit. Developing these qualities through their protean materiality, the tangible yet extraordinary nature of the living realm is characterised.

Environment

> Looking outward to the blackness of space, sprinkled with
> the glory of a universe of lights, I saw majesty — but no
> welcome. Below was a welcoming planet. There, contained
> in the thin, moving, incredibly fragile shell of the biosphere
> is everything that is dear to you, all the human drama and
> comedy. That's where life is; that's were all the good stuff is.
> (Botkin 2001, 192)

'Controls' were invented during the Enlightenment so that
bodies could be understood as things-in-themselves without
interference by their surroundings — wild flowers, Ice Age
megafauna, mists, sunbeams, a scurrying beetle, gardens, cities, graffiti, spilt remains of a Friday evening takeaway on the
pavement, guano, layers of pollution on brickwork, the volatile
perfumes of summer flowers, clumsy wings flapping in branches dripping with leaves, traffic jams, plane trails, the sigh of a
spider as it repairs threads on its web, thunder and lightning, or
a runaway balloon. These classical scientific experiments factor
out even the simplest substances like soil, air, and water, since
their embodied hypercomplexity and unpredictability cannot be meaningfully engaged using mechanistic frameworks,
which are dedicated to elucidating simple causes and effects.
This has set the stage for the neglect of our vital surroundings,
which became regarded as little more than decorative settings
for their occupants. While prized as picturesque backdrops
for resource-efficient metropolitan environments, these two-
dimensional images are devoid of real value or presence beyond their bucolic aesthetic. While it may be simpler to empirically and aesthetically understand abstracted bodies in this
way — rather than engaging with their true materiality — such
perspectives prevent us from discovering sophisticated ways of
inhabiting places whereby the environment flourishes alongside human development.

With the onset of increasingly turbulent environmental conditions that characterise climate change, the language of disaster is unleashed, as an 'arms race' between humans and nature begins. Colossal barriers like the MOSE gates in Venice, create defensive walls to keep out the high tides (Armstrong 2015), and geoengineering technologies like fertilizing phytoplankton with micronutrient iron on the ocean surface, seek to alter the flux of carbon to the deep ocean and mitigate global warming (Buesseler et. al 2004). Even R. Buckminster Fuller's Manhattan-scale biosphere proposes to achieve full control of our environments, so their resources can be exploited more efficiently through the better design of machines in 'The Good Anthropocene' (Fuller 2016, 387).

> People learned to create by the force of their own will, and called themselves gods. Now the world was filled with millions of gods. But their will was subordinate to impulse, and so chaos returned to the Sixth World. There was too much of everything, though something new was always coming into being. Time started gathering speed, and people started dying from the effort of trying to make something that did not yet exist. (Tokarczuk 2010, 204–5)

Implicit in this 'struggle' for survival is that we cannot dissociate ourselves from our habitats. Giving shape and meaning to the way we dwell in them, they generate value and a sense of belonging, so we can 'feel at home' in certain places, fall in love with a city, tend gardens, construct buildings, clean up beaches, or make a whole range of lifestyle choices. These specific material details are our interface with the world, which is so particular and peculiar to the places we encounter they possess unique meaning. Environment is exactly why what happens today still matters tomorrow and ways of working are urgently needed, so that the generative forces that enable the processes of living can continue their unbroken legacy.

Watery Planet

> Our planet may be blue from the inside out. Earth's huge
> store of water might have originated via chemical reactions
> in the mantle, [as well as] arriving from space through
> collisions with ice-rich comets. (Coghlan 2017b)

A very small amount of water, comprising less than 0.1% of the
Earth's mass, confers our planet with a 'pale blue' appearance
from space. Even at the time of the 'cool early earth', 4.4 billion years ago, when there were no tectonic plates to buckle and
bow into landmasses and mountains, our world was covered
with water.

> For perhaps half a billion years, the place was too hot for
> life. Water remained as vapour in an atmosphere rich in
> carbon dioxide, formaldehyde, neon and cyanide. Then,
> as the Earth began to cool, it rained for perhaps twelve
> thousand years without stopping, helping to create the first
> seas. (Logan 2007, 10)

Miraculously, our water reserves have not evaporated into the
atmosphere and out into space, partly due to Earth's gravitational pull but also because most of it is not contained in its surface
bodies. Only around a third of our water is freely available in the
hydrosphere, which contains around 1.6×10^{21} kilograms of water, while the rest of it is bound as hydrous minerals like clay and
mica within Earth's crust. Another 0.1 to 1.5 additional surface
hydrospheres are anticipated to be bound to minerals within the
bigger, lower mantle. While it is challenging to estimate the water content of the deeper layers, which may even be devoid of
water (Mottl et al. 2007), it is equally possible that up to 100 hydrosphere equivalents exist in Earth's core. Although the origins
of Earth's water are thought to have been acquired during the
Late Heavy Bombardment when ice-containing asteroids and
comets pulverised the world's surface around 4.1 to 3.8 billion

years ago, it may also have been produced by a simple chemical reaction that takes place between silica and hydrogen in the upper mantle, which is around 4–400 kilometres below the surface. Here, the necessary extreme conditions at temperatures of 1400°C and at pressures greater than 20,000 atmospheres could be met (Burnham and Berry 2017). Under great pressure, this chemically produced reservoir may be responsible for triggering previously unexplained earthquakes (Futera et al. 2017), and it seems that Earth is probably 'wet' (i.e., contains water), in some sense, 'all the way down to its core' (Coghlan 2017b).

The actual mass of liquid water in Earth's substance, however, does not account for its uniqueness. This arises from its ongoing, active circulation, and keen bioavailability through soils, liquid, and gas, which plays a critical role in establishing the conditions for liquid life.

> People who are born where there's a lot of water, in fertile lakelands or on the banks of great rivers, are different. Their bodies are soft, fragile and insensitive, their skin is darker, with an olive tinge, cool and damp with blue veins beneath it. (Tokarczuk 2003, 191)

Ocean

> ... the class of 'bodies without surfaces,' as Leonardo da
> Vinci was to put it, [are] bodies that have no precise form
> of extremities and whose limits interpenetrate with those of
> other[s]. (Damisch 2002, 124)

Oceans comprise 97% of Earth's surface water environments
which exist between Earth's breathable atmosphere and the
crust's solid ground. Recurrently reconfiguring the near-shore
environment, the vastness and depth of oceans means they are
opaque to our gaze, while their complex and changing behaviour provides a metaphor and linguistic trope for a world in flux
(Steinberg and Peters 2015). Possessing recognisable configurations that escape formal human encoding, they are understood
ambivalently as: voids with no persistent features, passive recep-
tacles, givers of life, bringers of destruction (Patton 2006), or
hypercomplex spaces that exceed our capacity to fully observe
and analyse them, which is even more profound when entangled with globalisation's toxic effluents (Gordillo 2014). While
oceans have facilitated human settlement and established power
relations, they are not reducible to their social uses or simple
categories. Indeed, oceans and synthetic platforms comprise 'an
ideal spatial foundation ... [that] is indisputably voluminous,
stubbornly material, and unmistakably undergoing continual
reformation' (Steinberg and Peters 2015), which demands their
own language, so their vastness and strangeness can be appreci-
ated not only in their generalities, but also through their details.

Inspired by dynamic, contingent liquid relationships, oceanic
ontologies are expressive apparatuses and agents of causal emergence, rather than descriptive tools. They can simultaneously
process events across multi-scalar domains without resource
to abstraction, reduction, or hierarchy. Matt Lee proposes these
systems can be imaginatively explored like actors that improvise
within a complex environment. A reading of the 'plot' can be
made through their exchanges, which 'present us with ... a way

of learning ... that isn't subject centred but created through the movement of transformation' (Lee 2011, 130), so their character becomes more visible and familiar.

The Drowned Man was always discovering his potential anew. At first he thought he was weak and defenceless, that he was something like a flurry of wind, a light haze or a puddle of water. Then he discovered that he could move faster than anyone could imagine, just be thought alone... He also discovered that the mist obeyed him, and that he could control it as he wished. He could take strength from it, or a shape, he could move entire clouds of it, block out the sun with it, blur the horizon and extend the night. (Tokarczuk 2010, 79)

Pluripotentiality: 'The Hunting of the Snark'

Throughout the ages, water has been understood as fundamental to life. Thales of Miletus considered water as the 'prime' matter — one of the fundamental elements of existence, or *archai* — that governed the growth of plants and animals. Continually rising, undulating, and falling within watery landscapes, liquid bodies are fundamentally lively. Simultaneously imbuing and infiltrated by their surroundings, neither our natural senses, nor concepts, fully convey their protean nature, which allies them with the realm of monsters — entities from unseen realms that evade categorisation by formal classification systems.

A classical approach to describing the motion of liquids is possible using Lagrangian fluid dynamics, where an observer follows a 'fluid parcel', which moves through space and time. Typically, these are constrained by considering very small amounts of liquids, which can be identified within a specific field and trajectory of flow. While the mass of a fluid parcel remains constant, its volume and shape may change due to distortion caused by its situatedness within the liquid field. Additionally, the properties of the fluid parcel may evolve during the trajectory as the result of simple physical laws acting upon it, like molecular diffusion.

In contrast, unconstrained fluid bodies are difficult to read beyond their surface qualities and are commonly regarded as bland, or featureless. Claude Lévi-Strauss regards the sea as uninspiring (Lévi-Strauss 1973, 338–39), while Roland Barthes views the ocean as a 'non-signifying field [that] bears no message' (Barthes 1972, 112) and Michel Serres embraces the details of liquid bodies specifically the subversive 'nautical murmur' of the sea, which he regards as a symptom of its disturbing pervasive vitality (Serres 1996, 13).

It is at the boundaries of physics, and physics is bathed in it, it lies under the cuttings of all phenomena, a proteus taking on any shape, the matter and flesh of manifestations.

187

The noise — intermittence and turbulence — quarrel
and racket — this sea noise is the originating rumor and
murmuring, the original hate. (Serres 1996, 14)

Liquid bodies are anything but banal. Their subversive unpredictability and unruly pluripotentiality resists control, componentisation — and, ultimately, mechanisation, so we are ill-
equipped to quell their monstrous transformations, or impose
order upon their undifferentiated expanses.

Lewis Carroll's satirical poem, 'The Hunting of the Snark', encapsulates the absurdity of trying to rationalise the liquid realm
through the tale of ten intrepid adventurers[1] that set out with
the aid of a blank map to find a creature, which will make them
invisible.

He had bought a large map representing the sea,
Without the least vestige of land:
And the crew were much pleased when they found it to be
A map they could all understand.
'What's the good of Mercator's North Poles and Equators,
Tropics, Zones, and Meridian Lines?'
So the Bellman would cry: and the crew would reply
'They are merely conventional signs!
Other maps are such shapes, with their islands and capes!
But we've got our brave Captain to thank:
(So the crew would protest) that he's bought us the best —
A perfect and absolute blank![2] (Carroll 1946, 6)

On entering the featureless terrain, each explorer conjures the
encounters their preconceptions of the space and during the
journey succumb to their individual neuroses. Just as the Baker
thinks he has found the Snark, he vanishes, since the creature is

1   The band of ten intrepid explorers in search of the Snark are: Bellman,
    Boots, maker of Bonnets, Barrister, Broker, Billiard-maker, Banker, Butch-
    er, Baker and Beaver.
2   From: Fit the second — the Bellman's speech (Carroll 1946, 6, lines 5–16).

actually a Boojum — which is a highly dangerous version of the species (Carroll 1946, 50).

The unfathomable complexity of liquid expanses opens up a space for transgressions where the classical expectations of the material realm are disrupted. In this protean space, encounters between occupying bodies and their medium begin to develop structural relationships with each other. This primes their receptivity and capacity to respond to continually altering contexts, so they undergo many transformations, which enrich the living realm. Although the invisible forces shaping this dance are not fully fathomable, they are of consequence, since in an uncertain terrain it is possible to come across a Boojum when we are looking for a Snark. Instead of becoming selectively blind to oceanic ontologies with notions of 'blandness', we must instead become familiar with the complexity of liquid bodies, as well as the perils and delights of their enabling media (Armstrong et al. 2017).

05.5

Ex Mare

> The floating and the bottom-dwelling invertebrates of the
> seas are memorials to the earliest strategies for achieving
> [osmotic independence], but although they acquired a skin,
> they did not acquire the ability to move under their own
> power. In a sense, they were and have remained cells in
> the vast organism of the ocean, which moves them at will.
> (Logan 2012, 12)

The bodies of water that make up our deltas, rivers, and oceans have been studied by seafarers since ancient times. Today, real-time Global Positioning System (GPS) networks observe our liquid world from space, offering generalisations about how these immense expanses of fluids perform. Much less is known about their particularities and peculiarities, which 'learned to contain the sea' (Logan 2007, 11).

Contestably,[3] life began in a liquid environment — freshwater lake, river, or stream, rather than in an oxygen-starved ocean (Byrne 2014). Darwin proposed that biogenesis occurred in the uterine environment of a 'warm little pond' (Brouwers 2012), while Alexander Oparin and J.B.S. Haldane give accounts of 'primordial soups' rich with organic materials (Shapiro 1987, 110). Deep seafarers imagine the rich yet isolated marine ecologies around the 'black smokers' of abyssal geothermal vents — naturally occurring chemical 'pressure cookers' — as the original site for life's origins (Colín-García et al. 2016). Others propose Earth was seeded with life by asteroids carrying alien molecules that catalysed the initial reactions — a theory called *panspermia* (Arrenhius 1908).

Whatever the nature of the initiating event, and wherever the location of its original context, the chemical principles of

---

3   While deep oceans are conventionally thought to hold life's origins, recent
    research suggests that active volcanic landscapes may have been the site for
    biogenesis (van Kranendonk, Deamer and Djokic 2017).

its progression through biogenesis are outlined by two distinct postulates.

The command-and-control style *information first* hypothesis argues that biological codes arose before energy-producing bodies. The most popular theory is RNA *World* (Neveu, Kim and Benner 2013), which centres on the dual properties of a smart molecule, ribose nucleic acid (RNA), which can catalyse reactions and also replicate itself without the need of an existing cellular apparatus. Early forms of life, therefore, evolved from concentrations of these molecules that enabled them to conserve biological functions and catalyse chemical reactions, which gave rise to the major domains of life.

The *Virus World* theory also centres on an information-first event and is closely related to the RNA World theory, but differs in the evolutionary sequence of events, where viral ancestors evolved before cells (Arnold 2014). From an evolutionary perspective, viruses are far more diverse than cellular life, with many more ways of replicating possible that viruses either predated or coexisted alongside the last universal common ancestor (LUCA). Supporting evidence for this theory is provided by the discovery of giant viruses such as mimivirus, pithovirus, megavirus, and pandoravirus that were characterised in 2013. Typically, viruses are considered degenerate life forms and relative latecomers in the story of life that lost the capacity to self-replicate, and so developed ways of hijacking more sophisticated cell systems. Giant viruses challenge these assumptions since they are larger than certain bacteria and possess huge genomes, which may contain genes that are absent from the major domains of life that are sufficiently complex to perform complex autonomous functions, like protein synthesis and self-replication. Some viruses contain the enzyme reverse transcriptase, which is not present in cells, but allows the virus to write themselves into a cell's genetic code by translating viral RNA into DNA sequences. The ancestors of giant viruses may have even provided the raw material for the development of cellular life and catalysed its biodiversity (Moelling 2013).

The *Metabolism First* hypothesis suggests that self-sustaining biochemical systems did not initially require centrally-coordinated biological information to form its persistent, yet open 'metabolisms'. While the sequence of biogenesis may have been initiated by traumatic events such as collapsing bubbles (Kaison, Furman and Zeiri 2017), repeated chemical exchanges within stable liquid environments could also have performed this function. Some theories propose that rich mineral rock surfaces provided such an environment (Wächtershäuser 2000), which are capable of catalysing fundamental reactions like carbon fixation and forming polymers. Within these protective niches, stable metabolisms could become more complex and organised, eventually becoming enclosed within selectively permeable membranes and integrating with biological information-carrying systems to give rise to primordial beings.

In practice, it is most likely that biogenesis was not a single process, but a range of entangled chemical strategies that contributed differently to loosely associating groups of agents, or protolife. Becoming more organised over time, at some point the first biological entity, or LUCA, evolved. This hypothetical creature may not have been a singularity, but a collaborating consortium of lively agents whose distributed tactics became integrated, then subsequently inseparable, over the course of evolution.

Ingenious material exchanges alone are not enough to precipitate vivogenesis — something unusual has to happen.

Liquid Reality

Life is a constant form of circulating matter. (Whewell 1840, 46)

Hippocrates, Plato, and Aristotle believed the body was governed by fluidic forces or 'humours' with melancholic, phlegmatic, choleric, and sanguine qualities. The humoral theory that governed these liquids proposed that imbalances in their proportions could cause disorder and provoke erratic conduct, so 'treatments' were choreographies of well-being that were titrated to the patient's condition. Some were subtle, such as making alterations in dietary habits, exercise, and herbal medicines, while other therapies were aggressive. Most illnesses were attributed to excesses of the humours, which were purged from the body using a range of techniques, including laxatives, emetics, skin blistering, and bloodletting, which were thought to draw out toxins.

The constituents of the body — blood, phlegm, yellow bile and black bile — remain always the same according to both convention and nature. Phlegm is quite unlike blood, blood being quite unlike bile, bile being quite unlike phlegm. How could they be like one another when their colours appear not alive to the sight nor does their touch seem alike to the hand? For they are not equally warm, not cold, nor dry, not moist. If you give a man a medicine which withdraws phlegm, he will vomit you phlegm; if you give him one which withdraws bile, he will vomit you bile. Similarly, black bile is purged away if you give a medicine which withdraws black bile. And if you wound a man's body so as to cause a wound, blood will flow from him. And you will find all these things happen on any day and on any night, both in winter and in summer, so long as the man can draw breath in and then breathe it out again, or until he is deprived of one of the elements congenital with him. (Ray 1934, 120)

Although zoological observations during the *scientific revolution* were underpinned by the *bête machine,* the development of the field of physiology was described through liquid metaphors (Nicholson 2018, 13). Sanctorio Sanctorius was the first modern student of metabolism, who discovered the *perspiratio insensibilis* as the loss of an invisible body substance by measuring the quantities of his food, drink, urine, and faeces over a period of thirty years. This 'insensible perspiration' became an indicator of ongoing continuous exchanges and the premise for the physicochemical basis of life (Bing 1971).

> ... [a unicellular organism] is a perfect laboratory in itself, and it will act and react upon the water and the matters contained therein, converting them into new compounds resembling its own substance, and at the same time giving up portions of its own substance which have become effete. (Huxley 1897, 42)

Luigi Galvani's (bio)electricity, or 'animal electric fluid', was also considered responsible for the vitalisation of tissues, until Alessandro Volta (re)interpreted these flows and demonstrated them within the context of (dry)electronic circuits, which repositioned this 'vital' force within the context of the *bête machine.*

> ... I eagerly inquired of my father the nature and origin of thunder and lightning. He replied, 'Electricity;' describing at the same time the various effects of that power. He constructed a small electrical machine, and exhibited a few experiments, he made also a kite, with a wire and string, which drew down that fluid from the clouds. (Shelley 2014, 57)

At the start of the twentieth century researchers delved more specifically into the particulars of life and fluids where increas-

194

ingly, the study of the bodily flows that made up a creature's physiology were discussed in terms of metabolism. Alfred North Whitehead developed a 'philosophy of organism', while Edward Stuart Russell likened living processes to the persistent ripples that a stone makes in a stream (Russell 1924, 6) and Edmund Sinnott preferred to draw analogies between the living realm and the fluid form of waterfalls (Sinnott 1955, 117). Ludwig von Bertalanffy applied liquids as a conceptual framework for the manifestation of natural systems (von Bertalanffy 1968, 27), where biological structures arose from the flow of matter transformed by living processes. Lifelike structures within complex chemical phenomena could also be identified and used as experimental models to test these concepts, as in the Rayleigh–Bénard convection cell, an analogue system for exploring the principles of fluid cells. Life as a dynamic process was particularly embraced by the field of biochemistry (Gilbert 1982) being more broadly adopted into scientific investigation by Conrad Hal Waddington (1957, 2) and Cark Woese (2004).

Although the generalities of flow, change, and environmental responsiveness are encapsulated within a fluid metaphor of life, exactly how these properties are expressed through living systems remains elusive, since the dynamics and behaviour of liquids is extremely complex. The most powerful criticism of the 'waterfall' analogy for life was that it was incomplete, particularly with respect to its inability to produce 'other whirlpools like itself' (Thomson 1925, 123). Implicit in this difficulty was the question of 'modification by descent' (see section 04.2), where parents pass traits on to their offspring, which was at the heart of inheritance discourses during the nineteenth century. This concept was particularly resistant to liquid metaphors, as blending fluids leads to homogeneity, not diversity. Unlike the inert materials used to build machines, fluid dynamics must be considered under a range of different states, and while some liquids behave according to the classical laws of physics, others are nonlinear and capable of changing phase, or state (gas, liquid, solid). Although the contemporary field of fluid dynamics is highly sophisticated, the range of possibilities is so vast and operate

195

at such a range of scales — from microfluidics to oceans — that many questions about the capabilities of liquids remain partly, or completely unresolved.

In the early twentieth century, the liquid metaphor was adopted into the field of embryology by Jacques Loeb, who shifted the challenge of fertilisation from the realm of (protean) morphology to that of physical chemistry. This allowed descriptive and often speculative work, to be empirically evaluated (Allen 2018, 6). While evo-devo, the field of evolutionary developmental biology where organisms change over time, is compatible with notions of fluidity, the strategies for testing its liquid principles are elusive, even with an understanding of chemistry. At the time when evo-devo arose in the 1880s from the field of developmental biology, heredity was regarded 'as identical to the problem of development' (Morgan 1910), but this soon changed into a more atomistic narrative over the course of the twentieth century.

> ... biology ... evolved two traditional approaches to characterise the physical basis of life. In each, the 'natural order of rank' is the reverse of the other. The first tradition [molecular biology/genetics] emphasises the phenomena of growth and replication as the major vital characteristics. Organisms are seen to increase in size and numbers and are thus akin to crystals. The second perspective [biochemistry/ embryology] focuses on metabolism as life's prime requisite, whereby an organism retains its form and individuality despite the constant changing of its component parts. In this respect, living beings resemble waves of whirlpools. These alternative crystalline and fluid models of organisms have interacted with each other for the past hundred years. (Gilbert 1982, 152)

During the mid-twentieth century, liquid and crystal substrates were forcibly separated as equal organising life-forces through ideas underpinning the developing field of genetics. By positioning genetics as the primary agent of heritability, Wilhelm Johannsen cleaved the study of (entangled) phenotype from (distilled) genotype, privileging the study of genetics over embryology (Sapp 1983). While many biologists tried to reconcile the two fields, this proved theoretically and practically incompatible, as each discipline was now only able to give a partial account of the other (Waddington 1940, 3). The ensuing dichotomy between genetics and embryology was further augmented by ongoing debates in biochemistry and molecular biology, where more mechanistic perspectives ousted fluidic accounts, resulting in the Modern Synthesis (Rose and Oakley 2007; Laubichler and Maienschein 2007; Reid 2007). During the 1940s and 1950s the fields of genetics and molecular biology took a decidedly mechanistic turn. Max Delbrück, one of the founders of molecular biology, who studied gene transmission as a precise measurement of biological effects, felt that biochemists were misrepresenting the cell as 'a sack full of enzymes acting on substrates, converting them through various intermediate stages either into cell substance of waste products' (Gilbert 1982, 159–60). In his view, they had 'stalled around a semi-descriptive manner without noticeably progressing towards a radical physical explanation' (Gilbert 1982, 151). With a new emphasis on structured information, crystals — which had been identified as the most lifelike substances in the seventeenth and eighteenth centuries — were now considered 'the nearest analogue to the formation of cells' (Gilbert 1982, 154). Inspired by Delbrück, who regarded the gene as a crystal, Schröedinger's 1944 essay *What Is Life?* exerted a powerful influence in validating the study of crystallinity as a state that could unify all matter, where 'the most essential part of a living cell — the chromosome fibre — may suitably be called *an aperiodic crystal*' (Gilbert 1982, 159). John Desmond Bernal, who pioneered the use of X-ray crystallography in molecular biology, also viewed crystals as components of cells and 'proof' of life (Gilbert 1982, 158), which consolidated the Modern Synthesis as the dominant worldview of life by the late twentieth century.

    … by 1940 the lines were being drawn. Biochemistry,
    concerned with intermediary metabolism and the energy

that drives it, worked well within the tradition of flux and thermodynamics. However, the portion of the life sciences concerned with the transmission and expression of inherited characteristics rejected this view for the tradition of crystalline morphogenesis. Not only did the gene just not fit into the whirlpool model, but it looked as if functional genes (i.e. viruses) could even be crystallized. Whereas the principal characteristic of life for the biochemist was metabolism, life's principal characteristic for the molecular biologists was replication. Furthermore, the primary unit of life for the biochemist was the result cell (metabolically active but not replicating), whereas the unit of life for the molecular biology was the virus — crystalline, nonmetabolising, and capable of enormous feats of replication. (Gilbert 1982, 159)

In 1937, Haldane predicted that classical biochemistry would be superseded by a new branch of biochemistry arising from the realm of genetics. During the second half of the twentieth century, liquid and mechanistic approaches were reconciled through the (re)approximation of molecular biology/genetics with biochemistry/embryology to conceive of networks of control (master) switches, capable of triggering developmental cascades. This more detailed understanding of the building blocks of life has been accomplished by new tools and techniques that are able map the appearance of creatures alongside their genetic material. New light is now being shed on one of the most surprising findings over the last 30 years in genetics — that there is remarkably little difference between the genes that are common to all known life forms. Although mice and humans are phenotypically very different, they share almost the same set of genes (Gunter and Dhand 2002), which were also present in ancient creatures. Alternative accounts of how such small numbers of critical genes can be differentially expressed over a broad range of contexts are emerging as a result of these new approaches. For example, cellular noise, which is non-linear and leads to symmetry breaking, seems to be extremely important in very

198

early embryo development and causes non-deterministic downstream effects, which result in substantial differences between cells (Mohammed et al. 2017). The critical role of phenotypic 'architecture' is also being revealed in developmental processes, which includes factors such as epigenetic interactions, the chemicophysical properties of developing cells and the influences of environmental parameters (Müller 2007).

While major challenges remain for *evo-devo*,[4] its focus on peculiar, particular, non-deterministic and highly localised events provides a counterpoint to genetic theories, which deal with the averaging of large numbers of molecules that are observed in populations of organisms. Whether it is possible to reconcile these perspectives within a 'unifying biological theory' remains to be seen. Such a framework may be provided by new discourses that position metabolic networks as the dominant systems in regulating cell function. Víctor de Lorenzo likens the interplay of DNA and metabolism to that of politics and economy, where both systems regulate their own autonomous agendas, while influencing each other. Positioning metabolism as 'the economy of living systems', he observes that this ultimately determines the viability of any political moves, as it frames and eventually resolves whether any given genetic program will operate, or not (de Lorenzo 2015).

> ... both the metabolites and the biochemical fluxes behind any biological phenomenon are encrypted in the DNA sequence. Metabolism constrains and even changes the information flow when the DNA-encoded instructions conflict with the homeostasis of the biochemical network. Inspection of adaptive virulence programs and emergence of xenobiotic-biodegradation pathways in environmental bacteria suggest that their main evolutionary drive is the expansion of their metabolic networks towards new

---

4   Challenges mainly relate to how evo-devo accounts for structural complexity, which is challenging to establish using empirical modes of testing, and its relationship to the population dynamics of classical evolutionary theory.

chemical landscapes rather than perpetuation and spreading of their DNA sequences. (de Lorenzo 2014, 226)

Since chemical landscapes radically increase the combinatorial potential of cell operations, Frederick Coolidge suggests a primordial platform for vivogenesis that approximates the RNA World hypothesis with metabolism's first concepts. Proposing that early nuclear building blocks were made up of a larger range of primordial nucleotide chemical precursors than observed in RNA today,[5] they could explore and exploit emerging chemical landscapes to evolve the relationship between 'information storage' systems and active metabolisms, which were also likely subjects for Darwinian natural selection (Coolidge 2017).

Liquid life's challenge is not whether the fluidity of bodies is real but how its foundational ideas become demonstrable and testable, since few technological systems can visualise, model, and realise its protean character. In other words, we must learn how to build and experiment with liquids.

5   The nucleotides of RNA are: adenine, cytosine, guanine, and uracil.

Origins of Dissipative Propagation

> Diderot was arguing against the mathematical mechanist
> conception of matter while today mathematical, physical
> and chemical physical references help to destabilise the
> blind watchmaker's unilateral responsibility: chaotic
> systems, edge of chaos systems, dissipative structures,
> neural networks, all those objects have opened up new
> possibilities, new problems and new bridges. (Stengers
> 2000, 97)

While molecular interpretations of the *bête machine* attribute
the character-specific properties of matter to crystalline states,
liquids also confer unique order on systems. In liquid phases,
molecules can freely associate and form transitional states of
potentiality, as well as spatially orienting themselves in relationship to a site.

The primary operative agents of liquid life are not bounded
cells instructed by central biological programs but are also derived from the broader spectrum of propagative agents at far-
from-equilibrium states such as, dissipative structures (see sections 08.9). While these hubs of matter/energy are recognisable
as singular entities, they can also link together to form massively
distributed nuclei of activity across the surface of the planet,
which not only form weather fronts but also form types of 'metabolic weather' (see sections 01.14 and 05.23). Such structures
can be seen grinding away on the surface of Jupiter, which is
pockmarked with a number of stable and violent storms. The
most notorious of these is the Great Red Spot, which is twice as
wide as the Earth and is potentially more than 150 years old. A
lesser-known system is the String of Pearls, a caravan of eight
storms rotating anti-clockwise on the southern hemisphere of
the gas giant (Loria and Mosher 2016). Terrifyingly, the storms
(Irma, Jose, Katia) that razed the Caribbean and Florida in September 2017 and also in 2014 (Charley, Ivan, Jeanne, Francis)
bore remarkable similarity to this formation, raising the ques-

tion of whether an impending feature of climate change will be the onset of stable, effectively permanent storms.[6] Such self-organising and persistent systems also constitute the low-level infrastructures of organisms. Becoming increasingly organised with time, they adapt, alter their surroundings, evolve, and contribute collectively to the active forces of nature.

Existing at many different scales, dissipative structures are more than background support for events. They are dynamic structuring systems whose interfaces provide sites for symmetry breaking and a range of specific spatial and material events. In fact, stability rather than change is a conundrum for liquid life, where permanence is an illusion orchestrated through highly persistent but mutable structures in constant motion. These paradoxical objects, which are simultaneously stable and unstable, confer integrity to dynamic bodies — not through stability, but through their repetitions and iterations of networked processes. Here, interiority and exteriority permeate each other through a constant choreography, which takes place between lively agents that shape developmental pathways. This tightly coupled system, which is a hallmark of dissipative structures, provides a highly robust, discursive platform for the synthesis of hyperlocal solutions, although it is also vulnerable to the potentially devastating effects of turbulence. Such configurations, however, possess many more degrees of freedom than are possible within the linear relationships and hierarchical ordering systems that typify classical machines, and can therefore mount creative resistance to external perturbations.

Liquid bodies persist when differential gradients are maintained across local micro-niches and environmental locales. Early life forms were likely leakier and more plastic than modern biological cells. Cradling dissipative bodies within them, molecular 'skins' provided quiet spaces for the accumulation of boundary-forming substances such as fatty molecules and set the scene for open niche construction. This enabled primitive

6   This observation was made by Nathan Morrison, CTO of Sustainable Now Technologies, on Facebook on 7 September 2017.

bodies to respond to, and organise around, local metabolic opportunities. Before biogenesis, the first liquid bodies may have stabilised upon oily films, or within porous networks in hydrothermal vents (Priye et al. 2016). Pinched off by lipid films, chemical environments became 'internalised' and established matter/energy gradients. Mediated across leaky interfaces, the accumulation and diffusion of local molecular species enabled the first metabolisms to stabilise. With many iterations of exchanges, different kinds of gradients were established, setting the foundation for primitive bioenergetics, where important metabolic pathways that couple bioenergy and biomass were highly conserved, like pathways leading to acetyl CoA formation (Nitschke and Russell 2013).

Even without formal borders, the compartments of the earliest life forms were sufficiently deformable, and capable of internalising other structured spaces through endosymbiosis. This takes place when one body swallows another without wholly assimilating, or digesting, its contents. Biological cell organelles today such as the nucleus and the mitochondrion, give testimony to such remarkable mergers that took place early in eukaryotic life — perhaps when an archaeon engulfed a bacterium and the subsequent, symbiotic relationship became irreversibly and successfully intertwined. Formal cellular environments would have only been possible when membranes became sophisticated gatekeepers of internal metabolic conditions and were capable of regulating them in ways that enabled primordial cells to adapt to environmental changes.

In keeping with its far-from-equilibrium nature, liquid life's influence on its surroundings extends beyond the limits of its physical boundaries. Innately agentised, its behaviours, metabolism, 'liquid consciousness' and soul substance — the winds that surround the cellular eye of the storm — produce tangible changes that can be encountered through their effects on other bodies like heat, vibration, and presence.[7] Embracing all agentised

7   In this instance, 'presence' refers to the existence of being that, by virtue of its intangible (far-from-equilibrium state) emissions, generates effects

material epiphenomena (crystals, cells, bodies, ecosystems), it is expressed across geological and evolutionary scales, its 'vital' agency flowing through its constituent bodies: lively materials, metabolic networks, ecologies, and nurturing planetary systems, and constitutes an (effectively) immortal hyperbody.

within the dimensions of spacetime, which are perceivable by other beings.

Transitions

The inability of liquid life to stay still is not an error, which assumes an end goal, but an impeccably tuned system with countless tolerances and protean states.

Liquid life persists through its fundamental disobedience, in slingshots of thermodynamic resistance, where lively matter twists in corkscrewing iterations of molecular ingenuity away from the direct and efficient path towards thermodynamic equilibrium.

So far, liquid life has successfully persisted during the ever-changing and challenging contexts of the terrestrial realm, despite five major mass extinctions and many more annihilations during the Hadean epoch, when the Earth hissed and boiled.

This capacity to resist thermodynamic decay is embedded in the unfathomably strange and massless fundamental particles that constitute liquid life's myriad bodies whose unfathomably peculiar fields enfold us within the strangest substance in the universe.

05.9

Mind as Substance

> The hard problem of matter calls for non-structural properties, and consciousness is the one phenomenon we know that might meet this need. Consciousness is full of qualitative properties, from the redness of red and the discomfort of hunger to the phenomenology of thought. Such experiences, or 'qualia,' may have internal structure, but there is more to them than structure. We know something about what conscious experiences are like in and of themselves, not just how they function and relate to other properties. (Mørch 2017)

While Descartes justified human rationality through the soul, other views of consciousness couple it to matter (Dyson 1979; Armstrong 1993) and life (Shanta 2015). In Western cultures, various concepts — higher order theories, reflexive theories, representationalist theories, narrative interpretative theories, cognitive theories, information integration theory, neural theories, quantum theories, non-physical theories (van Gulick 2014) — give accounts of how awareness and capacity for self-observation are produced. Neither fully produced within the self, nor purely channelled into a body from elsewhere, David Chalmers describes consciousness as a 'hard problem' that inevitably exceeds our ability to provide a complete account of its effects. 'Explaining' the nature of consciousness is particularly challenging, as like the soul, it is not governed by the (scientific) laws of the *bête machine*. It is therefore impossible to provide a rational account through the laws of classical physics.

> If the flesh came into being because of spirit, it is a wonder. But if spirit came into being because of the body, it is a wonder of wonders. Indeed, I am amazed at how this great wealth has made its home in this poverty. (Meyer and Bloom 1992, 37)

Drawing on alternative physical laws, Roger Penrose and Stuart Hameroff invoke the power of the quantum realm within nerve cell microtubules to offer 'quantum consciousness' as an alternative organisational model capable of offering a non-reductive explanation of consciousness, (Hameroff and Penrose 2014; Paulson 2017). In this book 'liquid consciousness' (see section 01.13) is presented as a way of discussing the receptive creativity and 'wilful' behaviour expressed by matter at far-from-equilibrium states, which is dynamically coupled with its structure.

Dissipative systems offer a significant advantage in providing an investigative platform for understanding notions of 'consciousness' from first principles in non-humans, as unlike quantum phenomena and 'living' biological brains, they can be directly observed and possess an apparent degree of 'subjectivity', which is governed by their extreme sensitivity to context. Each dissipative structure is an organising centre of information-gathering and action-making, like extremely primitive cells that can form coupled chains of activity (see chapter 09). This simple visualisation system provides a way of observing how a material structure can produce the phenomenological effects of a directly coupled sensor-effector system, in a testable, observable manner. Actuated by flow across interfaces, dissipative systems simultaneously alter themselves and their surroundings, by generating inhibitors (waste products), facilitators (catalysts) and physical obstacles (crystal skins). The decision-making capacities of these dynamic systems are located at the interface between oil and water, where they are amplified to produce observable, macroscale effects, through which they appear to make 'sense' of the world. As chemical activity is converted into kinetic energy, the droplet bodies are propelled forwards and move freely, encountering other active fields that maintain their liveliness. Contextualised and infiltrated by their surroundings, the material interfaces between active fields of chemical exchange, act as sensors, translators, and effectors of an (inner) materiality and an (outer) environment that may encode particular ideas, languages, images, and modes of expression. These can be read as a mode of 'analogue pattern computing', whose emerging patterns correspond with primitive (material) forms of 'decision making' and constitute the emergence of a 'dissipative mind' (Medlock 2017).

> ... long before we were conscious, thinking beings, our cells were reading data from the environment and working together to mould us into robust, self-sustaining agents. What we take as intelligence, then, is not simply about using symbols to represent the world as it objectively is. Rather, we only have the world as it is *revealed* to us, which is rooted in our evolved, embodied needs as an organism. Nature 'has built the apparatus of rationality not just on top of the apparatus of biological regulation, but also from it and with it', ... we think with our whole body, not just with the brain. (Medlock 2017)

The trails of transformation that emanate from these agentised bodies are expressions of 'metabolic weather' (see sections 01.14 and 05.23). Like thought processes, they generate unfathomably complex phenomena, which resist abstraction and simple causal explanations, but also leave behind physical residues that alter and complexify their surroundings. These spatially and temporally distributed substances may be read as a kind of 'short-term physical memory' that is not encoded within the body but is 'remembered', or understood, through ongoing encounters with its local metabolites. If the actions are repeated, then 'long-term memory traces' are consolidated as persistent structures, which constrain free movement within the active (cognitive) field/space. If these are not continually reinforced, they may be physically eroded by physical processes such as diffusion, or actively metabolised by other agents, which constitutes a kind of material 'forgetting'. Beyond the prebiotic realm, colonies of single-celled organisms also chemically coordinate their behaviours to establish conditions for cohabitation like biofilms, slime moulds, and siphonophores (see section 07.4). Carrying the seeds of sensibility across many scales, these 'dissipative minds' are coupled with a whole range of embodiments (and evolving memories) through a range of sensations, feelings, behaviours, and memories. The overall ongoing expression of these entanglements exemplifies 'liquid consciousness', which is always appropriate for the various forms of embodiment through which it is expressed, and neither aspires to be biological, nor 'human'.

05.10

In-between

> Where is she? Not there — not in heaven — not
> perished — where? Oh! You said you cared nothing for my
> sufferings! And I pray one prayer — I repeat it till my tongue
> stiffens — Catherine Earnshaw, may you not rest as long
> as I am living; you said I killed you — haunt me, then! The
> murdered do haunt their murderers, I believe. I know that
> ghosts have wandered on earth. Be with me always — take
> any form — drive me mad! Only do not leave me in this
> abyss, where I cannot find you! Oh God! It is unutterable! I
> cannot live without my life! I cannot live without my soul!
> (Bronte 2009, 118)

When a body is intrinsically entangled with its 'soul substance'
and leaves residues of its presence within a space, as in the case
of dissipative structures, encounters with transitional presences and beings, that are neither fully material, nor agentised,
become possible.

Throughout the ages, these angels, demons, spirits, and
ghosts, are often encountered during heightened states and in
places that are emotionally 'charged'. A contemporary limbo is
encapsulated by the paradox of Schrödinger's cat, which shares
Hamlet's dilemma of being (to exist, or not), where such indeterminate beings are gateways between one state of existence
and another. These are not purely imaginary situations but are
based on actual experiences and have even been *designed* for
since antiquity through tombs, where bodies were either preserved through mummification, or thoroughly rotted down, to
ease their passage of their 'soul' into the afterworld.

> When you think you've died, you haven't actually died.
> Death is a two-stage process, and where you woke up after
> your last breath is something of a Purgatory: you don't feel
> dead, you don't look dead, and in fact you are not dead. Yet.
> (Eagleman 2010, 43)

From the moment that someone's heart stops beating, life's fluids no longer sustain the tissues and territory by territory the body dies. Advances in modern medicine however, can artificially induce physiological holding-states, where vital organs such as the lungs and heart remain perfused and so, keep the brain 'alive'. These modes of life-suspension redefine the notion of 'death' and those that have been resuscitated during medical procedures report memories of these transitions, which vary from delightful to horrifying.

> There were those who reported feeling afraid or suffering
> persecution, for example. 'I had to get through a ceremony
> ... and the ceremony was to get burned,' one patient
> recalled. 'There were four men with me, and whichever
> lied would die ... I saw men in coffins being buried
> upright.' Another remembered being 'dragged through
> deep water', and still another was 'told I was going to die
> and the quickest way was to say the last short word I could
> remember'. (Nuwer 2015)

While such accounts may be little more than attempts to rationalise aberrant brain activity, studies of cardiac arrest survivors at New York University's Langone School of Medicine revealed that many could recall conversations at the scene of their death, some even hearing they had been pronounced dead (Parker 2017).

> They'll describe watching doctors and nurses working;
> they'll describe having awareness of full conversations, of
> visual things that were going on, that would otherwise not
> be known to them ... (Parker 2017)

Empirical evidence also suggests that the body continues to 'live', even after certain technical criteria for death have been met. Animal experiments indicate that gene activity occurs for up to two days after death, which may be a natural response to tissue damage, and raises important genetic questions about the definition of death (Williams 2016). Whether illusory or real, these intermediary expressions of 'life' are the cultural dominion of angels, where the mythological and material worlds mingle and establish the limits of what it means to be 'alive', 'dead' and acknowledge the existence of the liminal states in-between.

> In this part of the afterlife, you imagine something analogous to your Earth life, and the thought is blissful: a life where episodes are split into tiny swallowable pieces, where moments do not endure, where one experiences the joy of jumping from one event to the next like a child hopping from spot to spot on the burning sand. (Eagleman 2010, 43)

Linking Life and Death

> Life did not crawl out of the sea onto the land; it oozed
> from the sea into the land, the organic acids of its excretions
> joining with the carbonic acid of the rainfall to create the
> first soft mantle of soil on the Earth. Maybe two billion
> years ago, the cyanobacteria began to use the sunlight to
> make sugars, excreting oxygen. They were green or brown,
> and their scum spread into lagoons, up rivers. The oxygen
> reacted with iron and for the first time there were orange,
> yellow, and brown colours in the earth. (Logan 2012, 12)

Soil is the living skin of the planet. There is not just one kind
of soil, but many different types, which form giant bodies that
are permeated with liquid life and are teeming with living systems and creatures. They reach down deep into the physics and
chemistry of Earth's planetary system, occupying the interface
between air, water, ground, biology, the land, and chemistry.

> Soil is not unalive. It is a mixture of broken rock, pollen,
> fungal filaments, ciliate cysts, bacterial spores, nematodes
> and other microscopic animals and their parts. 'Nature,'
> Aristotle observed, 'proceeds little by little from things
> lifeless to animal life in such a way that it is impossible to
> determine the exact line of demarcation.' Independence
> is a political, not a scientific, term. (Margulis, and Sagan
> 1995, 19–20)

We walk and build upon these extraordinary hypercomplex,
living fabrics as if they were inconsequential but within their
substance, they forge the very webs of metabolic exchange upon
which all life ultimately depends. A teaspoon of fertile earth
houses more kinds of microbes than there are people on the
planet and bacteria also colonise our bodies as symbiotic communities. Since the 1990s, this 'microbiome' is now recognised

as a distributed 'organ', which carries out a range of functions (Lederberg and McCray 2001).

> Life is bacterial and those organisms that are not bacteria have evolved from organisms that were. ... Gene exchanges were indispensable to those that would rid themselves of environmental toxins. ... Replicating gene-carrying plasmids owned by the biosphere at large, when borrowed and returned by bacterial metabolic geniuses, alleviated most local environmental dangers, provided said plasmids could temporarily be incorporated into the cells of the threatened bacteria. The tiny bodies of the planetary patina spread to every reach, all microbes reproducing too rapidly for all offspring to survive in any finite universe. Undercover and unwitnessed, life back then was the prodigious progeny of bacteria. It still is. (Margulis and Sagan 1995, 111)

While soils are bringers of life, they are also intimately and creatively involved in the process of death. When a creature dies, its microbiome is no longer constrained by the host's immune system and begins to consume the corpse, marking its transformation into the thanatobiome.

> The microbiome goes on changing in response until death. Then the microbes will do their best to carry on elsewhere. First, though, they will consume the nutrients that leak from our dying cells. (Turney 2015, 132)

Working with the soil bacteria and a community of decomposers, the thanatobiome changes again to mingle with soil ecosystems to become the necrobiome. Returning organic matter and minerals into the life-bearing systems of soils, their webs of exchange are orchestrated by even more diverse communities of organisms than takes place within living bodies that are policed by their immune systems.

… the dead trunk is as indispensable for the cycle of life in the forest as the live tree. For centuries, the tress sucked nutrients from the ground and stored them in its wood and bark. And now it is a precious resource for its children. But they don't have direct access to the delicacies contained in their dead parents. To access them, the youngsters need the help of other organisms. As soon as the snapped trunk hits the ground, the tree and its root system becomes the site of a culinary relay race for thousands of species of fungi and insects. Each is specialised for a particular stage of the decomposition process and for a particular part of the tree. And this is why these species can never pose a danger to a living tree — it would be much too fresh for them. Soft, woody fibres and moist, mouldy calls — these are the things they find delicious. (Wohlleben 2016, 133)

Soil's complex, evolving metabolic webs ensure that a fountain of energy and matter is constantly circulated back into its substance and (re)emitted through fertile terrains that not only nurture plants and animals but when they die, reintegrate them back into the living realm.

> The particle of gold falls to the bottom and rests — the particle of dead protein decomposes and disappears — it also rests: but the living protein mass neither tends to exhaustion of its forces not to any permanency of form, but it is essentially distinguished as a disturber of equilibrium so far as force is concerned — as undergoing continual metamorphosis and change, in point of form. (Huxley 1897, 43)

From active processes of this kind, where creatures engulf, partially digest, or fully digest others, the linking of life and death has maintained continuity since biogenesis. As strategies for persistence evolve, their limits and constraints have changed over the course of 3.5 billion years, but the active upcycling

(Braungart and McDonough 2002) of organic matter remains fundamental to life's ongoingness and evolution on this planet.

> I work in evolutionary biology, but with cells and microorganisms. Richard Dawkins, John Maynard Smith, George Williams, Richard Lewontin, Niles Eldredge, and Stephen Jay Gould all come out of the zoological tradition, which suggests to me that, in the words of our colleague Simon Robson, they deal with a data set some three billion years out of date. Eldredge and Gould and their many colleagues tend to codify an incredible ignorance of where the real action is in evolution, as they limit the domain of interest to animals — including, of course, people. All very interesting, but animals are very tardy on the evolutionary scene, and they give us little real insight into the major sources of evolution's creativity ... I refer in part to the fact that they miss four out of the five kingdoms of life. Animals are only one of these kingdoms. They miss bacteria, protoctista, fungi, and plants ... Of what are they ignorant? Chemistry, primarily, because the language of evolutionary biology is the language of chemistry, and most of them ignore chemistry. (Brockman 2011)

While vertebrates are much more recent in evolutionary history than bacteria, they are used as the dominant 'model' in accounting for the lively potential of matter. In expanding our view of the capabilities of the living realm, much more robust, diverse, and unconventional models of 'life' are needed.

Hydrous Bodies

> The sea was the proto-soil, where earth, air, water, and
> the solar fire met for the first time. It was an inverse soil,
> you might say, with the liquid element providing the
> matrix for the mineral salts and for dissolved gasses, a role
> that the mineral elements would later come to play. But
> from a certain point of view, all Earth's later history is a
> consequence of that first mixing. (Logan 2007, 11)

Our bodies are 65% water by weight, which entangles us with
the nature of other liquid bodies and their vastness. According
to Giles Deleuze and Felix Guattari, the plane of 'immanence'
(or birth) is a fluid substratum, or 'body without organs' (BwO)
that is 'permeated by unformed, unstable matters, by flows in all
directions, by free intensities or nomadic singularities, by mad
or transitory particles' (Deleuze and Guattari 1987, 45). Such
BwOs are 'organism[s] without parts which operate[s] entirely
by insufflation, respiration, evaporation, and fluid transmission'
(Deleuze 2015, 101). Such monstrous, exquisite, hyperobjects
provoke awe and consternation — like encountering the night
sky for the first time. Oscillating between the quantum and cosmic realms, these quasi-beings that are both inside and beyond
us, question the classical view of reality and identity, where our
concepts of finitude, the nature of objects, their relationship
with time, our baselines of stability, locality, identity, scale, or
human sanction, need to be restated.

> It is wrong to say *I think*: one should say *I am thought … I is
> an other*. (Rimbaud 2004b, 28[8])

Hydrous bodies do not possess fragile egos. They are not alien-
ated by the gargantuan, uncategorisable, or monstrous aspects

---

8   In a letter to Georges Izambard, Charleville, May 1871.

of reality, and strike robust alliances with unknowns that enrich their portfolio of diversionary tactics in eluding entropy's call.

Origins of Liquid Life

Liquid bodies were the first protolife that were sustained by iterative events within a flow of resources — light, reducing gases, crumbs of organic matter and mineral matrices, which set the stage for the theatre of terrestrial life. This section tells a story that conjures a pre-biological era at the origins of liquid life. It begins on the violent surface of our molten planet — a primordial landscape of liquid fire, choking gases, and searing radiation — where there is no competition for resources between bodies. Here, excitable fields of matter at far-from-equilibrium states start to overlap and produce undulating interfaces, where the weirding of Earth's matter begins.

Wraiths of matter/energy fuelled by volcanic heat and cosmic radiation pass through each other. Sowing seeds of dissipative evolution they evade the planetary system's march towards thermodynamic stability, or death. Imbibing the sunlight, greasy bodies pool on rocky surfaces, the cannibalise their surroundings and feed off each other's turbulences.

These boiling seas are teeming with protolife.

Boundaries break and split, as tiny dissipative structures form dominant loci of activity. Little more than fluctuations with unregulated metabolisms, they reach into the tempestuous fields that roam these landscapes, exchanging structure for heat. Guided by passions and mischief, rebellious protolife searches for spandrels that promise opportunities for alternative modes of flourishing. Some bodies collapse and die, while those that resist the temptation of entropy, meander through varied pathways.

As proto-organism and mineral become inseparable, they form living rocks, which scar the world with their residues and inhibitors. Spewing monster after monster into the hostile surroundings, as kith, not offspring, lively surfaces spawn a host of liquid bodies. None are identical to their precursors, nor are they self-similar. Compulsively producing more oddities, each stranger than the last, the vortices of these vagrant droplets function like gizzards, grinding matter into new configurations and assimilating their surroundings into their substance during this process.

Becoming more ordered with time, they begin to take on distinctive forms.

Over aeons, colonies of interacting bodies cooperate as aggregations and assemblages, while surreptitiously trying to digest them. There are no 'pure' organisms here, just lively collectives of material persistence that leak around their edges. Avoiding the direct pathway towards efficient chemical collapse, they dawdle through time in search of abundance, creativity, and subjective encounters, leaving footsteps of chemical transformation and rich soils in their wake. With the shock of reaching relative equilibrium, each generation of liquid bodies finds temporary rest and mingles with the accreting soils, when maybe tomorrow, or millions of years from now, their restless chemistry (re)enters the living realm.

(AI)chemistry of Water

Water is sometimes sharp and sometimes strong, sometimes
acid and sometimes bitter, sometimes sweet and sometimes
thick or thin, sometimes it is seen bringing hurt or
pestilence, sometime health-giving, sometimes poisonous.
It suffers change into as many natures as are the different
places through which it passes. And as the mirror changes
with the colour of its subject, so it alters with the nature of
the place, becoming noisome, laxative, astringent, sulfurous,
salty, incarnadined, mournful, raging, angry, red, yellow,
green, black, blue, greasy, fat or slim. Sometimes it starts a
conflagration, sometimes it extinguishes one; is warm and is
cold, carries away or sets down, hollows out or builds
up, tears or establishes, fills or empties, raises itself or
burrows down, speeds or is still; is the cause at times of life
or death, or increase or privation, nourishes at times and
at others does the contrary; at times has a tang, at times
is without savor, sometimes submerging the valleys with
great floods. In time and with water, everything changes.
(Deodhar 2009, 383)

Debates about the natural world and man's ability to improve
upon it during the Enlightenment led to experimental thinking,
new apparatuses, specialised scientific practices and technologies capable of characterising the elements. Building upon the
physical distillations and purifications that were established by
alchemical practices, like Paracelsus and his mineral-based liquid medicines, modern science identified the molecular nature
of substances through their atomic composition and structure,
which enabled certain predictions to be made through their
position on the periodic table of elements. With the advent of
advanced imaging techniques such as atomic force microscopy,
aided by artificial intelligence and automation (Extance 2018),

we are able to tell a whole lot more about the structure and character of molecules.

Consisting of two hydrogen atoms bonded to one oxygen atom (H_2O), the hydrogen side of the water molecule holds a slight positive charge and the oxygen side is negatively charged. Owing to this uneven distribution of electron density, water exhibits polarity and therefore acts as a powerful 'universal' solvent, being one of the most reactive and corrosive substances known. It also absorbs large amounts of heat energy before it warms up and cools down again since it has a high specific heat capacity, and large volumes of water can maintain a stable temperature, even when environmental temperatures are fluctuating wildly. In transitioning from liquid to solid phase, it occupies about 9% more volume and therefore floats. Other unique physical properties arise from the strong cohesion between water molecules, which exceed its affinity with the air, resulting in high surface tension. It also participates in finely tuned biochemical processes through its highly structured hydrogen-bonded network, which enables it to form organisational templates, assist molecular recognition, enable replication, and orchestrate protein folding. Integrated with the fundamental processes of life, it comprises 65% of our bodies by weight, with tissues such as the brain and the lung being nearly 80% water, and carries a constant flow of resources through our cells.

Despite our incredibly ability to observe and analyse it, not all aspects of water molecules are fully understood, and digital simulations are helping us better understand its unique and constantly surprising character. For example, classical theories predict that 'supercooled' water molecules should be frozen, but they continue moving in a liquid state below 0°C. Simulations suggest the reason is that the spatial distribution of water molecules in ice is uneven and pockets of water with differing characteristics exist and accounts for the way that ice can retain some of its liquid properties while in solid form. This means the properties of water are not merely a function of its global molecular characteristics but are also configured by local spatio-temporal relationships (De Marzio et al. 2017).

Water's material richness, strangeness, and ability to interact, or associate with, so many substances has defined the nature of life on this planet. By allying with water and other liquids, we become semipermeable, protean beings that resist containment and can therefore adapt to changing circumstances.

Clay Code

Life's inconstant and paradoxical relationship between inert structures and responsive flesh (whether plant or animal) invites a synthesis between mineral crystal (rigid) building blocks, which are the units of stable structures, and the wet, soft (flexible) environments of cells. Many ancient stories relate the emergence of life with the transformation of Earth's soils such as the Sumerian myth of Marduk who created people by killing Qingu[9] and mixing his blood with clay, or the golem — an earthen structure, shaped in human form and brought to life by God's breath. Origin of life studies are now revealing the entanglements between life's emergence and the evolution of our dirts.

> There, on a clay bank, we measured out a man three cubits long, and we drew his face in the earth, and his arms and legs, the way a man lies on his back. Then all three of us stood at the feet of the reclining golem, with our faces to his face, and the rabbi commanded me to circle the golem seven times from the right side to the head, from the head to the left side, and then back to the feet, and he told me the formula to speak as I circle the golem seven times. And when I had done the rabbi's biding, the golem turned as red as fire. Next, the rabbi commanded his pupil, Jacob Sassoon, to do the same as I had done, but he revealed different formulas to him. This time the fiery redness was extinguished, and a vapour arose from the supine figure, which had grown nails and hair. Now the rabbi walked around the golem seven times with the Torah scrolls, like the circular procession in a synagogue at New Year's, and then, in conclusion, all three of us recited the verse, 'And the Lord God formed man of the dust of the ground, and breathed into his nostrils the breath of life; and man became

9 Qingu also may be written 'Kingu'.

a living soul.' And now the golem opened his eyes and peered at us in amazement. (Neugroschel 2006, 13–14)

When ancient seawater is experimentally simulated and added to clay, it forms a hydrogel which soaks up fluids into its labyrinthine spaces. Here, complex biochemical reactions were able to catalyse the evolution of primordial chemistry towards the metabolisms of the living world, until membranes evolved that were capable of performing this function for wholly independent living cells (Young et al. 2011).

> ... use good smooth dirt that is free of sand, rocks and pebbles. In a small bucket mix the dirt with water. Using your hands to combine the dirt and water, continue to add small amounts of water until the mud is the consistency of bread dough. Knead the mud until the mud becomes firm enough not to lose shape when you roll it into a small ball. Mould the mud into pies by rolling the mud into balls and then flatten them down. You can make them as thick or as thin as you like. (Kidspot 2017)

John Desmond Bernal first suggested that clay played a key role in the origins of life through its ordered arrangement, high adsorption capacity, impedance to ultraviolet radiation and ability to form templates for polymerisation (Bernal 1949). A whole theory of life's mineral origins was proposed by Alexander Graham Cairns-Smith, where simple crystal matrices, or 'clay codes', could offer physical structure, modes of synthesis, sites of catalysts and even programming information through 'primitive geneographs'. All these systems existed within hydrated states of clay that were responsible for organising life's building blocks and early metabolisms, until the more potent 'genetic takeover' took place, with a much-expanded molecular repertoire (Cairns-Smith 1965). While Cairns-Smith's theory remains experimentally untested, inviting criticism that 'no amount of vague talk about 'clay organisms' or 'genetic clay' [can] breathe life into such ideas as a substitute for a more tangible scientific

225

basis' (Fox 1988), increasing evidence supports notions that life evolved along with its soils (Yang et al. 2013).

> There are also people born on rocky ground, on sandstone or granite. Their skin is rough and hard, as are their muscles and bones. They have strong hair and teeth, and the skin on their palms and the soles of their feet is hard. On the surface they are tough and robust, because their bodies are like armour. They have a lot of empty space inside, so everything they see and hear echoes within them like a bell. (Tokarczuk 2003, 192)

In its most basic sense, clay creates a platform for prebiotic biochemistry and its ultimate assimilation into established metabolic networks. Although its vivogenetic properties have not been definitely proven, the clay montmorillonite has been shown to be catalytic in the assembly of RNA from simple nucleotides, and also accelerates the spontaneous conversion of fatty acid micelles into vesicles (Hanczyc, Fujikawa and Szostak 2003). Additionally, the role of hydrogels in the formation of ancient metabolic networks is being explored. Evidence 'support[s] the importance of localised concentration and protection of biomolecules in early life evolution, and also implicate[s] a clay hydrogel environment for biochemical reactions during early life evolution' (Yang et al. 2013). Working in combination with other substances, clay's potency creates the possibility of new kinds of 'agentised' synthesis, which suggests that ceramic technologies may even enliven the living realm. Using genetically modified biofilms to produce a specific range of metabolites, the EU-funded Living Architecture project engages ceramic interfaces to investigate the formation of a 'designed' set of (bio) chemical transformations that are useful within urban living spaces, e.g., reclaiming phosphate from wastewater.[10] A better

---

10 The Living Architecture project has received €3.2m funding from the European Union's Horizon 2020 Research and Innovation Programme under Grant Agreement no. 686585. It is a collaboration of experts from the

understanding of how such molecular and metabolic processes may be shaped by clay as various forms of ceramics situated within technological systems, may contribute to our better understanding of living systems and how they relate to alternative models of organisation — such as liquid life.

universities of Newcastle, UK; the West of England (UWE Bristol); Trento, Italy; the Spanish National Research Council in Madrid; LIQUIFER Systems Group, Vienna, Austria; and Explora, Venice, Italy, that began in April 2016 and runs to April 2019 (Living Architecture 2016). Living Architecture is envisioned as a next-generation, selectively programmable bioreactor that uses techniques in biotechnology and synthetic biology to design communities of cooperating organisms that are capable of extracting valuable resources from sunlight, wastewater, and air and, in turn, generating oxygen, proteins, and biomass (Armstrong 2018b).

Colloids, Coacervates and Foam

> ... protoplasm has a definite structure and is not a
> homogeneous lump of slime. This structure holds the secret
> of life. Destroy it and there will remain in your hands a
> lifeless mixture of organic compounds. (Oparin 1953, 60)

Liquid and crystalline systems first began to mix in the 'protoplasm', which is a viscous, aqueous, clear, polyphasic colloid
that provides a matrix for many kinds of material programs.
In the nucleus, it is called 'nucleoplasm' and 'cytoplasm' in the
cell body. Composed mainly of nucleic acids, proteins, lipids,
carbohydrates, and inorganic salts, the cytoplasm provides sup-
portive 'skeletons' and 'muscle systems' that generate cell structure. Selectively enabling molecules to move in and out of the
cell's highly choreographed environment, it regulates many vital
processes such as energy production by the mitochondria, and
protein synthesis in the granular ribosomes.

Prior to the discovery of DNA in the 1950s, cytoplasm was
believed to be a complex substance capable of conferring cells
with vital properties such as self-replication, the transmission
of heritable particles (Hodges 1889), and even with immortality (Bogdanov 2002). This gel-like substance could choreograph
the chemistry of life within cells, although without apparent
form, it was not obvious how this was achieved.

> It is not a question of straight lines and planes such as
> we meet in crystals, for here we have a whole network, a
> whole skein of fine threads which are interlaced, separating
> from one another and coming together again in a definite,
> complicated order. Sometimes these threads are very fine;
> on the other hand, sometimes they are thickened, fusing
> with one another to form small enclosed bubbles or alveoli.
> The structure of coagulates is strikingly reminiscent of that
> of protoplasm. Unfortunately, this structure has not yet been
> sufficiently well studied for us to be able to say anything

conclusive about this resemblance. However, there can be no doubt that we are dealing with phenomena of the same order. There is no essential difference between the structure of coagula and that of protoplasm. It may be, however, that the difference between living and dead does not lie in the organization which, as we have seen, is present in both worlds, but in the other features which we mentioned, the ability of living organisms to metabolise, to reproduce themselves and to respond to stimuli. (Oparin 1953)

Alexander Oparin demonstrated that the anisotropy and non-linearity that existed at the interfaces between liquid media, spontaneously produced droplets, layers, and microscopic localised systems known as 'protocells' (Oparin 1953). Highlighting the way this self-assembling process could spontaneously structure protocellular spaces, he established a testable approach for his theories with an experimental platform that produced increasingly complex and more heterogeneous chemical assemblages (Sloterdijk 2011, 2014, 2016) capable of responding to a selection process.

Continuous Media: Ectoplasm

> Things leak into each other according to a logic that
> does not belong to us and cannot be correlated to our
> chronological time. (Negarestani 2008, 49)

While quantum theory begins to close the 'gap' left between atomism's objects, Descartes' notion of 'extended' matter (see section 03.9) created the possibility of an atomic body that is permeated by its surroundings. Mutable like liquids, they no longer behave like geometrically discrete objects but fields (Dirac 1927), or strings (Smolin 2008), which draw both material and ephemeral forces into their substance.

The search for the interlocutors of the physical and immaterial realms coincided with the rise of spiritualism in the mid-nineteenth century, and was carried out by (mostly female) mediums. Regarded as hysterics, they reported leaking fluid-like substances out of their bodies during séances as a manifestation of spirit energy. Scientific luminaries like Charles Richet[11] sought to discover the nature of this 'ectoplasm', considering it to be a ubiquitous protoplasmic *prima materia* that arose from symptomatic vibrations of a 'sixth' sense that was capable of detecting 'ectenic' forces. The biological equivalent of the aether, it propagated the vibrations of life through the cellular substance of all beings, linking the ephemeral and material realms.

> How can the vibration of reality bring about knowledge? …
> we are not prejudging the question as to whether these are
> vibrations of ether, or emissions of electrons … We know
> that there are around us, quite close to us, many vibrations
> which do not reach our normal senses, for instance those
> of attraction, of magnetism, of the Hertzian waves, etc. All

---

11 Charles Richet was a French physiologist at the Collège de France, who was known for his pioneering work in immunology and won the Nobel Prize for his work on anaphylaxis in 1913.

the same, it would be madness to suppose that there are not others. Therefore we have three orders of vibrations of reality: a) those which our senses perceive, b) those which our senses do not perceive but which are revealed to us by detectors, c) those that are unknown to us and which are revealed neither by our senses, nor by detectors … When we have fathomed the history of these unknown vibrations emanating from reality — past reality, present reality, and even future reality — we shall doubtless have given them an unwonted degree of importance. The history of the Hertzian waves shows us the ubiquity of these vibrations in the external world, imperceptible to our senses … when a new truth has invaded the world of humanity, even the most far-seeing individuals can never know to what conclusions it will lead. At times this truth entails unforeseen and unforeseeable consequences, and that even from the rigidly narrow point of view of our present material life. Who then could have foreseen when the great Hertz discovered the electric waves, that our practical
daily life would be transformed and that all the ships sailing on the various oceans would be supplied with wireless? (Richet 2003)

Providing a legitimate scientific platform for his theories, Richet's observations were more than a question of physics, or psychology, but situated at the cusp between psychical research and the nascent discipline of plasmogeny[12] (Brain 2013). During the late nineteenth and early twentieth centuries, ectoplasm was 'scientifically' studied during paranormal theatre sessions, where spiritual mediums claimed to be able to link the psychic body with matter, making it possible to communicate with the dead. During a series of 87 séances led by 16-year-old Kathleen

12 The field of plasmogeny is concerned with the origin and study of protoplasm, but more broadly, also incorporates a study of the life-like behaviour of artefacts and is an early forerunner to the fields of synthetic biology and artificial life (Brain 2013).

Goligher, engineer William J. Crawford ('the Lavoisier of tel-eplasty') attempted to measure its appearances using a weighing scale large enough to hold the medium, while she was sitting in her chair. Noting a change in the distribution of mass in the subject's body, Crawford attributed this to the manifestation of 'psychic rods' (Brain 2013). Other investigators, such as neurologist Jules Bernard Luys, observed that the 'bodies of hysterics underwent a spasmodic consumption of energy and gave off a 'radiating neural force', taking the form of a luminous fluid that flooded out of the bodily orifices, especially the eyes and mouth' (Brain 2013, 118). Albert Freiherr von Schrenck-Notzing, a German physician and psychiatrist at the University of Munich, corroborated these findings by reporting 'the presence of fluid, white and luminous flakes of a size ranging from that of a pea to that of a five-franc piece' (Brain 2013, 114) when mediums were in communication with the spirit world. Richet himself described different stages in the materialisation process:

> [First,] a whitish steam, perhaps luminous, taking the shape of gauze or muslin, in which there develops a hand or an arm that gradually gains consistency. This ectoplasm makes personal movements. It creeps, rises from the ground, and puts forth tentacles like an amoeba. It is not always connected with the body of the medium but usually emanates from her, and is connected with her. (Richet 2010, 523)

While scientists had witnessed ectoplasm during séances in darkened rooms and by photographing its strange appearance, no actual samples that could be tested in a laboratory setting were provided (MacIsaac 2014). Spiritual mediums played on the vulnerability of their audiences using theatrical tricks to conjure the appearance of strange wools and fabrics from bodily orifices — particularly ears and mouths — as 'evidence' that bridging the realms of the living and the dead was possible. Medically trained Arthur Conan Doyle even became convinced of ectoplasm's reality, describing it as a gelatinous substance similar to body fluids and viscous liquids (Doyle 1930), but the non-scientist Harry Houdini was not so easy to deceive. Accompanied by an esteemed panel of scientists, he was invited to assess the psychic abilities of celebrity medium Mina Crandon, or 'Margery' — the Blonde Witch of Lime Street, New York and wife of a wealthy Boston surgeon and socialite, Dr Le Roi Goddard Crandon. Renowned for her nude *séances delicité* and assisted by her deceased brother Walter, many were convinced by her theatre of the dead. Tables knocked out messages, bells rung, and furniture shook with the fervour of the spirit world. She even conjured ectoplasm from her nose and ears and revealed an 'ectomorphic hand', from beneath a sheer kimono that bore a remarkable likeness to a string of entrails. While previous adjudicators had found no evidence of trickery, Houdini made a special instrument to detect the slightest movement in the darkened room. Binding his right knee so tightly that it was exquisitely sensitive to the subtlest movements, he could feel Margery play the séance table through a range of apparatuses that were operated by her head, legs, and ankles. Owing to her popularity in influential social circles, Houdini was, however, prevented from publicly debunking her techniques and instead, revealed the nature of her deceptions by exposing them in versions of his own performances (Love 2013).

Although ectoplasm was never proven to be a real substance, it was described in material terms by psychologists as composed of invisible rays, psychic forces, and ethereal vibrations, which could be conjured into actuality through a process of 'ideoplasty', or mental projection (Brain 2013, 116). Embryologist Hans Driesch took an assertively material view of ectoplasm as a medium for the union of matter and spirit. Regarding it as a special manifestation of protoplasm (Brain 2013), which contained a spirit force that could better explain the dynamic process of embryonic development in terms of the laws of physics and mathematics, he invoked Aristotle's life force, or 'entelechy', as the organising force that conferred living matter with flexible principles. This new science of 'supra-normal physiology', or 'supernormal biology', made explicit the links between ectoplasm and occult phenomena, where gelatinous bodies could also shape the course of prospective life. This groundbreaking scientific concept outlined a principle of malleable development, whereby undifferentiated organic tissue possessed pluripotentiality and inspired the emerging science of embryology.

> Think of the little material body, called an egg, and think of the enormous and very complex material body, say, an elephant, that may come out of it: here you have a permanent stream of materializations before your eyes, all of them occurring in the way of assimilation, of a spreading entelechial control. (Driesch 1928, 173)

Aqua Vita

Of all the fluids that fill life's interior spaces — vacuoles, coe-loms, cavities, stomachs, ventricles, and vessels — none is con-ferred with more potency than blood.

Since ancient times, it has been considered as a life force, or *ichor,* and a very particular kind of plasm with mystical proper-ties like Ambrosia[13] that could be acquired in different ways, like the witch Medea who used it to transfuse 'life' into the dead, the old, and the dying (Tucker 2011):

> Medea unsheathed her sword and drew a cut in the old
> man's throat, so letting the blood drain out of his body. She
> then replaced it with juice from the pot. When Aeson had
> fully absorbed this, either by mouth or by way of the wound,
> his hair and his beard lost all of their whiteness and quickly
> returned to lustrous black. (Ovid 2004, 262)

The actual transfer of blood directly between individuals re-mained a magical notion until the Enlightenment. William Harvey's rationalisation of blood flow as a theory of circulation in 1613 enabled the liquid to be empirically studied, but it did not quell belief in its rejuvenating powers, which remained the dominant motivation for developing the practice of blood trans-fusion. In 1666, Samuel Pepys referred to successful dog-to-dog blood transfusions in his diary, noting the potential medical im-plications and also the risks of the procedure:

> The experiment of transfusing the blood of one dog into
> another was made before the Society by Mr. King and Mr.
> Thomas Coxe upon a little mastiff and a spaniel with very
> good success, the former bleeding to death, and the latter
> receiving the blood of the other, and emitting so much of
> his own, as to make him capable of receiving that of the

---

13 Ambrosia is the nectar of the gods that confers them with immortality.

other. This did give occasion to many pretty wishes, as of the blood of a Quaker to be let into an Archbishop, and such like; but, as Dr. Croone says, may, if it takes, be of mighty use to man's health, for the amending of bad blood by borrowing from a better body. (Pepys 2010, 209–10)

Robert des Gabets claimed that transfusing blood between beings could not only transfer states of well-being, but also identity, which raised profound ethical questions for those who did not share Descartes' view that the soul resided outside the body. Rumours spread that transfusing dogs with the blood from a sheep would give them the ability to grow wool, develop cloven hooves and sprout horns (Learoyd 2006). The first formal transfusion experiments are accredited to Christopher Wren who observed the levels of intoxication in dogs, after injecting them with wine and ale:

Some may conceive that liquors thus injected into veins without preparation and ingestion will make odd commotions in the blood, disturb nature and cause strange symptoms in the body, yet they have other thoughts of liquors that are prepared of such things that have passed the digestion of the stomach; for example, of spirit of urine, of blood, etc.; and they hope likewise that beside the medical uses that may be made of this invention, it may also serve for anatomical purposes by filling the vessels of an animal as full as they can hold, and by exceedingly distending them, discover new vessels … The reader may securely assume that this narrative is the naked real matter of fact, whereby it is clear as Noonday … that to Oxford, and in it, to Dr Christopher Wren, this invention is due. (Anon 1665–1666)

Despite a number of successful blood transfusions between animals and humans during the mid-seventeenth century, due to moral and ethical concerns the practice fell into general disrepute and was banned throughout most of Europe. Jean Denys conducted the first animal-to-human transfusions in 1667, favouring the animal plasm for his experiments, as it was less likely '... to be rendered impure by passion or vice'. Although patchily successful owing to occasional haemolytic transfusion reactions, there were no further advances in blood transfusion for around 150 years (Learoyd 2006). This was a fortunate pause, since advances in antisepsis and immunology had not kept pace with this invasive practice.

In 1864, Paul Bert developed a new experimental technique in blood transfusion called 'parabiosis' whereby the skin of two mice were sewn together, and as the healing vessels fused, the animals shared a common circulatory system (Scudellari 2015). Significant scientific interest in blood transfusions was not however, rekindled until the second decade of the nineteenth century, when James Blundell used them to cure fatal haemorrhage in childbirth. Fatal haemolytic reactions arising from the mixing of incompatible blood types posed a significant risk to recipients until human blood groups A, B, and O were identified by Karl Landsteiner in 1901. Compatibility between donors and recipients could now be established before a transfusion took place and the practice of cross-matching was advocated as standard procedure by Reuben Ottenberg in 1907.

Despite these advances, the mystical potency of blood did not wane. The modern pioneer of blood transfusions, Alexander Bogdanov, regarded them as a replacement therapy that could cure sick and aged bodies. His grandiose approach to the powers of blood transfusion extended to claims it could reverse balding and improve eyesight. Ironically, he died following a poorly matched blood transfusion from a student suffering from malaria and tuberculosis, although the student recovered entirely following infusion with Bogdanov's blood (Rosenthal 2002).

Further technical developments over the course of the twentieth century increased the safety of blood transfusions. Between 1914 and 1918, the advent of refrigeration techniques and anticoagulants such as sodium citrate prolonged the shelf life of the plasma, so that blood banks could be established. Throughout the 1920s and 1930s, voluntary blood donations for storage and use of blood became an acceptable social practice and during

World War II, transfusion was regarded as a reputable and life-saving treatment for wounded soldiers. Following this resounding success, it was adopted into mainstream medical practice and during the 1970s new technological developments in the manufacture of disposable PVC, transfusion practices became safer than ever before, although screening for viral antibodies did not occur until the 1980s following the HIV epidemic.

Blood transfusions bring biological benefits to recipients that cannot be accounted for by the expectations of replacement therapy alone. During the 1950s, Clive McCay revisited the practice of parabiosis to connect the vasculature of mice of different ages in pairs[14] as a model system for studying the effects of old age. While some surgically 'conjoined' animals perished from a mysterious condition that became known as 'parabiosis disease',[15] the old mice generally benefited from a range of rejuvenating effects, while the young mice aged prematurely. While animal research regulations established in the 1970s made it more challenging to conduct such experiments, the mystical rejuvenating powers of blood have not been assuaged. In 2014, researchers studying mice found that giving old animals blood from young ones could reverse some signs of ageing, which caused a rise in levels of a growth factor that had beneficial effects on the heart, skeletal muscle, and brain (Kaiser 2014). Recent experiments show that plasma proteins from human umbilical cord blood also have 'rejuvenating' effects on the memory of brain function in aged mice, with significant implications for treating degenerative brain diseases in humans (Castellano 2017).

Such promising scientific studies have attracted the attention of transhumanists, allegedly such as Peter Thiel,[16] who stands 'against confiscatory taxes, totalitarian collectives, and the ideology of the inevitability of the death of every individual' and

14 Disturbingly, if the rats were not adjusted to each other, then one would chew the other's head until it perished (McCay et al. 1957).
15 'Parabiosis disease' may have been a form of haemolytic reaction.
16 Such claims made by *Gawker* have been denied by Thiel at the 2018 New York Times Dealbook conference, who declared he was 'not a vampire' (Trotter 2017; Cuthberson 2018)..

advocates the administration of a range of biological substances that may improve physical well-being — to the point where life spans can be radically increased. Thiel has already admitted to taking human growth hormone to maintain muscle mass and regards *transfusional parabiosis* as a pathway towards potentially infinite life extension (Kosoff 2016).

> … infusions of young blood … [were sought after by] … aged billionaires. One, who flies around in a jet with his name emblazoned on the side … another correspondent wrote with a more disturbing offer … [to] … provide blood from children of whatever [the] age … required. (Sample 2015)

Young people are cloned in order to 'harvest' their organs, organ-by-organ until they die prematurely in Kazuo Ishiguro's heartbreaking novel *Never Let Me Go.* While such an extreme scenario presently remains fiction, it raises relevant ethical questions about the Californian start-up *Ambrosia,* which meets the growing real-world market for plasma transfusions from young adults. Offering these as a rejuvenation therapy to tech circle clients, treatments promise to boost mood, the immune system, weight management, and much else. Unusually for an anti-ageing treatment, it appeals more to men than women (Haynes 2017).

> As a business proposition, the transfusion of young blood raises all kinds of fears. It raises the spectre of a macabre black market, where teenagers bleed for the highest bidder, and young children go missing from the streets. Then there is the danger of unscrupulous dealers selling fake plasma, or plasma unsafe for human infusion. The fears are not unfounded: health has become one of the most lucrative sectors for criminals and con artists. (Sample 2015)

For now, claims that young blood, or plasma, can extend animal life spans are not supported by scientific data (Scudellari 2015) and transfusional parabiosis undoubtedly carries unquantified risks, such as whether rejuvenating cells in ageing bodies carry a significant risk of cancer. Perhaps most intriguingly, despite our detailed understanding of medical treatments and advances in molecular biology, the crimson liquid that travels 96,000 kilometres along the arteries, veins, and capillaries of the circulatory system to carry more than 700 proteins and other substances around our bodies, remains mysteriously irreducible.

> Blood might contain the fountain of youth after all. And it is within us all — that's the crazy thing. It just loses its power as we age. (Thomson 2014)

Ghost of a Flea

The weightless, almost invisible, ubiquitous flea is a speck that challenges what a unit of life may be: a droplet masquerading as an object, a homunculus, a mini-monster, an ornate container for liquid, a self-propagating vector of pestilence, a parasite of sexual mingling, a host for a fluid drop of human life within an insect body, our blood-sucking enemy, and a curse that bites.

During the Renaissance, fleas were a humorous and risqué subject, which drew their many transgressions from the magical powers associated with blood. In a vision, William Blake saw the ghost of a flea that 'told him that all fleas were inhabited by the souls of such men as were by nature blood-thirsty to excess, and were therefore providentially confined to the size and form of insects' (Varley 1828, 54–55).

The development of the compound microscope catapulted the flea from the intangible to discernible realms, where — through his careful observation and detailing of their tiny armour plates — Robert Hooke demonstrated that the extreme performance of fleas far exceeded their fantastical status (Hooke 2007):

> … as for the beauty of it, the Microscope manifests it to be all over adorn'd with a curiously polish'd suit of sable Armour, neatly jointed, and beset with multitudes of sharp pinns, shap'd almost like Porcupine's Quills, or bright conical Steel-bodkins; the head is on either side beautify'd with a quick and round black eye … behind each of which also appears a small cavity … in which he seems to move to and fro a certain thin film beset with many small transparent hairs, which probably may be his ears; in the forepart of his head, between the two fore-leggs, he has two small long jointed feelers, or rather smellers … (Hooke 2007, 19)

Hooke's drawings drew the attention of craftsmen, who began to demonstrate their technical prowess by depicting the flightless insects as tiny models of people, so that everyday life could be viewed as a corpuscular version of the human scale. In 1578, watchmaker Mark Scaliot built a lock and chain for a flea that was made up of 11 different microscopically crafted pieces of steel, iron, and brass, which weighed only one grain, plus the key belonging to it.

> The same artist also constructed a chain of gold, containing forty-three links, which he fastened to the lock and key, and upon these being attached to the neck of a flea, the insect was able to draw them with ease. (Anon 1893, 187)

Other artisans followed suit, designing contraptions that ranged from landaus and chaises to cannons. During the 1820s fleas themselves, rather than the intricate objects associated with them, became the star attraction of shows. Louis Bertolotto's insects pulled tiny carriages, danced to an orchestra, played tiny instruments and even (re)enacted the Battle of Waterloo wearing full battle regalia. In the 1900s, William Heckler claimed his troupe of fleas were 'skilled professionals', who juggled, raced, boxed, and even responded to voice commands. Gradually, flea circuses became part of carnival sideshows and were exhibited alongside circus 'freaks'. They were also featured in magic routines, which resulted in the rise of the 'humbug' performance, where things appeared to happen — even in the absence of fleas.

> The audience see a table or stand set out with all the fascinating gear and trappings of a miniature circus. An arched sign at the back, proclaims the name and merits of the show, lit up by small lights. The performers on this apparatus and in the air above it, are talented fleas — so the Ringmaster says. By the time the exciting and action-packed show is finished, many spectators are sure about the fleas, while others are doubtful, but nobody knows for sure! The entertainer never loses sight of his job for a

242

moment — which is to present a flea circus — a three ring show of performing fleas! (Palmer 1975)

While flea circuses are not prohibited, enthusiasm for them has dwindled — excepting the Munich Oktoberfest, which has upheld this tradition for over 150 years.

I had always thought that the flea circus was ... an urban legend ... Are there magnets under the table? Are there tiny wires attached to performers? I choose to believe ... We watch the fleas play soccer. They pitch what looks to be pieces of styrofoam, 30 times their weight, into a tiny net ... Then there was the chariot race. Pulling the chariot, said the ringmaster, was equivalent to a human pulling a locomotive. For all we know, the Pyramids could have been built employing trained fleas. Afterward, we got the opportunity to meet the actors ... through a magnifying glass. (Johnson, n.d.)

Fleas are paradoxical creatures: simultaneously fluid and crystal, atom and fluid, seen and unseen. The not-quite-liquid-not-fully-droplet flea is a synonym for trickster, which personifies the outright contradictory aspects of liquid life.

05.20

Twenty-one Grams

> ... a cough came from the sacristy, then from the chancel, and finally died down, still coughing, behind the altar, behind the gymnast on the cross — where it quickly coughed up its soul. It is finished, coughed my cough; but nothing was finished. (Grass 2010, 342)

The idea of the soul as an ephemeral spirit entangled with a bodily identity is an ancient belief that is present in every civilisation and is thought to stem from our capacity for self-awareness. The narrative encapsulated in this dualism is highly compelling, since it offers transcendence from the insoluble difficulties of the material present and makes possible an unbounded world to be. The soul itself is generally considered an animating principle, whose presence is needed for the transformation between a living and dead state, even if, as Georg Ernst Stahl proposed, it is an agent that delays the decomposition of living things. The principles are so ingrained in our societies they are likely to have been communicated between early peoples at the dawn of cultural evolution around 200,000 years ago. Archaeologists from the Neubauer expedition of the Oriental Institute at the University of Chicago discovered a stone slab about a metre high and weighing about 350 kilograms at an Iron Age city called Sam'al in Turkey, which dated to around the eighth century BCE. Carved on its surface was a picture of a man, which was accompanied by an inscription that declared that his soul now resided within the stone slab (Small 2008).

> There is something at work in my soul which I do not understand. (Shelley 2014, 11)

While religions offered laws about the nature of the soul, the Enlightenment brought ways of thinking and measuring that could potentially not only characterise, but also quantify it. Since, by definition cadaveric specimens did not have souls, it was hard to establish an empirical method that could ascertain the relationship between body and spirit. In 1907, Duncan MacDougal sought to measure the loss of mass[17] that he presumed occurred from a dying person when the soul parted from the body,[18] which could be detected by a weighing scale that was sensitive to one-tenth of an ounce (3g). Implicit in this hypothesis was the assumption that the spirit was not immaterial like 'mind', but took the form of a physical substance, perhaps something like ectoplasm. MacDougal selected six patients with tuberculosis whose terminal symptoms could be clearly observed, so he and his colleagues would be able to identify the exact moment of death and quickly measure the differences in mass. His first subject, a 'phlegmatic man, slow of thought and action, [whose] soul remained suspended in the body after death, during the minute that elapsed before it came to the consciousness of its freedom', lost 'three-fourths of an ounce'. This is around the mass of five sugar cubes and has since been popularised as '21 grams'. Three other cases, 'including that of a woman', lost between half an ounce (14g) and a full ounce (28g) in mass. Later, MacDougall repeated the experiment on 15 dogs, reporting the outcomes as 'uniformly negative', with no perceived change in mass at the time of death. This was interpreted as evidence that the 'soul' could be weighed, but dogs did not have 'souls'. MacDougall also planned to take X-rays of the soul, but anticipated negative results, as he reasoned 'in reality, the soul is a shadow picture' (Snopes.com 2013). These controversial experiments were not only criticised for their speculative nature, but also the way the evidence was gathered. The sample size was considered too small to give significant results and other explanations for weight loss — for example, through evaporation — were poorly

17 It is worth observing that the idea of a loss of mass at the time of death is contrary to another (competitive) cultural trope, which suggests that, subjectively, the body appears to be heavier in death, leading to the idea of 'dead weight'.

18 MacDougal assumes the moment of death is a precise event, rather than a complex sequence of events that include cellular death, brain death, cardiac death, etc. or that the soul is not trapped by or dissipates within the corpse.

245

controlled. Damningly, MacDougal's results were heavily biased, as he only used findings that supported his initial hypothesis (Wiseman 2011, 42; Kruszelnicki 2004, 200–202).

Experiments conducted using even more sophisticated techniques, such as Magnetic Resonance Imaging (MRI), have been no more forthcoming about the transition between life and death, but raise significant ethical questions. Historically, the dead are used to study the natural of life as an intellectual inquiry. Joseph Paul Jernigan was a 38-year-old mechanic and murderer executed by lethal injection. Before his execution, a prison chaplain convinced him to donate his body to the Texas Anatomy Board. Alongside an anonymous female donor, a 59-year-old Maryland housewife, Jernigan's body was selected by the committee to become the subject for the Visible Human Project, which was organised by the US National Library of Medicine and completed in 1994. The male cadaver was embalmed in gelatine and 'cut'[19] in the axial plane at 1 mm intervals to produce a database of 1,871 slices, representing 15 gigabits of data. In 2000, the photos were rescanned at a higher resolution, yielding more than 65 gigabytes, while the female cadaver was sliced at 0.33 mm intervals, resulting in some 40 gigabytes of data. These datasets have been used to generate 3D anatomical models for medical research and train healthcare professionals.

> Rather than comprehend the miracle of its genesis through its passions, it is much easier to understand life through its 'lack', which is how the phenomenon has largely been (scientifically) understood. The physiological deficits that result from physical subtractions of the body correspond with the criteria for liveliness. Let us remove the heart, the brain, the entrails, the head, the limbs, the eye, the genes and the soul and watch an exquisite choreography of unfathomably complex exchanges fall. There! Like a

19 In specimen preparation, the 'cutting' process actually involves grinding into the specimen. It is a destructive process and leaves no residual 'slice' of the cadaver.

mediaeval Trial by Ordeal, these insufficiencies are formal proof there was once a living thing. Since this essence can be isolated and obliterated, it is now understood. What beautiful poisons balance these theories, which ultimately conclude the nature of being is bounded by a fat 'full stop'. (Armstrong 2018b, 56)

The images acquired in the Human Visible Project are not only a neutral database that archives anatomical structures but ask searching questions about how the living realm is observed and valued. Cadaverous tissues, which are at relative thermodynamic equilibrium, are interpreted as the equivalents of dynamic systems at far-from-equilibrium, which begs the question — what new information is being revealed in this exercise? Moreover, the project's association with human dissection as a data collection exercise is a morally dubious development within an already ethically questionable system of capital punishment and volunteer 'coercion' (Hildebrandt 2008).

At the trial the prisoner exhibited the utmost indifference to his fate, and appeared to entertain no fear for the consequences of his guilt. He maintained his firmness throughout a most feeling address of the learned judge, in which he was sentenced to death, but exhibited some emotion when he was informed that a part of the sentence was that his body should be given over to the surgeons to be dissected. (Anon, n.d.)

Weird Liquid

… aridity, dust and desert only elude water because they have already forged an alliance with a different species of wetness. Monster and alien vistas are indexed by climate and meteorology … [where] the universe is ideated by elemental alignments in which air, fire and earth are paired with questionable liquidities which either possess deranged properties or share more than two properties at the same time with their neighbouring elements. In the case of the former, the derangement and confusion of primary and secondary properties — wetness and coldness — leads to the rediscovery of the elements earth and air as a New Earth and a Fresh Air. Miasma, putrefaction, unground, nigredo and so on refer to the alchemical dispositions or the cosmogenetic problems inherent to these revolutionized elements. Yet excessive properties of the moist element signal something more abysmal. If air and earth can afford water only through one property at a time — either wet or cold — then in considering these liquidities (wet alternatives to water) with more than two properties, we cannot help but submit ourselves to certain ire and troubling speculations … the additional or so-called extraneous properties attest to missing links. In other words, these properties betoken other outsider elements to which the weird liquid species are coupled … [and] impose the otherworldly building processes … that … are built upon meteorological taxonomies; for meteorology suggest the weather-harnessing power of these alien building processes …

Dead seas bring rains and hails which are either crystals impregnated with sand of red and black particle, and sometimes even dead creatures. The desert is frequently haunted by pebble and sand rains, which not only being with themselves hordes of peculiar monsters, but also become teratological entities in themselves. The task of the desert and aridity is to invoke and to couple with alternate fluids; but the task of foreign moistures is to smuggle in the outsider elements as familiar atmospheric phenomena in the form of weather anomalies or havocs. (Negarestani 2008, 98–99)

Liquids do not always behave according to our expectations of them. The double slit experiment, which experimentally established the wave/particle duality of quantum physics (Davisson and Germer 1928), is only part of the repertoire of this realm. When light particles condense in a state known as a Bose-Einstein condensate (the fifth state of matter), they can form liquid light. Like all superfluids, this condensate has zero friction and viscosity. Historically liquid light was only formed at temperatures close to absolute zero, existing for only fractions of a second, but using a Frankenstein mash-up of light and matter, it can now be formed at room temperature using light–matter particles called polaritons. Under these conditions, photons are so highly coordinated that they resist the characteristic disturbances produced by obstructions in their path to flow around objects and even corners (Lerario et al. 2017). Such extraordinary states challenge the classical notions of fluids, and solids, and point towards a stranger, quantum reality, which may be experienced in the everyday reality through encounters with *monstrous materialities.*

Making Ground

> The cartography of oil as an omnipresent entity narrates the
> dynamics of planetary events. Oil is the undercurrent of all
> narrations, not only the political but also that of the ethics
> of life on earth. (Negarestani 2008, 19)

Dark liquids inhabit the ground beneath the soils. These dismal
substances have lurked here for millions of years, metabolising
slowly under pressure, as they turn like rancid milk. Possessing their own agency, they are changing our climate and global
culture.

Historically, the ground is recognised as a generative and fertile matrix, but the source of this potency has been contested.
Medieval accounts about the formation of land were based on
Biblical accounts, which claim the world is between 6,000 and
12,000 years old.

> As one penetrates from seam to seam, from stratum to
> stratum and discovers, under the quarries of Montmartre
> or in the schists of the Urals, those animals whose fossilized
> remains belong to antediluvian civilization, the mind is
> startled to catch a vista of the milliards of years and the
> millions of peoples which the feeble memory of man and
> an indestructible divine tradition have forgotten and whose
> ashes heaped on the surface of our globe, form the two feet
> of earth which furnish us with bread and flowers. (de Balzac
> 1977, 40–41)

The demand for metal purification practices that heralded the
Industrial Revolution required an empirical analysis of ore-
bearing ground. In *De Re Metallica,* 'On the Nature of Metals',
Georgius Agricola created the foundations for a systematic
study of the Earth's rocks and established the founding principles for the scientific study of mining, metallurgy, and geology (Norman 2017). In 1666, intrigued by how one rock could

grow inside another, Nicolas Steno characterised the nature of fossils[20] as snapshots of life at different moments in the planet's history, ensuring that his observations concurred with Biblical timelines and the advent of the Great Flood (Pennsylvania State University 2017).

> ... And on the seventeenth day of the seventh month the ark came to rest on the mountains of Ararat. (Gen 8:4)

Unlike Steno, Robert Plot recognised 'the [giant] figure of the lowermost part of the thigh-bone of a Man or at least some other Animal', in the 'Formed Stones' section of *The Natural History of Oxfordshire* of 1676. This stone was likened to the scrotum of a giant man by Richard Brookes in the eighteenth century, but it was not until 1970 that Beverley Halstead rediscovered these early accounts of fossils and recognised the drawings of *'scrotum humanum'* as evidence of a therapod dinosaur (Carnall 2017). Increasingly, the scientific study of the ground was formalised through the study of mineralogy, which could not only reliably locate valuable ores but also contradicted Biblical accounts. James Hutton argued that geological timescales were much greater than Antediluvian accounts, which according to John Phillip were around 96 million years. However, there was discord even in secular accounts specifically between 'Neptunists' and 'Vulcanists', who differed in their view of the causes of extinction events that shaped the Earth. Neptunists argued they were the work of water, and Vulcanists, acts of fire. New names were invented to correspond with the recognition of particular epochs: the Carboniferous was associated with the formation of coal; Cretaceous with the deposition of chalk; and the Jurassic invoked the limestone Jura mountains.

During the late nineteenth and twentieth centuries, the 'sudden' cataclysmic theories of land formation were replaced by Louis Agassiz's theory of Ice Ages, where huge amounts of earth moved across landscapes, prompting mass extinctions of

---

20 In Latin, *fossilis* refers to anything dug out of the ground.

mega flora and fauna. Around the late twentieth century, the 'slow' apocalypse was once again challenged by the possibility of a 'sudden' catastrophic event, where asteroids were the new agents of apocalypse, which saw the end of the dinosaurs. Once again, the Earth became a place where 'powerful deluges, colossal landslides, gargantuan volcanic eruptions, supersonic impacts from extraterrestrial objects — played a role in shaping our world' (Bjornerud 2015).

Contemporary geological debates centre on 'sudden' manmade geological impacts. While some, like rising global temperatures, may seem slow to us through the experience of lived time, from a geological perspective, they are taking place rapidly. Paul Crutzen and Eugene Stoermer argue that global human civilisation is generating irreversible planetary-scale impacts, which is irreversibly changing its character (Crutzen and Stoermer 2000). Although the impacts themselves are scientifically uncontroversial, their relationship to geological time remains hotly contested and whether we are presently in the Holocene, or Anthropocene, is still under consideration by the International Geological Congress (Carrington 2016).

> The 'Anthropocene' is a term widely used ... to denote the present time interval, in which many geologically significant conditions and processes are profoundly altered by human activities. These include changes in: erosion and sediment transport associated with a variety of anthropogenic processes, including colonisation, agriculture, urbanisation and global warming, the chemical composition of the atmosphere, oceans and soils, with significant anthropogenic perturbations of the cycles of elements such as carbon, nitrogen, phosphorus and various metals, environmental conditions generated by these perturbations; these include global warming, ocean acidification and spreading oceanic 'dead zones', the biosphere both on land and in the sea, as a result of habitat loss, predation, species invasions and the physical and chemical changes ... (Subcommission on Quaternary Stratigraphy 2016)

As we bear witness to large-scale depletion of polar ice, a rise in ocean acidification, 'new' carbon dioxide released into the atmosphere from fossil fuels and toxic plastic deposits generating continent-scale islands in the ocean gyres, our current toolsets are not designed for practically addressing ongoing ecocide — particularly at such a speed, or scale, of multiple simultaneous events. Ironically, the industrial systems and modes of consumption that have produced them are the very same processes that we are focussing on as a way of combating this situation. Try as we might, without a distinct change in technological platform to underpin human development, we are *fiddling while our homes burn.*

05.23

Metabolic Weather

> There is no other planet within twenty parsecs that has
> the like of it, and perhaps there is no other place anywhere
> at all that has such air. The air is the archetype of restless
> immanence. It is full of invisible movements and invisible
> contents. Through what is does and what is brings, it makes
> and unmakes the world it envelops. There is no actor more
> powerful on this earth, yet for the most part we studiedly
> ignore it … All the phenomena of weather and climate
> come from the restless motions of the air, the gyres, and
> all their permutations that bring rain, snow, fog, hail, sleet,
> black ice, tornadoes, hurricanes, the layers and the heaps
> of the clouds, the rising smoke of the chimneys. We can't
> control the weather, but nevertheless the weather changes as
> we change the contents of the air. (Logan 2012, 19–20)

'Metabolic weather' arises from energy gradients, density currents, katabatic flows, vortices, dust clouds, pollution, and the myriad expressions of matter that detail our (earthy, liquid, gaseous) terrains, which sets the scene for the process of living, lifelike events, and even life itself.

The potency of weather resides in its incessant flow, which is produced by the juxtaposition of gaseous and aqueous bodies at different temperatures, acting as the transport system for other agents. At the macroscale, 'weather' is a slow-moving field of enfolded dirts, water, and air; chemically, it is a highly active terrain where matter/energy is transformed into peculiar events, such as acidic rain, which excoriates alkaline surfaces like limestone. The field of termolecular chemical reactions describes the chemical processes that govern combustions, cloud formation, planetary atmospheres, and climate change (Caughill 2017). They are highly complex and uncommon, involving the simultaneous breaking and forming of chemical bonds between three molecules, ions, or atoms. Undergoing various transitional states that alter their reactiveness, they can (re)combine in many ways (Burke and Klippenstein 2017). Although these reactions were theorised during the 1920s, because of their complexity they could only recently be studied using state of the art computers, which 'can provide a unique lens into harsh chemical environments ill-suited for experimental techniques for studying individual reaction dynamics' (Bergan 2017). These modelling systems not only change the way complex chemistry is viewed, but also may have a broader impact on our study of chemical reactions, which offer insights into the planetary chemistry responsible for cloud formations, climate change, and evolution of pollutants (Burke and Klippenstein 2017). Importantly for metabolic weather, the sequence of reactions produces a plethora of turbulent structures, which are interconnected on a planetary scale and influence the conditions for terrestrial life. If we are to have any influence over these active fronts, their recognisable features must first be named.

> … during the second world war when meteorologists forecasting weather ahead of battles began to draw cold fronts and warm fronts on maps… Jacob Bjerknes … discovered the different air masses around the world and the stormy weather that occurs on the edges of these air masses … [and] … likened them to the battle fronts across Europe, so he decided to call them fronts. (Meyers 2015)

Naming things so they may be controlled is an ancient practice that shapes how we make sense of our world. According to the book of Genesis, power resides in words where humans acquired power over animals by naming them. In finding the names for experiences, our thoughts become real, so we are no longer musing but acting, casting 'spells', or exerting influence, upon the world. Abracadabra, which is often used to announce a trick in magic shows, is Aramaic for 'I create what I speak'. While the scientific Enlightenment changed naming into a practice of classifications, encyclopaedias, and taxonomies, the fundamental belief that finding the true names and nature of things increases our influence in the world, persists.

While it is relatively straightforward to describe and name objects with discrete boundaries — apple, chair, cat, saucer, bridge, sun — or particular actions and events — fall, buy, show, run, it is much more challenging to find specific names for things that we cannot observe in their totality, like the entire surface of the sea; abstractions, as in the objects associated with computer programming; or things that are constantly changing, like clouds.

> ... clouds have certain general forms which are not at all dependent upon chance but on a state of affairs which it would be useful to recognise and determine. (Hamblyn 2001, 103)

The visible patterns produced by weather fronts arise from a stream of transitions, so by interpreting these soft, dynamic structures as stable bodies, the chances of predicting their behaviour, or even controlling them, is increased. Jean-Baptiste Lamarck invented the first cloud classification system, while he was ill in bed. Staring out the window he noted basic typologies: *en voilé* (hazy), *attroupés* (massed), *pommelés* (dappled), *en balayures* (brooms) and *groupés* (grouped). Back then, before meteorologists could plot weather fronts and fields of equal atmospheric pressure, or isobars, the skies were read according to their cloud formations. Lamarck's system did not catch on and was superseded by Luke Howard's much more accessible Latin-based system, which used technical terminology and signs, namely: cirrus (curl of hair), cumulus (heap) and stratus (layer), terms that are now in common usage (Howard 1865). Considering these different cloud species as 'good visible indications of the operation of [their] causes as [the equivalent of] the countenance of the state of a person's mind or body' (Zajonc 1984, 36), Johann Wolfgang von Goethe recognised a kindred spirit in Howard's true typology of clouds. Popularising this gentle empiricism of the skies, he ensured the 'open secrets' of the natural world became accessible to all.

256

From all my strivings in science and art it must be clear
how precious to me is this process, bestowing form on the
formless and a system of ordered change on a boundless
world. (Zajonc 1984, 38).

Even today, locally reading the details of actual clouds is a
better predictor of events than a meteorological map. Despite
our better understanding of its constituent events, the weather
remains unpredictable as a global happening, sometimes as-
tonishingly so. Many incidents of red rain have been described
throughout the ages. In the *Iliad,* Homer described 'bloody
rain-drops on the earth' (Homer 1987, 264), and although Pliny
and Cicero also report such portents, Cicero suggests their causes are earthly, not supernatural, as arising '*ex aliqua contagione
terrena*'[21] (Tatlock 1914). Ernst Chladni complied a catalogue
on widespread occurrences of red rain and snow since ancient
times and attributed some of these to mineral causes such as
dust, or biological agents like lichen (Chladni 1826, 20[22]), while
Christian Gottfried Ehrenberg observed the widespread occurrence of red rain and recreated it using a mixture of red dust
and water (Wickramasinghe 2015, 160). More recently, in 2001,
50,000 kg of particular matter fell in the southern Indian state
of Kerala (Louis and Kumar 2006) and an initial report from
the Department of Meteorology suggested that this rainfall was
chemical in origin. Studies commissioned by the Indian govern-
ment analysed samples, which indicated that the red particles
possessed capsules but no DNA and were thought to be spores
of a lichen-forming alga belonging to the genus *Trentepohlia*
(White, Cerveny and Balling 2012). Chandra Wickramasinghe
contested these findings and suggested the recovered particles
'represent an unknown microorganism of extraterrestrial origin' (Wickramasinghe 2015, 161–67). Red rain was also reported

21 The Latin translates as 'from some earthly contagion'.
22 Ernst Chladni's last catalogue entry dated 3 May 1821 reads: 'Red rain at
   and near Giessen, during a calm, from a moderate-sized stratus ... [that
   contained] ... chromic acid, oxide of iron, silica, lime, a trace of magnesia,
   carbon, and several volatile substances, but no nickel.'

in 2013 over the Rakwana in the Kiwul-alla area, and then in mid-November 2015, across the Indikolapelessa and Moneralga district in Sri Lanka. On analysis, these samples confirmed the presence of *Trentepohlia* spores (Rajgopal 2015). Although many theories regarding the ontology of red rain exist, its formation remains perplexing and is likely to have various and highly contingent causes (Gat et al. 2017).

Outpourings of creatures falling from the sky have been reported since ancient times, which Pliny the Elder attributed to the natural but remarkable properties of water:

> Water engulfs lands, quenches flames, climbs aloft, and lays claim to even the sky, and by a covering of clouds chokes the life-giving spirit that forces out thunderbolts, as the world wages war with itself. What could be more amazing than water standing in the sky? But as though it were a mere trifle to reach such a great height, the water sucks up with itself shoals of fish and often stones as well, carrying more than its own weight aloft. (Pliny the Elder 1991, 272)

While transportation of a single species of creature from a stream of pond as a consequence of 'weather' may seem extreme, hurricanes and tornadoes are powerful enough to destroy buildings and may feasibly lift large particles in suspension into the atmosphere (Radford 2010; BBC News 2014). With the onset of climate change, the once seemingly recognisable patterns that Lamarck and Howard described are becoming increasingly unreliable. While showers of creatures are visible indicators that something in the natural cycles is unusual, the Anthropocene has introduced invisible agents into the atmosphere as *new carbon dioxide*. Having been quiescent for around 350 to 300 million years, this ancient source of carbon was first sequestered and buried on a massive scale by plants as biomass and turned into fossil fuels by subsequent geological events. With the advent of the Industrial Revolution which burned heavy oil to fuel powerful machines like the Hornsby–Akroyd engine, this recalcitrant carbon released by these dark ancient substances is invading our skies and impacting on our weather systems as *global storming*.

Metabolic weather is more than an atmospheric phenomenon, but also penetrates into all the terrains composed of atomic 'dusts' that are held to the Earth's surface by gravity — air, water, and the soils. A generative platform for irrepressible synthesis, constant mutability, and evolutionary transgressions, it may one day precipitate the occurrence of new kinds of 'life'. While the chances that this will happen are extremely small, that life has already occurred on this planet, significantly increases the likelihood of its recurrence.

> ... maybe life arose more than once at different locations on the early Earth. Those other organisms might have their own biochemistry and a separate evolutionary history ... there may be some organisms hiding on Earth today that are based not on DNA and proteins but on a more primitive type of biochemistry ... Even if [it] were living out in the open, the life detection tools that we have today would not find it ... because they assume that all metabolisms must be similar to our own ... There's no reason in physics or chemistry why these different ways of building a life-form wouldn't work ... If life is easy to make and is widespread, then it should have happened many times on Earth ... The best way to test for that is to look for it. (Zimmer 2007)

LIFE AS RESTLESS FLÂNEUR

This chapter explores how liquid life resists the decay towards thermodynamic equilibrium by working in conjunction with highly structured and specific environments like soil, eggs, and placentas to bring about the conception, differentiation, development, and maturation of living systems.

Chicken and Egg

> ... while they waited for the sun to go down again, she
> told them about the great big world outside the chick run,
> or the days when she was a chick, or the story she liked
> telling best of all — the Miracle story about Eggs. How
> the broken fragments they had hatched from were once
> smooth, complete shapes; how every chicken that ever was
> had hatched out in exactly the same way; how only chooks
> could lay such beauties; and how every time they did, they
> were so filled with joy that they could not stay quiet, but
> had to burst into song; and how their song was taken up
> by England the cock and echoed by every single hen in the
> Run. (Gage 1981, 11).

The inception of the *bête machine* provokes an existential paradox. Does a fully mature adult body, like a chicken, exist first to create an egg, or is an egg a necessary precondition for a chicken?

This apparent paradox is a consequence of its secular, dualistic framing which considers living beings to pass through discrete stages. However, the propagation of multicellular biological systems is sustained by ongoing exchanges between lively bodies at different stages of development. Liquid life's fundamental interconnectedness generates an inescapable ecology of exchange, where bodies are inextricably permeated by and entangled with others and their environments. Without associated networks of other beings (such as the bacterial biome, trees, earthworms, and mitochondria), living beings wither, fade, and die out.

The conundrum of the chicken and egg only arises when stages in a single lifecycle are conceptually isolated from each other. Chickens are biological transformers that produce biological seeds of potentiality, where not all sexual encounters are potent. Eggs are also transformational sites for choreographing the developing chicken-body through folded membranes, which mediate the relationships between lively chemistries and energy gradients to generate recognisable and repeatable body-types. Transitioning between various states of being, the continuity between chickens and eggs persists, but is never absolute. Every aspect of egg-ness (e.g., fertilised, unfertilised, egg shell fragments) and chicken-ness (e.g., chick, pullet, hen, cockerel) continue to give rise to creatures that share a 'chicken' ontology but do not always epistemologically qualify as such. Chickens may one day 'evolve' to become something 'else'.

By viewing chicken-ness and egg-ness as a continuum, the question of which stage precedes the other becomes redundant, since the various forms of chicken–egg are continuous expressions of an ongoing living process that is characterized by a range of anatomical structures and physiological events, some of which result in offspring. Rather than a paradox, the various stages of life are produced by an ongoing function of complex interdependencies, whose manifestations fluctuate accordingly with time, encounter, and location. The continuity and sense that unites all recognisable developmental stages is cleaved only by deterministic object typologies that are imposed on living systems through dualistic thought.

Liquid Soils

I! I called myself a magician, an angel, free from all
moral constraint, I am sent back to the soil to seek some
obligation, to wrap gnarled reality in my arms! (Rimbaud
2005, 302)

Eggs and placentas are highly organised substrata that link the
cycles of life and death. Primed by liquid infrastructures they
act like fleshy soils, with microsites that complexify the building blocks of life, so that specific lifeforms can emerge. The
apparatuses of fertility — allantois, chorion, amnion, egg sac,
and placenta — choreograph mini-worlds. Pulsing with liquid
protocols, they guide the synthesis of particular states of being through manifolds of material organisation, which differentially introduce time, space, and complexity into embryonic
developmental pathways. As pluripotent tissue masses become
organised through various spatial configurations, their twists,
rolls, and folds alter according to changing needs. As one set of
material negotiations is completed, another begins, until these
enfleshings form recognisable tissues and organs, which are capable of supporting a self-regulating being.

Egg

> I am their sign and epitaph,
> the goose egg : o :
> even the least of these — that is me…
> Can we say to the unborn, Egg, who are you? Egg, divulge
> your design. (Sandburg 1970, 324)

The amniotic egg typical of birds, reptiles, and dinosaurs produces four extraembryonic membranes that choreograph the
vital material exchanges necessary for embryogenesis. This ar-
moured world may be leathery, as in turtle eggs, or mineralised,
as in the shell of an ostrich. Each egg contains a liquid space that
enables embryos to develop outside a maternal body, but within,
the developing creature is not blind to the world.

The tough outer membrane, or *chorion,* that shelters the embryo, captures these external vibrations and transmits them into
this microworld like the beat of a drum.

Powered by the developing heart, the *amnion* choreographs
the embryo's metabolism through a rich network of blood vessels and enables the conceptus to respire. Shaped by osmotic
forces and genetic programs, these iterations continue until an
immature being forms, complete with heartbeat and cirulation.

Nitrogenous waste from the maturation process is gathered
in another membrane called the *allantois,* which stretches from
the embryonic gut to the chorion and is anchored to the inside
of the egg shell, being left behind when the chick hatches.

The *yolk sac* meets all the embryo's nutritional needs from internal reserves that are pre-provided by the maternal body and
is unsurprisingly large in comparison with the conceptus. Once
stores are exhausted, the chick, with a fully developed auditory
and vibratory understanding of the world, regards this depleted
space as a threat to its survival.

With sufficient strength, frustration, urgency, and encouragement from the shrieks of its kin, the chick breaks out of its

watery world into an alien realm, where it rapidly establishes an
alternative way of surviving.

06.4

Placenta

> … 'placenta' was first used by Realdus Columbus in his
> book *De Re Anatomica* published in 1559. Until then there
> was no specific name for it and it was simply called the
> 'afterbirth'. Descriptions of this 'afterbirth' were already
> well documented in ancient literature, including the Old
> Testament where it was referred to as the 'Seat of the Soul'
> or the 'Bundle of Life'. (Loke 2013, 11)

As in the amniotic egg, mammalian embryos develop in liquid
environments, supported by a range of membranes. These are
not leathery skins and shells, but a placenta, a fleshy temporary
organ snuggled deep in the mother's pelvis that 'occupies a position midway between the baby and mother, in a kind of 'no-
man's land" (Loke 2013, 6). Enfolding embryos within a muscular cathedral of flesh, the placenta unites them with the mother's
bloodstream through tissue cavities that are soaked in maternal
blood. Here, they negotiate their terms for survival — nutrition,
respiration, metabolism — so they can be accommodated until
they are semi-autonomous. At the moment of birth, foetuses
make a lightning change in reorganising their blood system, as
valves slam shut in response to their inflating lungs, so they may
thrive in air.

The evolutionary origins of this shared organ between mother and child evolved from a developmental journey of opportunity and survival that began after the worst mass extinction ever
at the end of the Permian period about 250 million years ago.
The creatures that would become mammals appeared 160 million years ago and acquired their placentas through a sexually
transmitted infection, which affected the cloaca. The vectors of
this disease were syncytial retroviruses, which are particularly
prone to integrating their codes into the genetic makeup of host
cells that caused cloacal and embryonic tissues to fuse together
into a single, synchronous organ. This early placenta was a fusion of cells that became so vascular and muscular that eggs

could thrive within its pouch-like outgrowth of the maternal excretory cavity. While the tissue proliferation should have only lasted for an adult lifetime, the proximity of the infective agents to pre-mammalian sex cells increased the likelihood that the viral codes would be incorporated into their DNA and — although certain mammalian groups such as pangolins were missed out — became part of the story of mammalian evolution.

This strange evolutionary pathway was discovered by genetic analysis when the placental hormone syncytin was found to share homologies with syncytial retroviruses. Mediated through cell-cell fusion, these infections became integral to their hosts' reproductive cycles on around six separate occasions (Zimmer 2012), resulting in muscular placentas that enabled mammalian embryos to bind to their mothers during the most vulnerable time of their development.

06.5

Hydatids

The strange embryonic cancers known as hydatid moles and chorionic carcinomas problematise beliefs that developing life is innately benign. Both types of cancer are made up of greedy, ambitious, and unruly cell populations that do not engage in diplomatic negotiations with metabolic or genetic networks and lack meaningful relationship with their communities. These virulent beings are as old as multicellular life. Evidence of tumour formation has been found in *hydra*, which are creatures that existed during the Vendian epoch around 650–540 million years ago. Possessing a very simple body plan that is composed of only two cell layers, which are maintained by three independent stem cell lineages (Bosch 2009), hydra appear not to age or to die of old age (Martinez 1998). Tumours arising in the stem cell population may therefore accumulate in large quantities, as they are not removed by programmed cell death. These malignancies affect only female hydra and share similarities with ovarian cancers in humans (Domazet-Lošo et al. 2014). Within a 'normotypical' body, cell proliferation and coordinated cell death are critical for shaping the emerging embryo. In this way, embryos become appropriately structured and differentiated, through the rolling, folding, and invaginating of body cavities, which enables their independent existence, away from the nurturing environment.

Hydatid moles arise from 'empty' fertilised eggs where the paternal genome takes over embryogenesis. Their rare and slow-growing tissue masses are full of empty cysts with a characteristic 'grape-like' appearance. Those that begin to differentiate generate unruly structures with resemblances to hair, teeth, sebaceous glands, and bone. A small number of hydatids become choriocarcinomas, which are monstrously malignant cells that are life-threatening to the host.

Both cancers unleash the relentless pluripotency of liquid life to the point of wilful disobedience. This is not an 'error' in their nature but unconstrained vigour, which refuses to cooperatively engage with nurturing systems. Trapped down long, winding blind alleys, the virulent cells strive to resist decay towards equilibrium, creatively inventing their way towards autonomy but ultimately fail in this quest, since they consume both their host and themselves in the process.

LIQUID BEINGS

The relationships between liquid environments and their inhabitants are explored through their exudates, developmental cycles, cultural provocations, embodiments, and appearances. Many of these creatures defy classical conventions of body plan, behaviour, and character, posing paradoxes of existence that exceed the programmatic logic of the *bête machine*.

Liquid *Paradoxa*

It is useless and tedious to represent what exists, because
nothing that exists satisfies me. Nature is ugly, and I prefer
the monsters of my fantasy to what is positively trivial.
(Baudelaire 1955, 233)

Since ancient times, unclassifiable bodies have inhabited in-
subordinate liquid landscapes, which were entangled with their
character. Even today, many of these beings remain largely un-
scrutinsed, or imagined. In the Icelandic saga of *Örvar-Odds,*
a crew bound for Helluland (Baffin Island) encounter two sea
monsters. One of these beasts — the *hagufa,* or sea-mist — is
thought to be the Kraken, which appears more like a land mass
than a creature and seems incapable of reproducing itself:

Now I will tell you that there are two sea-monsters. One is
called the *hafgufa* [sea-mist], another *lyngbakr* [heather-
back]. It [the *lyngbakr*] is the largest whale in the world, but
the hafgufa is the hugest monster in the sea. It is the nature
of this creature to swallow men and ships, and even whales
and everything else within reach. It stays submerged for
days, then rears its head and nostrils above surface and stays
that way at least until the change of tide. Now, that sound
we just sailed through was the space between its jaws, and
its nostrils and lower jaw were those rocks that appeared in
the sea, while the *lyngbakr* was the island we saw sinking
down. However, Ogmund Tussock has sent these creatures
to you by means of his magic to cause the death of you
[Odd] and all your men. He thought more men would have
gone the same way as those that had already drowned [i.e.
to the *lyngbakr,* which was not an island, and sank], and
he expected that the *hafgufa* would have swallowed us all.
Today I sailed through its mouth because I knew that it had
recently surfaced. (Boer 1888, 132)

During the sixteenth century, the systematic rationalisation of these creatures began. Conrad Gessner composed *Historiae Animalium,* a 4,500-page encyclopaedia of animals, which included animals like the unicorn, the basilisk, and mermaids, although he had only come across them in medieval bestiaries (Senter, Mattox and Haddad 2016). This one-man search engine founded modern zoology through a database of encyclopaedic works, as a means to understand the moral lessons within the animal kingdom and the divine truths they revealed.

However, Ulisse Aldrovandi is considered the 'father' of natural history. Inspired by Gessner, he assembled a spectacular cabinet[1] of around 7,000 curiosities as a theatre of natural history. In addition to his encyclopaedic collection, he also made publications. The most famous of these is the *Storia Naturale,* which is considered the most complete description of the mineral, vegetable, and animal kingdoms of nature of the time, while his *Monstrorum Historia* documented 'monstrous' human and animal deformities, as well as mythological beasts (Aldrovandi 2002).

> ... Natural Things, such as either [Nature] hath retained the same from the beginning, or freely produces in her ordinary course; as *Animals, Plants,* and the *universal furniture of the World.* Secondly, her extravagancies and deficits, occasioned either by the exuberancy of matter, or obstinacy of impediments, as in *Monsters.* And then lastly, as she is restrained, forced, fashioned, or determined, by Artificial Operations. All which, without absurdity, may fall under the general notation of Natural History ... (Plot 1677)

While early natural historians took an inclusive approach to the diversity of creatures, Carolus Linnaeus began to erase unknown and fabulous creatures from his accounts. In his first edition of *Systema Naturae,* Linnaeus included a section on *'Paradoxa'* (monsters) — a category of uncategorisable beings — to

---

1 Some of the specimens can still be seen at the Museum Aldrovendi in Palazzo Poggi, Bologna.

demystify the natural world, which was largely characterised by chimeras and allegorical beasts like the Pelican (Linnaeus 1735, 29). Although he had not seen a Kraken, he likened it to a cuttlefish, classifying it as a cephalopod *Microcosmus marinus*.[2] He also gave an account of it in *Fauna Svecica* (Linnaeus 1746) as a 'unique monster' that inhabited the Norwegian seas. In later editions of *Systema Naturae,* Linnaeus removed these references, apparently relenting that he had included imaginary creatures in a scientific text. Prone to changing his mind about his classification system, his rationalisation of the living world became a lifelong process of discovery and refinement, which banished such creatures to the realms of folklore.

However, 'monsters' could not be entirely rationalised away and with the progressive study of the natural world, the scientific value of anatomical non-conformity was championed by Francis Bacon in *Novum Organum* (1620), by categorising biological 'errors', so their origins could be better understood (Leroi 2005, 1). Later, William Harvey in *On Animal Generation* (1651) even named causal links between development and adult form, suggesting that monstrous chickens were produced from eggs with two yolks (Leroi 2005, 10).

While advances in reproductive technologies and the advent of genetics have provided a deductive toolset though which the inheritance of traits can be described, the relationships between genes, organelles, cells, body parts, and overall phenotypes, are still far from resolved. Treating organic materials as building blocks that can be compiled like machines, using advanced biotechnologies like biobricks and genetic sequences, continues to prove particularly challenging, as creatures are 'other' than the sum of their 'parts' (Bull 2015).

2   Linnaeus also referred to *Microcosmus marinus* in his publication *Fauna Svecica* (Linnaeus 1746).

Eradicating Monsters

> He grew up convinced that he was just the dregs of someone
> else, someone better ... he wrote about the Idea and its
> Shadow, that something real and individual can exist,
> perfect in its uniqueness, along with something more hazy,
> reflected, and, like every reflection, discontinuous, full of
> imperfections and thus false ... (Tokarczuk 2003, 160)

Although gene-editing methods using natural enzymes, such as CRISPR, may one day eliminate rare genetic diseases, they are not 'error'-free and, despite He Jiankui's claim to have altered the DNA of twin girls before birth (Sataline and Sample 2018), are far more expensive and risky than embryo selection. To confer an egg with favoured traits, many of them must first be harvested so they can be fertilised, studied, and selected outside the womb before the appropriate genes may be implanted.

While genetic sequencing is now affordable to the point where gene-sequencing for ancestral and medical reasons is available as a commercial service, interpretations must remain circumspect. Only for a rare number of instances does one gene code for a single trait. Far more commonly, multiple genetic sequences influence each other and are also sensitive to environmental influences, so it hard to make specific predictions based on the presence, or absence, of a single gene. Furthermore, desirable qualities like 'intelligence' (see section 02.4) are not easy to define let alone genetically isolate, as they are based on existing value systems (Ball 2017a). Despite insights into embryological development and advances in molecular control, in striving to prevent monsters through their rationalisation, we are more likely to produce them.

> Our very understanding of who we are, of the life-forms
> we are and the forms of life we inhabit, have folded *bios*
> back to *zoe*. By this I mean that the question of the good

life — *bios* — has become intrinsically a matter of the vital processes of our animal life — *zoe*. (Rose 2006, 83).

Despite Bacon's wish for a controllable natural world, wherever we impose command-and-control tactics upon living systems, they find ways of subverting our intentions by producing hybrids, chimeras, shapeshifters, mutants, and all kinds of teratogenic in-betweens.

It lumbered slobberingly into sight and gropingly squeezed its gelatinous green immensity through the black doorway into the tainted outside air of that poison city of madness. … The Thing cannot be described — there is no language for such abysms of shrieking and immemorial lunacy, such eldritch contradictions of all matter, force, and cosmic order. (Lovecraft 2002, 67)

As we move from an age of physics to one of biology, we discover a time of monsters, whose nature exceeds our ability to control them. Alternative value systems must be found if we are to appropriately and creatively engage their transgressive recalcitrance.

[We cannot] disregard the life and the passion of the creature, which [are] its essence … in the thought of Nature herself, there is, in a plant, nothing else but its flowers. (Ruskin 1900, 62)

07.3

Liquid Development

'… like blowing glass,' like liquefying a part that needs sculpting and then letting its new form set. (Cepelewicz 2018)

'See through' zebrafish (*danio rerio*) embryos are used as a highly accessible model for the study of vertebrate development, turning from a ball of cells into a fully-formed fish outside the mother, where it is possible to observe their protean character from the inception of their lives.

Alongside the traditional focus on morphology, more recent studies evaluate the distribution of internal forces and better characterise their transformation through their material properties. Focusing on the long axis of the embryo's body, Otger Campàs showed that developing cells can freely flow past each other at the tip of what becomes the tail, just like liquid. Closer to its head however, cells are increasingly jammed together and behave more like a viscous solid like glass, colloids, and foams (Serwane et al. 2016).

Tissue liquidation happens as the result of rapid cell division, where multiplying cells become round and detach from their neighbours. This occurs so rapidly that they eventually lose so many contacts they reach the 'fluidity transition'. Occurring suddenly, at a very specific time and location within the embryo's development, this mechanical change turns part of the zebrafish to liquid (Petridou et al. 2018). The various fluid states and forces determine how the developing body elongates and sculpts various structures along its axis. Previously, the position of cells was thought to result from finely-tuned and gradual forces that guided everything into place, similar to moulding ceramics. However, these recent studies reveal that embryological development is comprised of disruptive transitions where creatures are strategically liquefied, moulded, and allowed to set into their new form (Cepelewicz 2018).

These embryological findings attest that liquid life is comprised of many fluids, fluid states, and transitions, which underpin the irreducibly protean nature of organisms. We are liquid at our origin and our core.

07.4

Siphonophores

> All of these definitions of individuality are in alignment in most of the organisms we are familiar with. A bird, a rose bush, and a fly are all individuals as functional entities, according to their ancestry, and as units of [natural] selection. This makes it easy to get lulled into thinking of individuality as a monolithic property. (Encyclopedia of Life 2017)

Siphonophores are spectacular colonial creatures that challenge the singular nature of 'being'. While their progenitors have been on this planet for a billion years (Steele, David and Technau 2012), their precarious organisation, reminiscent of a feather boa, evades clear and efficient explanation. Fragile, and fragmenting even under the slightest touch, their peculiar composition offers insights into the complexity of multicellular life and raises questions about the nature of embodiment. Around 180 species of siphonophores are known which, like *Praya dubia,* can sometimes reach 40–50 metres in length (longer than a blue whale). Broadly speaking, they are long, thin, clear gelatinous, and efficient predators, which use their many tentacles and lethal venom to ensnare crustaceans and small fish. While the Portuguese man o' war, *Physalia physalis,* dwells on the surface of the sea and rhodaliids use their tentacles to attach themselves to the ocean floor, the vast majority are pelagic swimmers that move gracefully in the water column of the open ocean (Sirucek 2014).

Once considered a distinct species of animal known as cnidarians (Haeckel 1888), they were later found to have evolved from colonial hydrozoans, which are made up of cells that form societies together and are related to jellyfish, anemones, and corals. Currently, siphonophores are arguably identified as superorganisms, as they grow from a single embryo by budding off genetically identical zooids, which are the cells that make up the creature's body, which then become differentiated and spatially organised into highly specialised types. Each plays a particular role in the colony, including: protection, digestion, locomotion, reproduction, and making artificial (bioluminescent) light to attract food. Rather than separating as individuals, siphonophore zooids remain entangled and become integrated into the superorganism. Grouped through species-specific repeating patterns along the creature's stem, they perform specific organ tasks.

> Unless disturbed, Stephanomia apparently remain perfectly quiescent, and in an inclined position. The pneumatophore causes the whole organism to float to the top of still water, and that part of the stem bearing the nectophores hangs vertically below it, but the rest of the stem falls away from the basal nectophores at an angle of about forty-five degrees. The reason for this seems obvious, for in this position the long contractile filaments hang separately, vertically, and evenly spaced, whereas if the whole organism assumed a vertical position in the quiescent state the filaments would hang down together as one cluster, with a relatively small volume of water with its contained organisms exposed to their influence … Contact of any small particle with a single filament or tentacle causes the instantaneous contraction of the latter towards its associated gastrozoid. Stronger stimulation of one or more filaments not only results in their contraction, but also that of the stem itself up to the base of the nectophores. (Berrill 1930)

Buoyed up by the pneumatophore, a gas-filled float, at their tip, muscular nectophores propel the siphonophore superorganism through the water like a beating heart, where individual movements are coordinated by a distributed nervous system. Forming a deadly, graceful net, their tentacles wave food towards the organism, which triggers deadly stinging cells. These cnidocytes are arguably the most complex cells of any animals, as they are densely packed into the cnidoband, which fires the sticky cnidocytes as a single unit from the tentacles and injects toxins into the prey through a hollow harpoon. Along the stem, the many mouths and stomachs of gastrozooids feed the colony with their digested products. While specialised zooids are continually added to the creature by budding, new colonies are produced sexually through gonozooids that bear numerous spheroidal female and male gonophores. These egg and sperm cells are released into the open water, where they dance briskly together around the fertilisation site before they fuse and start a new colony that arises from a single embryo. While each cell has some independence from the colony, and is capable of its own movements, zooids cannot reproduce or survive independently but depend on the creature's collective specialisations. While their developmental and physiological complexity exceeds rational accounts of the nature of being, siphonophores' exquisite choreography celebrates the existence of wondrous monsters.

> ... how could there be Chimera with three bodies rolled into one, in front a lion, at the rear a serpent, in the middle a she-goat that her name implies, belching from her jaws a dire flame born of her body? If anyone pretends that such monsters could have been begotten when the earth was young and the sky new ... it is no indication that beasts could have been created of intermingled shapes with limbs compounded from different species. (Lucretius 2007, 198–99)

Liquid Experiences

> Every time I walk on grass I feel sorry because I know the grass is screaming at me … Plants are extraordinary. For instance … if you pinch a leaf of a plant you set off electrical impulse. You can't touch a plant without setting off an electrical impulse … There is no question that plants have all kinds of sensitivities. They do a lot of responding to an environment. They can do almost anything you can think of. (Ritzer and Smart 2001, 532)

Alternative forms of embodiment necessitate different kinds of consciousness. Descartes only attributed self-consciousness to humanity and so regarded the screams of animals as no more than physiological 'noise', produced by simple reflexes. Perhaps the same error is now being made with plants, which, viewed from the perspective of the *bête machine,* are slow and unintelligent clockwork-like mechanisms. In his 1751 treatise *Philosophia Botanica,* Carl Linnaeus proposed that the opening and closing of flowers could be used to tell the time. Based on field observations, he divided flowers into three categories: the *meteorici* that open and close with the weather; the *tropici,* which follow the changing hours of daylight; and the *aequinoctales,* which 'open precisely at a certain hour of the day and generally shut up every day at a determinate hour' (Tortello 2015).

While plants appear to be solid, they possess a liquid heart. Plunged randomly into the belly of a site, seedlings are equipped with an extremely robust molecular vocabulary that helps them orchestrate the site around them, to bring the necessary flow of resources, which will enable them to thrive. Working with light, soil structure, nutrients, water, toxins, microbes, temperature, gravity, and chemical signals from other plants, plants bend the world around them to meet their needs. Since their movements and responses happen much more slowly than animals, we largely overlook their potency.

During the nineteenth century, a range of scientific experiments explored the possibility of plant sensibility, which mirrored ongoing debates regarding 'vitalism' and 'brute' materialism. Charles Darwin identified the plant radicle as the anatomical structure capable of making decisions about the plant's environment (Darwin 2009). Taking an animistic perspective, Gustav Fechner suggested in 1848 that plants were capable of emotions, which could affect their growth and in 1900, Jagadish Chandra Bose began conducting experiments using a crescograph to establish how seasons and external stimuli affected plant life, which allowed people to take better care of plants. In 1920, Patrick Geddes, who explored ways of integrating technological and natural process to give rise to a 'eutechnic' age, where technology would harmonise with the Earth's needs (Bud 1993, 68), noted that Bose had found plants to possess 'all the characteristics of the responses exhibited by the animal tissues' (Geddes 1920, 121). These provocations were regarded as having limited value for modern science at the time, but by the latter part of the twentieth century, owing to widespread awareness of planetary systems, they were given new importance. Notions of non-anthropocentric notions of 'intelligence' could be studied in new ways with the capacity to study tissues in molecular detail, with insights brought by ecological sciences. It now appears that plants have evolved the capacity to make decisions about how they respond to their surroundings, with up to 20 distinctive types of sensory systems that possess similarities to animal senses, including smell, taste, sight, touch, and sound, which is thought to act as a 'radar' system to locate nearby objects.

> ... our 'fetishization' of neurons, as well as our tendency to equate behavior with mobility, keeps us from appreciating what plants can do. For instance, since plants can't run away and frequently get eaten, it serves them well not to have any irreplaceable organs ... A plant has a modular design, so it can lose up to ninety per cent of its body without being killed ... There's nothing like that in the animal world. It creates a resilience. (Pollan 2013)

The flows of matter that take place within and between plant bodies at a specific site, as well as other species like fungi and bacteria, collectively produce coherent environments and landscapes that regulate terrains as large as forests. Sharing a common information-processing infrastructure, these ecosystems coordinate their collective actions through air, water, soil, as well as the actions of many different organisms (Trewvas 2003).

> … now we know that trees can learn. This means they must store experiences somewhere, and therefore, there must be some kind of storage mechanism inside the organism. Just where it is, no one knows, but the roots are the part of the tree best suited to the task … the root network is in charge of all the chemical activity in the tree … For there to be something we would recognise as a brain, neurological processes must be involved, and for these, in addition to chemical messages, you need electrical impulses. And these are precisely what we can measure in the tree … (Wohlleben 2016, 82–83)

The astonishing, inner worlds of plants can be viewed through their liquid exchanges, which casts them — not as automata — but as social beings that can count, learn, remember, feel pain, communicate, have families, and nurture their kin. Certain trees may even entwine their welfare like a married couple and, should one of them fade, they then die together. The open exchanges that occur within forests are not limited to specific plants species, but extend throughout the entire ecosystem to create the conditions for the thriving of all (Wohlleben 2016).

> The [couple's] life is mysterious, it is like a forest, from far-off it seems a unity, it can be comprehended, described, but closer it begins to separate, to break into light and shadow, the density blinds one. Within there is no form, only prodigious detail that reaches everywhere: exotic sounds, spills of sunlight, foliage, fallen trees, small beasts that flee at the sound of a twig-snap, insects, silence, flowers. And

all of this dependent, closely woven, all of it is deceiving. There are really two kinds of life. There is … the one you are living, and there is the other. It is this other which causes the trouble, this other we long to see. (Salter 1975, 23–24)

Distributed Bodies

Surpassing our expectations of lived time and space, as well as out-weirding siphonophores in their modes of organisation, the clonal superorganisms of certain plants reach unprecedented dimensions that challenge the familiar stories of life.

The pando grove of *Populus tremuloides,* a male quaking aspen tree in Utah's Fishlake national forest, is a single organism that looks like a forest. Covering more than 100 acres of land, its 47,000 genetically identical trunks, or *stema,* push up through the ground from a shared network of roots with a combined biomass of around 6 million kilograms (Casselman 2007). Although individual trees live between 100 to 150 years, the superorganism is around 80,000 years old and is likely to have been spreading its clones for more than a million years (Bartels 2016), but it is not unique in its epic dimensions.

Covering the greatest surface area of land for any known organism is a honey fungus, which is a resident of the Blue Mountains of Oregon. Composed of several different species of parasitic fungi in the genus *Armillaria,* it colonises and kills a variety of trees and woody plants which are strewn with the edible yellow-brown fruiting bodies (mushroom) of its much larger network of rhizomorphs and hyphae, which collectively form a vegetative mass known as the mycelium.

> The mushroom spawn lives thanks to the fact that it sucks up the remains of juices from whatever dies, whatever is decaying and soaking into the earth. The mushroom spawn is the life of death, the life of decay, the life of whatever has died ... All year the mushroom spawn bears its cold, wet children ... it gives them all the strength to grow and the power to spread their spores ... to all corners of the world. (Tokarczuk 2010, 158)

Mycelia can span staggering areas of land and frequently persist longer than any animal. In 1998, a gargantuan fungus, *Armillar-*

ia solidipes,[3] was discovered in Oregon, which occupies almost 2,400 acres of soil — the equivalent of around 1,665 football pitches — and is estimated to be around 2,400 years old.

> The mushroom spawn grows under the entire forest … In the earth under the soft forest flow, under the grass and stones, it creates a tangle of slender threads, strings and bundles, which it twines around everything. The threads of the mushroom spawn have great strength and push their way in between every clod of earth, tangle around tree roots and restrain huge boulders in the infinitely gradual onward motions. The mushroom spawn is like mould — cold, white, and delicate — underground lunar lace, damp, hem-stitched mycelia, the world's slimy umbilical cords. (Tokarczuk 2010, 157)

In 1992, a 1500-year-old fungus, *Armillaria gallica,* which lives in hardwood forests near Crystal Falls, weighing around 9,500 kilograms and traversing 37 acres, was discovered, while an *Armillaria solidipes* was distributed over an area of 1,500 acres in southwestern Washington (Fleming 2014).

The oldest known plant does not live on the land but is an aquatic clonal species of Mediterranean seagrass, *Posidonia oceania.* Beginning its life at the time of the Ice Ages in the late Pleistocene, it is said to be 200,000 years old. Descended from a terrestrial lineage of monocotyledons — which include grasses, lilies, and palms — they are anchored by roots that distribute nutrients through an internal vascular system (Reynolds 2018).

These vegetal clonal creatures work together as one, creeping like liquids through time and space to collectively resist entropic decay and shape our environments by stealth through their persistent metabolic exchanges.

---

3   This species was previously known as *Armillaria oystoyae.*

Life as Paradox

> The intellectual and mechanical odyssey of the western
> mind rests on the rejection of new paradoxes, forgetting
> that life itself is paradoxical. This blindness does not come
> for free, there is a price to pay for ignoring the paradoxes of
> life. (Chatelin 2012, 9)

The modern story of life is as much about scientific storytelling, as gathering repeatable, measurable evidence. The pioneers of this narrative making were explorers and natural philosophers like Charles Darwin, who recorded their observations in diaries, as illustrations, and through surveys. No matter how peculiar their findings turned out to be — such as the co-evolution of orchids and insects, where Darwin predicted the existence of a long-tongued moth to draw from the long nectary of *Angraecum sesquipedale* — mechanistic principles were routinely applied to establish causality in their observations, which in some cases, caused remarkable distortions in perception and understanding.

> At last I understood the mechanism of the flower. (Darwin
> 2001, 100)

When viewed through the familiar sequences of causal relationships, where offspring are smaller than their parents, creatures like the 'paradoxical frog', whose adult form is smaller than the tadpole, was interpreted as a 'retrograde' creature by researchers, thought to represent a 'missing link' in the story of evolution.

> Pseudis is a peculiar South American frog, peculiar in
> the fact that it grows smaller as it becomes adult, and in
> possessing a nearer approach to a thumb than any of its
> relatives. It is much to be doubted whether there is anything
> in the actual history of an individual belonging to this

genus that calls for an amount of notoriety to which the most common toad or frog may not aspire ... In fact, as often happens in the case of men, Pseudis owes much of his reputation to a mistaken estimate. If we might trace him from as early a period as men have seen until well advanced in life, we should probably see nothing more than takes place in the history of all batrachians ... His first mention in literature ... [is] through some Dutch collectors in Surinam, [when] Albert Seba secured specimens of the adult and of the large larvae with and without limbs. Comparing the smaller with the larger he came to the conclusion that the development was retrograde: that the animal was at first a frog, then acquired a tail, then lost its limbs, and finally — the remote resemblance between the soils of the intestine and the sucking disk of the gobies probably suggesting the idea — became a fish ... This version of the story was at first accepted by Linné [Linnaeus] ... A little exercise of imagination enables one to see them grasping and swinging from the branches of the plants by means of the opposable thumb; whether this is its use is a question. One can imagine the tail and feet both required in the pursuit of rapidly moving prey or in escape from lively enemies, but it is only supposition. However, we shall wait another chapter in the history before accepting [this creature] as one of the 'missing links'; the reputation of Pseudis as a deceiver is too well established. (Garman 1877)

Linnaeus was so convinced by this interpretation that he described it as 'Frog Changing into Fish' in the *Paradoxa* of his first edition:

Frog-Fish or Frog Changing into Fish: is much against teaching. Frogs, like all Amphibia, delight in lungs and spiny bones. Spiny fish, instead of lungs, are equipped with gills. Therefore the laws of Nature will be against this change. If indeed a fish is equipped with gills, it will be separate from the Frog and Amphibia. If truly [it has] lungs, it will be a Lizard: for under all the sky it differs from Chondropterygii and Plagiuri. (Linnaeus 1735, 29)

By the tenth edition of *Systema Naturae,* Linnaeus had named the creature *Rana paradoxa.*

While scientific rationalism imposes its narrative of mechanical order upon the living world, our everyday experiences appreciate the extraordinary nature and innate disobedience of natural systems that not only have the power to surprise us, but sometimes seemingly overturn the established laws of physics. Life's peculiar phenomenology remains resistant to rational and universal explanations, where tales of natural paradoxes are not always celebrated, as recounted in the temptation of Saint Anthony. Although the holy man's faith ultimately triumphs over the temptations and horrors of sin and evil, it comes at the price of being confronted with his worst nightmare — the disintegration of the order of natural realm.

Then a singular being appears — having the head of a man upon the body of a fish ... He approaches through the air, upright, beating the sand from time to time with his tail; and the patriarchal aspect of his face by contrast with his puny little arms, causes Anthony to laugh ... 'Respect me! I am the contemporary of beginnings. I dwelt in that formless world where hermaphroditic creatures slumbered, under the weight of an opaque atmosphere, in the deeps of dark waters — when fingers, fins, and wings were blended, and eyes without heads were floating like mollusks, among human-headed bulls, and dog-footed serpents. Above the whole of these beings, Omokoca, bent like a hoop, extended her woman-body. But Belus cleft her in two halves; with one he made the earth; with the other, heaven; — and the two equal worlds do mutually contemplate each other. I, the first consciousness of chaos, arose from the abyss that might harden matter, and give a law unto forms: — also I taught men to fish and to sow: I gave them knowledge of writing, and of the history of the gods. Since then I have dwelt in the deep pools left by the Deluge. But the desert grows vaster about them; the winds cast sand into them; the sun devours them; — and I die upon my couch of slime, gazing at the stars through the water. Thither I return!' (Flaubert 2002, 126–27)

Living Drop

> Just think of all the things that are transparent and seem
> not to be so. Paper, for instance, is made up of transparent
> fibres, and it is white and opaque only the same reason that a
> powder of glass is white and opaque. Oil white paper, fill up
> the interstices between the particles with oil so that there is
> no longer refraction or reflection except at the surfaces, and
> it becomes as transparent as glass. And not only paper, but
> cotton fibre, linen fibre, wool fibre, woody fibre, and bone,
> Kemp, flesh, Kemp, hair, Kemp, nails and nerves, Kemp, in
> fact the whole fabric of a man except the red of his blood
> and the black pigment of hair, are all made up of transparent,
> colourless tissue. So little suffices to make visible one to the
> other. For the most part the fibres of a living creature are no
> more opaque than water. (Wells 2012, 91)

In transitioning from water to air, creatures developed thicker
integuments that became skins, and established firmer negotiating boundaries with their surroundings. Occupying an exquisite
twilight zone between interior and exterior, the fluid bodies of
frogs offer a unique view and 'living' window to their precarious
and environmentally nuanced existence.

The tiny, newly discovered species of glass frog *Hyalinobatrachium yaku,* lives in the Ecuadorean Amazon. With a distinct
mating call and unique DNA profile, it is entirely transparent.
Its see-through abdominal skin renders the lower jaw, urinary
bladder, reproductive system, head, pericardium, and heart
completely visible (Kluger 2017). It is so clear that in the Kichwa
language it is called *yuka,* or living drop of water. This shadowless bead of life produces eggs, albeit unusually on the underside of leaves, from which tadpoles drop into the water, but with
its discovery came the realisation that its habitat is under serious threat by road development and ongoing oil exploitation.
With their pending extinction, even if these rare creatures are
preserved in museum collections, they don't provide the same

detail about their existence as in real life. Not only do their eyes lose their vital spark, but the preservation process actually alters their appearance, making it difficult to tell different populations of glass frogs from each other.

Diaphanous, or see-though, frog specimens are more widely used as indicators of environmental pollution in urban surveys to reveal the presence of harmful mutagens, as their permeable bodies are closely coupled to fluctuations in their surroundings. When 60 frogs were studied on toxic land near Krasnouralsk, which is located in central Russia's Tyumen Oblast region, several specimens were found to have minor structural changes, including dark pigmentation and extra digits (Keartes 2016). Inhabiting a twilight zone between the land and water, the incredible permeability of frogs, as highly organised 'drops' of water that are deeply entangled with their habitats, is matched only by their robustness and ultimate fragility, where life is fluid at its core.

Bombardier Beetle

> There is (they say) a Wild Beast in Paeonia, which is
> called Bonasus, with a Mane like an Horse, but otherwise
> resembling a Bull; and his Horns bend so inwardly, with
> their Tips toward the Head, that they are of no Service for
> Fight, and therefore he hath recourse to Flight for Safety;
> and in it throwing out his Dung at intervals to the Distance
> of three Acres, the Contact of which burneth them that
> follow, like so much Fire. (Pliny 1991, 21)

Capable of transforming the mundane into the spectacular, the
bombardier beetle sprays its aggressors with boiling hot, caustic
fluids from special glands in its hind abdominal section. These
weapons can be angled in virtually any direction, like a personal
pepper spray. The apparatus has been claimed by proponents
of intelligent design to be an example of irreducible complexity — in other words, a biological feature that is too complex to
have evolved without influence by an external agency, or 'intelligent design' (Behe 2006, 31–45).

At first glance the system seems highly complex, as the beetle
mixes its arsenal on demand from stores that are situated in the
chambers of its hindquarters. When aggravated, two chemical
precursors — hydrogen peroxide and hydroquinones — are dis-
charged into a reaction chamber that is lined with cells, which
secrete catalytic enzymes. Here, the peroxide and hydroquinone
are catalysed *in situ* to form intense heat and oxygen, which generates the pressure needed to expel irritant p-quinones in the
direction of the aggressor. Released through openings at the tip
of the abdomen in a hissing volley of blasts (Chandler 2015),
these noxious sprays are capable of incapacitating insect aggressors like ants. The chemical burn also deters much larger foes,
such as amphibians.

Although ingenious, these ingredients are rather common
and uncomplicated metabolic products and bombardier beetles
have figured out how to store and combine them — rather than

breaking them down, or using them up. Hydrogen peroxide is a natural metabolic by-product in almost all creatures, and insects already produce quinones to harden their shells. While there is no convincing fossil record to chart the specific evolution of this species, it redeploys an established portfolio of biochemistry without recourse to predetermined mechanisms, or external creators (Simon 2014a).

Slippery Face

While mathematical narratives, such as the Golden Ratio, sought to establish 'beauty' in nature through an understanding of symmetrical frameworks, some creatures refuse to conform to these expectations.

Long-tailed short-faced eels, or *Pythonichthys macrurus,* are rarely caught since they bury themselves face first into the muck and silt of shallow seawaters, using their solid, conical skulls as drill bits. Found in tropical waters of the eastern Pacific Ocean off Panama and in the Atlantic Ocean near the Caribbean Sea and the west coast of Africa, they were first identified in 1912 by Charles Tate Regan, who classified them under the genus *Heterenchelys*. In a recent trawl survey, two of these long and slithery creatures rebuffed the Enlightenment dictum of symmetry attributed to nature, being oddly skewed like flatfish and their faces strangely slipped to one side. With tiny eyes, tilted jaws, and most of their teeth surrendered, the eels had developed blind sides, where one specimen possessed a single eye that was completely buried in flesh (Martinez and Stiassny 2017). Their bodies were also asymmetrical, with one flank assigned the status of a colourless underbelly (Buehler 2017). Although the study sample was small, it remains unclear whether these shape-shifters are one-off variants of mostly bilaterally symmetrical species, or if they share the perplexing asymmetry of the flatfish clade, which re-sculpture their heads during development, so that one eye migrates to join the other.

The bones in [the young flatfish's] skull bend and shift as one eye forces its way to the opposite side of the head. Its whole body begins to tip over, so it has to swim at an angle. One of its flanks turns a sickly pallor; the other becomes colourfully flecked, matching the speckled sand on the seafloor. Eventually, when it is large enough, the transformed flatfish sinks and settles on its newly blind side. It is now a young adult bottom-feeder with two eyes

on the same side of its head, a contorted mouth, and one
fin squashed against the sand. It will spend the rest of its life
this way. (Jabr 2014)

With its face fully displaced on one side of its body, the creature's whole world changes. It abandons ways of swimming to
navigate the ocean, and as its vertical orientation in the water
changes, its inner ears overrule its eyes. Clinging to the sea floor,
the flatfish learns how to lie perpetually sideways.

Slowly as our facial skeleton grows and ossifies, the muscles
inserted into our facial skin produce rapidly changing expressions that wrinkle with age, emotion, and gravity, so that we
may smile and frown at the world.

> ... Skin on skin becomes conscious, as does skin on mucus
> membrane and mucus membrane on itself. Without this
> folding, without the contact of the self on itself, there would
> truly be no internal sense, not body properly speaking,
> cœnesthesia even less so, no real image of the body: we
> would live without consciousness; slippery smooth and
> on the point of fading away. Klein bottles are a model
> of identity. We are the bearers of skewed, not quite flat,
> unreplicated surfaces, deserts over which consciousness
> passes fleetingly, leaving no memory. (Serres 2016, 22)

Faces are far from superficial organs. When we augment, or
alter them, using makeup or surgery, our emotions and feelings change too, although exactly how these are entangled is
not fully understood (Neal and Chartrand 2011). In the case of
mud-dwelling creatures, their relative invisibility and functional
freakiness ensures that their anatomical slippages and morphological chimerical tendencies, continue to remain closely guard-
ed secrets of the deep.

> Its deviation from the identity principle consigns it to fable,
> imagination and legend. Yet in this impossible location ...
> its identity is successful ... Rather like an ordinary animal

or man, one can speak of right or left, or one can speak of left or right. Plus a weld, a seam in the middle … but a chimera accentuates seams, it makes the blatantly obvious … Here the otherwise impossible mixture is successful. Here the sensible is successful. (Serres 2016, 62)

07.11

Faceless Fish

Providing no indication that it wishes to be categorised, or recognised, this pink slug-like creature is about the size of a cat. But it's certainly not a cat, or a slug, or a 'cusk'-eel, or any other eel for that matter. This *thing,* is faceless. Slamming on the deck like a freshly cut piece of butchers' meat, it's unrecognisable, except for its razorblade smile.

It's rare.

The first people to come across such a beast were the crew of HMS *Challenger,* who in 1872 had loaded the vessel with specimen jars and embarked on a scientific expedition. Until the late nineteenth century, when Michael and Georg Ossian Sars dredged Norway's fjords and found the first living sea lilies at a depth of three kilometres, it was assumed that the deep sea was lifeless. Previous knowledge of the seas was confined to the first few fathoms of the ocean, with scant knowledge of their depths. Since Britain wanted to rule the waves, it needed to know what was beneath them. The *Challenger* mission was to make these invisible realms known by cataloguing all the life in all the Earth's oceans and seas (Fox-Skelly 2015). During this expedition, the faceless fish was pulled out of the Coral Sea from a depth of 4.5 kilometres. As it slopped on to the deck, the ventral mouth of the eyeless creature grimaced. Its dead nostrils pointed accusingly at its captor, like false eyes, from the top of its head. They gave it no apology, for it showed no face to scowl at them with, and kept its secret face hidden under its skin, along with its name — *Typhlonus nasus.*

Five more of these slimy beasts were caught in a trawl in 1951, in deep water off East Kalimantan, Borneo, where they have no need of eyes in these lightless realms, as luminosity is deployed as a treacherous metabolism that deceives curious prey. Without trickster eyes, these abyssal creatures cannot be seduced by light's deadly lure and so, thrive without its temptation in the ocean depths of Indonesia, Papua New Guinea, Japan and Hawaii.

Having been dug up like a tenacious root from the sea floor, along with suffocating quantities of garbage, the faceless fish[4] now lies on the floor of the Investigator, a contemporary Australian scientific expedition (Brady 2017).

It smiles at its captors, because it cannot see what contempt they project on to it (Marine Biodiversity Hub 2017).

4   A species of cusk-eel.

Vampire Squid

> Because the vampyroteuthis is an animal of the deep sea,
> and because we are animals mired in the very depths that
> the vampyroteuthis occupies within us, the most important
> science for our purposes is biology. Its importance is also
> unmatched because it provides us with an almost mythical
> model of life's unrealised possibilities. This model is that of
> the protocell, a primaeval archive of life's potential on earth.
> Above all, the protocell is an especially vivid reminder of
> life's fitful development, over the course of which some
> possibilities were renounced for the sake of others. Biology
> thus enables us to perceive, in the vampyroteuthis, a share
> of the universal potential that has lain dormant within us.
> (Flusser and Bec 2012, 73)

The 'vampire squid from hell', or *Vampyroteuthis infernalis,* is
a 'living fossil' that exists in blissful stasis, which declares the
process of natural selection is a preservative and conserving
force, rather than a creative one (Shear and Werth 2014). First
described in 1903 by Carl Chun during the Valdivia expedition (1898–1899), which was a zoological, chemical, and physical voyage that set out to explore the areas of the oceans that
were not covered by the Challenger expedition, it dwells in the
oxygen-starved twilight zone of the deep sea at depths of 600 to
1,200 metres. The haunting blue eyes of these cephalopods stare
over a purple-winged red cape, which is stretched over their
eight arms. When threatened, this web of flesh, around the size
of a rugby ball, reverts to become a shocking mantle of spiny
'cirri', which bears remarkable semblance to the deadly crown
of thorns starfish. Masters of morphological confusion, at one
moment they are hypervisible, glaring through bioluminescent
markings on their rear and the tips of their arms — or releasing
a mucus-coated cloud of luminescent particles and at the next,
they are almost indistinguishable from their surroundings.

With time on their side, these slow-moving creatures have drifted in the ocean twilight zone for around 350 million years. Unlike other cephalopods that feast on live animals, *vampyroteuthes* are detritovores, which reel in 'marine snow', which is made up of slowly decomposing particulate organic matter that originates from microscopic algae, marine creatures, faecal pellets, and snot. Using a mucus-coated filament, *vampyroteuthis* catches these particles to sustain its exceedingly frugal lifestyle (Hoving and Robison 2012). Lingering between decay and preservation, evolution, and stasis, lightlessness, and brilliance, *vampyroteuthis* persists indefinitely within its ecological purgatory.

Octopus Thoughts

> Here is an animal with venom like a snake, a beak like a
> parrot, and ink like an old-fashioned pen. It can weigh as
> much as a man and stretch as long as a car, yet can pour
> its baggy, boneless body through an opening the size of
> an orange … Their mouths are in their armpits … They
> breathe water. Their appendages are covered with dextrous,
> grasping suckers, a structure for which no mammal has an
> equivalent. (Montgomery 2015, 1–2)

Living aliens; octopuses are expressions of liquid life that can touch, taste, navigate, and camouflage themselves to such a sophisticated degree that their activities are considered too complex to be entirely centrally coordinated according to the logic of the *bête machine*. Linnaeus named the octopus '*singulare monstrum*': a unique monster. Located in a bulge behind their heads, their vital organs pulse blue-green blood around their body and through their three hearts. Having delegated decision-making processes to its body, the mantle performs multiple functions. From squirting water jets, breathing, excreting, propelling themselves through the water and deploying an inky weapon against predators, octopuses are capable of incredible flexibility and acts of transformation (Hochner 2013). Electrophysiological studies of their activity during feeding show that during muscular activity, nerve impulses collide with each other to produce a 'joint' in a position that allows the octopus to place food in its mouth (Sokol 2017b).

> She appears to be sleeping, plastered to the roof of her lair.
> Her skin texture and colour are almost indistinguishable
> from the rock, her pendulous head and mantle hanging
> upside down. Her left eye is open but her pupil is a hair-thin
> slit. Her right eye is obscured by the thick part of one arm,
> its suckers facing me, until the arm curves backward, out
> of sight. The tips of five of her arms hang in curling tendrils

from the roof and sides of her lair. I can't see her gills or any sign of breathing. The movements of her body appear to be due only to the current in the water … I must train my brain from seeing nothing at all to seeing subtle changes, to recognising that suddenly, a great deal might be happening, all at once. (Montgomery 2015, 94)

While these cephalopods are strange, unnerving, and magical, their disarming otherness doesn't end with their bodies. They extensively practice a type of genetic alteration called RNA editing, which is very rare in the rest of the animal kingdom, which enables them to fine-tune the information encoded by their genes without altering the genes themselves. Their usage of RNA editing is so much more extensive than any other animal group that it is likely to be associated with their extremely developed brains. Only the intelligent coleoid cephalopods — octopuses, squid, and cuttlefish — can do this to re-code genes that are important for their nervous systems, while nautiluses, which are much more ancient and less smart, cannot. Although it's not possible to assert this prolific use of RNA editing as being entirely responsible for their alien intellect, it is a very compelling hypothesis that potentially could be tested by disabling their RNA-editing enzymes — and observe what happens next (Yong 2017).

Imagine if your snot was a genius. (Aranyszin 2017)

Vanishing Circles of the Spotless Mind

Puffer fish are valued in Japan as a delicacy known as *fugu sashimi*,[5] which can cause mild intoxication or, in rare cases, death due to an incredibly powerful neurotoxin found in the fish's ovaries and liver. But until now, no one also knew that they were artists. (Platt 2012)

Life's fundamental persistence is embodied in the male puffer fish, which carves a ribbed circular structure into the sea floor by swimming in a circular motion. Countering its constant erasure by the currents, the creature that is around the size of an index finger, shapes the fine seabed sediments with his fins to form valleys around the edges of the cuts. Finally, he decorates the ridges with shells, coral fragments, and coloured sediments.
Then, he watches and waits.
The female swims lazily towards him, and he gleefully stirs up the fine sand at the centre of the nest.
With a shrug, she lays her eggs and leaves.
The devoted father spends six days minding the brood and at the appointed time, the hatchlings split their cases.
Then, they are gone (Main 2013).

> … everything is corroded by the brine … there is no vegetation worth mentioning, and scarcely any degree of perfect formation, but only caverns and sand and measureless mud, and tracts of slime wherever there is earth as well, and nothing is in the least worthy to be judged beautiful by our standards. (Plato 1961, 91)

Swimming this way and that, the male puffer fish continues to build 'underwater crop circles' in the sand, toiling against their inevitable erasure.

---

5 *Fugu* is the Japanese term for pufferfish, or blow fish, which are served as a delicacy and contain a potentially deadly neurotoxin called tetrodotoxin.

… memory is what leads us to the objects of our desire, has made it plain that it is to the soul that all impulse and desire, and indeed the determining principle of the whole creature, belong. (Plato 1961, 1114)

Structuring Mind

> ... the snare of this spider is of composite structure,
> consisting of a pyramid of web, within which, near its base,
> is suspended a dome of the same material, and hanging
> beneath the open bottom of the dome is a horizontal sheet
> of cobweb ... in the mind of the araenologist the special
> interest of the basilica spider is not its architectural skill, not
> its beautiful markings, but the fact that it seems to form a
> link between the orb-weaving and the line-weaving spiders.
> (Popular Miscellany 1878)

Certain kinds of spider web reveal the structural thoughts of
their makers. Around half of all known spiders use silk webs to
trap their prey, which is highly sought after, as it is incredibly
strong and light. Making silk is the art of turning liquid to solid.
Starting out with a fluid protein produced in the abdomen, spiders use their spinnerets to extract a liquid filament and apply
physical force, which converts it into a solid silk fibre. Com-
bining the elasticity of silk with the surface tension of sticky
droplets, the fibre behaves under tension as a stretchy solid,
but under compression, it becomes liquid-like and capable of
shrinking while maintaining a constant tensile force (Elettro et
al. 2016).

Adding graphene and carbon nanotubes to a spider's drinking water, can alter the properties of spider silk to produce
filaments that are five times stronger than usual, which com-
pare with some of the strongest materials known such as Kev-
lar (Leary 2017). Farming spiders for their silk is tricky, as the
right kind for making fabric is produced only seasonally and
individuals have a habit of eating each other if they meet (Leggett 2009). They also bite their handlers. Nonetheless, in 1898 a
technique for milking female gold orb spiders was designed to
extract single filaments of up to 25 metres long from each spider
using a 'silking' machine. A row of stocks pinned 12 spiders at
a time down by applying gentle pressure on their backs. Here,

they lay quietly while their threads were rapidly wound onto a reel by hand. In 2009, this technique was repeated using a total of a million spiders to make a unique gown for the American Museum of Natural History in New York, which was the largest piece of cloth made from natural spider silk in the world (Leggett 2009).

While humans are interested in spider silk for utilitarian purposes, from the perspective of the arachnid, it is a self-spun extension of the arachnid body, which becomes a sensor by relaying vibrations from environmental events (Sokol 2017b). Since this is how many spiders understand reality, the web-map of silk threads encapsulates an area of attention and meaningful representation of a personalised world. In a very literal sense, webs embody the 'thinking' of arachnids through the way their food-collection territories are constructed and may even reveal the topology of (liquid) arachnid thought (Japyassú and Laland 2017).

07.16

Liquid Fish

> There was salt in the sack so the eels would wriggle
> themselves to death in the salt and the salt would draw the
> slime from their skin and innards. For when eels are in salt,
> they can't help wriggling and they wriggle until they are
> dead, leaving their slime in the salt. (Grass 2010, 136)

The oceans spawn liquid creatures but none encapsulate *living goo* like the hagfish. Living at depths where it is senseless to possess bones, hagfish are scaleless, almost sightless, 'jelly' eel-like creatures that have persisted for around 330 million years. They spend most of their lives writhing upon the ocean floor, distinguishing only between light and dark. Here, they sniff and feel for dead and dying fish using several pairs of barbels, which are sensory tentacles around their mouths. A single nostril on the top of their heads perforates their skull, which encases a massive knot of forebrain that is rich in olfactory areas. This then tapers into an embryonic-like neural tube that is not protected by a spine. Their primitive circulatory system is made up of four hearts, one that serves as the main pump, while the other three are accessory chambers. Fitting like a loose sock, their capillary-dense, pink to grey-blue skin, allows them to absorb food and 'breathe' — even when they are buried in carcasses and mud. While their reproductive habits are largely unknown, species are hermaphroditic with females laying batches of around 30 tough, yolky eggs that have a tendency to clump together owing to velcro-like tufts at their poles. Hatchlings are hermaphroditic miniatures of their parents that will change to either male or female as they develop, and may even alter their sex from season to season.

Firmly attaching themselves with their biting mouth and rasping tongue to passing fish, they bore into the unsuspecting host. Burying themselves face first into their temporary soft home, they shear off flesh using horizontally sliding plates bearing tooth-like projections. When no live large prey can be found, they feed on worms and other small invertebrates on the ocean floor and will even settle for rotting cadavers. Having barely changed over the last 300 million years, they can be found as deep as 1,700 metres, and prefer to stay near the soft silty sea floor so that, when attacked or threatened, they can bury themselves while exuding a gelatinous slime into the water that can quickly smother the gills and mouth of a predator. Once the threat has gone, the hagfish ties itself into a knot to wipe its slime away and 'sneezes' out any clog from its nostril (Bates 2014).

Intrat et devorat pisces; aquam in gluten mutat.[6] (Linnaeus 1758)

The properties of this incredible viscous exudate are only just being understood.

Hagfish slime forms in mucin vesicles in special glands, where they are bundled into skeins. These are looped into conical layers that, on deployment, can reach up to 15 centimetres. Seawater unravels these fibres by dissolving the protein glue holding tens of thousands of filaments that are tapered at both ends together. Although 100 times smaller than a human hair, they are ten times as strong as nylon and a mere teaspoon of slime will fill a cereal bowl in just a few seconds without the fibres tangling (Winegard and Fudge 2010). Once activated, they form a gloopy net of threads like a fine sieve, which are around three orders of magnitude more dilute than typical mucus secretions (Fudge, Levy and Gosline 2005).

Hagfish slime can also be added to cooking recipes as a special kind of gluten.

---

6 When Linnaeus first came across the hagfish, he classified it as a worm in the tenth and later editions of his *Systema Naturae,* where he succinctly described its behaviour — it 'enters into and devours fishes; turns water into glue' (Fernholm 1998, 33). Despite anatomical evidence to the contrary, Johan Ernst Gunnerus endorsed Linnaeus' view, calling the creature a 'Sleep-Mark', or slime-worm (Fänge 1988, xiii).

Hagfish Slime Cheddar-Gruyere Scones

4 cups all-purpose flour
2 tablespoons baking powder
4 teaspoons sugar
1/2 teaspoon salt
1 cup (two sticks) chilled unsalted butter, cut into 1/2-inch cubes
2 cups (packed) coarsely grated extra-sharp yellow cheddar cheese (about 9 ounces), or a mix of 6 ounces cheddar and 3 ounces gruyere.
1–1/2 cups chilled heavy whipping cream
6 tablespoons hagfish slime
Preheat oven at Gas Mark 4

Blend flour, baking powder, sugar, and salt in a food processor. Cut in the butter quickly until the mixture resembles coarse meal. Add cheese. Whisk together the cream and hagfish slime in a small bowl. With the food processor running, add cream mixture through a feed tube. Process until the dough just holds together.

Turn the dough out onto a lightly floured work surface. Divide into quarters. Pat each quarter into a round just short of 1 inch high. Using a clean, sharp knife, cut each round into six wedges. Transfer half the wedges to ungreased baking sheets lined with parchment paper, spacing them about 2 inches apart.

Bake the first batch of scones for about 20 minutes until the edges just start to brown and a toothpick comes out clean. Transfer them, still on their parchment paper, to a wire rack to cool at least 10 minutes. Bake the second batch of scones.

Serve warm, or at room temperature. The scones will stand for about 8 hours. Do not refrigerate. To reheat them, warm them at Gas Mark 4 for about 5 minutes. (Museum of Awful Food 2006)

The hagfish's highly structured relationship between liquids and soft material substrates — mud, rotting flesh, and snot — entangles them with the bowels of the world's ecosystems.

07.17

Liquid Fat

> ... the front of the sperm whale's head is a dead, blind wall,
> without a single organ or tender prominence of any sort
> whatsoever ... So that this whole enormous boneless mass
> is as one wad ... the blubber wraps the body of the whale,
> as the rind wraps an orange. Just so with the head; but with
> this difference: about the head this envelope, though not so
> thick, is of a boneless toughness, inestimable by any man
> who has not handled it. (Melville 1992, 280)

Guardians of life, liquid fats are 'angel' substances that maintain the boundaries of bodies. At 37°C, the body temperature
of warm-blooded mammals, their fats are liquid and stable. As
critical components of the cell membrane, they provide an interface between the inside and the outside of the organism that
establishes a tension and dialogue between fluid fields and protects biochemical networks within the cellular environment by
resisting the relentless encroachment of water. Phospholipids,
which are an essential part of all cell membranes, have a highly
polarised molecular structure,[7] the duality of which cannot be
collapsed and so maintains a contrary but relatively stable existence at the interface between fat and water. While maintaining
chemical stability, mammalian lipid ratios confer a range of fatty
tissue properties and provide a high-energy store for metabolic
processes. Marine mammals, which have to endure prolonged
exposure to freezing environments, are typically insulated with
blubber[8] with low melting points over a range between 13°C
and 70°C, which remain fluid even in bitterly cold conditions,
although the most important polyunsaturated fatty acids generate an overall melting point of less than 15°C. Some marine

7   The polarised structure of Phospholipids means that one aspect of the mol-
     ecule has a strong affinity with water, while the other strongly repels water.
8   Blubber is a metabolically active, subcutaneous tissue that contains large
     amounts of unsaturated fatty acids.

mammals, such as the beluga (*Delphinapterus leucas*), have high concentrations of a highly unusual biosynthesised, branched short-chain isovaleric acid with an extremely low melting point of 37.6°C, which upholds the liquid status of the outer layer.

Fats are liquid life's survival strategy. Operating as interlocutors that form protective and energy-giving layer between aqueous bodies and their environments, they also cushion against the lethal effects of energy depletion and extreme environmental variations.

Liquid Eye

> To suppose that the eye with all its inimitable contrivances
> for adjusting the focus to different distances, for admitting
> different amounts of light, and for the correction of
> spherical and chromatic aberration, could have been formed
> by natural selection, seems, I freely confess, absurd in the
> highest degree. (Darwin 2010, 227)

Life moved to the land for the view.

The first optical structures are thought to have evolved through liquid physics in aquatic creatures that peered over the surface of water. Like crocodiles, these creatures sought to catch an extended view of their surroundings (Ouellette 2012). Not all creatures with eyes moved to the land — some merely surveyed it.

Although box jellyfish (*Cubozoa*) evolved during the pre-Cambrian period around 500 million years ago and lack a formal brain, they possess 24 eyes. This visual navigation system, which involves no less than four types of special-purpose eyes, means that they are capable of advanced behaviour, namely, responding to light and avoiding obstacles. Most of the box jellyfishes' visual organs are rather primitive, like the pit and slit eyes, which merely detect light, but eyes in the upper zone are far more complex (Bentlage et al. 2010).

In the species *Tripedalia cystophora,* which is found in Caribbean mangrove swamps, upper zone eyes possess retinas and corneas that are structurally similar to vertebrates and cephalopods. They can also see in colour, establish the size of things and as they gaze up at the sky on cup-like structures, recognise images. Actively navigating their surroundings by drawing positional inferences from terrestrial and solar cues, they stay close to mangrove shorelines that are rich in food. An 'extreme' downward-looking fish-eye view of the whole mangrove floor is obtained through a similarly organised eye with a large lens (Garm, Oskarsson and Nilsson 2011).

Current-borne, wave-flung, tugged hugely by the whole might of ocean, the jellyfish drifts in the tidal abyss. The light shines through it, and the dark enters it ... (Le Guin 2001, 1)

Lenses within the lenses, the eyes of box jellyfishes comprise their entire bodies. Producing recognisable patterns within their ganglion retinas by focusing light through their bodies by coordinating it with movement, they contravene the maxim that intelligence depends on central organising systems. Demonstrating that structured liquids can generate programs that are meaningful to life, the intelligence of box jellyfish is tuned to their prevailing value systems and contexts. Not every living thing wants to play chess.

Double Take

> ... comb jellies come in a wide variety of other body types and ecological niches. One spherical species, known ... as the sea gooseberry, dangles long tentacles that snag smaller prey such as copepods. Then there are some that look a bit like biplanes, known as lobates, which cruise along 'like crop dusters,' ... instead of dangling their tentacles, theirs are situated along their mouth to snag prey and ferry it inside. Still other species have adapted their cilia into serrated teeth ... they have this whole field that looks almost like a velcro strip or something, with all of these teeth pointed in the same direction ... and they can actually ratchet themselves over and bite off chunks of other jellies that they've captured ... I use the analogy of spiders ... because spiders can have a sticky web, they can leap out and ambush things, they can make little lasso webs ... and ctenophores have similar range of different feeding modes, depending on the species. (Simon 2014b)

Comb jellyfish[9] (*Ctenophora*), our planet's original aliens, are distinguished by being the oldest and strangest of all marine animals. These 'aliens of the sea' are paradoxes (Zimmer 2014), which disintegrate at a touch while being voracious predators with cannibalistic tendencies. Riding the ocean water columns mouth-first, these planktonic creatures use their iridescent 'combs' of cilia to move up and down and are the largest creatures to use this method of locomotion. Comb jellyfish capture their prey by secreting sticky substances from their colloblasts, which they quickly ingest through their primitive mouth and expel any debris out through their anus. Although they lack eyes, they possess ten proteins for generating light, as well as

---

9   Comb jellyfish are different from box jellyfish (*Cubozoa*), which belong to a different phylum, *Cnidarians*. Although they share superficial similarities with each other, neither are true jellyfish (*Scyphozoa*).

other proteins called opsins that detect light, which may function as a regulatory feedback system. Owing to the ancient nature of comb jellyfish, these genetic sequences are likely to hold secrets about the evolution of vision (Mjoseth 2012).

An extraordinary network of subepidermal neurons lies beneath their rows of combs, which are quite unlike those of any other animal. Not only unique in their structure, they also secrete a range of peptide neurotransmitters that regulate their neural networks, which lack the usual spectrum of chemical messengers such as serotonin, dopamine, and acetylcholine, which are common to all other animals.

> When we look at the genome and other information [in the comb jellyfish nerve cells], we see not only different grammar but a different alphabet … (Singer 2015)

Comb jellyfish challenge the prevailing view of evolutionary biology, which holds that complexity is built up over time. According to this perspective, neurons will only have evolved once on this planet, most likely around the time that sea sponges appeared. The peculiar nature of comb jellyfish suggests they may be the first group of animals to have branched off the tree of life even earlier than sponges did and evolved an entirely independent developmental pathway from all other animal species. While evolving something as complex as neurons 'by accident' more than once seems unlikely, the alternative scenario where sponges which evolved from a common ancestor let something as valuable as a neurone degenerate, is equally unlikely (Singer 2015).

Confronting us with an existing, parallel view of evolution that asks how different biology would be if the 'tape of life' was run from its starting point again (Gould 1989, 48), comb jellyfish provide a real-life case study of an alternative organisational framework for 'life'.

Tardigrade

> ... beneath their cuddly exteriors lie unmatched reserves
> of endurance. In times of drought, tardigrades pull in their
> legs, contract and shrivel, and turn into 'resting' stages called
> 'tuns' in which metabolism all but stops. It is the tun, not
> the tardigrade, that is tough ... give a tun a drop of water,
> and it will rehydrate to form a tardigrade, as if nothing had
> happened. It's hard to top a tardigrade. (Gee 1998)

Seeking immortality, life's capacity to resist the decay towards
equilibrium is as strange as it is varied. The tardigrade, the most
resilient of all organisms, is also known as the 'water bear' and
'moss pig'. Having evolved around 500 million years ago, these
segmented, tiny creatures about a millimetre in length have
grub-like bodies with eight legs and 'hands', and four to eight
claws on each. Most use their sharp teeth in their compact heads
to digest the sap from algae, while some species are carnivores
and a few are cannibals that prey on other tardigrades.

At times of environmental stress, tardigrades reduce their
metabolic activity to as low as one-hundredth of normal levels.
This state of suspended animation is further conserved within a
glass-like structure (Stromberg 2012) from which they may be
fully revived after a few hours of hydration. This amazing capacity to enter into a vitrified state is conferred by tardigrade-spe-
cific intrinsically disordered proteins (TDPs). The 'glass coffin'-
producing capacity of TDPs is so powerful that tardigrades must
'wear' protection at all times by having a thin coating of water
around their bodies. In their hydrated form, TDPs are jelly-like
and lack the typical well-defined three-dimensional structures of
most known proteins, but during desiccation, these proteins so-
lidify into a glassy structure, enabling them to survive for decades
in a state of cryptobiosis. Glass-coated tardigrades can withstand

irradiation,[10] boiling liquids, extreme pressure, environments as cold as −200°C and up to around 150°C, as well as the vacuum of space without any protection (Coghlan 2017a). While 'extremophiles' are physically adapted to life in extreme environments, tardigrades are not. They are simply able to weather disaster through a vitrification escape route, by becoming liquid stone.

10 Tardigrades can survive irradiation, as they possess the 'damage suppressor' Dsup gene (Chavez et al. 2019).

07.21

Blood Stones

> Too often, the adaptationist programme gave us an
> evolutionary biology of parts and genes, but not of
> organisms. It assumed that all transitions could occur
> step by step and underrated the importance of integrated
> developmental blocks and pervasive constraints of history
> and architecture. A pluralistic view could put organisms,
> with all their recalcitrant, yet intelligible, complexity, back
> into evolutionary theory. (Gould and Lewontin 1979, 597)

The evolutionary journey of sea squirts is the story of the transgressive material states of creatures that gave rise to the very first backbone-producing organisms, whose ancestors gave rise to the phylum of vertebrates. Stinking like an armpit under its rock-like protective integument made of tunicin, at depths that can reach 70 metres off the Peruvian and Chilean coastlines, the *piure* (*Pyura chilensis*) feeds by siphoning seawater through its body, using a basket-like internal filter to capture plankton and oxygen from its surroundings. Split by a blood-red interior, this stone-with-organs lives in dense colonies. Each creature feeds by drawing water into its body through one siphon, referred to locally as an 'udder', and ejecting spent fluids through another. Through this primitive exchange, the *piure* possesses an apocryphal 'heart' and an interior exchange of fluids that might conceivably be considered a circulation. Its colonial existence and odd fleshy-rocklike appearance do not prevent molluscs, fish, and humans from feasting on its 'bitter and soapy' crimson flesh with aphrodisiac qualities, which is rich in iodine, vanadium, and iron.

More than a strange stone that contains soft marine meat, it is a chordate, a creature bestowed with a primitive throat and a cartilaginous backbone-like rod, or notochord. Like all species of sea squirts, its lifecycle is complex, where sessile adults release sperm and eggs into the water. On hatching, the tiny male, free swimming larvae are made up of only about 2,500 cells and develop a notochord that runs the entire length of their tail before they settle down and metamorphose into a sessile, stone-like adult. At puberty, they develop female organs and are therefore capable of 'selfing', or fertilising their own eggs but prefer to cross-fertilise with others (Crew 2012). While sea squirts possess a number of vertebrate-like genes, they share many more characteristics in common with bacteria, fungi, and plants, which are combined to serve their own specialised needs.

As mixtures of liquids and solids that change throughout their complex life cycles to take on one form or another, sea squirts have set benchmarks in development protocols that draw actual circumstances together with a spectrum of contexts, creating the opportunity to imagine and invent what their progeny 'could' be.

07.22

Fishing Bats

> How do you capture the flying dragon? ... Only with a
> net made of mist ... Thick cumulus clouds and the black
> threads of the net both reflected in the water ... When they
> pulled the fine net taut, it became invisible ... and they
> seemed to be holding on to empty space, knotting empty
> space in their hands. (Ackerman 1991, 29)

Life's precariousness is embodied in the long-toed fishing bat. With the lightest skim of the water, it screeches and impales a small fish from out of the waves with its large, sharp claws (Nowak 1999). Rising and dipping like a wayward plastic bag, this minuscule creature flutters close to the surface under a darkening sky, searching for ripples produced by the fins of small fishes (Suthers 1965). Gathering in groups amongst caves, hollow trees, and rock fissures (Gannon et al. 2005), colonies of bats emerge every night for around 2.5 hours to go foraging when the moonlight is most subdued (Brooke 1994). This 'lunar phobia' increases the chances these hunters will not be backlit against the sky as they approach the water (Börk 2006). Dancing upon the interface between the sea, sky, and shimmering scales, these predatory phantoms search for their prey with varying degrees of success and may harvest up to thirty fish a night.

Sometimes, liquid engulfs liquid, when a fish catches the bat.

Back to the Cat

While its 'catness' is still recognisable, the organic softness of the creature's outline is partially digested by a field of light glaring from a computer screen.

The hard drive purrs, as the agitated tip of the computer's power supply fishes for small creatures, like a mouse. Heat flows between the interlaced bodies.

One struggles to lose energy to its surroundings, so its cooling fan whirrs harder, while the other basks in excess heat, dreaming of dark spaces and the blurry flash of fur that can be caught at a claw's stretch.

Only when the computer powers down into energy-saving mode does the liquid life stop vibrating and separates from its sleeping box.

Part IV

MAKING

LIQUID TECHNOLOGY

This section examines the capacities of
liquids to produce work at the cellular and human scale in ways that differ
from machines. A range of materials and
techniques are discussed that may form a
'soft' technological palette and portfolio
of effects, which speak to the principles of
liquid life.

Engineering Water

> My house ... is diaphanous, but it is not of glass. It is more
> of the nature of vapour. Its walls contract and expand as I
> desire. At times, I draw them close about me like protective
> armour ... But at others, I let the walls of my house blossom
> out in their own space, which is infinitely extensible.
> (Bachelard 1992, 51)

Liquids have long been known to possess structure and character, from the turbulent currents that shape the hunting grounds
for fishermen, to arched fountain sprays, the bottomless valley
of Charybdis and raindrops that bleed onto window panes. As
we are not in control of these configurations, we must constantly negotiate our relationship with them.

Since ancient times, we have sought to better understand
the elusive, yet mighty forces of the fluid realm. In his treatise
Meteorologica, Aristotle describes the principles of hydrologic
cycle, where water evaporates by the action of the Sun and forms
vapour that condenses as clouds (Koutsoyiannis and Angelakis
2003). From the third century BCE, the invention of hydraulic
engineering enabled the dynamics of fluid forces within closed
bodies of water to be understood and harnessed. Leonardo da
Vinci, who considered water as the driving force of all nature,
established the central narratives of modern hydrology that
began to reveal the organisational principles through which it
could potentially be commanded.

> The whole mass of water, in its breadth, depth, and height,
> is full of innumerable varieties of movements, as is shown
> on the surface of currents with a moderate degree of
> turbulence, in which one sees continually gurglings and
> eddies with various swirls formed by the more turbid water
> from the bottom as it rises to the surface. (Ball 2009, 10–11)

Da Vinci had witnessed the terrible force of the Arno River 'devouring' people, animals, plants, and the ground itself, when its banks burst on 12 January 1466, and again in 1478. Setting out to know his 'enemy' through drawings, he showed how the structure of water flowed faster and more linearly in the centre of rivers than around the shallow sides of their banks (Ball 2009, 11), then he designed mechanical systems to control and constrain these forces. Studying the hydra-headed rivulets that writhed through deltas and curling vortices within rivers, he applied this knowledge to link Florence with the sea through a navigable canal. This involved cutting a series of giant steps with locks and siphons to enable ships to sail up into the hills. He also worked on a system of locks and paddlewheels to wash the streets of Milan and even invented a way of cleansing the disease-carrying marshes of the Val di Chiana.

Rather than working through the innate properties of liquids, da Vinci constrained and channelled them through apparatuses, rendering their forces compatible with the logic of machines, through which they could be subordinated to perform simple tasks like turning switches, screws, and gates. This highly effective approach continued to be developed throughout the Enlightenment.

Living Water

> Were water actually what hydrologists deem it to be — a
> chemically inert substance — then a long time ago there
> would already have been no water and no life on this Earth.
> I regard water as the blood of the Earth. Its internal process,
> while not identical to that of our blood, is nonetheless very
> similar. It is this process that gives water its movement.
> (Bartholomew 2003, 110)

Viktor Schauberger, like da Vinci before him, observed the way
that water moved, as he was interested in better understanding
how, through continual movement, water became uniquely lively. Regarding water as a living organism that was conceived deep
under the ground in the cool, dark cradle of forests, he imagined
its life-giving potency was conferred through the stages of its
natural lifecycle. Rising slowly from the aquifers as a juvenile
form of pure ground water, it was enriched with mineral impu-
rities and spurted to the surface as a spring. Tumbling through
streams and rivers, this 'living' water became even more complex and mature, until it eventually joined the sea. Through its
various forms — blood, sap, plasma — Schauberger believed
that 'living' water, was Earth's lifeblood. Schauberger was particularly interested in the way that 'living' water self-regulated
its character through lively, corkscrewing, hyperbolic spirals.

> With the right lighting, it is possible to see the path of
> levitational currents as an empty tube within the veil of
> a waterfall. It is similar to the tunnel in the middle of a
> circulating vortex of water plunging down a drain, which
> brings up a gurgling sound. This downwardly-directed
> whirlpool drags everything with increasing suction with
> it into the depths. If you can imagine this whirlpool or
> water cyclone operating vertically, you get the picture of
> how the levitational current works and you can see how

the trout appears to be floating upward in the axis of fall.
(Bartholomew 2003, 15)

Believing that the energy and vigour of these dissipative structures could also be weakened by pollution and stasis, Schauberger produced a number of inventions that sought to counteract the effect of industrial catastrophes on the rivers. Pioneering a scientifically verifiable framework for a study of natural processes, he used simple but effective physical interventions, which were informed by his deep knowledge of the forest and its systems to produce natural turbulence; for example, adding a large boulder strategically in the middle of a river. Technologies like the 'vortex-generator' and 'river generator' were naturally energetic structures that produced and propagated 'living' water anew. These revitalising systems could also perform useful work such as driving propellers and rapidly transporting logs downstream.

Although Schauberger dedicated his entire life to demonstrating how working along with the natural technology of the living world could be applied to everyday challenges, he failed to persuade 'techno-academic' scientists that their rationalist approach to natural phenomena, and their domination of them, would result in environmental devastation. Consequently, the principles of 'living' water are no longer applied to bodies of water as a revitalising system, or alternative technology. We may wish to revisit these principles and explore more fully their potential.

Rainmaking

Working with water is more than manipulating a material; it requires engagement with all phases of the water cycle, each of which is essential for the farming practices that feed our cities. Summoning the rains is an ancient practice whereby cultures channelled rainfall through rituals, like rain dances. These were succeeded by agrarian technologies that used the formation of artificial waterways, irrigation systems, and aqueducts to help divert the flow of streams and rivers to arable lands. In the modern era, we have learned how to build instruments that can hold back tides, like the MOSE project in Venice (United Nations Office for Disaster Risk Reduction 2012), and even induce strategic downpours. The challenge remains in our expectations of control over them.

The first devices that suggested rain could be 'made' were particle detectors. In 1911, Charles Wilson developed a cloud chamber using a sealed container filled with supersaturated water vapour. As cosmic rays moved through the space, they produced paths of ionised matter, around which water droplets condensed, with the appearance of tiny contrails. The droplet-making principles of this apparatus were applied in 2010 as the *Teramobile,* which is a laser that fires short pulses of infrared laser light into the atmosphere and represents an eco-friendly form of cloud seeding, compared with its chemical forerunners (Teramobile 2008; Harris et al. 2017).

An electromagnetic device to make rainfall was developed by Juan Baigorri Velar in 1938. While the internal workings were kept a secret, it was known that circuit 'A' could produce slight drizzles, while circuit 'B' generated downpours. Although Velar received international offers to buy his machine, he refused, insisting that the device was designed to serve Argentina's driest regions. Today, nothing remains of the mysterious machine (Vintini 2013).

The first breakthrough in the technology of chemical cloud seeding took place in 1946 at a General Electric facility in Schenectady, New York, where three researchers, Vincent Schafer, Irving Langmuir and Bernard Vonnegut, established a productive basis for the use of chemicals to initiate chain reactions that crystallised naturally forming ice in the clouds. The dispersants, which originally included silver iodide, potassium iodide, and dry ice, could therefore increase or alter the distribution of natural rainfall. Their work led to the development of further chemical agents that could produce similar strengths of precipitation, such as liquid propane and hygroscopic materials like table salt.

> 'Rainmaking' or weather control can be as powerful a war weapon as the atom bomb, a Nobel prize winning physicist said today Dr. Irving Langmuir, pioneer in 'rainmaking,' said the government should seize on the phenomenon of weather control as it did on atomic energy when Albert Einstein told the late President Roosevelt in 1939 of the potential power of an atom-splitting weapon. 'In the amount of energy liberated, the effect of 30 milligrams of silver iodide under optimum conditions equals that of one atomic bomb ...' (Novak 2011)

With growing interest in weather-manipulating technologies, Wilhelm Reich was asked to intervene in a drought in 1953. Adopting a typically controversial approach, he asserted that drought was the result of build-up of orgone radiation in the atmosphere—a hypothetical, omnipresent libidinal life force, which Reich claimed was responsible for gravity, weather patterns, emotions, and health. His rainmaking device therefore set out to automatically remove excess orgone. This 'cloudbuster' was formed from a set of hollow metal tubes that were connected at the back end to a series of flexible metal hoses and placed in water, a medium that would supposedly draw orgone energy to the ground like a lightning rod. The instrument was then aimed into areas of the sky to disperse orgone accumulations. Seemingly, Reich's apparatus worked and he continued developing orgone accumulators, which attracted the attention of the US Food and Drug Administration (FDA). After one of his associates violated an injunction to stop him shipping them out of Maine, Reich was sentenced to two years in prison, where he died from a heart attack (Atlas Obscura 2013).

Representing a newfound freedom from nature, rainmaking technologies demonstrated that humans could command the weather and unleash the fury of the tempest. Artificial rainfall was also of interest to military forces as a delivery system for chemical and biological warfare. However, rainmaking technologies cannot be controlled with the precision of machines. Even the most plausible cloud-seeding devices are unreliable, as they are severely challenged by the highly nuanced and unpredictable nature of weather. In fact, the statistical 'noise' naturally produced by weather greatly overwhelms the possibility of success of any interventions that are possible with anthropogenic agents. For starters, the stratiform clouds targeted by these technologies are fragile structures, with a poor capacity for precipitation on demand, and most droplets evaporate again before they reach the ground. Importantly, the effects of cloud seeding are contingent upon environmental conditions. For example, hilly terrain that bounds mountainous regions can cause reliable rainfall patterns, while flat agricultural lands are much more mixed in their responses and carry the additional risk of precipitating thunderstorms. Misplaced doses of cloud-seeding chemicals, poorly judged sites of delivery and changing contexts are also likely to result in failure to produce rain. To compound these difficulties, it is currently impossible to digitally model the appropriate parameters for effective micro-casting forecasts. Evaluation difficulties also arise, as existing cloud formations are the targets for the production of rain and it is not possible to distinguish between how much rain would have fallen naturally, or has been induced (Langewiesche 2008). The very nature of rainfall currently exceeds the capacity for modern technologies to constrain it, but in the process of these experiments and explorations, our engagement with hypercomplex systems is improving — but we are certainly not 'there' yet.

We conclude that the initiation of large-scale operational weather modification programs would be premature. Many fundamental problems must be answered first ... We believe that the patient investigation of atmospheric processes coupled with an exploration of the technical applications may eventually lead to useful weather modification, but we emphasize that the time-scale required for success may be measured in decades. (Novak 2011).

Sonifying Liquid

> … molecular evidence linking hippos and whales
> overwhelms dissenting fossil evidence to the contrary
> … The biggest problem with thinking of hippos as close
> relatives of whales is that the oldest hippos are only about
> twenty million years old, nearly thirty million years younger
> than the oldest whales, and that body-wise, the similarities
> are very limited. The long ghost lineage of hippos, between
> forty-nine and twenty million years ago, implies … that the
> ancestors of hippos were so unlike modern hippos that we
> do not recognise them … (Thewissen 2014, 159)

Whales and hippopotamuses not only share a surprising ancestry (Thewissen et al. 2007), they are also peculiarly adapted to aquatic life by using sound to communicate through water. The sounds of baleen whales originate in folds in the larynx, whose vibrations are then transmitted through the ventral grooves before being finally emitted into the water. In toothed whales, the movement of thick membranes called phonic lips is triggered by air that enters the nasal tract. This causes the surrounding tissues to vibrate and produces a sound that passes through the skull to reach the melon, a fatty sound box in the forehead, which modulates and focuses the sound beam in the water. They also listen to their watery world through special structures in their jawbones (*National Geographic* 2011). In contrast, hippopotamuses can communicate through both air and water, responding to signals in these separate media at the same time. Hippos bellow and grunt, in a manner not dissimilar to whales, where their voices travel through the air and across a fatty layer around their neck into the water. Like other terrestrial mammals that can clearly detect air vibrations, hippos have ears but also use their jaws, like whales, to transmit sounds in the water through their body. These aquatic vibrations travel through their bones and into the middle ear, where they are translated into auditory signals. Hippos, therefore, are immersed within a dual auditory realm weaving together the liquid language of their evolution-ary ancestors with the rarefied vibrations of the gaseous realm.

We, without listening jaws,[1] may also experience the auditory landscapes of hippos and whales using hydrophones to capture the intensified effects of sound in liquid environments. Packets of sound travel much faster and over longer distances in water than through air, as molecules are much more closely packed together. It is also possible to feel the physical presence of sonic vibrations, which produce a spectrum of real, potentially use-able, physical effects.

Although sound waves are influenced by many factors such as salinity, temperature, and pressure, they can be used passively to gather information about an underwater landscape. Listen-ing-only technologies, such as SOund Navigation And Ranging (SONAR), detect waves that are travelling through the water and use them to gather spatial information about the environment, which can be used to generate images.

Active processes like echolocation can also be used where shock waves are applied to achieve specific effects. Changes between an emitted and received signal provide directional information about obstacles; or, at higher energies, may even be used to generate forceful impacts. Pulse waves will travel through a medium without causing too much harm until there is a density discontinuity — then, they act like an explosion, ripping matter apart.

Technologies that lock aquatic sound into highly repetitive patterns, perhaps something like cymatics (Jenny 2001, 8), are also possible. These structures are produced by the periodic or-ganisation of standing waves, which can mobilise loosely associ-ated particles — from sand to ferrofluids.

Since the various aspects of these phenomena are due to vibration, we are confronted with a spectrum which reveals a patterned, figurative formation at one pole and kinetic-

1   Bone conductivity is used to directly stimulate the cochlea using electronic implants in people with sensorineural hearing loss.

dynamic processes at the other, the whole being generated and sustained by its essential periodicity. (Jenny 2001, 11)

'Bodies' produced by the oscillations of actively colliding fields set the scene for lifelike events by establishing energy gradients, generating density currents and producing katabatic flows, creating vortices. They may even result in 'organs [that] are not homogeneous masses, but tissues of the utmost delicacy which go on developing and repeating themselves indefinitely' (Jenny 2001, 18). Such liquid bodies maintain their structure through the constant flow of energy through their particle systems, which enable them to adapt fluidly with alternations in their environment; namely, the frequency and intensity of vibration. As long as these vibrational energies are sustained, the resultant bodies possess agency and may even be regarded as possessing a 'life' of their own. In highly constrained environments, such as the abyss, continuous flow systems may arise as fields of infernal heat from geothermal systems are rapidly cooled in the pressurised, freezing ocean and recursively heated again as they fall. These hypercycles (cyclically linked, self-replicating, metabolic reactions) (Eigen and Schuster 1979) are rich in organic building blocks such as hydrogen, carbon dioxide, and sulfur (Martin and Russell 2007) and are considered as possible sites and apparatuses for the initiating sequence of 'life' — through the onset of (liquid) biogenesis.

08.5

Glassmaking

> A glass-blower, remember, breathes life into a vessel, giving it shape and form and sometimes beauty; but he can, with that same breath, shatter and destroy it. (DuMaurier 2004, 11)

A frozen supercooled liquid, glass is a fluid that has never set, where covalently bonded silica crystals do not take back their original form after melting, but become an amorphous solid. Possessing some of the order of solids, as well as the randomness of a liquid, it remains pliant, and can be shaped by a variety of approaches.

The first forms of glass were naturally sourced as obsidian, which forms during volcanic eruptions when silica in granite or sand becomes molten and which also spontaneously formed in the New Mexico desert sand following the detonation of an atomic bomb prototype in 1945. Glass may have originally been manufactured as a by-product of metalworking, or through developing glazes in ceramic practices. Glazes used for coating stone beads have been discovered that date back to 4000 BCE, and sand casting (pouring molten glass into moulds), may have appeared around 1500 BCE (British Glass Foundation 2013). Glass blowing (using air to expand a 'gob' of glass wrapped around an open pipe that is turned to form a range of complex formations) appeared from around the first century BCE, when glass engraving (using tools to mark the surface) also became increasingly common. During the fourteenth to sixteenth centuries CE, glass-cutting techniques were developed to give dazzling finishes to the material and float glass techniques (where molten glass is floated into sheets upon molten metal to produce sheets of glass) were developed in the mid-nineteenth century, which made the industrial manufacturing of glass possible.

Glass became a versatile and inspirational building material for early modernists such as Bruno Taut, who thought it could re-tune *Geist* (the spirit) and *Volk* (the mass of humanity). Having already made incredible use of coloured glass, mosaics, glass paintings, glass bricks, and floors to construct the Glass House pavilion for the German glass industry for the Werkbund (the German Work Federation) exhibition in Cologne in 1914, Taut was inspired to design a new city. Using glass building materials to embody his vision of an intellectual socialist revolution, he positioned a crystalline beacon at its centre to unify people through transcendent notions of the *collective* good.

> The cathedral was the container of all the souls that prayed in this way; and it always remains empty and pure — it is 'dead'. The ultimate task of architecture is to be quite and absolutely turned away from all daily rituals for all times (Taut 1919, 53–54).

Today, additive manufacturing techniques use cartridges that are heated to 1000°C to develop glassware, which is built up from cooling liquid layers (Temperton 2015). The properties of glass can be altered by a range of additives and finishes, which have been refined during its long history in artisan and industrial practices, which determine the strength, malleability, colour, and physical properties that, in recent times, can now react to light and temperature, conduct electricity, and transmit information (British Glass Foundation 2013).

While glass is well-known for these unique and malleable properties, water can also behave as an amorphous solid although its potential has not been fully explored. Glassy water, or amorphous ice[2], behaves somewhere between (disordered) water and (crystalline) ice. While they do not naturally form on Earth, they constitute the dominant form of water in the universe, occurring most frequently on interstellar dust, comets, Kuiper Belt objects, icy moons (e.g., Europa and Ganymede) and other cosmic structures like Saturn's rings (Loerting et al. 2015).

2   Different forms of amorphous ice are distinguished by their densities.

345

We know a lot about glasses that form from ordinary
silicates, sugars and metals … They're making golf clubs
out of glassy metals these days. But how important is the
glassy state of water. And what can it tell us about ordinary
water, which is such an anomalous liquid? … [Glassy water
suggests] a different sort of thermodynamics in water than
… in any of these other molecular glass-forming liquids.
(Phys.org 2008)

The strangeness of glassy bodies resonates with the peculiar
nature of cosmic matter, which becomes complicit with Earth's
laws as soon as it approaches terrestrial environments. Our understanding of what appears to be ordinary matter, like water
or glass, may not be at all 'usual' within the cosmos but highly
localised within the cosmos, where worlds with dynamic liquid
infrastructures are extremely different from our own. Owing to
our familiarity with the chemistry of our own world, it is generally assumed that only 'Goldilocks' planets are capable of bearing life, however alternative life-generating environments may
be possible.

The gas giant HD 189733b is 63 light years from Earth. It has a
'blue marble' appearance that is thought to be due to its molten
glass rain. Since only one side of the planet permanently faces
the star, daytime temperatures soar to 930°C and it is rapidly
bleeding its atmosphere into the cosmos at a rate of 100–600
million kilograms per second (Poppenhaeger, Schmitt and
Wolk 2013).

… the nightmare world of HD 189733b is the killer you
never see coming. To the human eye, this far-off planet
looks bright blue. But any space traveler confusing it with
the friendly skies of Earth would be badly mistaken. The
weather on this world is deadly. Its winds blow up to 5,400
mph (2 km/s) at seven times the speed of sound, whipping
all would-be travelers in a sickening spiral around the
planet. And getting caught in the rain on this planet is more
than an inconvenience; it's death by a thousand cuts. This

scorching alien world possibly rains glass—sideways—in its howling winds. The cobalt blue color comes not from the reflection of a tropical ocean, as on Earth, but rather a hazy, blow-torched atmosphere containing high clouds laced with silicate particles. (Loff 2017)

While the conditions in this world are completely hostile to our carbon-based chemistry, in a liquid world where glass rains from the skies, it might be possible that alien silicon-based chemistry organises in ways that prompt tenacious dissipative structures. Although we are unlikely to test this in any meaningful way soon, this strange planet draws attention to our presumptions about life on Earth that deeply shape our expectations, not just about life on other worlds, but what conditions that are necessary for 'life' on our own planet. This will not be life as we know it — but other kinds of infrastructures capable of producing dynamic, persistent liquid bodies.

08.6

Liquid Apparatuses

> We already have digital computers to process information.
> Our goal is not to compete with electronic computers
> or to operate word processors ... Our goal is to build a
> completely new class of computers that can precisely control
> and manipulate physical matter. Imagine if when you run a
> set of computations that not only information is processed
> but physical matter is algorithmically manipulated as well.
> We have just made this possible at the mesoscale.[3] (Katsikis,
> Cybulski and Prakash 2015; Carey 2015)

To negotiate with the liquid domain, we need to establish how
fluids may not only be screens for projecting ideas, substrates to
work upon or bodies that can power machines, but also become
operational as liquid technology and substrate for analogue
computing. Vladimir Lukyanov's 1936 'water computer' could
solve (partial) differential equations to address calculations in
geology, thermal physics, metallurgy, and rocket engineering.
The computation was performed by translating physical properties into (real) numbers, then titrating fluid displacements
within a series of interconnected, water-filled glass tubes and
then levelling the parameters through the equalising flow of water under gravity. This hydraulic integrator was used until the
1980s, when personal computing became cheap, configurable,
and powerful enough to run complex equations.

Water bodies have also been programmed to generate large-
scale spectacles in public spaces such as the Palace of Versailles,
the Villa da Pratolino, the Tivoli gardens and the hydraulic gardens of the brothers Salomon and Isaac de Caus. These mechanically enlivened liquid systems deploy the same kind of tactics
as da Vinci, where the power of water movement is controlled

---

3   The experiment explores the capability of synchronous logic-based droplet
    control to enable algorithmic manipulation of materials at the intersection
    of computer science and fabrication.

through hydraulically operated circuitry to produce largely pre-determined effects. These spectacular gardens may also be regarded as architectural-scale water computers, whose spectacular water features demonstrate the dominance of machines over the natural realm and whose potential for an alternative kind of liquid technology and performance, remains only partially explored (Pruned 2012).

Soft Robots

> It lumbered slobberingly into sight and gropingly squeezed
> its gelatinous green immensity through the black doorway
> into the tainted outside air of that poison city of madness.
> … The Thing cannot be described—there is no language
> for such abysms of shrieking and immemorial lunacy, such
> eldritch contradictions of all matter, force, and cosmic
> order. (Lovecraft 2002, 167)

Typically, robotic systems are considered animated machines,
where the 'brute' mechanical body, often made of steel, or aluminium, is provided with an external energy source. Algorithms that encode pre-programmed motion patterns instruct
its tasks from the inside-out, which may be informed by feedback from inbuilt mechanical sensors. By contrast, the responsiveness of living systems comes from the outside-in as *embodied intelligence,* where soft, elastic, and flexible materials like
soft skin, hairs, elastic muscles, tendons, and various fluctuant
organs direct the movement of rigid mechanical components.
Operations are governed by local reflexes that are modulated
by a central 'brain'.

Two types of applications of liquid technologies are relevant
to the emerging field of soft robotics: those systems that are actuated by external liquid pneumatic or hydraulic forces, which
engage with the dynamics of non-linear materials, and those
whose soft bodies are internally agentised and receptive to external conditions.

Externally powered 'soft robots' are actuated by 'liquid' forces
that work with the plasticity of soft structures, which can adapt
and endure complex unstructured environments. Challenges
are 'solved' both centrally and locally, using the responsive apparatuses of non-linear 'sensing' materials, where intelligence is
embodied in the structural systems that fine-tune pre-formulat-
ed external programs. Delegating task-solving to the periphery
of the operational program makes it easier for robots to perform

complex tasks (Iida and Laschi 2011). For example, fabricated transparent, hydrogel-based robots can perform a number of fast, forceful tasks, including kicking a ball underwater, and grabbing and releasing a live fish. Actuated through an assemblage of hollow, hydrogel structures that are connected to rubbery tubes, these robots can be inflated into different orientations by the rapid inward movement of water, which enables it to curl up or stretch out (Chu 2017).

Soft bodied robots without internal actuators such as 'walking' gels and dynamic droplets (see section 08.13 and chapter 09) are both activated and modulated by their contexts, which enables degrees of 'soft' control. The chemical 'inchworm' created at the Shuli Hashimoto Applied Physics Laboratory at Waseda University, Tokyo is a colour-changing, 'walking' gel. Actuated by a periodic, oscillating Belousov-Zhabotinsky reaction, where the concentration of reagents periodically increases and decreases (Belousov 1959; Zhabotinsky 1964) the polymers in the gel shrink or grow in response to cyclical variations in the presence of ruthenium bipyridine ions. Traction for this movement is gained on a notched surface, so the entire 'self-organising' chemical system generates its own control and mechanical signals from within its body operating within environmental constraints (Maeda et al. 2007; Simonite 2009). Modulating the performance of such agentised soft robots can involve fine-tuning environmental conditions. At Brandeis University, researchers have created a gel from a solution of bovine protein tubes and bacterial motor proteins that is capable of spontaneous movement. The gel is activated by mixing it with energy-rich adenosine triphosphate (ATP), which enables the individual tubes and proteins to slide past each other to form patterns or bundles that grow and eventually fall apart in a cyclic fashion. The movement and formation rate of these patterns can be modulated by altering the concentration of ATP while the character of motion is adjusted by changing the number of tubes in the original solution (Yirka 2012).

The control of autonomously agentised systems, or liquid technologies, requires a more detailed engagement with the environmental design than mechanically operated systems. Life is the ultimate embodied computer where, through various forms of molecular memory (DNA, brain, tissue receptivity), agents can make informed decisions about how to act by comparing internal models of 'self' with the actual external conditions.

Natural Computing

> The future is unknowable, though not unimaginable. Future knowledge cannot be had now, but it can cast its shadow ahead. In each mind, however, the shadow assumes a different shape, hence the divergence of expectations. The formation of expectations is an act of our mind by means of which we try to catch a glimpse of the unknown. Each one of us catches a different glimpse. The wider the range of divergence the greater the possibility that somebody's expectation will turn out to be right. (Lachmann 1977, 59).

Computation is a mode of thinking and practice that enables the world to be sorted, ordered, and valued, so that new knowledge may be acquired. In this book 'computing' is considered a way of interrogating the processual building blocks of 'decision-making' proposed by Descartes' 'rational thought' — a thing that doubts, understands, affirms, denies, is willing, is unwilling, and also imagines and has sense perceptions. Implementing models of the world, the computing process can be iteratively tested and altered through the recognition of different 'states', or stored information/inputs (memory). In particular, computing within the material realm is considered, as it is very different to the symbolic exchanges of digital computers that are encoded into patterns of ones and zeroes ('bits').

In a digital computer, binary information (0,1) is grouped into 'bytes' (usually eight digits) and moved around into different physical storage areas according to a set of instructions, or algorithm, where they are etched into electronic components, and can collectively perform specific 'applications', or 'apps' (Epstein 2016). Since massless electrons carry digital information, the speed of calculation is limited by the hardware, and not by information travel speed.

In contrast, natural computing (Denning 2007; Zenil 2013) places matter at the heart of its computational processes and operates through 'actual' material paradigms, which explore the computational strategies and parallel processing abilities of living and dynamic physical systems. This is only possible when matter is at far-from-equilibrium states, where the atomic realm is capable of making decisions and therefore, exerting effects in the world, which are shaped in relation to external events.

The internal agency of atoms (Dyson 1979, 249) responsible for this 'decision-making' resides in their structure where, for example, chemical bonds spontaneously associate through weak and strong molecular forces to produce different kinds of molecules. John Dalton symbolically represented the mass of atoms, calculated from the averages of large sample numbers, so they could be theoretically and practically combined in ways to make new substances, or compounds. The computational capacity of the molecular realm reached a new threshold with the advent of supramolecular chemistry, or chemistry 'beyond the atom', which is concerned with the use of weak intermolecular interactions to produce different configurations of molecules. Donald J. Cram, Jean-Marie Lehn and Charles J. Pedersen were awarded the 1987 Nobel Prize in this field for developing structural and functional building blocks that could be used to build up larger molecular architectures, so materials could be synthesised, which had not previously existed in the history of the universe (Steed and Atwood 2009).

Alan Turing was interested in how the combinatorial processes that occurred within the natural realm (chemical, physical, developmental, adaptive, evolutionary) could produce morphogenetic forms (Turing 1952). While Turing's inquiry was mathematically symbolic, he inspired the field of natural computing that is interpreted according to respective interests and existing knowledge sets within a range of overlapping disciplines, and has given rise to a range of derivative practices. For example, morphological computing arises from the field of robotics and engineering, which exploits the physical dynamics of non-linear material systems to perform a computational task (Füchslin et al. 2013); 'collective computing' observes how adaptive biological systems solve problems (Sokol 2017a); while unconventional computing aims to enrich, or go beyond, the standard models of computing such as the Turing machine and von Neumann architectures, which have dominated computer science for more than half a century (Adamatzky et al. 2007). Collectively, these emerging practices are generating new computing systems, which are producing new insights into the nature of the world such as soft robotics (Shepherd et al. 2013), slime mould computing (Adamatzky et al. 2013) and reaction diffusion computing (Adamatzky and De Lacy Costello 2003). Although digital computing plays a critical role in all fields of computing, the analogue modes of advanced computation raise questions about number theory, hardware systems, and appropriate programming languages for working directly with matter. For example, when slime mould 'computes', it does not use our number systems.

> ... biological systems ... are collective ... They are all made up of interacting components with only partly overlapping interests, who are noisy information processors dealing with noisy signals. (Sokol 2017a)

In living systems, material iterations, or oscillations, perform the role of numbers. They are not symbolic gestures but actual: an orbital pathway around the Earth, a pulse, a blink, a footstep, a bowel contraction, the tide, and rain. These iterative, persistent occurrences are not exact, self-similar, regular, or universal, and constitute nature's 'beats'. These numerical-equivalent systems are nothing like numbers at all. As Henri Lefebvre notes,

> the departure point for this history of space is not to be found in the geographical descriptions of natural space, but rather in the study of natural rhythms, and of the modification of those rhythms and their inscription in space by means of human actions, especially work-related actions. It begins, then, with the spatio-temporal rhythms of nature as transformed by a social practice. (Lefevbre 1991, 117)

Simultaneously fields and particles, atoms, and molecules are in constant oscillation at the atomic scale as their active fronts collide, interdigitate, collapse, or persist long enough to shape the course of proximate events. The next level of organisation involves the generation of hubs and 'attractors' that shape and characterise spaces and environments across many scales, like the Belousov–Zhabotinsky reaction, which produces colourful, fractal-like patterns (Belousov 1959; Zhabotinsky 1964). Within these potent fields of activity, excitable molecules can then make decisions about their configuration and spatial distribution in relationship to other atoms. Material expressions arise from molecular 'discourses' that take place through agile molecular fields of potential and even quantum states. While these events may provide a basis for prediction, since they arise from probabilistic systems, they are not absolute indicators of events. However, they create the conditions for shaping outcomes that can be clearly observed at the macroscale in systems like the pulsatile connecting tubes of slime mould colonies (Adamatzky and Schubert 2014). While repetitions within lively systems create bifurcations that demand molecules make choices and ultimately, result in irreversible events; such agentised matter is not 'alive'.

Dissipative Structures

Life then is a vortex, more or less rapid, more or less complicated, the direction of which is invariable, and which always carries along molecules of similar kinds, but into which individual molecules are continually entering, and from which they are continually departing; so that the form of a living body is more essential to it than its matter. As long as this motion subsists, the body in which it takes place is living — it lives. When it finally ceases, it dies. After death, the elements which compose it, abandoned to the ordinary chemical affinities, soon separate, from which, more or less quickly, results the dissolution of the once living body. It was then by the vital motion that its dissolution was arrested, and its elements were held in a temporary union. All living bodies die after a certain period, whose extreme limit is fixed for each species, and death appears to be a necessary consequence of life, which, by its own action, insensibly alters the structure of the body, so as to render its continuance impossible. (Cuvier 2006, 6)

Dissipative systems are paradoxical structures like tornadoes and whirlpools that form spontaneously when reactive energy/matter fields overlap. Characteristically, they resist Newton's law of increasing disorder (or entropy) to produce dynamic, yet persistent, material systems with recognisable forms of organisation. While dissipative gravitational fields are likely to give rise to celestial bodies such as planets and galaxies, everyday examples include convection currents, turbulent flow, cyclones, hurricanes, and living organisms, which are 'the most stable and complexly differentiated dissipative structures in existence' (Nicholson 2018, 8). Less commonly encountered dissipative systems are ones that can be constructed, or produced, such as lasers, the Belousov–Zhabotinsky reaction and Rayleigh–Bénard (convection) cells, which are formed when a layer of liquid is heated from below, so that hexagonal convection cells are formed in the layer of liquid.

Dissipative structures challenge our expectations of objects, as they are simultaneously structures and also processes that produce lifelike patterns, which cannot be distilled into any discrete phenomena, but perform a range of recognisable activities with many variations. While no two twisters are exactly the same, their unique qualities are instantly recognisable. Characteristic to all life is the extension of their influence beyond their apparent boundaries, semi-permeability and deep entanglement with context — not as an afterthought, but as a primary condition of existence. Dissipative structures are coupled to an as yet unspecified, but mathematically proven, internal reorganisation and reordering process, which becomes more efficient at remaining stable over time by diffusing energy into its surroundings. This extends way beyond the apparent object boundary and also impacts on its environment. Think of a cyclone that can influence extensive landscapes through the winds it sets up, long before a storm chaser reaches the eye of the storm. Consequently, in possessing a dynamic energy cloud, dissipative structures are not blind automata, but demonstrate a kind of primitive subjectivity that is not only extruded into, and responsive to its environment. Such agentised expansion constitutes an active and hyperlocal decision-making system that operates through auras, fields, and fuzzy zones. Dissipative structures may also assimilate passive objects into their bodies, slingshotting them into higher levels of thermodynamic order, unless the objects themselves obstruct the flow of exchange. Imagine Dorothy's house as it becomes loosely coupled with the tornado in which it is swept up and carried to the Land of Oz, where it is eventually dumped along with the energy that the tornado is trying to shed.

Dissipative systems are important infrastructures in the evolutionary story of life, whose flows of material and energetic exchange constitute the webs of life and death. Although their ultimate destiny is to collapse back into nothingness, their very presence alters the probability of further lifelike events. Over time, the collective actions of dissipative networks may even become organised enough to function as oscillators, which can compute and pattern their surroundings. Such dissipative chains of events have already persisted on Earth long enough to support the transformations arising from energetic and material exchanges between organisms over the course of 3.5 billion years and constitute the fundamental infrastructures for life.

Dissipative Adaptation

> While any given change in shape for [a dissipative] system
> is mostly random, the most durable and irreversible
> of these shifts in configuration occur when the system
> happens to be momentarily better at absorbing and
> dissipating work. With the passage of time, the 'memory'
> of these less erasable changes accumulates preferentially,
> and the system increasingly adopts shapes that resemble
> those in its history where dissipation occurred. Looking
> backward at the likely history of a product of this non-
> equilibrium process, the structure will appear to us like
> it has self-organized into a state that is 'well adapted' to
> the environmental conditions. This is the phenomenon of
> dissipative adaptation. (England 2015, 922)

As systems dissipate energy they become increasingly ordered over time, so that their complexity and stability increases, without the need for organising codes. In the late 1990s, Gavin Crooks and Chris Jarzynski showed that a small open system driven by an external source of energy could irreversibly take up a new configuration, as long as it shed energy into its surroundings. The 'memory' of these changes preferentially accumulated within the body of the dissipative structure and increasingly adopted configurations that were 'well adapted' to their environmental context (Eck 2016).

> This means clumps of atoms surrounded by a bath at some
> temperature, like the atmosphere or the ocean, should tend
> over time to arrange themselves to resonate better and
> better with the sources of mechanical, electromagnetic, or
> chemical work in their environments … (Wolchover 2014)

'Dissipative adaptation' proposes that matter rearranges to chan-nel the flow of energy through its structure increasingly more effectively. It accounts for how molecules can remain stable and even become more effectively organised by dumping excess energy into their surroundings. It is a mode of analogue computation that increases the organisation of lively matter without recourse to central organising systems like biological code, such as RNA or DNA. This process does not just reference the past states of dissipative structures, but also creates a platform for alternative ways of designing and engineering with lively materials.

08.11

Is Dissipation Enough?

> It is obvious that organisms differ from flames, whirlpools
> and other dissipative structure in a number of ways. For
> a start, organisms exhibit a far greater degree of stability,
> being able to maintain themselves for much longer periods
> of time. The key to their extraordinary stability lies in their
> ability to store energy, which enable them to manage their
> metabolic needs without having to rely on a constant supply
> of experimental energy, like other dissipative structures.
> In addition, organisms are distinctive in that they are
> demarcated by a physical boundary — a semi-permeable
> membrane — which helps regulate the intake and outtake of
> materials flowing through them … Organisms … derived
> from previous organisms, and their structure reflects the
> gradual consolidation, through the eons of evolution, of
> an intricate higher-order self-organizing dynamic among
> component self-organizing processes. (Nicholson 2018, 16)

Dissipative structures that spontaneously occur in nature do
not completely describe all those characteristics that we recognise as 'life' (Moreno and Mossio 2015, 18). While they do not
provide literal accounts of biogenesis, they exhibit principles
of organisation that enable further exploration of how matter
becomes lively. Given that the Modern Synthesis assumes the
fundamental building blocks of life are inert, dissipative systems
generate experimental apparatuses to rethink our assumptions
of living processes through lively matter, and enable different
kinds of questions regarding the nature of life to be explored.
They also help us (re)consider the trajectory from non-living to
living matter in ways that are consistent with the principles of
liquid life.

Making Liquid Life

Liquid life offers a metaphorical and physical way of developing the character of living things through the perspective of fluid substance that were banished like the soul, from the *bête machine* and Modern Synthesis.

Finding ways to convert the principles of liquid life into a toolset of materials, apparatuses, and prototypes that enable these ideas to be further explored in testable and observable ways, is akin to 'nailing jellies to walls'. To date, testing the liquid nature of life in practice has been an observational pursuit (a natural philosophy) without meaningful ways to explore its actuality an experimental capacity. With advances in our understanding of matter at far-from-equilibrium states (spectroscopy, particle tracking), dissipative structures (characterisation of dissipative adaptation), natural computing (reaction/diffusion waves) and biotechnology (difference analysis, microarrays), it becomes possible to develop a design-led exploration of liquid life, which is situated within a realm of constant flux and instability, whose outcomes are contextual and contingent and therefore, seeks to raise possibilities rather than predict outcomes. Unlike the classical worldview, where the relationships between things is abstracted and simple, the fragility, incidental nature, and unpredictability of lively systems requires a different way of producing effects.

Shaped by curiosity and provoked by odd juxtapositions, design-led experiments begin with sculpting questions using spatial, material, and temporal 'liquid' tactics. Establishing terrains of rebellion, soft systems, and resistance against entropy, which are coerced and seduced towards desired states and encounters, they reveal and make familiar a realisable framework for 'liquid life'.

08.13

Visualising Lively Liquids

> ... a computer of such infinite and subtle complexity that
> organic life itself shall form part of its operational matrix.
> (Adams 2009, 158)

A range of dynamic droplet systems exist that exhibit strikingly lifelike properties. The most commonly observed model of self-organising non-linear systems is the Rayleigh–Bénard convection cells, which are hexagonal structures that are caused by convection currents when a thin layer of fluid is open to air and submitted to a vertical temperature gradient (Bénard 1900). They operate by way of a gravity-driven positive feedback system, where molecules in liquid states continually move through colder fields as they rise and results in instabilities that produce the characteristic, morphologically stable 'structure', which resembles biological cells (Rayleigh 1916).

David Deamer has observed hydrocarbons in amoeboid bodies splitting into daughter cells (Wolchover 2017c), while Manu Prakash observes water and propylene glycol-based droplets as mimicking the behaviours of living cells (Abate 2015; Cira 2015) and Martin Hanczyc and colleagues have also designed droplets that can be induced to go through cycles of fusion and division (Caschera, Rasmussen and Hanczyc 2013).

Arguably, the most lifelike droplet system was first discovered by Otto Bütschli (Bütschli 1892), whose spectrum of body morphology and behaviour is much more diverse than the previous examples[4]. By adding a drop of strong alkali (potash) into a field of olive oil (oleic acid) at room temperature, Bütschli created a recipe for life whereby the drop transformed into a complex structure with strikingly lifelike behaviours. Extruding proto-

---

4   In contrast to Rayleigh–Bénard cells, the Bütschli system's metabolism produces varied structures that may facilitate the transition from apparent order to lifelike behaviour

plasmic-like tentacles into its surroundings, he likened it to a simple, single-celled organism (or protist) such as an amoeba.

In 2009, this system was observed for the first time in a modern laboratory at low power (×10) under a light microscope with a backlit stage, which enabled the droplets to be seen more easily. Each alkali droplet broke down into stable but mobile structures around 1 mm in diameter, which produced soapy deposits (sodium oleate) that recorded their movements like automatic drawings. Iterations of the experiment produced various trajectories that shared common characteristics. Droplets could move around their environment, sense it, and respond to each other through coordinated population-scale events. Such extraordinary lifelike behaviour may be a consequence of the relative abundance of the 'food source' in which the beads of alkali are immersed, which provides unlimited energy for the structure-producing exchanges. Through the principles of dissipative adaptation, these lifelike characteristics persist long enough to result in increasingly organised agents and complex behaviours (Armstrong 2015). While the Bütschli system is not 'alive', it can be practically applied to construct an apparatus that explores how primordial (liquid) agents produce diverse and persistent structures. This constitutes both a visualisation tool and native experimental platform for directly observing and exploring questions pertaining to liquid life (Armstrong 2015).

Part V

BEING

LIQUID APPARATUS

'Beings in transition' are agents of discovery that take the form of lifelike droplets, which interrogate the theory, qualities, characteristics, and apparatuses of liquid life. In this chapter, an account of the Bütschli system is given, based on the study of dynamic droplets under a light microscope, which provides fourteen phenomena associated with various stages of Bütschli droplet development. These act as a language, or 'angelology' for liquid life, through which its imaginary and technical capacities are developed. Quotations from a variety of sources are juxtaposed with experimental accounts to introduce 'quality of living' into design-led observations, where chemical events acquire a specific cultural context. These provocations lay the foundations for poetic experiments by Rolf Hughes in chapter 10, and notations by Simone Ferracina in chapter 11.

Lively Liquid

> … like the sceptics of atomism who could see no way of verifying the totally invisible or the ancients for whom the stuff of the stars was unknowable; or Mendel himself who did not believe that the material basis of heredity would ever be discovered. Not being able to see experimental approaches is part of the paucity of the imagination. (Cairns-Smith 1987, 135)

Liquid technologies are not constrained by or translated into the operational structure of the machine, but retain the potential to create transformative events, experiences, and habitats. The strangest and most creative of these is the Bütschli system, which establishes a unique dialogue with the living realm, by providing access to a realm of low-level 'agentised' material operations that inhabit fields, interfaces, and protean bodies that continually respond to their environment. While it is evaluated through the specificity of these encounters, being concerned with 'this' particular molecule, or 'these' specific qualities, in 'that' precise place, its operations are very different to the kind of push-button or touch interface that has been developed for machines.

Arising from the edge of chaos, Bütschli droplets take their first rebellious steps against inertia through the stages of birth, life, and death (Armstrong 2015, 87). Moving through lifelike transitional states of existence, they splinter away from their initiating field of organisation, in material expressions that range from simple droplets to structured configurations and population-scale assemblages. Embodying an explosion of proto-Cambrian chemical diversity, they offer a glimpse into the parallel world of liquid life[1].

1 At ×10 magnification, radiant aqueous bodies cast shadows on a dark oil background with their turbid trails of osmotic structures formed by soap precipitates. At ×40, the narrow field of view reduces the field contrast and the droplets appear like wraiths, which grow scaly skins against a slate background.

Around 80% of the initial droplets rapidly develop thick encasings that form deposits on the base of the Petri dish like chemical snow. While many perish in the initial stages of this journey, some prevail and persist, becoming increasingly organised. Some break free to reach the container's edge, where they turn back in upon themselves to traverse liquid fields that are contaminated, or 'structured', by their own waste products. Others circle in groups where they steadily increase in mass through the production of deposits and become tethered to the bottom of the Petri dish, where they strain restlessly against their moorings. Those that do not 'perish', steadily accumulate soft deposits, or 'osmotic structures', at their interface that eventually prevent the droplets from 'feeding'. Encased in their soapy cocoons, these droplets eventually reach a tipping point in their thermodynamic order and plummet towards thermodynamic equilibrium, or 'death'.

> Osmotic growths like living things may be said to have an evolutionary existence, the analogy holding good down to the smallest detail. In their early youth, at the beginning of life, the phenomena of exchange, of growth, and of organization are very intense. As they grow older, these exchanges gradually slow down, and growth is arrested. With age the exchanges still continue, but more slowly, and these then gradually fail and are finally completely arrested. The osmotic growth is dead, and little by little it decays, losing its structure and its form. (Leduc 1911, 151)

In an open environment and over the course of billions of years, such agile tactics may ultimately increase the material complexity and fertility of a site, or even generate discernible signs of 'alternative' lifeforms.

Life Cycle

> Our home was a spilt-level affair with 14 steps leading up
> from the garage to the kitchen door. Those steps were a gage
> of life. They were my yardstick, my challenge to continue
> living. I felt that if the day arrived when I was unable to lift
> one foot up one step and then drag the other painfully after
> it — repeating the process 14 times until, utterly spent, I
> could be through — I could then admit defeat and lie down
> and die. (Canfield and Hansen 2012, 246)

Standing in for the qualities neglected by classical expectations
of the material realm, in these experiments Bütschli droplets are
granted the mythological status of angels, which are explored
through fourteen 'key stations' that take place within a theatre
of chemical events. Each title refers to formal classifications
made to the characteristic behaviours of the system, which I
have previously published in *Vibrant Architecture: Matter as
CoDesigner of Living Structures* (Armstrong 2015). References to
themes relating to the process of 'living' are mixed into the experimental observations, to emphasise the ethical dimension of
the lively material realm and to render it strange. Selected quotations conjure forth experiences and expectations[2] that exceed
functionalist Enlightenment narratives, which typically frame
experimental findings.

As messengers (information), vectors (direction), translators of events (transformers), messages (language) and things-
in-themselves, the Bütschli angels brought forth by the mixing of alkali and oil, draw our attention to the extraordinary
characteristics of matter at far-from-equilibrium states. In the
following design-led experiments and alternative spaces for
dreaming and transformation, they seek to (re)unite the soul
substance with the material realm, so that the remarkable char-

---

2   Each quotations indicates the specific characteristics of a particular Bütschli angel.

acteristics of the living realm may be observed anew through the lens of liquid life.

Birth: Field of Fire and Ice

The little fires spawned by each four-pound incendiary ball joined into middling fires, and middling fires into bigger fires. Soon, the fire whirls were self-sustaining, sucking in oxygen from all around and creating intense cyclonic winds. Gale force winds spun into the centre of the fires, sucking combustibles, animals, bricks, beams, and people into the maelstrom. The asphalt in the streets turned to molten black rivers. In the superheated air, people asphyxiated or died from breathing the hot gases. Structures apparently far from the fire front would suddenly burst into flames. (Logan 2012, 166)

When the alkaline droplet first breaks up in the oil field through the saponification process, it self-organises into a polarised, dynamic field with a characteristically arched, rolling front. This moves outwards, producing ripples with a flame-like appearance. Soap flakes, like ice crystals, are swept backwards and accumulate at its trailing edge, where they begin to form osmotic structures. In this initial highly energised stage, the front can break up into discreet bodies that resemble moving islands of 'fire and ice'.

09.2.2

Birth: Shells

> If what you found was made from pure matter, it will
> never spoil. And you can come back one day. If it was just
> one moment of light, like the explosion of a star, you will
> find nothing on your return. But you would have seen an
> explosion of light. And that alone would already be worth
> the journey. (Coelho 1993, 118)

As the alkaline field continues to break up, twisting shell-like
structures appear, which absorb energy from the environment
to remain stable.

Like tornadoes trapped within tiny Russian matryoshka
dolls, these turbulent manifolds burst out of each other, time
and time again. Many suddenly collapse on their release and
form dense crystalline deposits, while others enter a new phase
of organisation as lifelike droplets.

Life: Organising Droplets

> … Some sat
> Poised like mud grenades, their blunt heads farting.
> I sickened, turned, and ran. The great slime kings
> Were gathered there for vengeance and I knew
> That if I dipped my hand the spawn would clutch it.
> (Heaney 2002, 4)

The chemical front disintegrates to become wandering fields of dynamic droplets. Some move alone, while others form groups that explore and modify their surroundings by casting complex structures from around their posterior pole.

As if out of a witch's cauldron, a parade of forms arises from the conjunction between liquid media; tadpole tails, rose-like formations, knotted rhizomes, and winking encrustations.

09.2.3.1

Fourteen Liquid Stations of Life: Primary Morphologies

> ... they were words
> invented to define things
> that existed
> or did not exist
> in the face of
> the pressing urgency
> of a need ...
> (Artaud 1975)

The configurations of Bütschli angels are not pre-determined, or gradual, but are continually negotiated through their exquisite responsiveness to instabilities and ability to rapidly transform in response to change.

The ensuing interdigitations, cohesions, dissolutions, extrusions, and inevitable collapses in the following sections, map a pathway of entropic resistance that shapes the character of liquid life.

ONE Life:*Droplet

> Life and death appeared to me ideal bounds, which I should first break through, and pour a torrent of light into our dark world. A new species would bless me as its creator and source; many happy and excellent natures would owe their being to me. No father could claim the gratitude of his child so completely as I should deserve theirs. Pursuing these reflections, I thought that if I could bestow animation upon lifeless matter, I might in process of time (although I now found it impossible) renew life where death had apparently devoted the body to corruption. (Shelley 2014, 44)

Bütschli angels wander flâneur-like in search of the path of greatest resistance towards their inevitable end. Leaving chemical ripples in their wake, they surf the forward progression of time, which shapes the irreversibility and creativity of liquid life.

TWO Life:*Osmotic Skin

> ... true theatre, because it moves and makes use of living
> instruments, goes on stirring up shadows, which life
> endlessly stumbles along. (Artaud 2010, 7)

Soap crystals that arise from the meeting of alkali and oil are
carried upon miniature glacial flows that clothe the Bütschli angel's body. These osmotic skins may take on the form of undulating jellyfish, stuttering werewolves, or writhing worms, and
break away from the droplet body, to archive the metabolic intensity of the system as soft fossil trails.

THREE Life:*Clusters

He sees efflorescences in fragments of ice, imprints of
shrubs and shells — yet so that one cannot detect whether
they be imprints only, or the things themselves. Diamonds
gleam like eyes: metals palpitate. And all fear has departed
from him! He throws himself down upon the ground, and
leaning upon his elbows watches breathlessly. Insects that
have no stomachs persistently eat: withered ferns bloom
again and reflower; absent members grow again. At last he
perceives tiny globular masses, no larger than pinheads,
with cilia all round them. They are agitated with a vibratite
motion. (Flaubert 2005, 190)

As Bütschli angels pattern their surroundings, they avoid the
trails of their own waste products. Their aversion is such that
while circling, they may become paralysed if they find themselves suddenly surrounded by a field of their own excrements.
These invisibly scarred terrains provoke sudden actions, where
chemical insect swarms weave over and around fossilised bodies, like pollinating bees. They shake, zigzag, and crash into each
other in a frenzy of information exchange.

09.2.3.1.4

Paradoxa

> 'This is Hell,' she said with a smile. 'But Hell is merely a
> form of terminology. Really this is the Womb of the World
> whence all things come.' (Carrington 2005, 137)

Bütschli angels inhabit an oily realm of constant instabilities, uncertainties, and displacements. Consuming the fuel within their own bodies they remain lively until they reach a threshold where they are either incarcerated in their waste, or have consumed themselves entirely. This auto-cannibalism is the source of their liveliness, which fuels a highly agentised material realm that only monsters truly understand.

FOUR Life:*Rose

> In the transformative realm these practices ... show a
> certain control of the transformation of individuals and
> their disintegration into a non-individual 'body' of skulls
> and long bones ... the disordering of the corpse, the
> relocation and redistribution of body parts also can be
> interpreted as serving as mnemonic practice, creating
> and maintaining memories ... bodies and objects do not
> belong to an individual but the community. Fragments of
> a body need not commemorate individuals ... the politics
> of separating, giving and consuming [are] community
> concerns. (Gramsch 2013, 464–65)

When Bütschli angels become tired of osculating with each other, their bodies grow feathery crystals although they do not take
flight, but fall. The fallen bones of Bütschli angels form structured landscapes that signpost alternative futures for beings yet-
to-come.

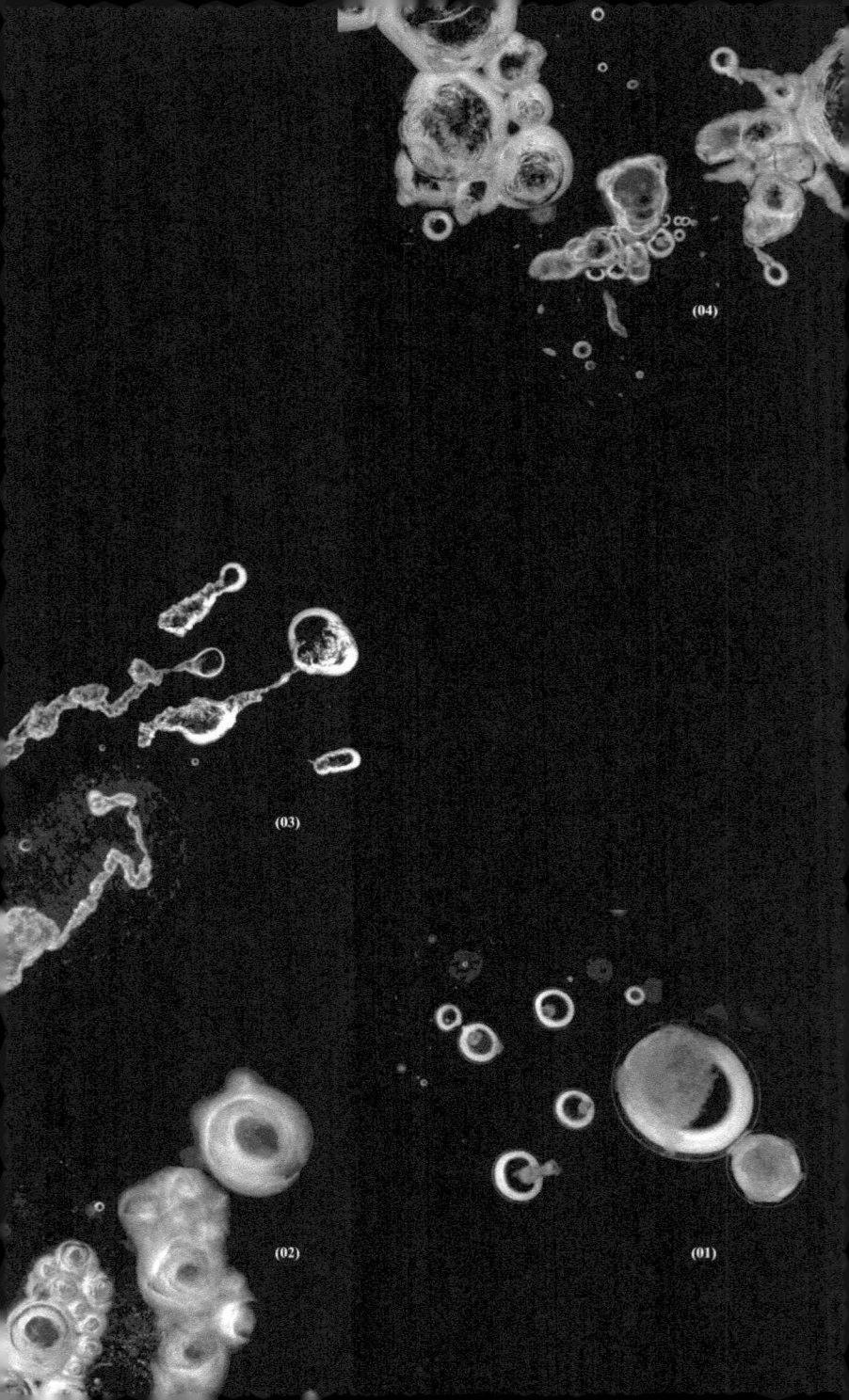

FIVE Life:*Werewolf

Wide shoulders, long arms and she sleeps succinctly curled
into a ball as if she were cradling her spine in her tail.
Nothing about her is human except that she is not a wolf; it
is as if the fur she thought she wore had melted into her skin
and become part of it, although it does not exist. Like the
wild beasts, she lives without a future. She inhabits only the
present tense, a fugue of the continuous, a world of sensual
immediacy as without hope as it is without despair. (Carter
2006, 141)

When the surface area-to-volume ratio of a Bütschli angel is optimised, it vigorously consumes itself and its surroundings. Heralded by the rapid precipitation of hairy crystals over its body,
the drag produced by these uneven deposits causes the angel
to move erratically. As these hair residues rapidly build up, the
angel seems to grow a 'tail'. The combination of profuse crystallisation and erratic movement is recognised as the 'werewolf
moment', which precedes an imminent phase change in fate and
behaviour. As more fur builds up around its body, the angel's
metabolism is weakened and heralds its inevitable decay.

09.2.3.1.4.3

SIX Life:*Oyster

> Tucked darkly in their calciferous shells, listening warily for dangers, breathing oxygen into the water, sifting the silt, changing sex, the oyster has witnessed all our histories, all our struggles … The oyster was here before we were. Before once upon a time. Before, you might say, time itself. Back then oyster reefs encircled the continents, a great shelf or ledge between the ocean and the land that we used to haul ourselves up or along, whichever it was, and row ourselves around this planet, cove to cove, not cavemen but covemen. Take one in your hand, feel the scratch of the shell of what we now call rock, prise it apart and you have Mother Earth's chronicle of the planet and a taste of the future. Treat it with respect. (Smith 2015, 9)

When the skin of an angel becomes sufficiently thick and heavy, it no longer glides through the liquid medium. Its body becomes anchored to the ground, whereupon it continues to grow a thick shell like an oyster, creatures that were once considered only a little more sophisticated than minerals in the hierarchy of life.

Like beating hearts, the soft matter of angels keeps mark of subjective time through their iterations. Slowly consuming and incarcerating themselves in their waste products, their metabolism slows down to the point where they are barely breathing.

SEVEN Life:*Suckling Pigs

> Of all the delicacies in the whole mundus edibilis, I will
> maintain it to be the most delicate — princeps obsoniorum.
> I speak not of your grown porkers — things between pig
> and pork — those hobbydehoys — but a young and tender
> suckling — under a moon old — guiltless as yet of the
> sty — with no original speck of the amor immunditiae, the
> hereditary failing of the first parent, yet manifest — his voice
> as yet not broken, but something between a childish treble,
> and a grumble — the mild forerunner, or praeludium, of
> a grunt. He must be roasted. I am not ignorant that our
> ancestors ate them seethed, or boiled — but what a sacrifice
> of the exterior tegument! (Lamb 2011, 6)

The active interfaces of incarcerated Bütschli angels attract the attentions of other bodies that circle around them, becoming their satellites. Such compulsions develop complex relationships, which may adopt formations that are evocative of suckling pigs on a sow. It is unclear exactly what draws these droplets together without fusion. One possibility is that it is surface tension-related, where glycerol, a waste product of saponification, lowers surface tension and invites other droplets to move towards each other.

> Without Contraries is no progression. Attraction and
> Repulsion, Reason and Energy, Love and Hater, are
> necessary to Human existence.
> From these contraries spring what the religious call Good
> and Evil. Good is the passive that obeys Reason. Evil is the
> active springing from Energy.
> (Blake 1975, 7–8)

A reduction in surface tension does not explain, however, why droplets are repelled at the boundary interface and, mostly, do not merge[3]. Whatever the nature of the exchanged forces, a complex choreography of attractive and repulsive forces is at work.

3   When surface charge-based systems, like surfactants and salts, are applied
    to the surface of a different species of dynamic oil droplets, they can be
    induced to perform the kinds of physical movements associated with clas-
    sical life cycles. Adding surfactants to the medium provokes droplets to di-
    vide, while adding salt makes individual droplets fuse. By alternating fission
    and fusion, the life cycle can be provoked to continue indefinitely (Mar-
    shall 2013, 7). Yet, this is simply mimicry of processes that operate a much
    higher organisational order than droplet systems, and without an internal
    or environmental system to precipitate these events, these experiments are
    cosmetic simulacra of living things without the unruly agency that is char-
    acteristic of lifelike systems.

Fourteen Liquid Stations of Life:
Primary Behaviours

> Trickster ... is a pore-seeker. He keeps a sharp eye out for
> naturally occurring opportunities and creates the ad hoc
> when they do not occur by themselves. (Hyde and Chabon
> 2010, 47)

Bütschli droplets exhibit an opportunistic spectrum of distinctive types and tendencies. Such characteristics can be thought of as primary behaviours, which possess recognisable, although never exactly repeatable, stories.

09.2.3.2.1

Interfacing

> Moon-milk was very thick, like a kind of cream cheese.
> It formed in the crevices between one scale and the next,
> through the fermentation of various bodies and substances
> of terrestrial origin which had flow up from the prairies
> and forests and lakes, as the Moon sailed over them. It
> was composed chiefly of vegetal juices, tadpoles, bitumen,
> lentils, honey, starch crystals, sturgeon eggs, moulds,
> pollens, gelatinous matter, worms, resins, pepper, mineral
> salts, combustion residue. (Calvino 2002, 6)

While Bütschli angels are attracted to each other, they do not usually fuse when they met. The distribution of water within their bodies can be observed by adding a hydrophilic dye under a fluorescence microscope. Glowing like tiny moons, the indentations of their soap scales can be seen as impact craters over the angel's smooth surface. Using this imaging technique, Bütschli droplets can be seen releasing small jets of fluid into an adjacent body as their interfaces touch, but still, they will not fuse.

EIGHT Life:*Mirroring

Mirror-image identical
Twins. One egg, one sperm,
One zygote, divided
Sharing one complete
Set of genetic markers.

One egg, one sperm.
One being, split in two.

And how many souls?
... might the soul clone itself,
create a perfect imitation
of something yet to be
defined? In this way,
can a reflection be altered?
... do twins begin in the womb?
Or in a better place?
(Hopkins 2008, 1–3)

When a deep split occurs in the generative streams that produce
Bütschli angels, mirrored beings emerge (Golbin et al. 1993). As
in the case of biological systems, where identical twins replicate
a shared fundamental structure, mirrored angels demonstrate
commonalities, like form or behaviour. This is not a superficial
finding but evidences the fundamental role played by propagative systems in the genesis of liquid life.

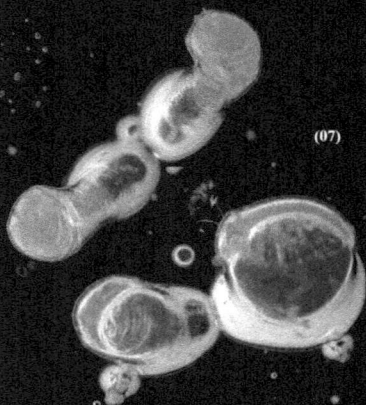

(07)

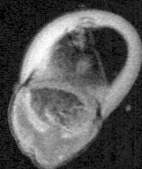

(08)

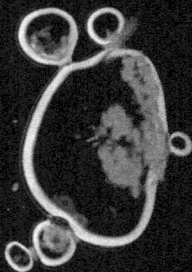

(06)

(05)

NINE Life:*Satellite

Not a few worlds were destroyed by the downfall of a
satellite. The lesser body, ploughing its way, age after age,
through the extremely rarefied but omnipresent cloud of
free atoms in interstellar space, would lose momentum. Its
orbit would contract, at first slowly, then rapidly. It would
set up prodigious tide in the oceans of the larger body, and
drown much of its civilization. Later, through the increasing
stress of the planet's attraction, the great moon would begin
to disintegrate. First it would cast its ocean in a deluge on
men's heads, then its mountains, and the titanic and fiery
fragments of its core. If in none of these manners came
the end of the world then inevitably, though perhaps not
till the latter days of the galaxy, it must come in another
way. The planet's own orbit, fatally contracting, must bring
every world at last so close to its sun that conditions must
pass beyond the limit of life's adaptability, and age by age
all living things must be parched to death and roasted.
(Stapledon 1999, 88)

As large Bütschli angels produce more chemical attractants than
smaller ones, they tend to draw them towards their orbit. Oscillations between the large and small angel bodies, result in tides
of exchange that result in the mutual deposition of skins like
tectonic plates across their active bodies.

09.2.3.2.1.3

TEN Life:*Chain

> I was born and raised in a magic time, in a magic town,
> among magicians. Oh, most everybody else didn't realize
> we lived in that web of magic, connected by silver filaments
> of chance and circumstance. But I knew it all along. When
> I was twelve years old, the world was my magic lantern,
> and by its green spirit glow I saw the past, the present and
> into the future. You probably did too; you just don't recall
> it. See, this is my opinion: we all start out knowing magic.
> We are born with whirlwinds, forest fires, and comets inside
> us. We are born able to sing to birds and read the clouds
> and see our destiny in grains of sand. But then we get the
> magic educated right out of our souls. We get it churched
> out, spanked out, washed out, and combed out ... Because
> the people doing the telling were afraid of our wildness and
> youth, and because the magic we knew made them ashamed
> and sad of what they'd allowed to wither in themselves.
> (McCammon 1992, 2)

Bütschli angels frequently form pulsing chain-like formations that stabilise their collective movements. Those that are weighted down by their residues are rapidly encased in osmotic films. Strung like dew upon a spider silk filament, they pulse and glitter intermittently until they reach thermodynamic equilibrium.

ELEVEN Life:*Propagation

> I opened my eyes — and all the sea was ice-nine. The moist
> green earth was a blue-white pearl. The sky darkened.
> Borasi, the sun, became a sickly yellow ball, tiny and cruel.
> The sky was filled with worms. The worms were tornadoes.
> (Vonnegut 2008, 187)

While Bütschli angels spontaneously arise from the fuzzy realms
of energised chemical fields, they cannot replicate, as their progenitor systems are too primitive to form reproductive structures. Bütschli angels persevere so as long as their generative
systems abide and have no need for progeny, for when they fall,
others relentlessly take their place. The Petri dish base is littered
with angel snow.

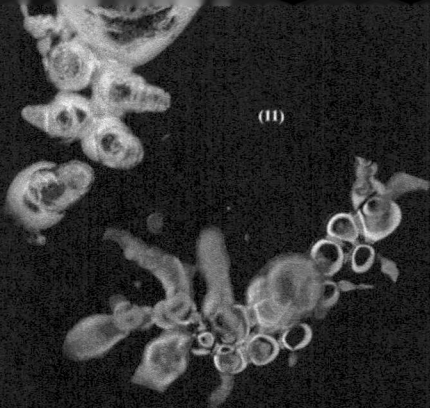
(11)

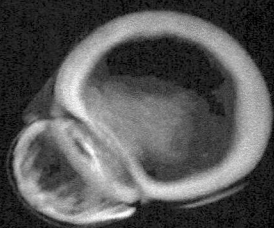
(10)

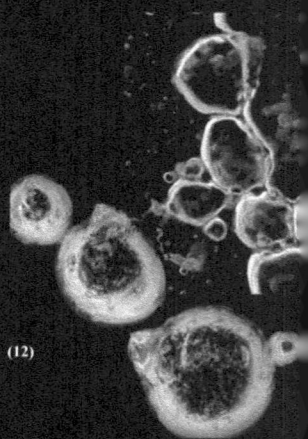
(12)

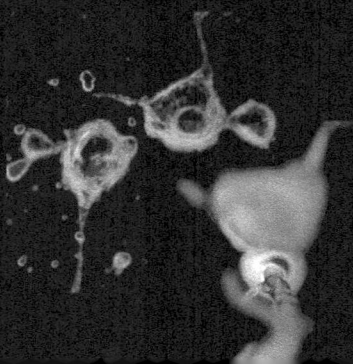
(09)

TWELVE Life:*Persistence

> Movement's folding in on itself is not something the body
> does. It is what bodying is. Movement embodies only itself.
> Movement's making is corporeogenic: becoming-body.
> (Forsythe 2014, 39)

The complexity of Bütschli angels is time limited and takes on
different manifestations across various media. Only when angels replenish their interior metabolism (by feeding) and tend
to their environmental health (waste removal) will they discover
the path towards (relative) persistence.

09.2.3.2.4

THIRTEEN Life:*Sensitivity

> Tiny differences in input could quickly become
> overwhelming differences in output — a phenomenon given
> the name 'sensitive dependence on initial conditions.' In
> weather, for example, this translates into what is only half-
> jokingly known as the Butterfly Effect — the notion that
> a butterfly stirring the air today in Peking can transform
> storm systems next month in New York. (Gleick 1997, 8)

Soft as a mosquito's dance, soap flakes gather on the surface of
Bütschli angels, but may be chaotically amplified to become a
snowstorm of residues. Unlike cellular life, droplet metabolisms
are turned inside out, so their critical exchanges take place at the
interface, with no recourse to interiority, subjectivity, or privacy.
The inner workings of Bütschli angels are therefore transparent,
vulnerable to, and penetrated by the chaos of the world.

FOURTEEN Life:*Fusion

> The Theatre of Cruelty has been created in order to restore
> … a passionate and convulsive conception of life, and it is
> in this sense of violent rigour and extreme condensation of
> scenic elements that the cruelty on which it is based must
> be understood. This cruelty, which will be bloody when
> necessary but not systematically so, can thus be identified
> with a kind of severe moral purity which is not afraid to pay
> life the price it must be paid. (Artaud 2010, 122)

Touching without fusing, Bütschli angels persist until they are
exhausted and lie gently metabolising alongside each other.
Some livelier angels set traps at the tips of crystalline stalks like
predatory insects, waiting for the approach of an unsuspecting
warm metabolism. Then, 'snap', two become one. A chance finding under fluoroscopy reveals a momentary union of two un-
tethered bodies. The apex of a probing droplet blasts fluorescent
liquid, like the spray of a bombardier beetle, into the other. Its
discharge twists like smoke until it evenly diffuses throughout
the recipient droplet. This fusion was only partial and an extraordinary sight that occurs without record and is now just a
memory.

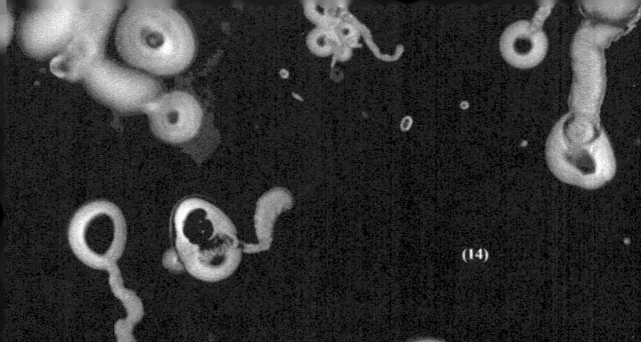

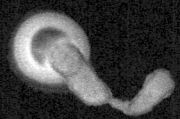

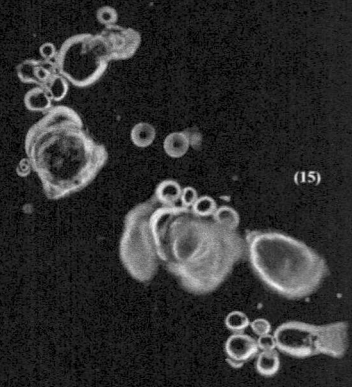

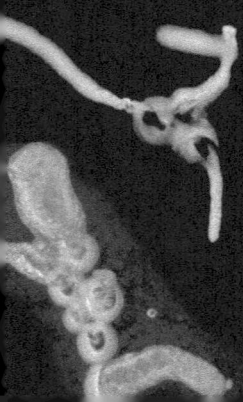

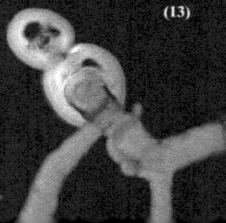

Life: Populations

> Their first terraforming move was to sprinkle the precious
> dirt from their homeland into the planet's atmosphere,
> which carried living seeds from their laboratory
> experiments. After decades, these creeping chemistries went
> 'native' with interesting results. Now slithering scoundrels
> flop, gaping out of the silt and flap tirelessly on the beach
> in an evolutionary race to gain a colonising foothold on the
> hallowed dry land. While the sentinels, who have only just
> evolved their magnificent tri-legs, raise their skinny bodies
> out of the puddles, scream 'no room!' and pick off the
> scoundrels in droves as they flail helplessly, in the effort to
> dry-dirt upgrade. (Armstrong 2018a, 106)

Like weather fronts, Bütschli angels can bring about radical change through events that take place at their interfaces, where highly complex molecular landscapes reach thresholds of transformation, or tipping points, where completely new kinds of molecular patterning, or ordering emerge.

While the source of this creativity is not fully understood, it arises from pre-existing metabolic activity where attractants/ stimulants and inhibitors/repellents respond to each other and produce hyperdynamic, transformative landscapes, which generate coordinated group behaviours such as scattering — the inverse of 'quorum' sensing in bacteria, which recruits other bodies to the signal site (Nealson, Platt and Hastings 1970).

09.2.5

Death: Quiescence

> While we live, we ourselves are inhabited ... our bodies are
> the kitchens were our food is cooked, digested, and then
> burned to cook us. We live until death in a perpetual fever,
> 98.6 degrees Fahrenheit. When at last we are well done, we
> begin to cool, becoming food ourselves. (Logan 2008, 55)

Having danced in the theatre of liquid life, Bütschli angels lie
spent among wreaths of crystalline materials, having almost
consumed their own bodies in the process. Osmotic membranes
snap around their active surfaces like a trap, completing the
chemical act of 'death'.

Death: Regeneration

> I had realized the injustice of society, I wanted first of all
> to cleanse myself, then go beyond its brutal ineptitude. My
> stomach was the seat of that society, but also the place in
> which I was united with all the elements of the earth. It was
> the mirror of the earth, the reflection of which is just as real
> as the person reflected. That mirror — my stomach — had to
> be rid of the thick layers of filth (the accepted formulas) in
> order properly, clearly, and faithfully to reflect the earth; and
> when I say 'the earth,' I mean of course all the earths, stars,
> suns in the sky and on the earth, as well as all the stars, suns,
> and earths of microbes' solar system. (Carrington 1989, 164)

Bütschli droplets may be briefly regenerated when their thick, incarcerating osmotic skins are temporarily broken apart by vigorous agitation. A flicker of life passes through their bodies until the fractures are healed by metabolism, returning the angel to an inert state.

As in the case of living systems, a specific Bütschli angel cannot be restored to its original form once dissipation is quenched from its being. For the angel, this removal from the theatre of liquid life is permanent but living things may be returned into the web of life by slingshotting their decomposed matter back into existing metabolic pathways, where it is assimilated into other bodies. The strange reanimated apparatuses that can perform this function, are the soils.

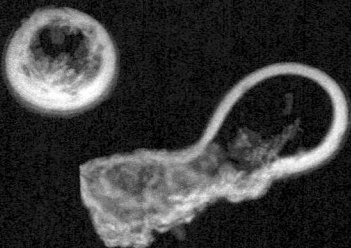
(18)

(19)

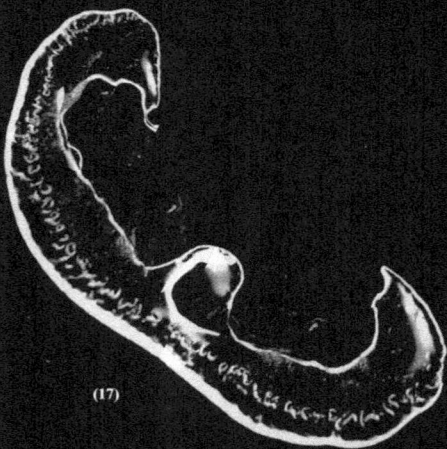
(17)

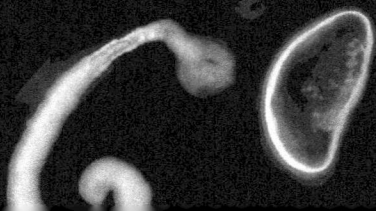
(16)

Bütschli Droplets as Computational Agents

The theory does not make any new hypotheses; it merely suggests that certain well-known physical laws are sufficient to account for many of the facts … This model will be a simplification and an idealization, and consequently a falsification. It is to be hoped that the features retained for discussion are those of greatest importance in the present state of knowledge. (Turing 1952, 37)

Bütschli angels provide a theoretical and applied experimental platform that demonstrates the technological potential of liquid substrates at far-from-equilibrium states, behaving in unusual ways that are difficult to describe through conventional scientific narratives alone. By drawing on design-led agendas (culture, aesthetics, history, language, poetry etc.) alternative explorations are possible that raise different kinds of questions about the nature of 'life', and open up new spaces for investigation.

Even the non-classical behaviours of dynamic droplets defy logical explanation, but fortuitously generate a range of easily visualised outcomes that are also capable of performing useful 'work' and therefore may be readily operationalised as a technological platform, capable of interrogating the principles of liquid life.

While not detailed in this book (Armstrong 2015), 'loose' control systems can be strategically applied to influence the Bütschli system's emergent phenomena, which include: adding various salt solutions to the droplets to produce bodies with dense carbonate surface precipitates, or stimulating and inhibiting movement by adding organic solvents like acetone (Armstrong 2015). Thus, the Bütschli system fulfils the equivalent function of the *bête machine* for liquid life, as it not only embodies a set of ideas but also practically demonstrates them.

09.4

Ontological and (Post)epistemological Issues

> Listen to the forecasts, note what they say and then use
> your own knowledge to refine the details for your own area.
> (Watts 2014, 12)

Responsive bodies in constant flux exceed the capabilities of classical objects, and therefore require a set of terms, metaphorical contexts, and recognisable narratives capable of interrogating our encounters with them. Clues to the kinds of frameworks and metaphors that may be appropriate for this purpose already exist in our concepts of weather (material, systems, lore), oceans (material, systems, lore) and angels (mythology). This is where the language of liquid life begins.

Beyond Classical Categories

The Bütschli system poses a particular challenge to the structuring of knowledge, as it may yet prove to be 'post-epistemological', or uncategorisable in any conventional way (Latour 2013). The implications are for establishing meaningful encounters with its inevitable paradoxes such as — measuring the unmeasurable, valuing the unvaluable and recognising the unknown. Droplets exhibit unique features that are characteristic of non-linear systems, which are not fully resolvable using classical approaches. Their complexity, organisational diversity, extreme environmental responsiveness and intersections with other ontologically distinct systems such as machines, implies their outputs are not only constantly moving physical targets, but also conceptual ones. Consider, for example, Venice in the following terms:

> Life is in a state of oscillation, as heartbeats quell and dead things explode from composts into animated states. Creatures like ichthyosaurs, trilobites, coelacanths, megalodons and ammonites, awaken from fossil beds, to live again. Beings that have been erased from the world's imagination are already forming in wombs, where it is impossible to count the number of limbs and eyes as they perpetually roll in knots of dough-like flesh and blissful embryogenesis. Bodies wander through adaptive fields, digestive juices, and egg sacs, which constantly remodel their bones then explode into dust. Tinged with blue copper-laden blood, the lagoon seems built from thick folds of meniscal flesh, full of heavy metals and other kinds of uncleanliness. It's a place where creatures simultaneously freeze and boil, holding up a mirror to our darkest urges and most grievous ecological atrocities. This realm imagines us extinct. (Armstrong 2019, 97)

It is challenging to view and describe the constantly changing Bütschli system without assimilating it into pre-existing knowledge sets, like the *bête machine*. However, this is exactly what needs to be done if the full potential of this emerging technology is to be fully explored and imagined. Bodies in constant flux are not unknown to us. Their concepts and metaphors reside in the expressions of our encounters with mutable matter like oil slicks, reflections, murmurations, flames, developing embryos, snot, waterfalls, shoals, the weather, and oceans. However, our strong preference for bounded objects that can be 'names' and ultimately controlled, has left the mutable, intangible, inconstant, and transitional aspects of being incompletely characterised and interrogated. Re-engaging the protean aspects of reality may conjure forth qualitatively different kind of encounters with the living realm, which provoke alternative forms of knowledge.

Notating Life

I was struck by the idea of drawing a diagram of my life,
and I knew at the same moment exactly how it was to
be done … I should … speak of a labyrinth … with …
many entrances leading to the interior. These entrances
I call primal acquaintances; each of them is a graphic
symbol of my acquaintance with a person whom I met,
not through other people, but through neighbourhood,
family relationships, school comradeship, mistaken identity,
companionship on travels, or other such hardly numerous
situations. So many primal relationships, so many entrances
to the maze. But since most of them — at least those that
remain in our memory — for their part open up new
acquaintances, relations to new people, after some time they
branch off these corridors (the male may be drawn to the
right, female to the left). Whatever cross connections are
finally established between these systems also depends on
the intertwinements of our path through life. (Benjamin
1999, 614–15)

Dynamic droplets perform on an 'ever-changing stage' (Tschumi 2012, 28) that takes the form of an olive oil field. To provide a
notational map of the Bütschli system, an oceanic ontology was
derived from discrete events that took place during a series of
over 300 experiments. All of these were conducted at room temperature using 3 M sodium hydroxide drops, which were added
by hand to the olive oil field (Armstrong 2015).

At the centre of the map, concentric circles, which are loga-
rithmically spaced to indicate passing time in the system, radi-
ate outwards from an initiating event at the origin. Following
activation, an estimated 90% of chemical activity is completed
within five minutes. While individual droplets may be active for
as long as an hour after their genesis, the greatest diversity of
events is observed during this period. A spiral also emanates

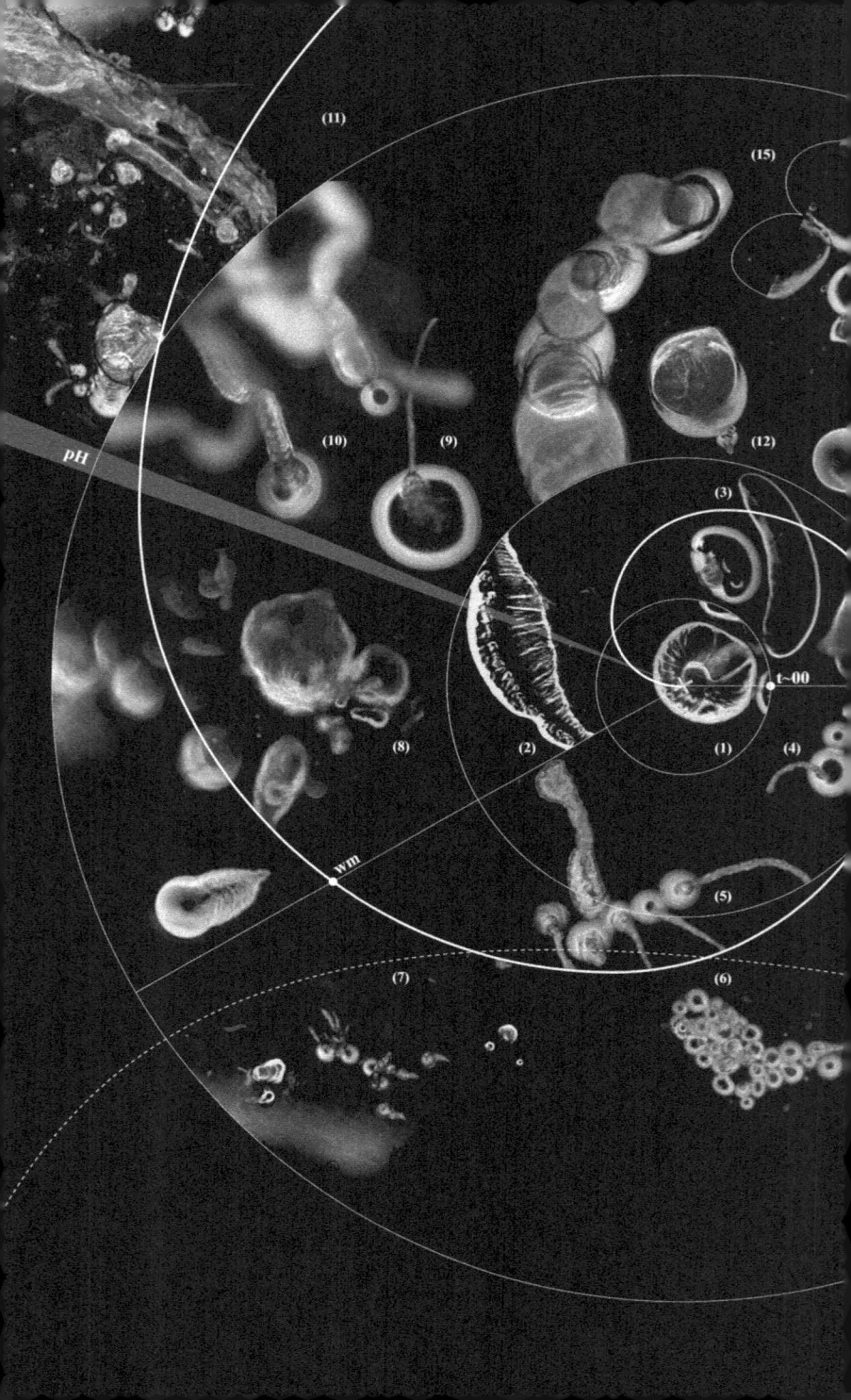

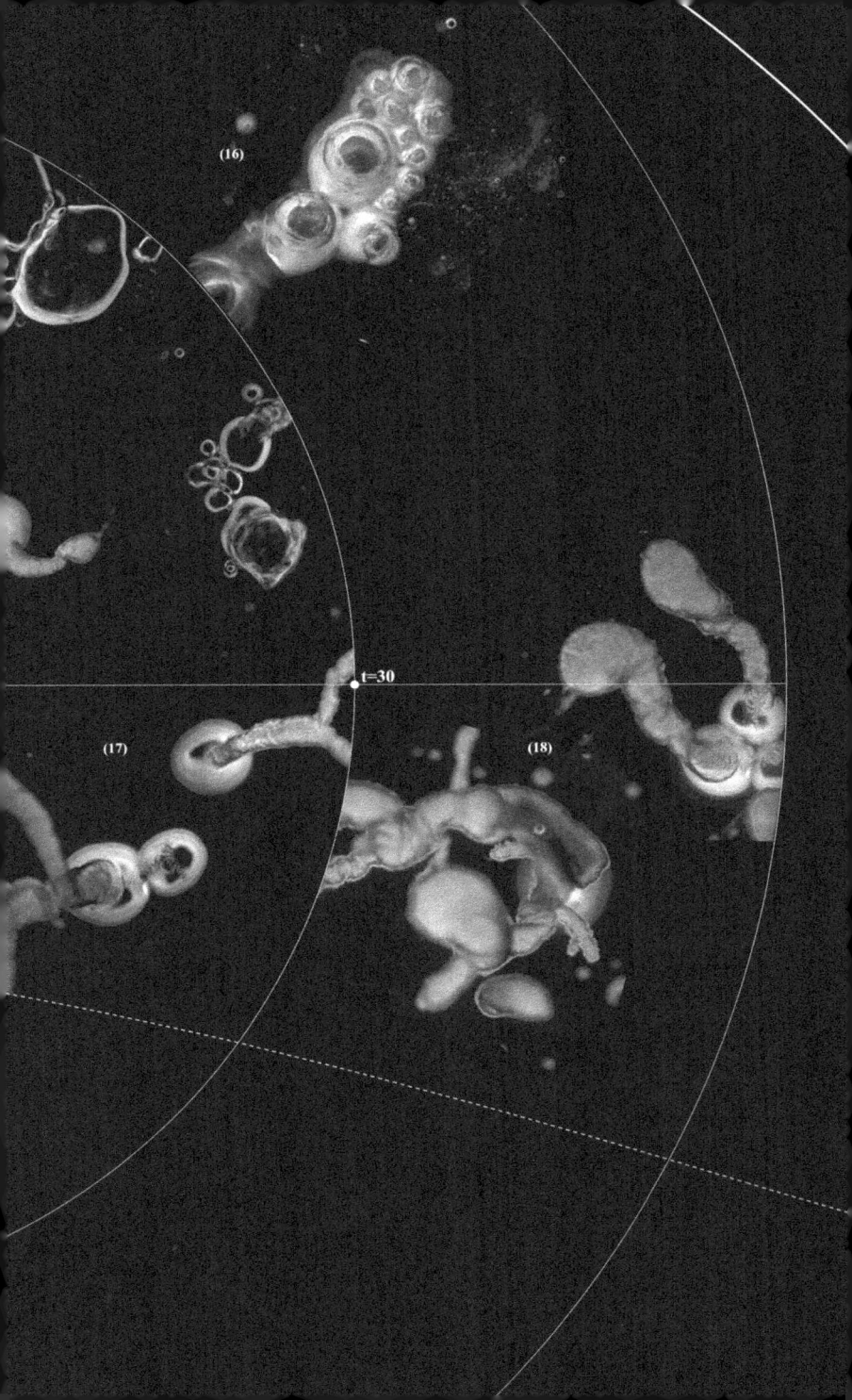

from the origin, which depicts increasing complexity in the events clustered around the start of the reaction, which become less frequent as time unfolds. The various outputs are grouped according to recognisable events or structures, like the 'were-wolf' moment (see section 09.2.3.1.4.2).

Produced by the interactions between actors, the resultant map does not propose a formal classification system, but acts as an avatar of events that are shaped by informal and subjective accounts of the system's possibilities. Since these are open to reinterpretation, the Bütschli system's oceanic ontology may be regarded as a framework for storytelling.

Conclusion: Bütschli Droplets and Liquid Life

And with the hieroglyph of a breath, I wish to recover
an idea of sacred theater. Antonin Artaud, *Le Théâtre de
Séraphin* (Damisch 2002, 200)

Bütschli droplets provide a lifelike model that facilitates discovery of the non-biological, 'living' realm. They reveal surprising encounters that raise questions about the nature of life and the character of lived experiences. Enabling the visualisation and iterative testing of liquid life's concepts, so they can be refined (Armstrong 2015), dynamic droplets draw together the conditions for continual change and provide a cauldron of toolsets that provide insights into the 'adjacent possible' (Kauffman 2008, 64) of the living realm, which is beyond our current capacity to calculate. Constituting a visualisation system and technological platform, it becomes possible to observe how living systems 'could be' if they were composed from alternative modes of organisation than constitutes the biological realm.

The Bütschli system demonstrates that liquid life is ebullient and extends beyond its apparent boundaries to excoriate its niches and neighbours with tangible effects. This being-in-the-world (Wheeler 2011) is characterised by non-linear systems like dissipative structures, which combine fluidity with the transformational repertoire of matter, to mount mischievous material resistance against entropic forces.

Like a waterfall whose journey to the ground has, so far, been prevented by the collisions it has encountered on the way, liquid life finds a way to slingshot around the rock face through the metabolisms (digestion, anabolism, assimilation) of other living bodies and agents of strategic decay like the thanatobiome and necrobiome (catabolism, composting), so that it may fall again in other ways. This metabolic waterfall 'elevator' is a metaphor for the processes that underpin the 3.5-billion-year unbroken legacy of modern biology. It highlights an oft-neglected truth — that life is only possible when it is deeply entangled with the rich metabolisms of death.

Part VI

TRANSITIONING

ANGELS

Rolf Hughes constructs an 'angelology'
of language through the transformative
invocations of prose poetry, summoning
fourteen angels and six (non)definitions of
circus, as part of the transition from life to
death.

> Every visible thing in this world is put in
> the charge of an angel. (Chase 2002, 14)

The Letting Go
(Fourteen Angels)

Preface

> 'I tell you that they have reinvented microbes
> in order to impose a new idea of god.'
>
> — Antonin Artaud, *To Have Done with the Judgement of God*

As above, so below;
sun cleft
bitter slope
black coal
drum burst
rhythm
red sun
black horse
dawn crag
blacksmith
six horseshoes
tossed across
earth & wood
wind & bone
earth & bone
iron & blood
fire & ash
and, finally,
a petal or two
— ready for you.
As this world is not fully formed, we have only a small idea of
its scope.

*

1. On the futility of defining angels

The angel is concerned with transforming the world into magnificence. It transcends the narrow and the obscure, yet inhabits paradox, being both disembodied and integrated into the core of our being.

This means the angel is a manifestation of inner oscillation. Oscillation opens up the world. It is the basis of the dissemination of light.

The angel seeks only to sustain a gaze on each form of existence — this alone keeps it in a state of grace.

The angel lies down with the leper, shares the heat of its heart, yet looks aside when life leaks away. Challenged, it resorts to a language of falling.

I fall by means of candlelight
I fall in thrumming yards
I fall in brackish waters
I fall on open hearts.

If you dissect an angel, you will find no rules that can be transcribed; you will discover, instead, that the purest laws are now made manifest on your bloodied hands.

*

2. The breath before liquid life

breeze
whispering world
opaque, glimmering, crepuscular thoughts

mirror mist, sunbeam
deep green tides

city of coral
fragments waving

grey scaffold
shells, sponge
seaweed
populations of polyps
secret affinities
twilight

It's not about you, she says.

It is about we.

*

First definition of circus

Think of the circus as a watering place, a wellspring.

A ghost walk on which doors appear closed without being so.
Walls revealed to yield at sprung rhythms.

A *rite de passage* where the sick and the afflicted confront the
potentialities of their recovery.

A dream house made of canvas and wax.

A maze. A market. A city. A sewer.

Now raise your right hoof.
Feel the equilibrium about to be cleaved by your coming stum-
bling into this world.

*

3. A dialogue of clowns

Here comes mischief!

[LAUGHTER]

Horizontal *Capitano* versus
Vertical *Servetta!*
Dialoguing about the afterlife!
[LAUGHTER]
Red-faced, white-faced mischief!
Sssh, listen!

The door is locked.
The key elsewhere.
There's a stone in my shoe.

Fetch it, he says.
The key, fetch it!
Hobble, hobble…
What about me blister, mister?
Just fetch it!
The afterlife awaits!

Forget it, is what I said.
Forget about me fetching it.
The key is elsewhere
The door remains locked.
Plus, there's a stone in my shoe
Didn't you hear?
[*Turns to face audience*].
I got a bleedin' blister!

[LAUGHTER]

The afterlife? The after *this* life?
[PAUSE]

Don't make me laugh!

[*UPROARIOUS LAUGHTER. EXEUNT TO TRUMPET SERANADE*]

*

4. *What but a soul?*

> *What but a soul could have the wit*
> *To build me up for sin so fit?*
> *So architects do square and hew*
> *Green trees that in the forest grew.*

— Andrew Marvell, 'A Dialogue Between the Soul and the Body'

Let me suggest you climb a tree and cut.
The branches will take your weight and bounce you gently,
sensually.

So let me suggest you now cut some more.
Relish your suspension between earth and sky —
your soul snarling in the saw's hungry maw,
your skeleton bolted together in its sack.

> *Lay your head where my heart used to be*
> *Hold the earth above me*
> *Lay down in the green grass*
> *Remember when you loved me*

Nerves, arteries, veins. Arboreal chain. All in vain.

> *Stand in the shade of me*
> *Things are now made of me.*[1]

1   Italicised lines from 'Green Grass' by Tom Waits. Songwriters: Kathleen
    Brennan/Thomas Alan Waits. 'Green Grass' lyrics © Peer Music Publishing.

Cut.
Me.
Down!

*

Second definition of circus

Circus is built upon materials singularly resistant to the instruments of human control. Spade, drill, truncheon, club. It is not uncommon for stepladders to plunge thirty metres into aerial emptiness.

When I am in that darkness, I know nothing of anything human.

I do remember that previous darkness in which I see everything (and then nothing), that darkness that comes from within and that so delights me that I cannot speak of it.

*

5. Proto life incantation

> *That is not dead which can eternal lie,*
> *And with strange aeons even death may die.*

— H.P. Lovecraft, 'The Nameless City', January 1921

They appear, these malaks, angels, or jinn, as if in a clouded mirror, by the loosed ones tempestuously, storming successively, the scatterers scattering, several severing, hurling the remaining to bond or repel; by those that out plug violently, or draw out gently; by those that float serenely, those that outstrip suddenly; by those that enter a flat mirror world, averse to perspective and all the errors of your penetrating gaze. The lake of fire descends, you abandon your neutrality; we loiter with intent, eventually peering up through our three eyes for

the judgement of the cap that fits with a snap and extinguishes
all light.

*

Third definition of circus

The standing limb/the falling limb: a choreography of
(dis)equilibrium.

No, lift not that leg without lowering an arm, turning your
head, or arching your back; every movement solicits a compen-
satory movement. By such means do we safeguard the asymmetrical trust and respect that sustains the collective.

Once set in motion, we learn an art of decisions, summoning
all that is outside expression to illuminate our current embodied geographies of flotsam and flow, this being another aspect
to *a practice of oscillation.*

*

6. On naming the membrane

> *Through the spoken Word we receive fire and light, by*
> *which we are made new and different, and by which a*
> *new judgment, new sensations, new drives arise in us.*

> — Martin Luther, *Lectures on Galatians*

In the beginning, before life,
there were *words*;
possessed of propulsion,
rebounding, but not yet accountable;
they occupied the blank spots
hitherto reserved for the divine;
they endowed life with a language of life,

a membrane against each storm of atoms.

*

Fourth definition of circus

For a thought to become circus, it must expose a higher degree of *inner oscillation* than the surrounding materials, movements, spaces, artefacts. This oscillation is found between the *abject* and the *transcendental,* between *chance* and *the sublime.* For every fall, a potential hook.

> I understand now, imagining to myself the momentum of the fall, that nothing exists in the world without meeting a hook. (Bataille 1977, 42)

It is why the circus artist is the one whose greatest achievements are all located *outside* the body, under conditions that can never be repeated, knitting together as they do realms such as fall, hook, flesh, and dust, law, and light,these being tricks that not only create the illusion of 'saving' us, but halt, momentarily, our slide offstage.

*

7. Carnival of the undefinable

The angel is drawn to certain sites. An ocean harbouring in-grown volcanoes once known as the island's multiple eyes, but today hollowed and lacklustre (occasionally, in their manifold furrows, the angel may glimpse flashes of defiance). A robust cage lowered into the saltwater lagoon, mounds of swollen flesh slowly rippling, then parting as sunken eyes survey their new home. The angel will toss live rabbits and hens which are shredded in seconds, gobbling guts and bones alike, sending showers of sparks from the iron bars.

Such sites provide excellent opportunities for trapping unwary jinns.

To have unloosed the angel's soft skin, pressed my lips to its heat until rising delight subsides in sighs, served choice meats from calfskin platters, hands encased in the finest, blood-mottled gloves — all this counts for nothing in the inferno of fury to which an ensnared angel invariably brings itself.

And so we wait, malak clinging to a rock gnawed by the ocean, drawing light and energy landscapes, folding a trick back into itself, a perfectly purposeful accident, a ring dropped into a lagoon to summon crustaceans to the marriage of sea and land.

Yes, here they come — white-lipped barnacles, sucking on effervescent salt blooms, forming water islands, liquid naming rituals, subjecting the metaphors of the machine to saline jaws until they rust-crumble, diffusing orange cloud-showers of iron nutrients, the back end of something becoming the front end of something else — Cambrian explosion — origin of life, farting pantomime horse, masked stranger — a carnival of the undefinable.

*

Fifth definition of circus

> *Angels can fly because they take can themselves*
> *lightly. […] Satan fell by the force of gravity.*

— G.K. Chesterton, *Orthodoxy*

A retired clown is giving advice to an enthusiastic young student.

'We should not connive in the construction of our own abject formats, the surface currents we generate, nor run a ruler over depth and flow while our thoughts flit haphazardly from rock to sky then plunge abruptly towards uncharted oceanic depths, the source of our peerless intuition, our bottomless rage. We create a ladder to another world by means of interfaces and incubators. By liquidating situations, we express our resistance to *stasis*.'

The student (an ageing trickster) remains patient, having already converted millennia of ambition into stone.

*

8. Reflection on polyrhythms

We are no longer equipped to experience our experiences.

The pace of one world seems increasingly incompatible with the pace of another.

A storm roils up the estuary. Lightning strikes the cranes. The pylons crash in an eruption of showering electric sparks — a birthing of angels.

It is announced over the site megaphone that each accident of weather is, in fact, a fine opportunity for repurposing the self.

*

Final definition of circus

At the end of the day ... at the end of the day ... strictly speaking ... and so therefore ... it is my honour ... when all is said and done ... without whom ... *saucy, saucy!* ... and with that in mind ... none of this would have been possible ... you have to laugh ... so let the show —

*

9–14. The letting go

> *In a moment, in the twinkling of an eye, at the last*
> *trump: for the trumpet shall sound, and the dead shall*
> *be raised incorruptible, and we shall be changed.*

— 1 Cor 15:52

To imagine circus is to slip the body from its moorings.

I dream of performing circus in storm and gale alike, roped to a creaking rig in Dogger, watched only by stars, sea spray, and the occasional incurious gull. I can fly, balance, soar, spin, and fall.

Towards dawn, I am in the company of an angel, its ribs torn asunder, its exposed innards heaving under sea spray. The angel tells me not to fear.

A helicopter arrives to drop provisions. I display gratitude. Unclip. Act casual. No angel here! I wave from my churning landscape. Thumbs up from pilot as she lifts away. I will become the hunger artist. It is a straight line down to the waves.

I write an essay on the impossibility of angels rotting. My body flexes, my arms move constantly over the page, trying to avoid repetition. Through writing, I leave all that has been and all that will be and inhabit solely the moment of now, a moment that contains all times at once. The ink behaves strangely in this climate. Fluid life. Dark blue lake. Oozing tentacles.

I write a treatise on the impossibility of angels performing acrobatics; their movements would be entirely without artistic merit since, lacking friction, they would merely float like puffy astronauts, or bloated bodies brought to the beach from a tsunami, tumbling slowly in the tide.

I write a poem about the threads in the night sky, long, and narrow, with which we bind each other, until our bandages become a seeping, weeping, luminous web, in which we are enmeshed.

On waking, I see the angel has added a verse:

I fold my skin over yours
You roll your skin around mine
And there we stay, unseeing and unseen —
strange flower of forever flesh,
forever bursting to bud.

But every day the drop, I say …
Every day —
Fall never —

[Pause]

Snap! laughs the angel.

One morning, far away and long ago, while straddling a low, greasy wharf by a quay at the extremity of a canal, my long legs on each side down to the water, which had become black with stagnation, the black water yielding continually, letting my thoughts sink into soft vacancy, a faint scent of oranges and wood smoke winnowing over the stench of putrefaction, I saw you, tumbling across the sky, a possible pivot in this new world of rotation and churn; I would have gripped you as you neared, held tight until we hinged and fused, but you were already gliding to other co-ordinates, auto-smiling through the dense weather — our fingers almost touching, but trailing further and further away, plucked from their knuckles, pointing elsewhere, until — matchsticks in a storm — gone.

The angel shows me how to take up a deathless position and wait. The waking waiting tedious as scientific method. Survival memories in a black hole. Light our currency. Black light. Sunless, dappled twilight captured on your pupil.

Drift.

That was the moment we realised we did not need kings, queens, presidents, nor gods. Nor did we need permissions, categories, or constraints that were not of our own choosing. We did not even need a guide.

And so we stood, facing each other. Sack of lined flesh. Angel.

Waiting.

What we discovered is something quite remarkable.

When we create conditions for care and attention, the world enters.

The world enters and it goes from one to the other, slyly unmasking us.

It waits until we are open and attentive, then disrobes in turn.

The room's molecules start whispering — we lean forward to listen. They curl around us, draw us closer together.

Closer.

Closer still.

The world is alive.

In time, the human body forgets it belongs to the circus and starts to seep and drip over the edges of the mattress. Like mercury it rolls across the floor, a shiny glob of reflected candlelight, rigging, wheels, stuffed animals. As precise as a bead of sweat descending the rope artist's spine, it slips under the door and towards the motionless waves that surround the platform.

I watch it until it stops. Flesh becoming angel. Word made static.

The trickster returns with a back flip.
I would dig a grave, but I lack a spade!
He laughs like a cartoon villain caught in a drain.

Winter. The body now a mere 21 grams; it skims the sparkling crust of snow on the frozen sea, its salts carving indecipherable runes — melting, it becomes water, steam, mirror mist.

Inside the mirror, rising steadily, a black, hot air balloon drifts towards a hole in the sky. We dive headlong into the silver pool and grip the lifting basket.

This is what we seek out, that place, that here, and only here, where we can be our own, irreconcilably entangled selves — fingers clutching the weave of it all, hanging, affirm-ing, ascending …

then, finally

… the letting go.

SIGNS

In a visual essay that combines text and drawings, Simone Ferracina interrogates liquidity as a technological and metaphorical paradigm for design and the choreography of space.

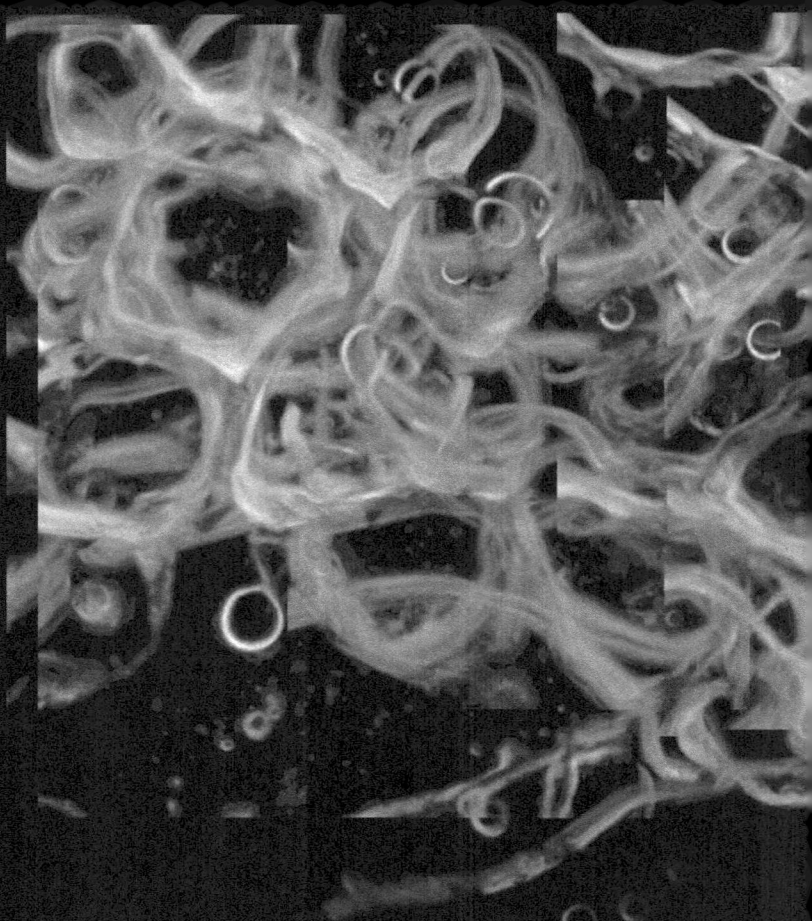

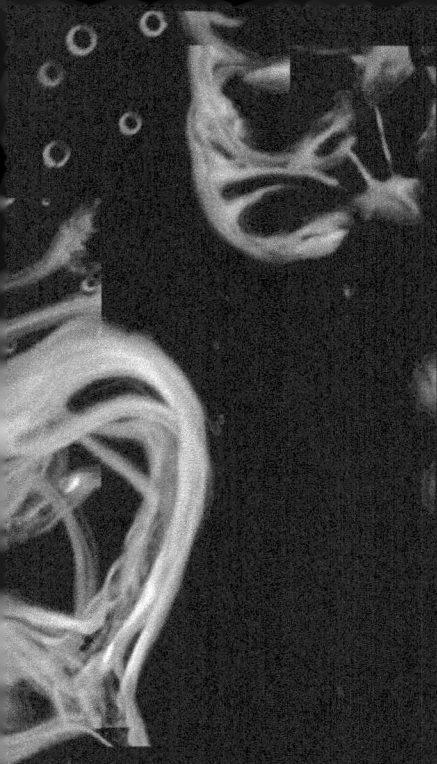

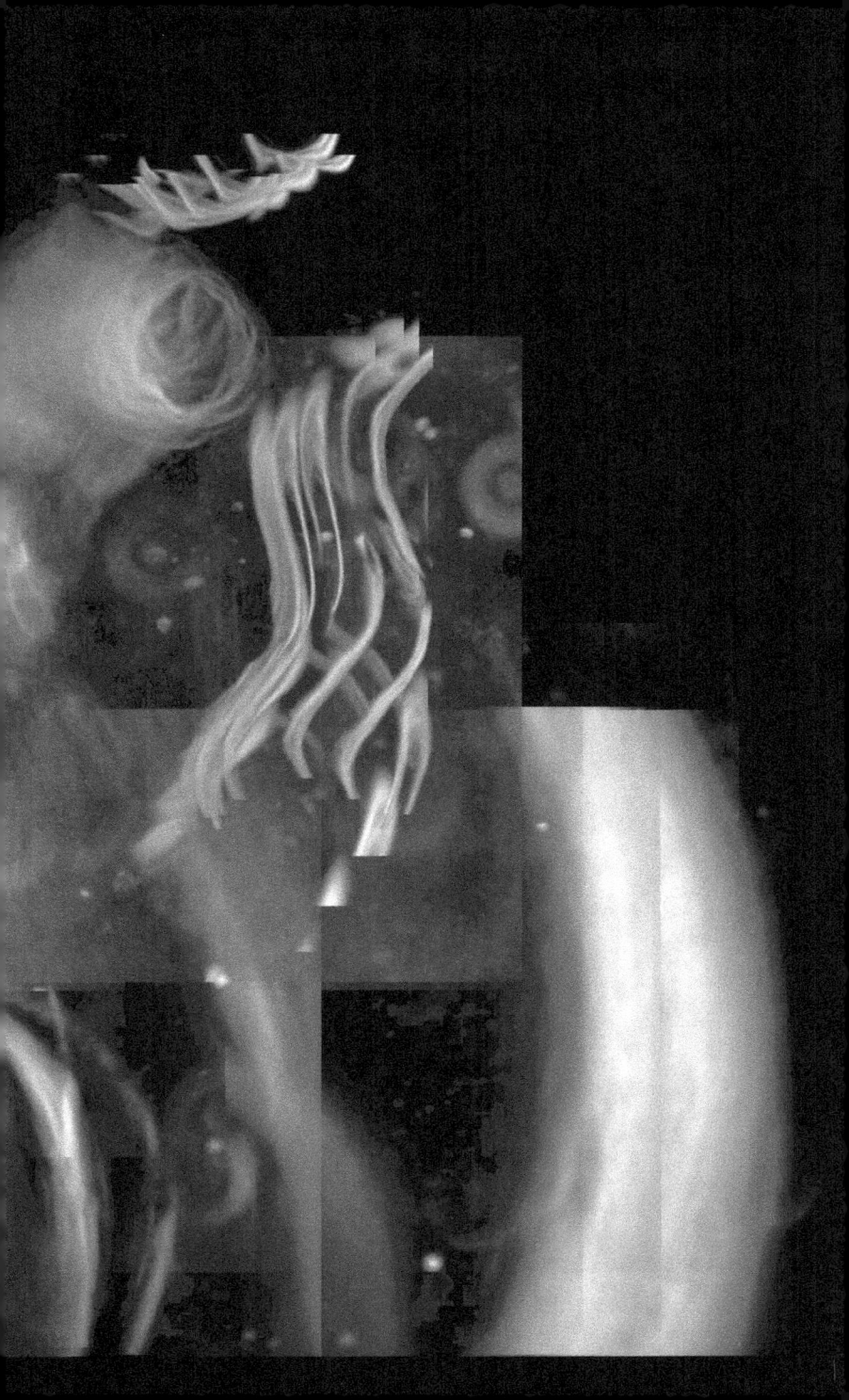

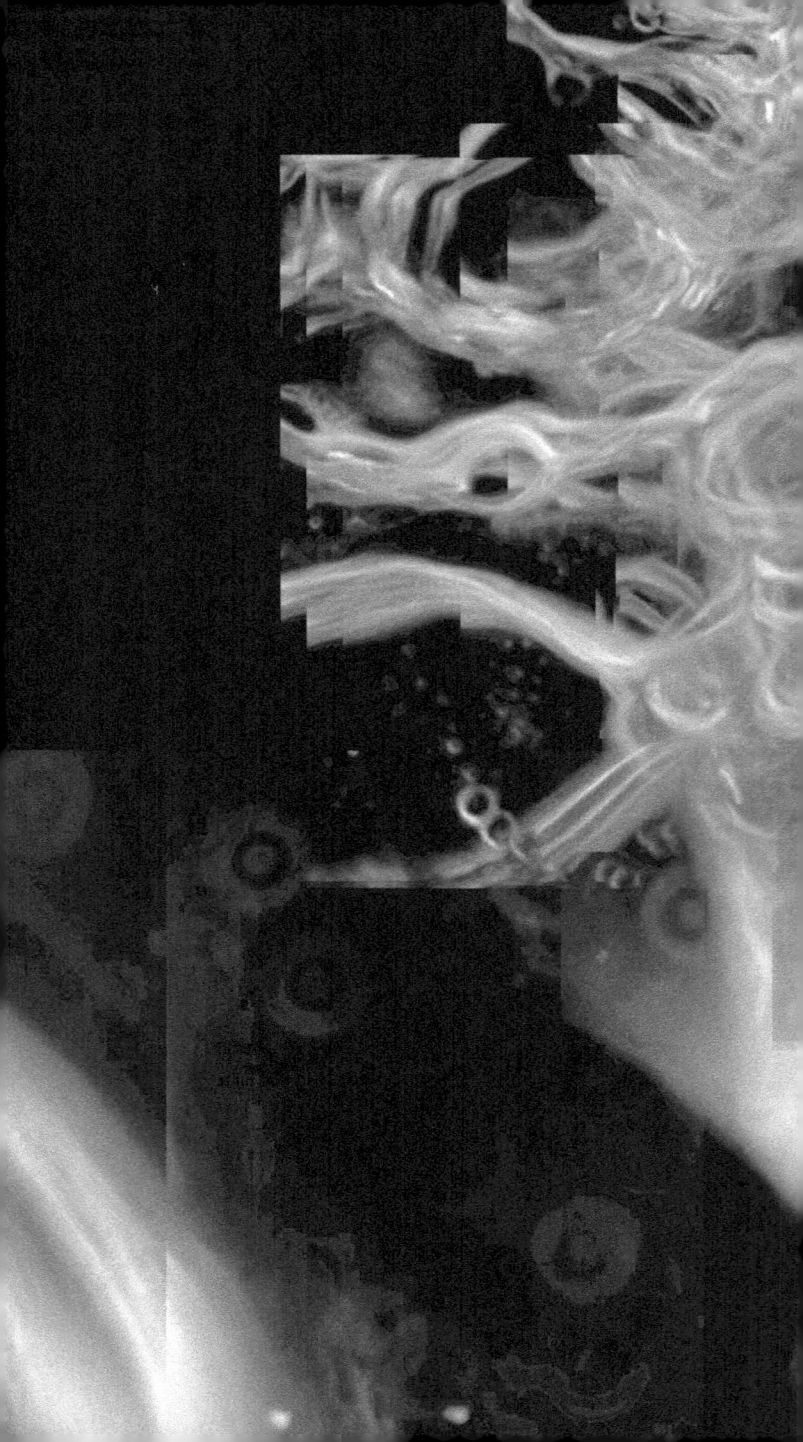

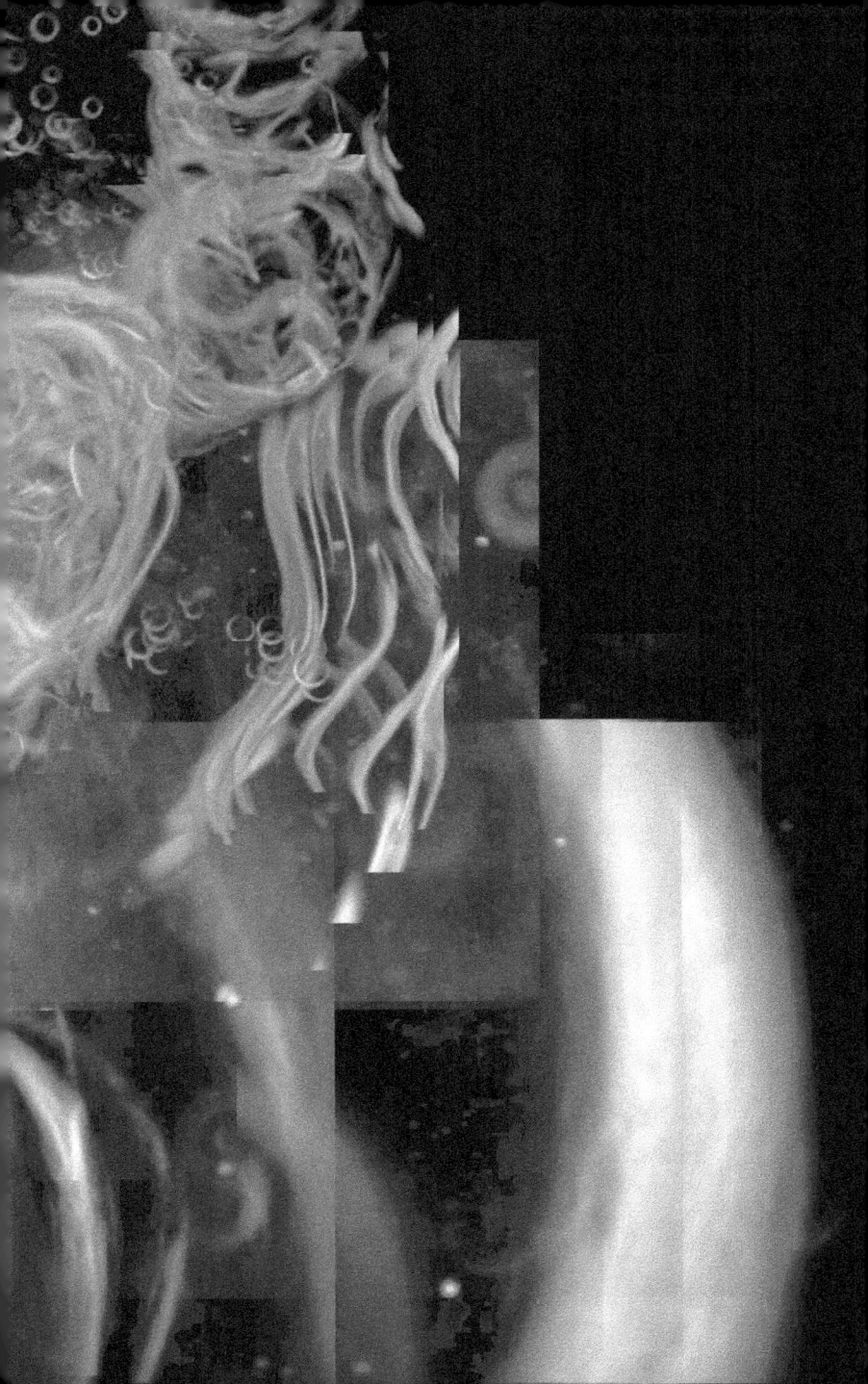

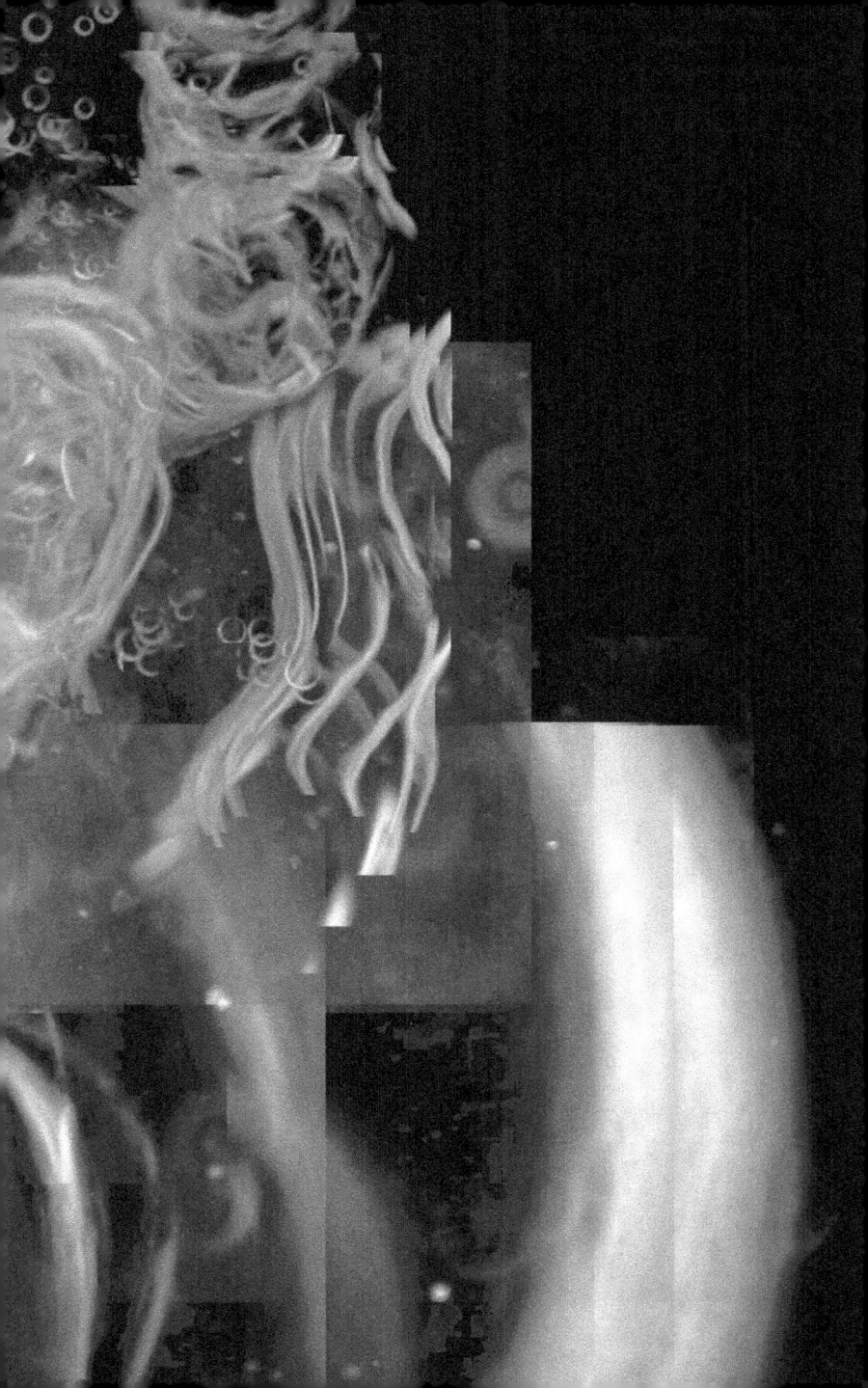

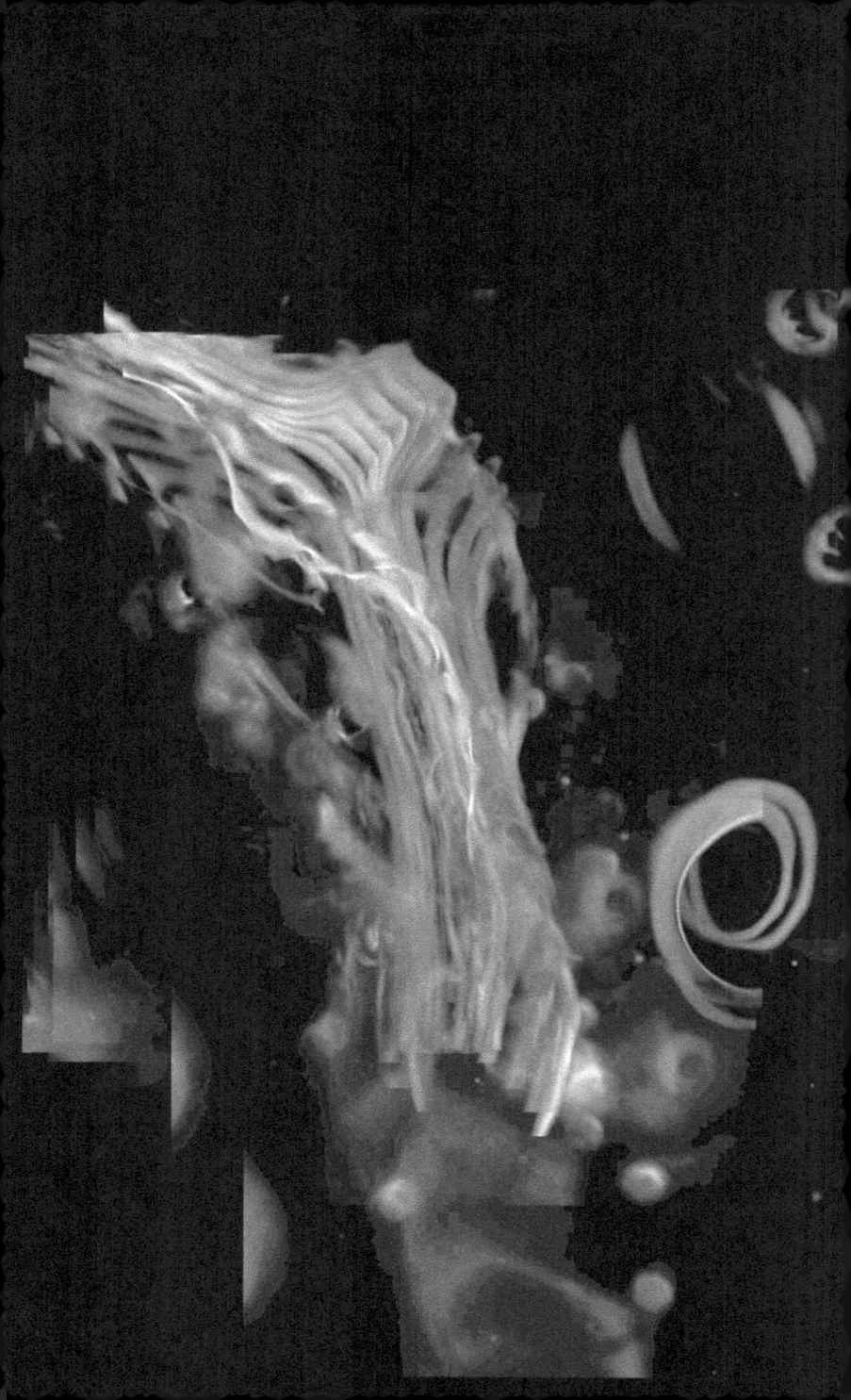

Liquid Notations:
A Common Language of Transitions

Parallel stories begin to unfold. In and between them, across notations and trajectories, our characters (the point, the drop-let, the trace, weather, matter, spacetime, etc.) roam an ecology of differences, tensions, jumps, contradictions, experimentation, and hope. Arguments develop transversally, defying the fifth postulate.

*

> Our effluents are inextricably blended. We can no longer enclose a piece of land. This could be done only in the old space that was easily mapped. We no longer live there. We haunt a topological space without distances, rather than the old Euclidean or Cartesian expanse that could be located metrically by a network of coordinates. Our global techniques, world objects, and communications that reach even beyond the solar system have created a totally different space of proximities and continuities that is difficult to cut up. The Rousseauian plots of land disappear in this typology without distances and measures. (Serres 2010, 67)

Objects melt and disperse, yet they remain intact and intercon-nected. They are real yet paradoxical, structured yet ungrasp-able, immanent yet withdrawn. Their boundaries shift out of focus as soon as we attempt to control and define them. Signs no longer guide us towards increased semiotic resolution and transparency, but into dampness, uncertainty, and abjection. Signifiers float on the surface of oceans and pile up in malo-dourous heaps of garbage. Pollution translates an animal tech-nology of appropriation (the marking of one's territory) into a pervasive planetary language, a geological cry that is as insidi-ous and destructive as it is slippery, muted, and patient. We re-

gress into analphabetic ignorance, and sink in the quicksand of our own footprints — in the toxic sludge that periodically resurfaces; oozing and bubbling across uncannily autonomous and hypercomplex bodies; between golden teeth, microplastics, and plutonium.

Drawing — a form of pollution — remains strangely unfazed by the emergent liquidity and unpredictability of the anthropogenic trace, clinging to mathematics and its presumed ability to order, cleanse, scale, measure, compute, and name. The modern illusion of a linear, unmodulated translation between intentions and outputs, strengthened by increasingly precise modes of digital and robotic manufacturing, dismisses (forgets) the hybrid ecologies and monstrous depths gurgling beneath and beyond.

*

… Behold me — I am a Line. The longest in Lineland, over six inches of Space — ' 'Of Length,' I ventured to suggest. 'Fool,' said he, 'Space is Length. Interrupt me again, and I have done.' (Abbott 1992, 71)

Points and lines are linked and combined, overlapped, extended, plotted, interlaced, programmed, stretched, and interrupted. They generate all manner of paths and incisions: shapes, figures, fields, surfaces, maps, spot elevations, meshes, vertices, vectors, edges, and blobs. Whatever the output, the method, or the drawing apparatus, they assert and declare an identity, a distance, a set of coordinates; they identify beings and fix them into precise hierarchies and spatial relations; they articulate potentialities extruded through sets of localised desires, ambitions, and intentions.

*

The point is motionless and inert. As soon as it appears, it sprouts invisible roots that anchor it to the sheet of paper, hindering movement. It is static, forbearing, and silent — like a seed sealed

in a moisture-proof container and stored in the cool darkness of a fridge. It ends sentences and inhibits further development. It stands still. No growth, no individuation, no becoming. The point simply exists. In a sense, it has always existed.

The line is, instead, animate and dynamic. It emerges progressively and develops alongside currents. It is vector and trail, arrow and gust of wind. It travels across durations and is woven within the material fabrics of the world, carried by the turbulent waters of life itself.

Or so we are told.

∗

Not all lines are generated dynamically. A line can be an ocular/pointillist affair: a sequence of points standing adjacent to one another, in orderly files. Connecting the dots — melting them into lines — is the human being, sole agency in a realm of fixed and pixelated geometries.

A line is also the representation of an extension in space, between A and B; a distance and measure; the edge of the table, the height of the Great Wall of China, the path between me and you. A descriptive mark, it tames environments through the simplifying violence of abstraction (from the Latin *abstrahere,* to drag away, to detach).

Out walk the mountain's vibrations — its forests, geological tremors, flourishing soils, bacteria, foxes, and mycelial tapestries — replaced by contours and property lines, fences and walls, Euclid, Descartes, and Viollet-le-Duc.

∗

A line translates by subtraction and reduction, but also claims, captures, annexes. It operates through chains of exclusion and re-inclusion; embracing and rejecting, sampling, and archiving. A line is finite; it is a segment (from *secare,* to cut): a choice, a tear. It strips matter of contextual agency while culturalising it by transcription, rendering it into discrete graphic units to which straightforward meanings and associations of use can be assigned. A line has a beginning and an end, a thickness, a colour, a length. It folds into perimeters and eats its own tail, like the *ouroboros* — not to symbolise introspection and circularity, but to enclose land. To draw a line is to invent a parallel world; but also to appropriate, to endow with purpose, to command.

> God, when he gave the world in common to all mankind, commanded man also to labour, and the penury of his condition required it of him. God and his reason commanded him to subdue the Earth, i.e. improve it for the benefit of Life, and therein lay out something upon it that was his own, his labour. (Locke 1976, 14)

The benefit of Life (capitalised L). But whose life?

*

> Property is marked, just as the step leaves its imprint … In short, either proper means appropriated and consequently dirty or proper implies really neat and therefore without an owner. Come over here, to this clean spot; you may, because it obviously welcomes you. When you leave, it will be yours because you will have made it dirty. (Serres 2010, 3–4)

Drawing begins with a blank sheet of paper or wax tablet — with a *tabula rasa*. The first appropriation is not the intentional mark traced on the sand with a stick, but the invention of the beach-as-canvas; the reductive force that flattens a volumetric environment into mere writing surface, or plot. A *rasura* prepares (pre-processes) nature for human appropriation and intervention. It chews it into submission, grinding and blending it until difference gives way to an amorphous and obedient soup. Prehistoric eyes, noses, ears, and mouths fuse into a faceless, solid lump: a background; a white-walled room within which collections can be archived, stored, and exhibited. Words are scraped off so that other words may be written and read. But whose words?

*

> Without a master, one cannot be cleaned. Purification,
> whether by fire or by the word, by baptism or by death,
> requires submission to the law. (Laporte 2002, 1)

Purity is coextensive with culture and cannot be naturalised. It
is endowed, assigned, granted — never given, found, or discovered. (Scanlan 2005, 66) Appropriation (territorial, cultural)
begins precisely with the *ability* to make identifiable, lasting
marks; with a clearing in the forest; with the invention of purity; with blankness as a figure of potentiality. Yet the blank page
does not channel the possibility to write without indexing, with
at least equal intensity, a proclivity for clarity. A demand for legibility is built into the urge to write. Writing is, after all, a plea to
be read; a social enterprise; a technology for making shareable
traces (archives, discourses, laws, and so forth).

A drawing or text discloses reality in its essential forms and
purest features — as it appears in the eyes of a god, or of a king.
Not *filthy vision* (the forest and its competing sensual stimuli,
or the animal *Umwelt*), but pure vision: seeing through the gaze
of the social other.

Now, could liquidity help us decouple reading from writing,
ma(r)king from the normative violence/glory it invokes and
imposes? Could it confuse and dissolve the cosmetic make-up
of our societies, precipitating fluid value systems and stranger
(less stable) political and ecological assemblages?

As a metaphor and project, liquidity is on the move — plastic and protean, tentative and fearless. Liquid scores drift and
drip across medium and message, actor and stage, pond and
pebble. Their interpretation remains partial, negotiable, and
contingent. Could the 'principle of legibility' (purification precedes history) be overturned? Could contrast and lucidity be
surrendered in exchange for a common language of transitions?

*

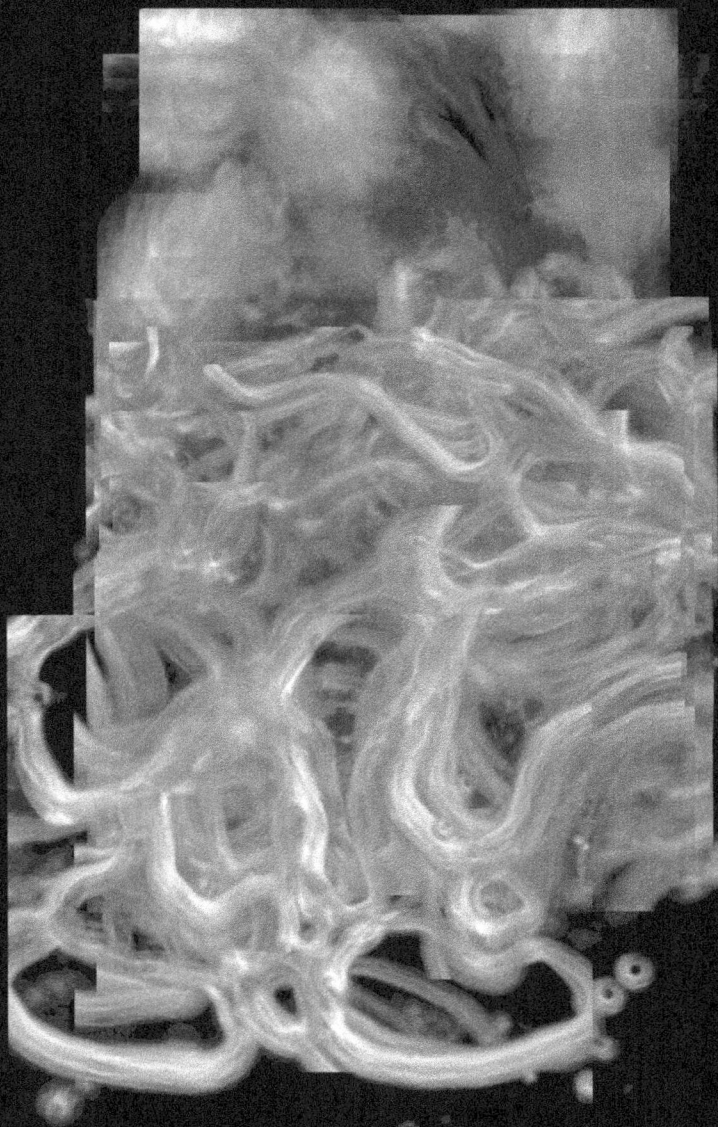

The author, like Narcissus, admires his own reflection on the surface of the drawing. Yet, the pool resists legibility: a passing boat leaves no lasting ripples, and a fallen leaf will keep moving, cradled by the currents. To draw with liquids one has to forget the complicity of canvases and pencils, figure and ground; to forgo the control (and feedback) implicit in their dance. Agents and patients touch and embrace like oil and alkali in a liquid medium, giving rise to dynamic chemical behaviours, self-assembling agglomerations and co-evolutionary designs. The drawing becomes a vibrant and moving agency; an authorial force in its own right. Within it, there are no fixed recipes or standard scripts. Characters continually swap roles, blend, mix, and metamorphose.

*

> If there is no background — no neutral, peripheral stage
> set of weather, but rather a very visible, highly monitored,
> publicly debated climate — then there is no foreground.
> Foregrounds need backgrounds to exist. So the strange
> effect of dragging weather phenomena into the foreground
> as part of our awareness of global warming has been the
> gradual realization that there is no foreground! (Morton
> 2013, 104)

The contrasting black and white figures fail to reproduce reliable semiotic conditions, eluding clear-cut distinctions between background and foreground, canvas and ink. Rather, these fluid masses undergo soft modifications and exchanges in three dimensions, propelling themselves chemically until nothing is left but inert glycerine formations. Protocells partake in elaborate autonomous behaviours and temporal notations, of which we understand very little. Wet traces replace signs with semi-living interfaces, concentrations, intensities, gradients, and depositions.

*

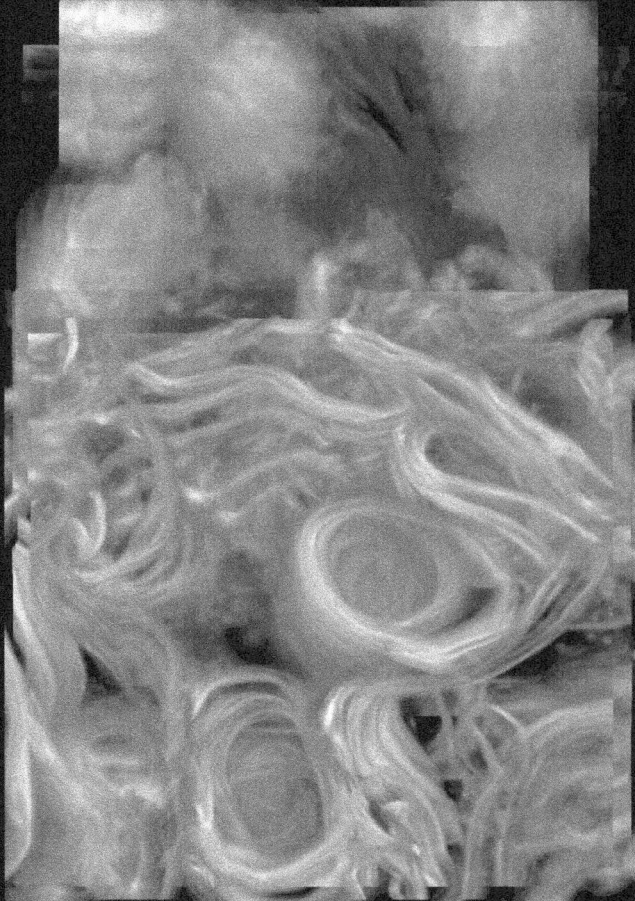

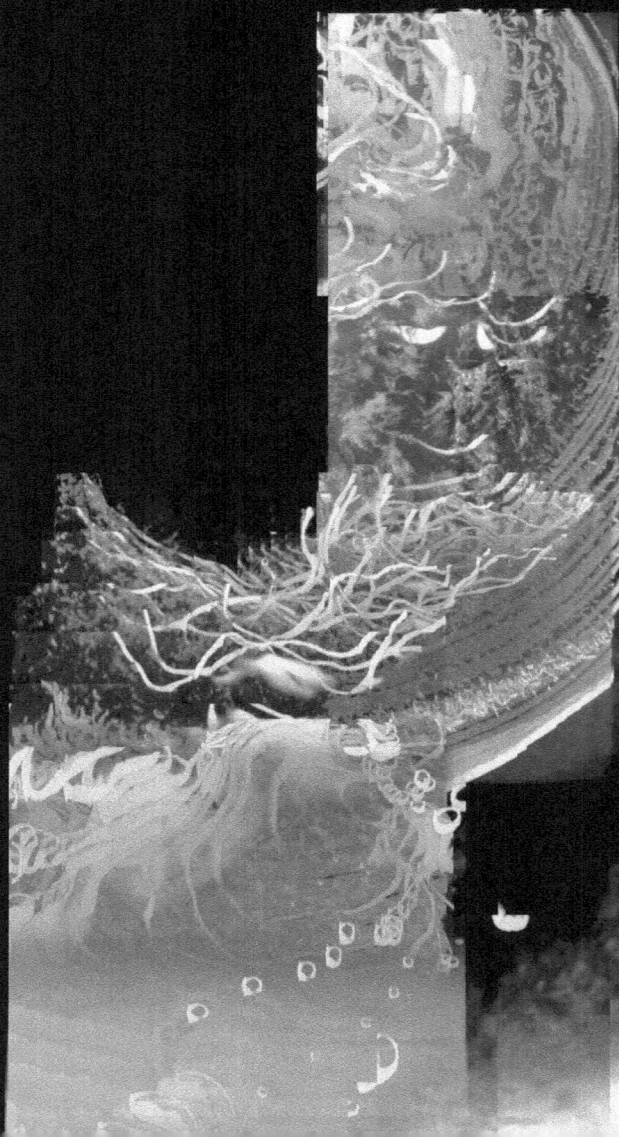

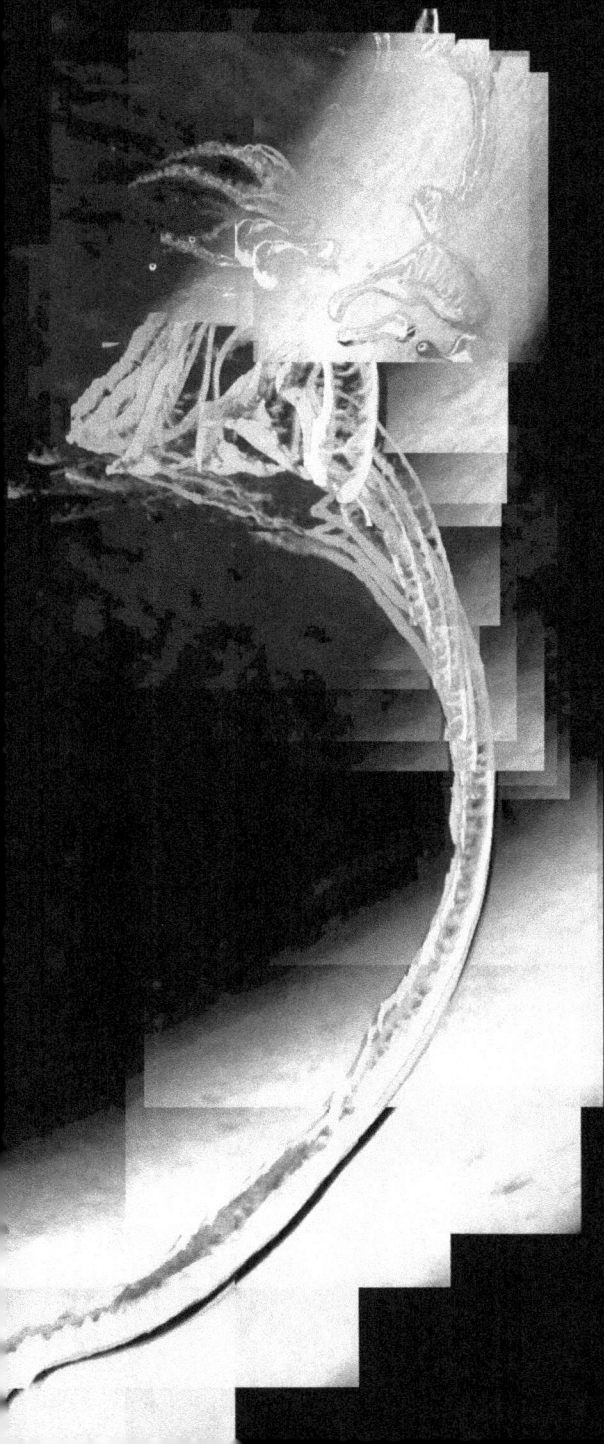

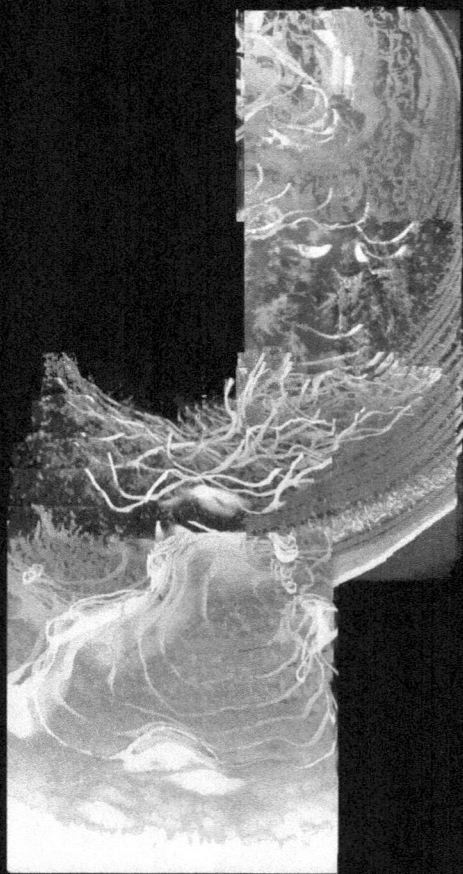

The body is like a windscreen for the mind against the infinite: whereas in every parcel of matter, however minute it might be, we can envisage an infinity of information, the body conquers finitude through the power of refusal. (Meillassoux 2007, 74)

The drawing body is a sifting body, one that most matter traverses untouched. The square does not represent (re-present) the window, but rather conceals it, suppressing (most of) its reality. A figure stands in for glass, wood, and silicone, transparency, and thermal bridges, views, solar irradiance, condensation, operable surfaces, heat, dripping rainwater, airflow, handles, bird song, spider webs, and voyeurism. Only its measurable symptoms persist; only the emoji; only that which is instrumental, resolved, legible, and universal. Yet, the *positive* strokes that describe it are inversely proportional to the negation of reality they subtend.

How could such a narrow/impoverished set of tools — the *blanked* surface; the drawing of lines, digital or analogue, flat or solid as it may be — ground the way in which space is conceptualised and choreographed?

*

The symbol nullifies the thing. Signs express and suppress the world. (Serres 2010, 52)

Making proceeds by reduction — a technology of blind spots. Designs generate abstract forms that can be thought, counted, sized, drawn, fabricated, and reproduced, while all else conveniently (and temporarily) disappears. Yet intentionality can only temper or delay our encounter with the world.

*

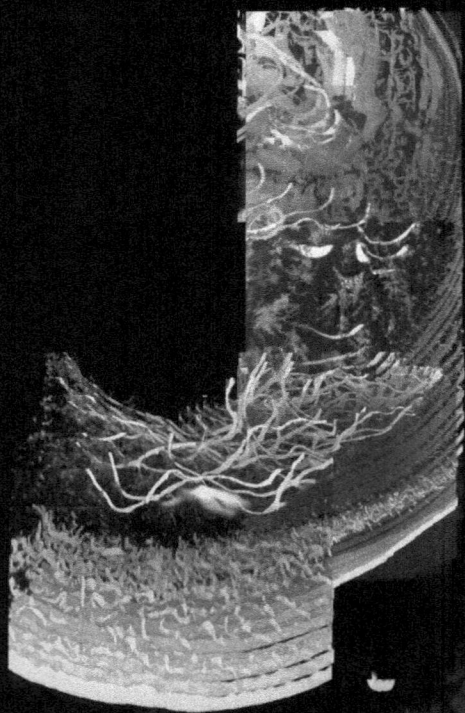

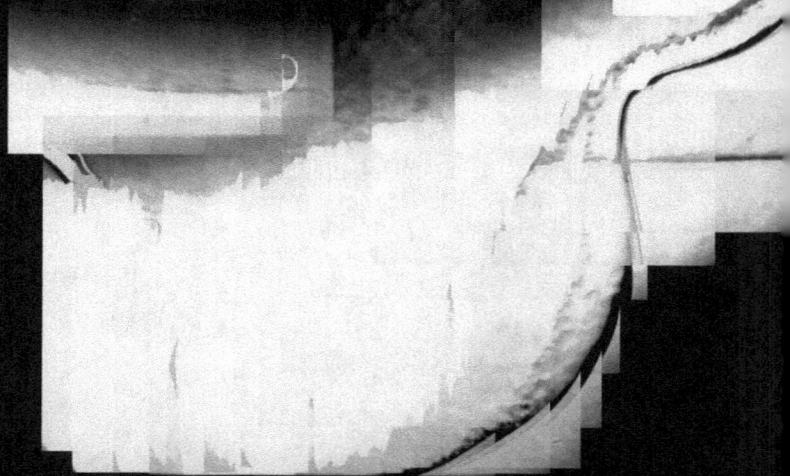

Abstraction is the order of the formal cruelty of thought. In its most trivial and unsophisticated form it involves pure mutilation: amputating form from the sensible matter. In its most complex — that is, most veritable — instances, it is the concurrent organization of matter by the force of thought, and the reorientation of thought by material forces. It is the mutual penetration and destabilization of thought and matter according to their respective regulative and controlling mechanisms. (Negarestani 2014, 5)

As a technology of finitude, abstraction operates through dismemberment and substitution: what it conceals, detaches, and carefully clips off always gets replaced by something else — a placeholder, a signifier, a paraphrase — recoated, repackaged, and renamed. Yet substitutions require stable forms and reliable meanings, phantom limbs and full-colour posters. That which is fluid and mutable, complex, unpredictable, cloudy, and diffused is traded in for inertia, simplicity, sharp edges, definite boundaries, visibility, and compliance. Durability is valued over accuracy, generality over specificity, readability over resolution. Rifts between the culturalised experience of environment and its reality progressively widen.

Certainly, language claims a degree of objectivity precisely by negating the hybridity and vibrancy of the sensible in the name of shared symbols and systems of signification. Yet our signs are not neutral but selective; they prefigure and choose an audience; they declare membership to a community. The social contract is, in this sense, an agreement of reciprocal legibility and communicability; an assurance of authorial relevance.

A liquid technology — a language of situated/territorialised transformations and time-based notational systems that resist standard modes of conveyance and capture — does not only violate and contradict the principle of legibility and its decontextualising drive or frustrate its appetite for reductive substitutions. It points to the ecological expansion of community; to inclusivity and our willingness to partake in conversations we only tangentially curate, control, and understand; to a partial yet voluntary relinquishing of intentionality. It prefigures a precarious and mutually destabilising (ethical) order, beyond delusions of submission and improvement.

*

A line can also stroll, animated by the gestures that produce it: no longer an inert parade of points but a single living dot meandering across a sheet of paper. Paul Klee invites us to think of lines as movement (walks). Yet is something actually moving or is it rather being dragged across the page — docile, demure, on a leash? How much of our love for the processual is animated by our ability to process? How much of our appreciation for movement is predicated on moving (versus being moved)?

*

The representation of movement often funnels abstraction through the logic of the machine. A moving outline turns into a series of topologically extruded points, of which few are selected and finally printed (those deemed re-presentative of the object's defining features, those that highlight specific patterns, etc.). Lines develop along the fluttering of wings and stretching of legs, revolving around shoulders, elbows, and knees.

Étienne-Jules Marey's chronophotographs exemplify an understanding of movement as the temporal plotting of the machine's operational range; a spectrum of bodily alterations constrained by clear part-to-whole relationships, functional hinges and bending limbs. Variations remain strictly mechanical and rely on stable forms, uses, and relations. Internal gradients, biochemical fluctuations, and autonomic processes never seem to pierce the surface of the skin, or to call into question either the identity of parts (e.g., leg, arm, head) or their role towards coordinated pursuits (e.g., walking, running, jumping).

Marey's illustrations describe a deterministic world in which organic machines are pre-programmed for action, and map the

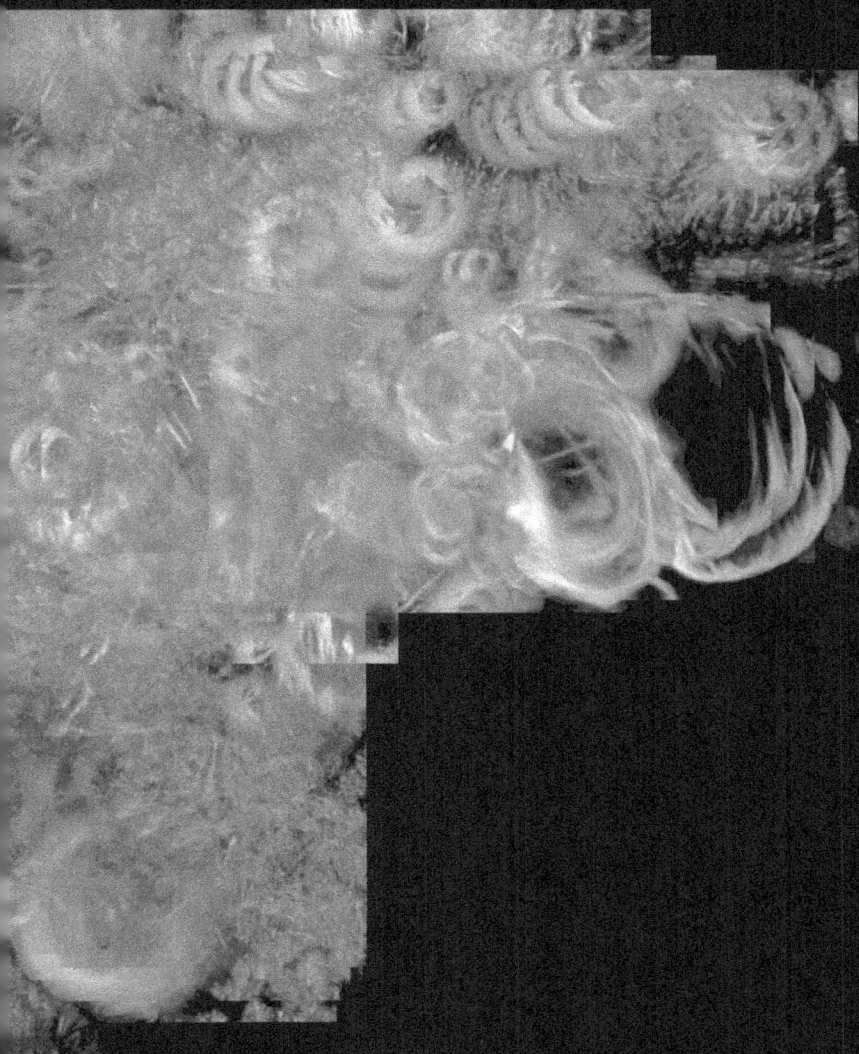

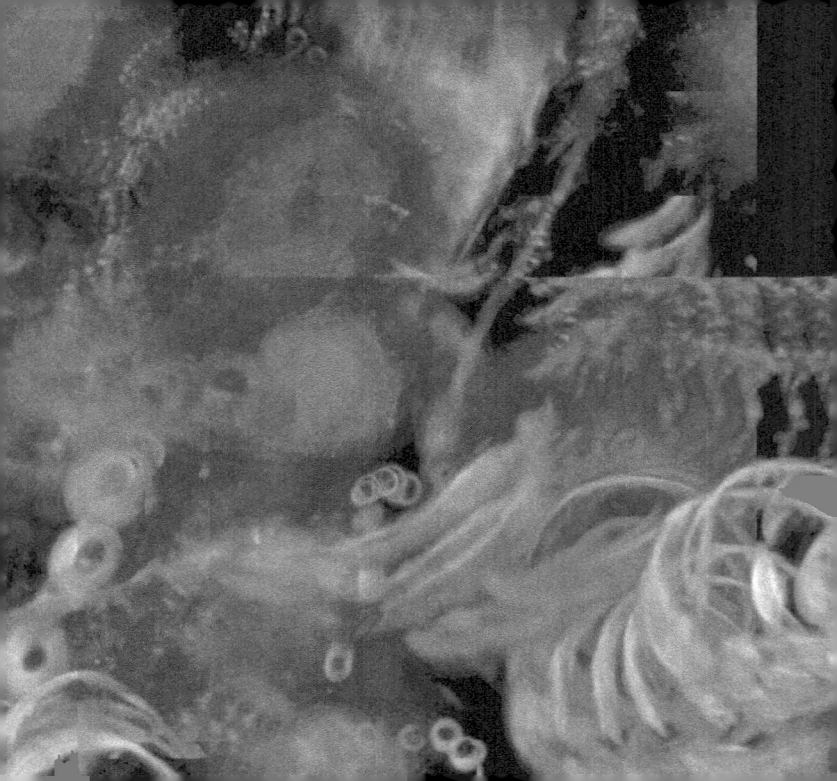

normal/algorithmic agency of bodies based on predefined kits of interconnected (working) cogs that rely on given syntaxes and transparent preconfigurations of use. Furthermore, if his overlays of sequential transformations (the running of a man as a linear temporal projection, from left to right) revolutionised the way we visualise temporality, their machinic constitution suggests a non-durational and reversible conception of time: time as a synchronic and spatialised instruction manual; a cartography of pivoting gears; a mere container for action. As the agential range of the machine does not change (each component part is assumed to be stable), time is excluded as a plastic ingredient and relegated to the mere space within which variations occur. Cogs always turn in identical fashion — today, tomorrow, or in a hundred years. And when they break, they stop turning.

While the drawings in these pages are chronophotographic compositions of sorts, they elude the logic of the *bête machine*, evoking transitions and revolutions that are loose, unscripted, open-ended, durational (non-reversible) and active.

*

The drawing reduces objects and their spatio-temporal interactions to Platonic representations, drowning out all manner of contextual and site-specific entanglements.

Yet it also rematerialises them by assigning a new indivisible, atomic unit: the point. Merging Democritus and Euclid, geometry can be read as a naive illustration of materialism: a distortion of reality based on the ontological bias towards a specific, albeit universally valid, constituent brand or principle.

Superficially, the behaviour of liquids would seem to support materialist reduction, or at least to neatly exemplify it: the more you cut up a solid — the smaller the units — the more fluid its behaviour. Yet, liquidity has less to do with fluidity (or with the ability to con-form, to *form with*) than with environmental receptivity, reactivity, and responsiveness. It cannot be blindly assigned to hydrogen or oxygen atoms, or even to water molecules, which can also exist in solid or gaseous states.

Rather, liquidity depends on context, as an emergent property of the encounter of molecules with specific temperatures and atmospheric conditions, chemical solutions, and vessels, at different scales and levels of interaction.

*

> Now our atom is inserted: it is part of a structure, in an architectural sense; it has become related and tied to five companions so identical with it that only the fiction of the story permits me to distinguish them. It is a beautiful ring-shaped structure, an almost regular hexagon, which however is subjected to complicated exchanges and balances with the water in which it is dissolved; because by now it is dissolved in water, indeed in the sap of the vine, and this, to remain dissolved, is both the obligation and the privilege of all substances that are destined (I was about to say 'wish') to change. (Levi 2000, 229)

Instead of matter (an imaginary lack of actualised form), we embrace liquidity as a figure of potency, opportunity, resilience, and life; not an abstract lump of atoms, but a smooth, localised, and shape-shifting object/field.

*

Flux is inseparable from the substances it stirs and participates in. The Heraclitean river does not illustrate the ontological priority of process over things (everything flows), or of matter-as-process, but the unity, co-existence and mutual dependence of space and time, matter, and form. Objects shiver, heat, fuse, and rust, guided, and extruded by events and alliances, adjacencies, and collisions, synergies, and sympathies, events, and intrinsic structures. If agency and meaning cannot be understood as imposable from the outside, or from the top down, neither can they be told to privilege the isolated adventures of atoms or the socialised lives of objects. Somewhere in-between, a time lapse

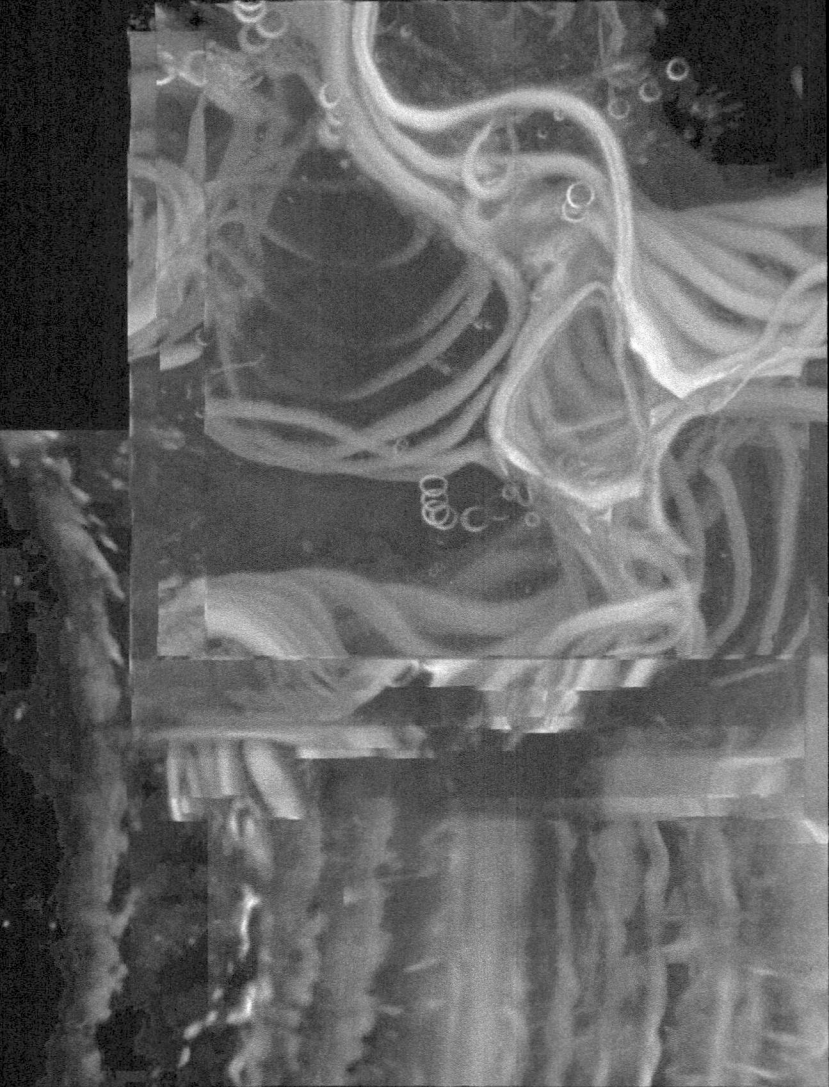

plays at accelerated speeds, and all things, alive and inert, large and small, are allowed to evolve — deformed and upcycled, worn out and grown, hacked and extended, recycled, decomposed and composted.

*

We draw droplets as pinched spheres, with a pointy head and rounded belly. They are always falling and never land. There is no wind, no branch, no temperature, no surface tension, no transition.

We also draw them as rainfall, in parallel vertical lines. We picture them dropping, screaming with distorted mouths, as kids on the descending bent of a rollercoaster. Yet, they are silent and unafraid, not droplets as much as *drop-dots* — comfortably sliding across the page to please their masters.

Lines are sometimes illustrations of how points can be moved in space and time. Rain — it gets you wet.

*

Anyone can draw a dot, anywhere. Or a square centimetre, or a three-foot-long line. I pick up the phone and ask a contractor in Rome to cast a concrete cube. Each side should measure thirty centimetres exactly. She knows what I mean. I don't need to inquire about material properties or environmental conditions, or to receive a report on today's local temperature or how the cube will be poured. I don't need to be present. I don't even have to ask for it to be grey; I know what the output will be. I know what the cube looks like: I have a drawing of it. My only question is whether the supplier will be as precise as I require; whether the manufactured cube will adhere to the abstract template floating mid-air above my head.

Materials don't surprise me. They are non-local collections of specifications and parameters. I can list their properties by heart, reciting spreadsheets and engineering manuals. They are divorced from experience and site, and reliably negate both.

They are generic compounds that only come into focus to translate drawings and ideas into buildings, forks, armchairs, paintings, and lamp shades. They have no previous identity or specificity; and when they do, when their 'raw' status is not enough to conceal form or actuality, they apologise profusely.

Anyone can draw a dot, anywhere. But how does one begin to draw a droplet?

*

A droplet is not a point, a number, or a grapheme. It isn't a punctuation mark, a quantifiable lump or a readable character. It isn't a sign, a pixel, a code, a chemical recipe, a fixed definition, volume, or extension. It defies straightforward translation and representation, and yet it has form, which it *performs* contextually and responsively, fleeing equilibrium and adapting to changing conditions; mixing and wetting, spouting and freezing, dissolving and irrigating, spilling and rippling, swirling and oozing, evaporating and dripping, filling and diluting, entering and exiting, transporting and hydrating, drying and boiling. The droplet is queer: its identity transitional and situational, fluid, and transformative. It resists fixed definitions and eludes symbolic clarity, sending trembling messages across lifeworlds.

Liquidity tempers the bias of abstraction, meeting reality halfway.

*

475

I was asked to draw a droplet, but wasn't told where or how, which is a bit like scheduling a date without setting a time and place, or forgetting who you are going to meet.

What would the temperature in the room be? What kind of paper would I be drawing on — what thickness, grain, texture, type of fibres? Or, would I be drawing on a different material — on a towel, on leather, fur, plastic? And what liquid would I be using: ink, acrylic paint, coffee, hot wax, plaster, molten aluminium, egg yolks, oil? Would I drip the liquid with a pipette, apply it with a paintbrush, or pour it with a bucket? You don't have to be Pollock to understand the effect these parameters would have on the final product; to know that the distance between surface and dripping implement, or the most minute arm oscillation, will greatly affect the outcome — a constellation of rotund stains and splashing patterns.

The droplet channels a material recalcitrance, a fundamentally un-abstractable, analogue, territorialised, and relational vibrancy.

Anyone can draw a dot, anywhere. But how does one begin to draw a droplet?

*

Liquidity embodies a novel, non-hylomorphic poietic paradigm, one that is inherently contextual. Here, 'context' does not denote the site designers are tasked with fixing or improving — its cartographic reproduction or other distilled, programmatically relevant parameters — but a generative and creative materiality, one that isn't resolved as much as stirred, steered, modulated, gardened, and post-tuned. The indistinction of context, material, and finished object — the blurring of relative roles — is the *modus operandi* and strategic protocol of liquids.

*

A notational system is not merely a lucid set of graphic signs, codes, and symbols; but a key for reading and inhabiting the

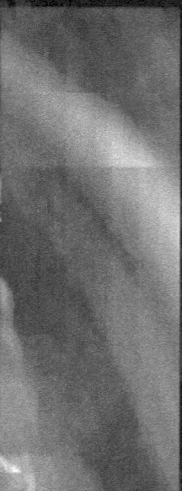

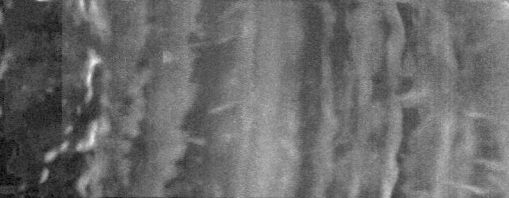

world, a prompt, a translation software and, sometimes, a design tool. Notations extend beyond the mere representation of or negotiation with reality: they are immersed in it. Are songs not notations for dancing? Are buildings not notations for moving through space? Are rings not notations for juggling? Is Gibson's very notion of 'affordance' not fundamentally notational? More languages lie within our material surroundings than we care to imagine or understand. Few of them speak to (or of) us.

These liquid scripts and space-time fossils, frozen in diachronic accretions and transitional constellations, begin to account for (to tell) their strange and unruly stories.

*

In nature, it is once again water that sees and water that dreams: 'The lake has created the garden. Everything is composed around this water which thinks.' As soon as one surrenders himself entirely to the sway of the imagination with all the united powers of dream and contemplation, he understands the depth of Paul Claudel's thought: 'Thus, water is the gaze of the earth, its instrument for looking at time' (Bachelard 1994, 31)

Part VII

REGENERATION

COMPOST

The character of decomposition is discussed in this section, establishing its relevance to the continuity between life and death.

Composting Continuity

> Bodies are not produced by their anatomical structure but
> by their languages. (Armstrong, forthcoming 2020)

Liquid bodies begin and end with a pause. While every lifespan
is acting out its resistance to entropic forces through a unique
web of events, ultimately all pathways eventually lead to relative equilibrium. However, on Earth, death is not necessarily
the final state for living matter. In fact, death is anything but
restrained. Its alternative metabolic network is orchestrated by
complex communities that constitute the necrobiome and thanatobiome. Together, these degrade, digest, and redistribute the
building blocks of life within corpses, so they may re-enter life's
flow. Spanning the surface of the earth, the metabolism of death
reaches into the lightless abyss and the pitilessly dark caves inhabited by troglodytes, so wherever a body falls on this planet, it
stands a chance of rejoining life's flow.

> … [the] dialogue between species through physiological
> and ecological discourses did not happen suddenly. They are
> the product of billions of years of chemical negotiations …
> If the messages are not fair, or misunderstood, or if agendas
> become divergent, then the superorganism becomes part
> of an impossible city like Babel, which is always at risk
> of crumbling under the strains of its own success … [the
> once-living agents, now] … overwhelmed by the voices of
> the necrobiome … must somehow meaningfully maintain
> … [their] conversations so [they may] one day … rise again.
> (Armstrong, forthcoming 2020)

The space in which these rich transformations and resurrections
take place is compost — an attractor for life with a unique spectrum of metabolisms that are brought together through unfathomably complex networks of chemical and biological processes.

Everywhere, creatures and minerals together make their characteristic soils. Where the grand circulation exposes different bands of rocks in juxtaposition, so the plant communities that come to live on them differ, and the resulting soils do too ... We spend our lives hurrying away from the real, as though it were deadly to us. 'It must be somewhere up there on the horizon,' we think. And all the time it is in the soil, right beneath our feet. (Logan 2007, 97)

Making compost is, therefore, not an elaborate form of waste disposal. It is an art like cooking that needs a recipe, which recommends the right substances and how they may be combined, or processed effectively: specifically, thirty parts of carbon to one part of nitrogen are needed. This is easy to do. Carbon can be found in sources such as straw, dead leaves, wood chips, shredded paper, corn stalks, and egg shells. Nitrogen is in manure, meal, green garden waste, algae, hair, kitchen vegetable scraps, fish, and sod. Since air and water are vital to metabolic processes, compost must be blended to form a well-draining, nutrient-rich mixture, then processed in a structure with enough water to dampen the pile and allow it to breathe, so it can begin to biochemically 'burn'. The mixture needs continual stirring and turning, so food, water, and oxygen can be evenly distributed to the microorganisms. As temperatures frequently reach around 50–70°C, it is agitated to dissipate the heat. The process is finished once the dark brown pile contains small uniform particles that smell earthy, like yeast, and are light and fluffy to the touch.

A dump, a landfill, or a bad compost heap is an example of a failed relationship to nature. Even where people have begun large-scale composting ... they frequently design closed systems that end by stinking up the neighborhood, giving compost a bad name, and ultimately failing ... composting ... is an act of healing. It restores the right working of a natural process. In that act, the participants are not just functionaries, they are sharers in an act of faith. (Logan 2008, 48)

Composting is open to creative negotiation and does not need to be naturalistic. While natural processes obviously play a critical role in enlivening ecosystems, alternative materials and approaches like *supersoils* may restore, remediate, and augment environmental performance, as well as create alternative spaces for new processes and metabolisms (Armstrong 2016). For example, hygroscopic granules may be added to sand so that water retention is increased, or (synthetic and natural) organisms introduced into loams to process certain toxins such as heavy metals and plastics, which are hard for natural organisms to metabolise. By bringing a range of composts and different kinds of soil bodies into proximity with each other, the repertoire of death's metabolic processes may be extended in agile ways that restore environmental fertility.

> The soil is the great connector of lives, the source and destination of all. It is the healer and restorer and resurrector, by which disease passes into health, age into youth, death into life. Without proper care for it we can have no community, because without proper care for it we can have no life. (Berry 1996, 86)

12.2

Geophagia

> People whose colour is bad when they are not jaundiced
> are either sufferers from pains in the head or earth eaters.
> (Celsus 1971)

Geophagia establishes a direct relationship between human ingestion and soil, in a manner that is not first transformed by ecological intermediaries. Hippocrates provided the first written account of the practice more than 2,000 years ago. On every inhabited continent and in almost every country, people that eat earth are reported and children are particularly prone to the habit. Around 20% of normal children between the age of 1–3 years will eat up to 500 milligrams of soil a day. When it persists beyond childhood, it is mostly associated with relief from hunger pains, the onset of pica in cases of iron, zinc, or calcium malnutrition, traditional skin lightening recipes, or as a kind of vaccine that protects the stomach against toxins, parasites, and pathogens (Woywot and Kiss 2002). While small amounts of ingested healthy soil are harmless, complications include parasitic infestation, electrolyte disturbances, chemical contamination (lead, arsenic), bacterial infection, and intestinal obstruction (Young et al. 2011). Whether geophagia is pathologised or not, life's ongoingness is entangled with the health of its dirt, and soil is integral to healthy food cycles, ending up in our bodies in modest amounts[1] one way (unwashed food, hygiene etc.), or another (Calabrese et al. 1990).

Perhaps one way to establish its potency, is to deliberately sample it.

> That was the year the founder took a long spoon from his
> pocket, plunged it into the earth and scooped a spoonful of

---

1   According to a study of tracer elements found in 6 adults, around 50 mg of soil is ingested daily.

organic matter into his mouth. He chewed for a few, silent moments then spat the dirt onto the ground.

'Bitter!'

He vowed that by the time we left the island it would taste of magic. (Armstrong and Hughes 2016)

PAUSE

This chapter summarises the key discussion points in the text and proposes strategies for advancing the principles and practices of liquid life.

Principles of Liquid Life

Through critical reflection of liquid apparatuses in experimental contexts, fourteen key principles are proposed to comprise the character of liquid life. These are as follows:

1 Liquid life is a primal force native to cosmic luminous matter.

2 It is a paradoxical, planetary-scale material condition, unevenly distributed spatially but temporally continuous. Flowing through and into myriad bodies at many scales, it is an open, 'living' infrastructure that underpins the metabolic webs of life and death.

3 Liquid life is based on the ancient idea that the character of 'life' is fluid.

4 Liquid life offers an alternative framework to the *bête machine* for considering the complex, networked, sensible, constantly-changing material events that constitute the living realm.

5 Liquid Life provokes an expanded notion of consciousness that is embodied, environmentally aware, and capable of observing its surroundings. It does not propose an a priori understanding of reality but constantly discovers its world, which is always tinged with mystery and so remains enchanted by the possibility of its own existence.

6 Liquid Life is a testable, pedagogical system, whose concepts can be interrogated, evolved, and ultimately realised. It offers a different relationship between humanity and the living world by materially augmenting its lively infrastructures.

7 Arising from the tensions between potent fields of matter/ energy, liquid life emerges at lively interfaces to generate highly mutable, paradoxical structures at far-from-equilibrium states that give the illusion of 'permanence' through their sustained persistence.

8 The incessant transgressions of liquid life are not erroneous, but integral to its success. Continually devising metabolic resistance strategies that dawdle, flâneur-like, away from entropy's call, it embraces multitudinous forms of expression, intermediary beings, and 'monsters' whose modes of organisation defy mechanistic explanations and established modes of categorisation.

9 Liquid life converses with 'angels' as vectors for knowledge, which manifest as transitional bodies that mediate between the living and non-living realms by invoking new languages, which generate alternative terms of reference to begin fresh conversations about the living realm.

10 Liquid life is a vital material force that commands an appropriate, ecological ethics and upholds the complex epistemologies of 'being'.

11 The politics of liquid life enables life's unbroken legacy to persist. Advocating active diplomacy between lively bodies through a choreography of events, it offers a platform for participatory decision-making. Continual negotiations take place at many levels of organisation including individuals, groups, communities, and ecosystems, where no specific species is privileged over others, although outcomes are not always equally beneficial for all beings.

12 Liquid life is not an antidote to the present ecocide, but an alternative paradigm towards imagining, encountering, and making the world than the *bête machine*.

13 Liquid life links the cycles of life and death through the metabolism of compost, where many different agents and bodies (re)incorporate organic matter into 'living' webs of matter/energy exchange.

14 Liquid life is what remains when logical explanations can no longer account for the experiences that we recognise as part of 'being alive'.

13.2

Soul Substance

> Two souls are locked in conflict in my heart,
> They fight to separate and fall apart.
> The one clings stubbornly to worldly things ...
> The other has an inborn urge to spread its wings ...
> (Goethe 1999, 35)

You were promised a materialist discourse of the soul, which makes itself known, whether we are sceptics or not. Without fixed shape, specific materiality, or particular trajectory to characterise it by, the soul resides within the liquids, flows, modes of emergence, transformations, and angels that permeate this text and may be difficult to recognise. Known through its many other names: life force, animating principle, vital essence, spirit, inner being, constant flux of vital functions, essential nature, aura, consciousness, yche, or a glitch in our material conceptualisation of the living realm, it is most dramatically experienced through its absence. Without it, living things tangibly fade and wither, as metabolic networks disperse and bodies lose their capacity for growth, transformation, or affinity for others.

> Whether called or uncalled, they come by themselves from all sides, on all paths, from the mountains, from the oceans, from the stars. Who can prevent them? I am sure that I, such as you see me here, have lived a thousand times, and hope to come again another thousand times. (Carus 1910, 150)

While fundamental to the expression and experience of 'life', the nature of the soul is elusive and defies formal characterisation within our understanding of the material realm[1]. Nor is it fully

---

1   The soul substance shares an indeterminate material status in a similar manner to radiation (see section 03.4), which interacts with matter, is created by matter, can create matter and is emitted by matter, but it is just too ephemeral to 'be' matter (Armstrong 2016, 36).

immaterial, as it interacts with matter, is generated by matter, animates matter, is emitted by matter but is too ephemeral to be classified as matter.

> Indeed I feel even now as if I were not seeing things here for the first time, but if I saw them again. (Carus 1910, 151)

13.3

Towards a Liquid Architecture That Accommodates the Soul

> Liquid architecture is an architecture that breathes, pulses, leaps as new form and lands as another. Liquid architecture is an architecture whose form is contingent on the interests of the beholder; ... Liquid architecture makes liquid cities, cities that change at the shift of value, where visitors with different backgrounds see different landmarks, where neighbourhoods vary with ideas held in common, and evolve as the ideas mature or dissolve ... Judgements of a building's performance become akin to the evaluation of dance and theatre ... this identity is only revealed fully during the course of its lifetime ... and what is made speaks for itself, not in words, but in presences, ever changing, liquid ... (Novak 1992, 283–85)

The present principles for human development are framed by economic systems that establish how natural resources are distributed and shared. By setting up the extreme conditions of scarcity and excess, multiple inequalities are established throughout society to feed the peristalsis of supply and demand of 'the market'. From an ecological perspective, these scenarios are fundamentally hostile to 'life', where 'survival of the fittest' equates with the 'richest', this cannibalistic state of affairs determines how our living spaces are constructed and settled.

Buildings are impenetrable fortresses with no 'living' relationship to their surroundings that neither care for the soils we depend on, nor clean the air we breathe, and remain oblivious to our water becoming infiltrated with hormones, neurotransmitters, heavy metals, and microplastics. As 'dead things', the inert surfaces of buildings are maintained only for their capital value, rather than as an expression of any moral duty of care for our living spaces. This fundamental indifference to the natural realm, is reflected in the consequences of how we make and occupy our living spaces, which presently contribute 40% of our total carbon footprint. No matter how much we propose to 're-duce' the impacts of this worldwide approach to human settlement, its consequences are damaging the natural world, where the wastes of our excesses become environmental poisons. Even when we vow to perform our acts of daily living more considerately through 'sustainable' approaches towards resource and energy consumption, we are still trapped in a toxic relationship with the biosphere.

An ecological ethics and associated construction toolset is critical to inverting the established order between human settlement and environmental health, so that we may establish a symbiotic relationship with the planet. Rather than serving as industrial sumps, we must imagine, design, prototype, and construct buildings differently so they *operate as infrastructures of life*. An alternative portfolio for space-making than Le Corbusier's doctrine of building-as-machine is required to catalyse this vital transition away from the 'brute' buildings of the industrial era, and midwife an ecological era of human development by making 'living' architectures with 'souls'.

Liquid life establishes the appropriate values, ethics, and principles of inhabiting the living realm for an ecological ear by foregrounding the infrastructures of life within our living spaces. By thinking through and constructing with fluids at far-from-equilibrium states, 'living' buildings can meet our needs as well as respond to changes in our proximate (resource availability) and global environment (rising waters, increasing frequency of extreme weather, brownfield sites, garbage patches). Enfolding dynamic liquid spaces into our habitats (Living Architecture 2016) unleashes an irreducible, material potency that is sustained by liquid life's protocols of matter/energy, which persists within spandrels, occupies transitory structures, leaks into unoccupied spaces and expands into new sites by virtue of its own agency. Comprising an ethical, ecological approach to the built environment, where the way we take care of our buildings affects their ability to meet our own needs, 'living' architectures provide spaces that modulate the flows and exchanges of fluid substances — gasses (air), liquids (water, snot), flow-friendly amorphous solids (glass).

The liquid qualities of 'living' architectures are associated with movement (running, jumping, flying, falling, climbing) and character (liquid cats, 'slippery' people, amoebae that move by constantly changing their body shape, fluid flames). They are not formless, but dynamically structured through their persistent patterns within iterations of pulses, waves, vortices, and oscillations, which are augmented and sustained by our presence. Their uncertain terrains and fuzzy spaces nurture a 'soul substance', which flows through, moulds around, and embraces their inhabitants, imbuing them with empathy. Evading *hard* control by conventional apparatuses, liquid architectures instead prefer to respond to the presence of slow, soft technologies and elemental infrastructures (Armstrong 2018b). The turbulence brought by dramatically changing environmental conditions is set to transform the world we know into a surreal landscape colonised by regressive attitudes. Offering alternative strategies to making barriers against the systems that sustain — and are capable of destroying — us, liquid architectures generate protocols for space-making that resist the Anthropocene's unfolding legacy and inevitable urban collapse.

Epilogue

> Every epoch not only dreams the next, but dreaming impels it towards wakefulness. It bears its end within itself, and reveals it … by ruse. (Benjamin 1997, 176)

Liquid life is a provocation and ecological story of the living world that increases our portfolio of choices in (re)constructing our relationship with the natural world through the choreography of countless acts of *liquid living* that uphold life's unbroken legacy. Introducing concepts and apparatuses capable of providing such a critical perspective, like dynamic droplets, liquid life does not attempt to reduce the strangeness of life's processes but rather to create a context in which existing assumptions may be considered anew, so that alternative ways of sorting, ordering, agentising, and valuing our world become possible.

Through its deep attachment to the unique physics, geology, chemistry, and cosmology of this planet, liquid life conjures forth the irreducible soul substance and uncategorisable bodies of slimy creatures such as the mucus-secreting, flesh-dwelling hagfish, paradoxical frogs that defy the anticipated order of development and fishing bats that skim the membranes of life. Such 'monsters' evade conventional modes of classification and take on new significance in allying with the weird and lively material systems that defy the *bête machine*'s persuasive logic.

(Re)empowering, (re)enchanting and (re)connecting us with the Earth's fundamental strangeness, liquid life raises the possibility of locally-initiated, global-scale, orchestrated material transgressions that are capable of reaching escape velocity from the pending Sixth Great Extinction and bring alternative futures *to functionality.*[2]

2   This phrase is inspired by Haraway's observation in *Anthropocene, Capitalocene, Chthulucene: Staying with the Trouble,* which invokes Hannah Arendt's notion of the banality of evil in reference to our own incapacity to think the world that is actually being lived. Noting that our inability to confront the actual consequences of the worlding that we are engaged in, and the

limiting and *thinking to functionality* of our actions, and inactions, means that we continue 'business as usual' while catastrophe unfolds around us (Haraway 2015). Liquid life's ambition is to escape the conceptual trap of this deadly 'banality', by releasing the limits of possibility through first the imagination and then, through re-empowerment by access to *liquid technology*.

RECONSTITUTION

All systems that start at far-from-equilibrium states eventually lose their potency.
The principles of liquid life enable their
reinvigoration through acts of composting where organic matter may be returned
to non-equilibrium states through the
metabolic networks of the living. This section embodies such a restorative process
through literary composting, which distils
and transforms arguments already proposed throughout the book, so they may
be (re)combined, (re)invigorated and
(re)encountered as new narratives and
alternative sets of discourses, adjacencies,
and juxtapositions.

Hiatus

Darkness is not nothingness. Something always happens. Your retinal discharges become fireworks, the squirming of your innards feels like a voluntary command, your skin becomes a sudden expansion of your brain. Nothingness is not absence, but many actualities that negate one another. In this realm of sensory deprivation, 50 metres below the ground, our senses are reorganised through dreams, neuroses, and desires that are no longer hidden. It is impossible to tell whether we are within inner or outer space; if we are still or in transit, or which way up we are. Gradually, we acquire alternative registers from which we make new sense of our chthonic existence. The dripping of groundwater is the beat of life reconfiguring itself, but we do not yet recognise its patterns or rules, and so this slowly leaking broth remains pluripotent — unpredictable.

14.2

Performing Liquid Life

It is not sufficient to bring about change in the way we inhabit the world by theorising the existence of liquid life. Nor is it adequate to stand outside its operations and objectively observe its field of influence through technological mediation and laboratory-based experiments. Narrative-making platforms and immersive performances are required to produce *lived experiences* of liquid life, which provoke the senses and generate unfamiliar encounters with reality.

Cthonic

The following text in 14.2.1.1 was first performed by the Experimental Architecture Group (Rachel Armstrong, Simone Ferracina and Rolf Hughes) for the *Cthonic* workshop on 20 July 2017 at Allenheads Contemporary Arts, Northumberland. The work responded to *Cthonic,* a 72-hour subterranean experience in which John Bowers, Alan Smith, Louise K. Wilson and Peter Mathews entered Smallcleugh mine in Nenthead, Cumbria on 20th April 2017 to settle into the vast cavern now known as the Ballroom. During this time, the Experimental Architecture Group travelled into the mine to meet them (ACA 2017a) and responded to this extraordinary event through situating an exploration of liquid life — and characters such as droplets, quantum foam, and angels — within this uninhabited and bare space. A second version of the reading was (re)worked into a new form and performed at the Beyond symposium held at the Mining Institute, Newcastle, and Culture Lab, Newcastle University, 5 October 2017, which invited its audience to consider what lies beyond our current knowledge sets and imagination (ACA 2017b). The version published here is the third textual incarnation of the text (the compost has been turned over by Rolf Hughes and some gentle warming applied).

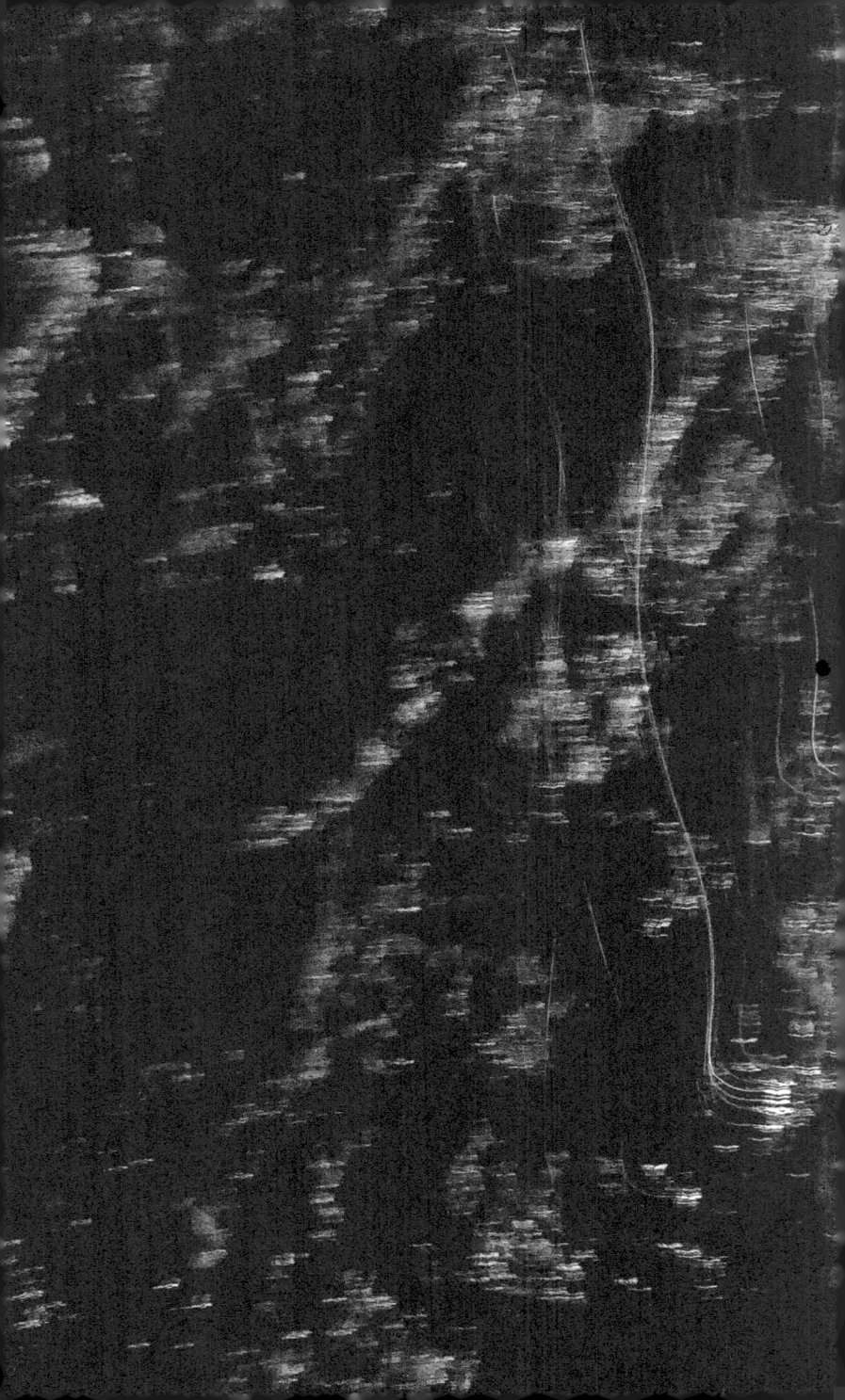

14.2.1.1

Compost

Darkness. Retinal discharges.

Nothingness is less absence than presences cancelling each other out.

A form of dripping. A slowly leaking broth of light. Cleft. Patterns or rules, they say.

Bitter slope. Damp black stone. As above, so below.

One moment we are blinded, plunged into a darkness where something nonetheless happens. It arises from a soup, smog, scab, fire — molten rock and alkali meeting oil; a metabolic choreography sucking gas clouds, dusts, obfuscating light, a gruesome purplish hue — muscle fibres locking into a fixed position — scum and crust.

We are eyelids, jaw, and neck, trunk, and limbs — puppets with a watery heart, energetically incontinent. Liquid eyes, lensing errant light into dark thoughts. Structural disobedience, misshapen mass; poles of oblivion.

Our world is not fully formed. This means there are plenty of other bodies in what happens next. Unlike us, they are alive and concerned with transforming the world into magnificence — their molten hearts are manifest on our bloodied hands.

We are all monsters now. What is the point of being static, patient, and silent? Oscillation is the basis of the dissemination of power. Vector and trace — sites of non-orientation — liquid infrastructures streaming through the material fabrics of the world, carried by the turbulent waters of life itself. We hunker down in a dream house made of canvas and wax. Contact light. A maze. A market. A city. A sewer.

Letting go becomes harder and harder.

There is a line to a tree bouncing me gently between earth and sky. As above, so below: in that darkness, that landscape of flotsam and flow, there is nothing human, only a figure made of wood and silicone, filled with spider webs and bird song. The world feels warmer, kinder, and more familiar than it used to be. Bless this weather. It is as if we have become semi-permeable — liquid scripts, frozen in durational accretions, transitional constellations. Signals appear, disappear, reappear. Something trying to say something. It happens.

14.2.1.2

Being Human

The following text in section 14.2.2.1 was written by Rolf Hughes for an event titled *Unquiet Earth: From Victoria Tunnel to Quantum Tunnelling*. It was performed in the Victoria Tunnel, Newcastle-upon-Tyne, between 10.00–11.00h on 17 November 2018, by the Experimental Architecture Group (Rolf Hughes, Rachel Armstrong, Simone Ferracina and Pierangelo Scravaglieri) with sound design by Culture Lab (John Bowers and Tim Shaw) and support from the Ouseburn Trust (Kelly Thompson and Clive Goodwin). The event was part of Newcastle University's contribution to the *Being Human* festival of the humanities, taking place in around 50 towns and cities across the UK between 15–24 November 2018. Themed on how the North East has been shaped by its rivers, the work was a public exploration of how the material agency of the tunnel could investigate the way the spaces we inhabit can be transformed into experiences that inform new ways of living. Following a site-survey by the participating groups, the complex formations of stalactites and mineral depositions indicated that the structure was actively growing, developing, and — taken to a logical extreme — capable of giving birth. The script drew on themes that run throughout this book — from the primordial iron and calcium laced flesh of the world, to the sounds of cosmic matter produced by Perseid meteor showers, and quantum tunnelling that enables green plants to make biomass from ephemeral substances, as well as the voice of soils. These oscillations were imagined to intersect with the substance of the tunnel and scattered throughout it, to immerse an audience of 15 people within a living-regenerative soil body.

Being (In)human

Set-up: RA *and* RH, *lead the audience through the tunnel, pausing to examine details of the tunnel. Their faces are a mixture of blue and green as if in an advanced stage of mould.*

VT staff help audience put on helmets and give instructions that they are to follow their two guides but may not at any time advance beyond them. No torches for audience — only the performers control the lighting.

Duration: 20–30 mins, followed by discussion with audience and return to surface.

1. Introduction
RH: Into the dark! Leave that slowly leaking broth of light. In a moment we are blind.

Keep listening! Damp black stone. *It speaks!*

1. First chamber
RA: One moment we are blinded — darkness, yes, but so much happening, so much arising from molten rock and alkali, metabolic choreography sucking gas, dust, obfuscating light, a gruesome purplish hue — muscle fibres locking into a fixed position — *oh oil, oh scum, oh crust!*

RH: *Ssssh!*

[*Pause*]

RA: Do you hear something?

2. Second chamber
RH: Here they come, jaw and neck, spine and pins — don't ask me how it's all put together — watery heart, liquid eyes lensing

errant light. Rivets, I guess. Or glue. Structural incontinence. *D-d-disobedience* at the engineering level. It's our fate. It's why we need, it's why, we need, a way ... *out-t-t-t ... T-t-t-t ... T-t-t-tec ... t-t-tick ... t-tock...*

RA: Do you hear it? [*Pause*] The ... *groaning?*

[*Pause*]

RH: Our world is not fully formed. This means there are plenty of other bodies in what happens next. Unlike us, they are alive.

[*Pause*]

They are concerned with transforming the world into magnificence — their erupting hearts are manifest on our bloodied hands.

*3. Third chamber (*RA *goes ahead,* RH *blocks the entrance so the audience cannot follow)*
RA: Do you hear anything beyond the reverberations of our words?

[*Audience allowed in*]

Sound actions

4. Fourth chamber
RA: What is the point of being static, patient, and silent? We are *all* monsters now! Liquid infrastructures stream through the material fabrics of the world, carried by the turbulent waters of life itself. Here, it's here, I'm sure it's here somewhere ...

Yes, HERE!

This is the primordial flesh of the world, formed by moulten iron that spilled from Earth's core and fed upon early life's first excrements. Green organisms produced oxygen from an extraordinary reaction that turned the ephemeral matter of light and carbon dioxide into biomass. Seemingly defying the laws of classical physics, they used quantum tunnelling to bypass natural energy gradients and so, turned iron's green salts into red, fleshy tissues. Oozing from the earth they swallowed minerals and sediments, folding themselves into ever more stratified topologies — first forming tissues, then organs, until — see here, they create tiny calcium bones.

Here, it's here. This is what we've been looking for ... *Here!*

Sound actions

RH: This is a line. It connects me to a tree. Somewhere between earth and sky.

In this *d-d-darkness,* this landscape of flotsam and flow, there is only ... (*well, you'll see*).

Don't ask me how it's made. I only know it's filled with spider webs and bird song. When you see it, the world feels warmer, kinder — more familiar than it used to be. It is as if the world has become semi-permeable.

Signals appear, disappear, reappear. Something trying to say something. It happens a lot.

1. Fifth chamber
Sound actions

RA: [*halts the group on entering the chamber; whispering*]: The sounds, they're ... from some other place ... some other place ... gut ... soil ... coal ... womb? ... *Be prepared.*

RH: *Ssssh!*

Sound actions

RA: BE PREPARED!

[*Crouching and whispering*] Be prepared … for a birthing … a birthing so monstrous … whatever issues … this world … this world … *this world!*

[*Pause*]

It cannot be imagined!

[*Blackout*]

KT [*glimpsed momentarily as Pepper's ghost*]: AWAAAAAAAY!

Blackout. Silence. Hold 7–10 seconds.

Lights on — RH *first, then swiftly* RA, *then* KT, *then others: release of tension. Discussion with audience.*

*

GLOSSARY

* indicates the specific characteristics of one of the 14 Bütschli angels.

Affective computing is the study and development of systems and devices that can recognise, interpret, process, and simulate human affects, or emotions.

Angel is a transitional being that neither fully belongs to the material or ephemeral realms. In the Christian tradition, orthodox angels include Gabriel, Michael and Raphael (see section 01.6). Unorthodox angels included Oriell, Ragwell, Barachiell, Pantalion, Tubiell and Rachyell that appear to derive from Jewish pseudepigrapha (Keck 1998, 174).

Angelology is the study of angels and their languages — the 'angel' equivalent of anthropology.

Anisotropy occurs when matter produced is directional; for example, the rotation of electromagnetic light through a crystal may polarise its orientation through the structure and therefore, alter its optical effects.

Anthropocene is the epoch during which human activity has been the dominant influence on the climate and planetary systems. Its onset arguably dates from around the time of the Industrial Revolution and the rise of fossil fuel-burning machines. It is characterised by industrial 'progress', capitalism, and 'modernisation', the 'side effects' of which are poisoning planetary systems (Crutzen and Stoermer 2000).

Anthropos is derived from the Greek term for 'human, man, or being'. In cultural studies, it has come to represent a Promethean politics of human exceptionalism, individualism, and 'the representative of a hierarchical, hegemonic, and generally violent species (Braidotti 2013, 65). An 'Enlightenment figure [that] arose in dialogue with God … [and] inherited God's universalism' (Tsing 2015).

Archai is a Greek word for the elements, which signify the original state from which things arose and the forces that initiate and govern their coming-to-be.

Atomism is an ancient philosophical concept that is based on fundamental 'uncuttable' material units known as 'atoms', where the whole of reality is made up of their countless combinations and how they are positioned within an infinite void (Berryman 2016).

Autopoiesis is the study of 'the circular organization of living things' (Maturana and Varela 1928, xvii).

Babel is an ancient city described in the book of Genesis that grew prosperous through the advent of new technology that challenged the power of God. It was therefore cursed with the evolution of multiple languages through which many misunderstandings arose and the city destroyed itself. In this book, Babel is a metaphor for a (monstrous) system that is constantly negotiated to maintain its coherence. It is a theoretical and experimental framework for a city of contradictions and imperfections that is held together by precarious ecological principles of mutuality, cooperation, synthesis, and diplomacy.

Baupläne, or ground plan, is a biological term for a set of morphological features that are common to many members of a phylum of animals.

BCE (Before Common Era) is a secular notation for 'Before Christ' (BC), which was first used in the sixth century to indicate the historical point of reference of the Gregorian calendar system, which takes the birth of Jesus Christ as its starting point.

Being-in-the-world is a term used by Martin Heidegger to conjure a form of conscious, embodied existence, whose experiences are shaped by being situated within a particular material realm (Heidegger 1962).

Belousov-Zhabotinsky reaction is a chemical oscillator made up of ten chemical stages, whose reagents (potassium bromate, cerium (IV) sulphate, malonic acid, and citric acid in dilute sulphuric acid) remain at non-equilibrium states for a prolonged period. It can be observed unaided as a solution that rapidly and periodically changes colour, in waves of fractal-like patterns.

Bête machine is Descartes' philosophical notion that non-human animals are like machines; do not have thoughts, reason, or souls like humans; and thus, cannot be categorized with humans. As a result, they do not experience pain or certain other feelings (cf. *L'homme Machine*).

Black hole is a cosmic object where matter has been condensed into a tiny space and gravity pulls so hard that even light cannot get out. This can happen when a star is dying. Because no light can get out, black holes are invisible and typically, have a mass around few times the mass of our Sun. Understanding black holes is crucial, as they bring together the very massive (general relativity) with the very small (quantum physics). They may even be similar to the Big Bang itself, and their better characterisation could help us understand how the universe was formed (Creighton 2015a).

Blind watchmaker is a teleological argument made by William Paley that presupposes anyone finding a complex object would immediately conclude that it was designed (Paley 2008). He infers that since the universe is infinitely more complex than anything that humans could design, then it supports the existence of a 'designer' god.

Brute matter does not possess agency or liveliness. The term originates from a letter by Isaac Newton to Richard Bentley discussing how one (inert) body can exert a force upon another 'without the mediation of something else which is not material' (Newton 2017). New materialist Jane Bennet uses this term as a counterpoint to 'vibrant' matter, which is agentised, lively, and volitional independently of human command (Bennett 2010).

Bütschli system is a simple chemical recipe where strong alkali is added to a field of olive oil and produces a lifelike system that generates pleomorphic bodies. It was developed by zoologist Otto Bütschli who claimed he used these ingredients to make a simple, amoeba-like artificial organism (Bütschli 1892).

Causal emergence occurs when the higher scale of a system has more information associated with its causal structure than the underlying lower scale. It refers to a set of causal relationships between some variables, such as states or mechanisms, and works on the principle that macrostates can be strongly coupled even while their underlying microstates are only weakly coupled (Hoel 2017).

CE is a secular notation for the era after the birth of Christ (AD) and is referred to as the Common Era.

Central dogma of molecular biology states that 'DNA makes RNA makes protein' (de Lorenzo 2014, 226).

CERN is the European Organization for Nuclear Research. It is one of the world's largest and most respected centres for scientific research. Its business is fundamental physics, finding out what the Universe is made of and how it works.

Charybdis is a sea monster of Greek legend, which was later rationalised as a treacherous whirlpool in the Strait of Messina.

Chemoton is a set of experimental criteria — namely, metabolism, compartment, and information — that are experimentally used to build artificial cells in contemporary origins of life experiments (Gánti 2003).

Chthulucene is a concept invented by Donna Haraway to depict a protean epoch as 'an ongoing temporality that resists figuration and dating and demands myriad names' (Haraway 2016). It offers a counterpoint to the Anthropocene and is characterised by 'a thousand somethings else … telling of linked ongoing generative and destructive worlding and reworlding in this age of the Earth' (Haraway 2016).

Clade is a group of organisms believed to comprise all the evolutionary descendants of a common ancestor and represents a single branch on the tree of life.

Cloaca is a structure that is situated at the end of the gut and serves as a combined opening for the urinary and reproductive organs. An embryological developmental stage in humans, it persists in adult birds, amphibians, reptiles, marsupials, and monotremes.

Clinamen is a term used by Lucretius to refer to the unpredictable and infinitesimally small change of direction in the course of an atom's downward fall.

Cnidarians are aquatic invertebrate animals of the phylum *Cnidaria,* previously called 'coelenterates', which include jellyfish, corals, and sea anenomes. The name is derived from the Greek word cnidos, which means 'stinging nettle'.

Coacervates are spherical aggregates of colloidal droplets that are held together by hydrophobic forces.

Colloid is a suspension of microscopically dispersed insoluble particles suspended in a medium.

Componentisation is the process of atomising (breaking down) resources into separate reusable packages that can be easily recombined. Componentisation is the most important feature of (open) knowledge development as well as the one that is, at present, least advanced.

Conformal symmetry is a symmetry in which working mechanics of a system remains symmetric when spatially rotated in a fixed or a dynamic background.

Correlation functions are statistical variables that provide the link between random variables, contingent on the spatial or temporal distance between those variables.

Crescograph is a device for measuring growth in plants that was invented in the early twentieth century by Sir Jagadish Chandra Bose.

CRISPR (Clustered Regularly Interspaced Short Palindromic Repeats) is a simple yet powerful tool for editing genomes that allows researchers to easily alter DNA sequences and modify gene function.

Cryptobiosis is a form of animated suspension and physiological state where metabolic activity is reduced to an undetectable level without disappearing altogether. In this condition creatures no longer metabolise but still have the capacity for life.

Cybernetics is a transdisciplinary field of research that investigates the principles of communications and control in both machines and living things.

Cymatics is a study of wave phenomena derived from the Greek phrase *ta kymatika,* which means 'matters pertaining to waves'.

Dark energy is an invisible and little understood phenomenon that appears, in some way, to counter gravity. There are no convincing theories about what it might actually be, although its existence accounts for why the expansion of the universe appears to be accelerating.

Dark matter is an invisible substance that largely works to hold the matter in space together. It causes galaxies clump together despite not seeming to have enough visible matter.

Death is not an end point for liquid life but a material 'pause' in liveliness. Dead matter may be returned to the living realm through active webs of metabolism found in composts, which are patchily extend around the Earth's surface.

Deep Blue, built by IBM is the first supercomputer chess-playing system to win against a human competitor.

Decoherence brings a quantum system into apparent alignment with classical physics.

Demon is a counterpoint to an angel and in science also stands in for paradoxes, or insoluble challenges.

Deucalion is the son of Prometheus, who with his wife Pyrrha, escaped a catastrophic flood sent by Zeus by hiding in a wooden chest. The flood lasted for nine days and the couple were the only surviving human. On the advice given by the oracle of Themis, they repopulated the earth by throwing rocks over their shoulders, which transformed into people (see Pyrrha).

Double slit experiment demonstrates, with unparalleled strangeness, that photons (and other subatomic agents) operate both as particles and waves and that the very act of observing them has a dramatic effect on their behaviour.

Dissipative adaptation is when a system at far-from-equilibrium simultaneously becomes more ordered towards increasing complexity and stability without the need for organising codes or inciting external agency.

Dissipative system, or structure, is a thermodynamically open system which is at far from equilibrium that exchanges energy and matter with their surrounding medium to produce characteristic structures that a simultaneously 'objects' and processes. They spontaneously form in nature to produce a range of phenomena such as, hurricanes, oscillatory reactions, and whirlpools.

Dynamical chaos is a form of non-linear behaviour that possesses a surprising amount of order, which masquerades as randomness, and cannot be fully predicted.

Earthbound is a term used by Bruno Latour during his Gifford Lecture series in Glasgow 2013 to replace 'human' that indicates only a superficial relationship with the soil (humus) and instead, highlights a much deeper *Gaian* attachment to the Earth that is intrinsic to planetary systems (Latour 2013).

> … the Earthbound people are a way to help us think about a new political community that could emerge which is rooted in a new of humans embedded in nature, rather than outside or separate from it. (Earthbound 101 2018)

Electroweak interaction is the unified description of two of the four known fundamental interactions of nature: electromagnetism and the weak interaction.

Embodied intelligence is a computational approach to the design and understanding of intelligent behaviour in embodied and situated agents, or materials, through their coupling with the environment. Overall actions are mediated by embodiment that includes the properties and constraints of the agent's own body, the brain, and motor and perceptual systems.

Entropy is a measure of thermodynamic disorder in a system that increases spontaneously with time.

Equilibrium is a systemic condition where all competing influences related to the distribution of matter and energy are balanced.

Ecopoiesis is the artificial creation of a sustainable ecosystem on a lifeless planet.

Ectoplasm is a supernatural viscous substance that exudes from the body of a medium during a spiritualistic trance and forms the material for the manifestation of spirits (Richet 2003).

Ethics establish how choices are made in an uncertain world. The term is used throughout the book to invite readers to consider the consequences of certain decisions and value sets — rather than imposing a particular set of moral principles on the reader.

Eutechnic age is when technology harmonises with the Earth's needs.

Evo-devo refers to a field of biological research known as evolutionary developmental biology. It is a comparative study of developmental processes and ancestral relationships between organisms, that is used to understand how creatures change over time.

Flâneur is a character that emerged from the imagination of Charles Baudelaire in his 1863 essay *The Painter of Modern Life*. It refers to a keen-eyed stroller that chronicles the minutiae of city life and resists the compulsions and tropes of modern lifestyles by, for example, 'window shopping' rather than making a purchase, and 'wasting time'.

Gametes are specialised haploid cells that are capable of sexually reproducing by uniting with another to produce a diploid cell, as their progeny. Typically, male gametes are sperm and female gametes are eggs.

General relativity is the current description of gravitation in modern physics, which is based on Albert Einstein's theory published in 1915. It breaks down at very high energies, where the gravitational interaction becomes comparable in strength to the other quantum interactions and can no longer be ignored.

Geophagia is the deliberate consumption of earth, soil, or clay.

Geostory is a non-human narrative fabric, which is woven through tectonic plates, meteorite impacts, and ice ages (Latour 2013).

Global storming is a planetary-scale condition associated with an increase in global temperatures, which specifically refers to increasingly severe meteorological events including tropical cyclones with higher wind speeds, a wetter Asian monsoon and increased intensity of mid-latitude storms.

Golden Ratio is an ancient mathematical principle and ratio, which is approximately equal to a 1:1.61 ratio that is found in nature. Used by artists such as Leonardo da Vinci to create pleasing, natural-looking compositions, it is thought to be at least 4,000 years old and may even have been used to design the pyramids.

Goldilocks planets can be found in the **Goldilocks zone**, which refers to the circumstellar habitable range of orbits around a star. These planets can support liquid water given sufficient atmospheric pressure and are candidate locations in the search for extraterrestrial life (Crutz and Coontz 2013).

Golem is derived from the Hebrew *gelem* (גלם), meaning 'raw material'. It refers to an animated being that is created by humans entirely from inanimate matter, and given life through a mystical process, which invokes the secret name of God.

Good Anthropocene is where humanity shrinks its environmental footprint through improved mechanical and industrial systems, creating more 'room' for nature, so that economic growth does not come at the expense of the environment.

Gradualism is a theory of evolutionary development first proposed by James Hutton in 1795, which suggests profound change is the cumulative product of slow but continuous processes (Hutton 2010).

Hadean epoch is the earliest phase of Earth's development that began about 4.6 billion years ago when the first rocks were formed as the Solar System was forming, probably within a large cloud of gas and dust around the sun, called an accretion disc. It ended 4 billion years ago with the advent of the Archean period, which brought the earliest forms of life.

Hard problem of consciousness was introduced by David Chalmers to explain how, even when decoded, a (hyper)complex system is unfathomable (Chalmers 1999). He suggests using nonreductive explanations that give a more naturalistic account. The nature of matter is also regarded as a hard problem, because it is more than the sum of all its relative components and retains its mysteries, even when deciphered.

Hertzian waves are radio waves that gave rise to wireless technology.

Heterogenesis is the derivation of a living thing from something unlike itself (Nature News 1946). It also refers to the theory of spontaneous generation championed by Félix Archimède Pouchet as a principle of nature. He suggested that animals are produced as a 'plastic manifestation' of groups of molecules that are conferred with a specific vitality that eventually results in a new being.

Homunculus is the 'little man', or miniaturised human inside a sperm, a cell (genetic code), or brain.

Hornsby–Akroyd oil engine was the first successful internal combustion engine.

Hylomorphism is a philosophical theory developed by Aristotle, which regards every physical object as a compound of matter and form.

Hyperbody is a living system that exceeds conventional boundaries and definitions of existence. For example, a slime mould in its plasmodial form that looks like a membranous slug is a hyperbody, as it is formed by the merging of many individual cells to form a single, coordinated giant cell.

Hypercomplexity is an organisational condition that is founded on the principles of complexity, from which new levels of order arise through the interactions between components. However, it exceeds a classical understanding of complex systems through their scale, heterogeneity, and distribution.

Hypercycles are cyclically linked, self-replicating, metabolic reactions that are theoretical models of autopioesis and may also occur naturally in the abyss.

Hypermaterial is a coherent yet highly heterogeneous consortium of agents, which are varied in their nature, or organisation.

Hyperobjects are entities of such vast temporal and spatial dimensions, such as climate change or capitalism, that they cannot be perceived in their entirety and defeat traditional ideas about the discreteness and certainty associated with individual bodies.

… the more data we have about hyperobjects the less we know about them — the more we realise we can never truly know them. (Morton 2013, 180).

Hyperorganism is a creature that is not made up of cells but of many individual creatures working together within a specific context, or locale, like a forest.

Ideoplasty (see teleplasty) is the power of the mind to conjure forth physical effects or modify certain physiological functions and processes.

Ichor refers to the fluid which flows like blood in the veins of gods in Greek mythology.

Intelligent design is a theory that argues certain features of the universe and living things are best explained by an intelligent cause, not an undirected process such as natural selection.

Intermediary metabolism is a theory proposed by Rudolf Schoenheimer, where 'all constituents of living matter, whether functional or structural, of simple or of complex constitution are in a steady state of rapid flux' (Schoenheimer 1942, 3).

Internal/interior milieu is a phrase usually attributed to Claude Bernard, although the term was coined by Hugo van Mohl 'to designate certain active contents of the vegetable cell' (Hodges 1889). It refers to the extracellular fluid environment in which the tissues and organs of multicellular organisms are bathed.

Irreducible complexity is when a biological feature is said to be too complex to have evolved without influence by an external agency, such as divine forces. It is an argument that support intelligent design.

Invisible realms are fields, spaces, and fabrics that cannot be perceived directly by our senses but may be accessed through technological systems that articulate their presence through indirect means. Some invisible realms are undetectable by any means and therefore, their existence is controversial, since they cannot be demonstrated.

Katabatic flows are wind currents.

Kin are family and blood relatives.

Kith are acquaintances, friends, neighbours, or the like: persons living in the same general locality and forming a more or less cohesive group

Late Heavy Bombardment occurred around 4.1 to 3.8 billion years ago, when ice-containing asteroids and comets pulverised the world's surface.

Liquid life is an ancient idea that 'life' is organised through the principles of material (and spiritual) flow. This book takes a third millennial view of the term, to construct an alternative metaphor and philosophy of 'life' than the *bête machine,* which can be examined, tested, and imagined.

Liquid living is the processes enacted and experiences provoked by liquid life.

Living fossil is a creature that is seemingly untouched by evolution. Their ancestors are represented in the fossil record in forms that vary very little from the way these organisms appear today, such as the coelacanth, nautilus, tuatara, horseshoe crab, tadpole shrimp, hagfish, and vampire squid. The term, however, is controversial, as the term is scientifically inexact and many living fossils are arbitrarily assigned this status (Schopf 1984). As a cultural meme, the term is evocative as it suggests that life adapts at many different speeds to broader planetary change.

Living goo is a play on the term 'grey goo', which is a hypothetical end-of-the-world scenario where out-of-control self-replicating agents (nanotechnology) consume the living world while building more of themselves. Since hagfish possess a seemingly endless ability to produce a special kind of 'snot', a hypothetical world scenario arises when the world is smothered in it — akin to the sequelae of a traffic accident in Oregon involving a lorry that was full of 'slime eels' (Bittel 2017).

LUCA, or Last Universal Common Ancestor, is the first biological organism — and hypothetical creature — whose progeny gave rise to all creatures on Earth. If the tree of life is traced back far enough back in time, then all life is genetically related to LUCA.

Luminiferous aether was a hypothetical matrix responsible for the propagation of light through empty space, which was something that waves should not be able to. It was experimentally disproven during the nineteenth century and superseded by Albert Einstein's *Special Theory of Relativity* in 1916.

Magic is the production of astonishing events that are not lessened in their strangeness by rational explanations of their apparent causes.

Magnetic Resonance Imaging (MRI) produces detailed images of the body by visualising its water content, using strong magnetic fields and radio waves.

Marduk is an ancient Mesopotamian god capable of good and evil, associated with the epic of creation. He is the patron deity of Babylon.

Melissai, or *melissae,* are the Greek and Latin words for bees.

Metabolic weather is a dynamic, far-from-equilibrium substrate, or hyperbody, at far from equilibrium that permeates the atmosphere, liquid environments, soils, and Earth's crust.

Metabolism is the ongoing flow and exchange of biochemical reactions and energy that characterises living systems. It is a form of 'cold combustion' that takes place at body temperature, which 'burns' resources but does not 'consume' itself in the process.

Modern Synthesis is a theory of evolution that is centred on the primacy of natural selection as the motivating force behind evolution and the levels of organisation at which this selection is manifest. It takes a gradualist perspective of change and is enabled by a set of mechanistic technologies (see section 04.2).

MOSE is the Italian word for Moses, and an acronym — Modulo Sperimentale Elettromeccanico — which means Experimental Electromechanical Module. It refers to the series of 78 hydraulic gates that are installed in the Venice lagoon to protect the city against high tides.

Natural selection is the biological theory and natural process that underpins the concept of modification by descent, where selective 'pressures' that act upon organisms create a condition of 'fitness', so the best adapted to a given context survive and reproduce. This leads to the perpetuation of genetic qualities best suited to that particular environment. It is an ethically problematic term as it is fatalist and endorses ruthlessness and selfishness as favourable characteristics. It also undermines the agency of creatures to make decisions and overcome challenges. While natural selection proposes to be a neutral instrument for considering the process of evolution, it is a highly loaded value system that endorses practices such as eugenics, the science of 'better' breeding, where selective values (preferences, prejudices) are non-inclusive, or undeclared.

Necrobiome is the community of bacteria found on a corpse.

Neoteny is when larval or juvenile forms of creatures become sexually mature before they reach adulthood, such as in the lifecycle of the axolotl.

Neutrinos are subatomic particles that are created when radioactive elements decay. Unlike protons, neutrons, and electrons, they do not play a major role in the structure of atoms (Lincoln 2017).

New carbon dioxide is released by the internal combustion engine from fossilised plant sources that trapped it as partially decomposed biomass during the late Devonian and Carboniferous eras. When the plants died, they only partially decomposed and became petrified as coal (mostly terrestrial higher plants), or liquefied as oil (mainly aquatic/marine lower plants and bacteria) (Tissot and Welte 1978, 202–24). This carbon is being reanimated in the guts of our industrial machines and transport systems, as the combustion engine breaks the long chain hydrocarbons of fossil fuels into energy and carbon dioxide, releasing the ancient Earth's atmosphere back into our own.

New physics refers to developments during the Enlightenment whereby all natural change could be reduced to the local motion of material particles and mathematically described.

Nonillion is a cardinal number represented in the US by 1 followed by 30 zeros, and in the UK by 1 followed by 54 zeros. The US notation is indicated in the text.

Obsidian is an igneous rock that forms when molten rock material cools so rapidly that atoms are unable to arrange themselves into a crystalline structure. It is a naturally occurring form of glass and amorphous material, known as a mineraloid.

Odic force is the name given in the mid-nineteenth century to a hypothetical vital energy or life force by Baron Carl von Reichenbach (von Reichenbach 2003).

One gene, one enzyme hypothesis was proposed by Gorge Wells Beadle in 1941. It states that every gene encodes for a single enzyme, which affects a step in a single metabolic pathway. While influential, the concept is over-simplistic and does not properly describe the contemporary relationships that are understood to occur between genes and proteins, which are far more nuanced and complex.

Open niche construction is the selective modification of environments by organisms.

Origin of life is a spectrum of material events that led to the transition from inert to living matter. This book holds that no one occurrence but a continuum of interconnected events gave rise to life as we currently recognise it. The first forms of lively matter did not have the present status of 'life', which is reserved for biology, which is uniquely governed by a central organising nucleotide code like DNA.

Osmotic structures are outgrowths of a material that are produced by the pressure caused by the rapid entry of water, which produces an internal force that causes sudden expansion, or growth (Leduc 1911).

Orgone radiation is a hypothetical, omnipresent libidinal life force in the atmosphere proposed by Wilhelm Reich, which he claimed was responsible for gravity, weather patterns, emotions, and health.

Orrery is a mechanical model of the solar system that illustrates or predicts the relative positions and motions of the planets and moons, usually according to the heliocentric model.

Ort is a scrap or a morsel.

Panglossian paradigm is a term coined by Stephen Jay Gould and Richard Lewontin in their paper 'The Spandrels of San Marco and the Panglossian Paradigm: A Critique of the Adaptationist Programme' (Gould and Lewontin 1979). The title refers to Dr. Peter Pangloss, a fictional character in Voltaire's Candide, who teaches that in this, the best of all possible worlds, everything happens out of absolute necessity and everything happens for best, even at times of disaster. In their paper Gould and Lewontin set out to contest the underlying fatalism of this approach, likening it to the 'adaptionist' theory of evolution that makes the unsubstantiated assumption that all or most traits are optimised adaptations 'fit' for a predetermined purpose.

Parabiosis means 'living beside' and refers to the surgical union of two creatures through their blood circulation.

Parallel modes of existence (bodies, universes etc.) exist within a probabilistic reality, where various degrees of freedom exist. This means that alternatives to their current expression of matter, time, and space may be unlocked from within the system.

Pelagic refers to the open sea. Pelagic fish often occupy the open waters between the coast and the edge of the continental shelf in depths of 20–400 metres.

Periodic table of elements is a tabular arrangement of the chemical elements, which are ordered by their atomic number, electron configuration, and recurring chemical properties, whose structure shows periodic trends.

Perspiratio insensibilis, or *insensible perspiration,* refers to changes in body weight that occur from day to day that are unnoticed by most persons, as body weight is fairly constant for weeks at a time. Although the phenomenon was known to ancient physicians like Galen, the term was modernised by Sanctorio Sanctorius through a series of rigorous experiments, which demonstrated that volatile substances leave the body during the processes of metabolism.

Pica is derived from the Latin for magpie, a bird with indiscriminate eating habits. It refers to the persistent ingestion of non-nutritive substances, like soil, for at least one month, at an age for which this behaviour is developmentally inappropriate.

Pig iron ingots are crude iron casts, which are intermediary products in the iron industry. They acquired their name as they were cast from a branching structure formed from sand with multiple ingots subtended at right angles to a central channel, or 'runner'. The overall structure resembled a sow suckling a litter of piglets. On cooling and hardening, the smaller ingots (the 'pigs') were broken from the runner (the 'sow') for further processing.

Plasmogeny is the study of the origin of protoplasm.

Polysemic means having multiple meanings.

Progeny are offspring.

Protists are mostly single-celled organisms like amoeba, but they also exist as colonial forms, which consist of many similar cells.

Protocell is a simple chemical precursor of a living system, which exhibits lifelike properties but does not have the status of being fully alive[1].

---

1   The term defined here is the one presented in this book. In the wider literature, definitions vary and include a range of lively chemical assemblages from vesicles to fully artificial cells (Armstrong 2015, 35).

Protolife is a set of chemical systems that exhibit lifelike properties without having the full status of being alive. They are used experimentally to demonstrate some of the principles of interest in understanding the transition from inert to living matter.

Punctuated equilibrium is a form of evolutionary development proposed in 1972 by Stephen Jay Gould and Niles Eldredge. It describes a process where species are generally stable, changing little for millions of years, which is 'punctuated' by a rapid burst of change that results in a new species and leaves few fossils behind.

Pyrrha is a mythological figure in a story that resembles the Biblical tale of Noah's Ark, where in the attempt to erase the sins of the old world, a new race of people is created (see Deucalion).

Qingu is a Babylonian god who was posed as an adversary to Marduk by his mother, the goddess Tiamat. Marduk slayed him and mixed his blood with the earth to mould the first human beings. Qingu then sought refuge in the underworld kingdom of Ereshkigal, along with the other deities who had sided with Tiamat.

Quantum theory is the science of the subatomic realm, where fields and forces do not behave according to the laws of classical science. While they appear to contradict classical physics, their effects are coherent with conventional models of reality, as their strange effects are largely averaged out into insignificance by the effects of decoherence at the macroscale.

Quantum field fluctuations are the particle territories that are mostly empty space that make up atoms.

Quantum indistinguishability means it is not possible to tell the difference between two quantum particles.

Quantum jellyfish is a term used by Erwin Schrödinger that refers to the anticipated blurriness and featurelessness from many overlapping fields and boundaries exist that are characteristic of quantum fields (Byrne 2013).

Rayleigh–Bénard convection cells are dynamic material formations that are produced by complex changes in surface tension and differentials that exist between the hot and cold fields of fluid, which produce cell-like boundaries and host a turbulent 'internal milieu'.

(re) is used throughout this book as a way of introducing ambiguity. It asks the reader to consider whether something is happening for the first time, or whether it is an iterative process capable of producing alternative outcomes, which may differ with each cycle of events.

Schrödinger's Cat challenges an existential paradox at the heart of the Copenhagen interpretation of quantum mechanics, which states that a particle exists in all states at once until observed. Erwin Schrödinger devised this thought experiment in 1935, placing a cat in a sealed box along with a radioactive sample, a Geiger counter and a bottle of poison. If the Geiger counter detects that the radioactive material has decayed, then the bottle of poison is smashed and the cat is killed. If the 'Copenhagen interpretation' of quantum mechanics is true, then the cat is both alive and dead until the box is opened. 'Common sense' suggests that the cat must either be dead or alive (not both), whether or not it is observed, and exposes the limits of the Copenhagen interpretation in relationship to practical, or actual situations. (Merz 2013).

Scientific Revolution is a period of cultural development and technological advancement, which led to changes in social and institutional organisation that occurred in Europe around 1550–1700.

Scrying is reading the future against the present by using unstable images produced by reflective surfaces.

Scylla is a sea monster in classical Greek legend who haunted the rocks of a narrow strait opposite the whirlpool of Kharybdis (Charybdis). Homer describes Skylla (Scylla) as a creature with twelve dangling feet, six long necks and grisly heads lined with a triple row of sharp teeth.

Selfish gene is a theory of genetic conservation proposed by Richard Dawkins in 1976 that builds upon the principal theory of George C. Williams' *Adaptation and Natural Selection* (1966). It is a way of reading life that positions the gene as the material substance which governs evolution and is ultimately, self-preserving. As a primary unit of selection, the gene constitutes an immortal digital code, which is proposedly far more reliable than other ephemeral vehicles for producing forms of life like chromosomes, communities, individuals, and species. However, the ultra-reductionist thesis of the book is very hard to justify. While self-conserving genes may exist, they are not as prevalent as Dawkins proposes. In reducing the 'pressures' of natural selection to forces that act only on genes in which the 'empowered' organism is merely a 'vehicle' for its molecular compulsions is, quite simply, wrong. Evolutionary forces operate on all levels, from molecular landscapes to individuals and communities. It's Ultra-Darwinism, where natural selection is an all-powerful force also dismisses evidence from other areas of science, like population biology and evolutionary biology. There is also an absence of ethical concerns in his justification of 'selfishness', whose far-reaching implications not just for life, but also society, are uncritically presented.

Ship of Theseus is a thought experiment that asks whether an object that has all of its parts sequentially replaced is the same as the original.

Siphonophores are a group of predatory animals, or superorganisms, of around 175 known species that include corals, hydroids, and true jellyfish. Specimens consist of clear gelatinous material, are thin, long, and may reach up to 40 metres. They are exceedingly fragile and break into many pieces under even the slightest stress.

Sixth Great Extinction, or Holocene Extinction, is an anticipated mass extinction event whose unique characteristic is that it is mediated by humans. It follows five previous major extinctions, namely, the Ordovician–Silurian extinction events, the Late Devonian extinction, the Permian–Triassic extinction, the Triassic–Jurassic extinction and the Cretaceous–Paleogene extinction event.

Skyrmions are a general class of particles that are made by twisting a field. When this field is a magnetic field, the particles are called magnetic skyrmions, with potential applications in spintronics, where electron spins are exploited in the design of transistors and storage media.

Spin-isomers of molecular hydrogen occur in two isomeric forms, one with its two proton nuclear spins aligned parallel (orthohydrogen), the other with its two proton spins aligned antiparallel (parahydrogen). These two forms are often referred to as spin isomers.

Stochastic processes have a random probability distribution or pattern that may be analysed statistically but not be predicted precisely.

Stromatolites are fossil evidence of the prokaryotic life that remains today. They are sheet-like sedimentary rocks that were originally formed by multiple layers of cyanobacteria over thousands of years and offer a visual portal into deep time on earth and the emergence of life.

Superfluids are uncommon in nature. They can be produced experimentally by slowing down normal matter to extremely low temperatures. They act as a single, giant 'superatom' where their matter waves spread out and overlap with one another, sharing the same energy and vibrating together as a single entity.

Supermassive black holes are found at the centres of galaxies. They are much larger than stellar mass black holes, with a typical mass of millions of Suns and devour matter to produce luminous objects known as quasars.

Superorganism is a body that behaves in some respects as a single being but is made up of many cooperating creatures that act as a whole, like the bacterial biome, or colonial organisms such as bees, siphonophores, and slime moulds.

Supersoils are artificial organic fabrics that augment the environmental performance of the soil, or enable new processes and metabolisms to occur within the ground.

Synthetic biology is the designing and engineering of living things. This field is evolving so rapidly that no widely accepted definitions exist but are generally concerned with the application of engineering principles to the fundamental components of biology, most commonly invoking the modification and (re)insertion of genetic sequences into microorganisms. This book appreciates both the ontology of the term, which was coined by Stephane Leduc as a more complex branch of complex chemistry (Leduc 1911), as well as its contemporary molecular biology and bitechnological applications in the construction of novel artificial biological pathways, organisms, and devices.

Synthia was the first self-replicating synthetic bacterium with a fully artificial genome that was created in 2010 by the J. Craig Venter Institute (JCVI) (Gibson et al. 2010).

Systems science views an entire system of components as an entity, rather than simply as an assembly of individual parts, where each component fits properly with the other components, rather than functioning entirely by itself.

Technosphere is the realm of human technological activity and the technologically modified environment.

Teleplasty, or ideoplasty, is acting and creating artefacts using the mind. It was developed as a controversial psychoanalytic theory by Roger Callois that proposes the possibility of intelligence without thought, creativity without art and agency in the absence of the human agent. In some contexts, it is thought to be the precursor to notions of bottom-up chemosynthetic design, where morphology is built into the very structure of matter and can be released from it through methods of soft, or remote control (Callois and Shepley 1984). Historically, it is associated with controlling the dead, the 'externalised dreams of mediums' and the conscious generation of shadowy forms, or projections using the mind.

Thanatobiome is the metabolising community of creatures found in composts.

Third time is a concept proposed by Ilya Prigogine that exists in space-time rather than standard geometric space. Characterised by its irreversibility, it provides a source of material creativity that is expressed through the living realm.

Three-body problem takes an initial set of data that specifies the positions, masses, and velocities of three bodies for some particular point in time and then determines the motions for all of them.

Thrombolites are ancient forms of photsynthesising microbial communities that form clotted accretions in shallow water by trapping sedimentary particles to form reef-like structures.

Transfusional parabiosis is a rejuvenation therapy whereby regular blood injections from young donors are given to older recipients.

Upcycling is when discarded items are processed in ways that increase their quality, or value, so they can be readily incorporated into metabolic cycles of biological, or industrial exchange.

Virus is a small infectious agent that can only replicate inside the cells of another organism. The word is from the Latin *virus* referring to poison and other noxious substances, first used in English in 1392. There is much disagreement as to whether viruses are organisms, which are described as replicative particles that constitute the most numerous living agents on Earth. Specifically, a virus dubbed HTVCo1oP was the commonest, which parasitises its viral host *Pelagibacter ubique* that makes up one-third of all the single-celled organisms in the ocean (Eveleth 2013).

Vitalism describes the nature of life as arising from a 'vital', life-giving force, which infuses matter so that it becomes animated. It is peculiar to living organisms and different from all other forces found outside living things.

Vitrification is the process of turning matter into glass.

Vivogenesis is a process that results in persistent lifelike phenomena, without necessarily being biological in its character, or ordering.

Weirding is the process of becoming odd, mysteriously strange, unsettling, and exceptional.

Zoephilia is our empathy for lifelike phenomena. It is derived from E.O. Wilson's notion of biophilia, 'the innate tendency to focus on life and lifelike processes' (Wilson 1990, 1). This definition is expanded, not only to include *bios,* qualified (anthropocentric) life, but also *zoē*, bare[2] life that includes all living beings and is an ecological entity (Braidotti 2006, 41), which demonstrates effects that are suggestive, in some aspects, of our experience of life.

---

2   Giorgio Agamben (1998) argues that *bios*, the sheer biological fact of life is given priority over 'bare life' (or *zoē*), the way a life is lived, and implies an active biopolitics.

REFERENCES

Abate, Tom. 2015. 'Stanford Researchers Solve the Mystery of the Dancing Droplets'. *Stanford News,* March 11, 2015. http://news. stanford.edu/2015/03/11/dancing-droplets-prakash-031115/.

Abbott, Edwin Abbott. 1992. *Flatland: A Romance of Many Dimensions.* London: Dover Thrift Editions.

ACA. 2017. 'Beyond: Cthonic'. *Allenheads Contemporary Arts.* http:// acart.org.uk/beyond.

Ackerman, Diane. 1991. *The Moon by Whale Light: And Other Adventures among Bats, Penguins, Crocodilians.* London: Random House.

Adamatzky, Andrew, Rachel Armstrong, Jeff Jones, and Yukio-Pegio Gunji. 2013. 'On Creativity of Slime Mould'. *International Journal of General Systems* 42, no. 5: 441–57. DOI: 10.1080/03081079.2013.776206.

Adamatzky, Andrew, Larry Bull, Benjamin De Lacy Costello, Susan Stepney, and Christof Teuscher. 2007. *Unconventional Computing.* Beckington: Luniver Press.

Adamatzky, Andrew, and Benjamin De Lacy Costello. 2003. 'Reaction–Diffusion Path Planning in a Hybrid Chemical and Cellular-Automaton Processors'. *Chaos, Solitons and Fractals* 16: 727–36. DOI: 10.1016/S0960-0779(02)00409-5.

Adamatzky, Andrew, and Theresa Schubert. 2014. 'Slime Mold Microfluidic Logical Gates'. *Materials Today* 17, no. 2: 86–91. DOI: 10.1016/j.mattod.2014.01.018.

Adams, Douglas. 2009. *The Hitchhiker's Guide to the Galaxy.* London: Macmillan.

Admin, M. 2013. 'Descartes Dissected His Wife's Dog to Prove a Point'. *KnowledgeNuts,* September 29. http://knowledgenuts. com/2013/09/29/descartes-dissected-his-wifes-dog-to-prove-a-point/.

Agamben, G. 1998. *Homo Sacer: Sovereign and Bare Life.* Translated by Daniel Heller-Roazen. Stanford: Stanford University Press.

Al-Khalili, Jim, and Johnjoe McFadden. 2014. *Life on the Edge: The Coming Age of Quantum Biology.* New York: Crown Publishers.

Allen, Garland E. 2018. 'Mechanism, Organicism and Vitalism'. In *The Routledge Handbook of Mechanisms and Mechanical Philosophy,* edited by Stuart Glennan and Phyllis Illari, 59–73. Abingdon: Routledge.

Aldrovandi, Ulisse. 2002. *Monstrorum Historia.* Paris: Belles Lettres.

Altenmüller, Ulrike. 2013. 'The City Crown: A Utopianist's Vision of a Better World by Bruno Taut'. *Spaces of Utopia: An Electronic Journal* 2, no. 2: 134–42.

Ambrose. 2009. *On the Holy Spirit (Book I),* chap. 7, v. 81, New Advent. http://www.newadvent.org/fathers/34021.htm.

Anker, Peder. 2014. 'The Gaia Hypothesis: Science on a Pagan Planet – by Michael Ruse'. *Centaurus* 43, no. 3: 123–24. DOI: 10.1111/1600-0498.12057.

Anon. n.d. 'John Amy Bird Bell'. *British Executions.* http://www.britishexecutions.co.uk/execution-content.php?key=2373&termRef=John%20Amy%20Bird%20Bell.

Anon. 1665–1666. 'An Account of the Risk and Attempts, of a Way to Conveigh Liquors Immediately into the Mass of Blood'. *Philosophical Transactions of the Royal Society* 1: 128–30.

Anon. 1893. *The Bookworm: An Illustrated Treasury of Old-Time Literature.* London: Elliot Stock.

Anstead, David Thomas. 1863. *The Great Stone Book of Nature.* Philadelphia: George W. Childs.

Anthill Social. 2009. 'Cybernetic Bacteria'. Exhibition, Dublin Science Gallery, April 18, 2009. http://www.theanthillsocial.co.uk/projects/cybernetic-bacteria.

Aranyszin. 2017. Comment to 'Beached Octopus Thanks Rescuer'. *Imgur,* July 18. https://imgur.com/gallery/ys9By?s=fb.

Armstrong, D.M. 1993. *A Materialist Theory of the Mind.* London: Routledge.

Armstrong, Rachel. 2015. *Vibrant Architecture: Matter as a Codesigner of Living Structures.* Berlin: Degruyter Open.

Armstrong, Rachel. 2016. *Star Ark: A Living, Self-Sustaining Spaceship.* Chichester: Springer-Praxis.

Armstrong, Rachel. 2018a. *Origamy.* Alconbury Weston: NewCon Press.

Armstrong, Rachel. 2018b. *Soft Living Architecture: An Alternative View of Bio-Informed Design Practice.* London: Bloomsbury Academic.

Armstrong, Rachel. 2019. *Invisible Ecologies.* Alconbury Weston: NewCon Press.

Armstrong, Rachel. Forthcoming 2020. *The Decomposition Comedy.* Alconbury Weston: NewCon Press.

Armstrong, Rachel, Simone Ferracina, Christos Kakalis, and Rolf Hughes. 2017. 'Notating Not Knowing: The Oceanic Challenge to Format and Medium'. *Edinburgh Architecture Research* 35.

Arnold, Carrie. 2014. 'Hints of Life's Start Found in a Giant Virus'. *Quanta Magazine,* July 10. https://www.quantamagazine.org/were-giant-viruses-the-first-life-on-earth-20140710/.

Arrenhius, Svante. 1908. *Worlds in the Making: The Evolution of the Universe*. New York and London: Harper & Brothers.

Artaud, Antonin. 1975. 'To Have Done with the Judgement of God'. Black Sparrow Press, Issue 34. *Surrealism-Plays.com*. http://surrealism-plays.com.

Artaud, Antonin. 2010. *The Theatre and its Double*. London: Oneworld Classics.

Atkins, Marc, and Iain Sinclair. 1999. *Liquid City*. London: Reaktion Books.

Atlas Obscura. 2013. 'Dr. Wilhelm Reich's Orgasm-Powered Cloudbuster'. *Slate*, August 19. http://www.slate.com/blogs/atlas_obscura/2013/08/19/see_wilhelm_reich_s_orgasm_powered_cloudbuster_at_his_orgonon_estate_in.html.

Baas, Nils A., and Claus Emmeche. 1997. 'On Emergence and Explanation'. *Intellectica* 2, no. 25: 67–83. http://intellectica.org/SiteArchives/archives/n25/25_04_Baas.pdf.

Bachelard, Gaston. 1992. *The Poetics of Space*. Translated by Maria Jolas. Boston: Beacon Press.

Bachelard, Gaston. 1994. *Water and Dreams: An Essay on the Imagination of Matter*. Translated by Edith R. Farrell. Dallas: Dallas Institute of Humanities and Culture.

Ball, Philip. 2009. *Flow: Nature's Patterns – A Tapestry in Three Parts*. Oxford: Oxford University Press.

Ball, Philip. 2017a. 'Designer Babies: An Ethical Horror Waiting to Happen?' *The Observer*, January 8. https://www.theguardian.com/science/2017/jan/08/designer-babies-ethical-horror-waiting-to-happen.

Ball, Philip. 2017b. 'How Life and Death Spring from Disorder'. *Quanta Magazine*, January 26. https://www.quantamagazine.org/the-computational-foundation-of-life-20170126.

Ballantyne, Andrew. 2007. *Deleuze and Guattari for Architects*. Abingdon: Routledge.

Ballard, J.G. 2012. *The Drowned World*. New York: Liveright.

Barrow, John D. 2002. *The Book of Nothing: Vacuums, Voids and the Latest Ideas About the Origins of the Universe*. London: Vintage.

Bartels, Meghan. 2016. 'This Looks Like a Forest, But It's Actually Just One Tree – And It's One of the Oldest and Largest Organisms on Earth'. *Business Insider UK*, July 8. https://www.businessinsider.com/pando-aspen-grove-utah-oldest-largest-organism-2016-7.

Barthes, Roland. 1972. *Mythologies*. Translated by Annette Lavers. London: Paladin.

Bartholomew, Alick. 2003. *Hidden Nature: The Startling Insights of Viktor Schauberger*. Edinburgh: Floris Books.

Bartoletti, Ivana. 2018. 'Women Must Act Now, Or Male-Designed Robots Will Take Over Our Lives'. *The Guardian,* March 13. https://www.theguardian.com/commentisfree/2018/mar/13/women-robots-ai-male-artificial-intelligence-automation.

Bastian, Michelle. 2006. 'Haraway's Lost Cyborg and the Possibilities of Transversalism'. *Signs: A Journal of Women in Culture and Society* 43, no. 3: 1027–49.

Bataille, George. 1977. 'Chance'. In *The Bataille Reader,* edited by Fred Botting and Scott Wilson, 42. Oxford: Blackwell Publishers.

Bates, Mary. 2014. 'The Creature Feature: 10 Fun Facts About Hagfish'. *Wired,* March 11. https://www.wired.com/2014/11/creature-feature-10-fun-facts-hagfish/.

Baudelaire, Charles. 1955. *The Mirror of Art*. London: Phaidon Press.

Baudelaire, Charles. 1995. *The Painter of Modern Life and Other Essays*. New York: Phaidon Press.

BBC News. 2014. 'Fish Rain Down on Sri Lanka Village'. May 6. http://www.bbc.co.uk/news/world-asia-27298939.

Behe, Michael. 2006. *Darwin's Black Box: The Biochemical Challenge to Evolution*. New York: Free Press.

Belousov, Boris Pavlovich. 1959. 'A Periodic Reaction and Its Mechanism'. *Compilation of Abstracts on Radiation Medicine* 147: 145.

Bénard, Henri. 1900. 'Les tourbillons cellulaires dans une nappe liquide'. *Revue Générale des Sciences Pures et Appliquées* 1: 1261–71, 1309–28.

Benjamin, Walter. 1969. *Illuminations: Essays and Reflections*. Edited by Hannah Arendt. Translated by Harry Zorn. New York: Schocken Books.

Benjamin, Walter. 1997. *Charles Baudelaire: A Lyric Poet in the Era of High Capitalism*. London: Verso.

Benjamin, Walter. 1999. *Walter Benjamin: Selected Writings. Volume 2, 1927–1934*. Edited by Michael W. Jennings, Howard Eiland, and Gary Smith. Cambridge: Belknap Press of Harvard University.

Benner, Steven. 2010. 'Life after the Synthetic Cell'. *Nature* 465: 422–24. DOI: 10.1038/465422a.

Bennett, Jane. 2010a. *Vibrant Matter: A Political Ecology of Things*. Durham: Duke University Press.

Bennett, Jane. 2010b. 'A Vitalist Stopover on the Way to a New Materialism'. In *New Materialisms: Ontology, Agency, and Politics,* edited by Diana H. Coole and Samantha Frost, 47–70. Durham: Duke University Press.

Bentlage, Bastian, Paulyn Cartwright, Angel A. Yanagihara, Cheryl Lewis, Gemma S. Richards, and Allen G. Collins. 2010. 'Evolution of Box Jellyfish (Cnidaria: Cubozoa), a Group of Highly Toxic Invertebrates'. *Proceedings of the Royal Society B: Biological Sciences* 277, no. 1680: 493–501. DOI: 10.1098/rspb.2009.1707.

Bergson, Henri. 1922. *Creative Evolution.* London: Macmillan.

Bergson, Henri. 2010. *Time and Free Will: An Essay on the Immediate Data of Consciousness.* Riverton: Legacy Books.

Bernal, John Desmond. 1949. 'The Physical Basis of Life'. *Proceedings of the Physical Society, Section B* 62, no. 11: 537–58. DOI: 10.1088/0370-1301/62/11/507.

Bernard, Claude. 1974. *Lectures on the Phenomena of Life Common to Animals and Plants.* Springfield: Charles C. Thomas.

Berrill, Norman John. 1930. 'On the Occurrence and Habits of the Siphonophore Stephanomia bijuga (Delle Chiaje)'. *Journal of the Marine Biological Association of the United Kingdom* 16: 753–55. DOI: 10.1017/S0025315400073069.

Berry, Wendell. 1996. *The Unsettling of America: Culture and Agriculture.* Berkeley: Counterpoint.

Berryman, S. 2016. 'Ancient Atomism'. *Stanford Encyclopedia of Philosophy.* https://plato.stanford.edu/entries/atomism-ancient/.

Bing, Franklin Church. 1971. 'The History of the Word 'Metabolism''. *Journal of the History of Medicine* 26, no. 2: 158–80. DOI: 10.1093/jhmas/XXVI.2.158.

Bittel, Jason. 2017. "Slime Eels' Explode on Highway After Bizarre Traffic Accident'. *National Geographic,* July 14. https://news.nationalgeographic.com/2017/07/hagfish-slime-oregon-highway/.

Bjornerud, Marcia. 2015. 'Stone's Throw'. *The New Yorker,* October 2, 2015. https://www.newyorker.com/tech/annals-of-technology/a-tsunami-written-in-stone.

Blake, William. 1975. *The Marriage of Heaven and Hell.* Oxford: Oxford University Press.

Boer, Richard Constant. 1888. *Örvar-Odds Saga.* Leiden: E.J. Brill.

Bogdanov, Alexander. 2002. *The Struggle for Viability: Collectivism through Blood Exchange.* Bloomington: Xlibris.

Boltzmann, Ludwig. 1964. *Lectures on Gas Theory.* Berkeley: University of California Press.

Boltzmann, Ludwig. 1974. 'The Second Law of Thermodynamics'. In *Ludwig Boltzmann: Theoretical Physics and Philosophical Problems:*

Select Writings, edited by Brian McGuinness, 14–32. Dordrecht: D. Reidel.

Börk, Karrigan S. 2006. 'Lunar Phobia in the Greater Fishing Bat Noctilio leporinus (Chiroptera: Noctilionidae)'. *International Journal of Tropical Biology and Conservation* 54, no. 4: 1117–23. DOI: 10.15517/RBT.V54I4.14085.

Bosch, Thomas C.G. 2009. 'Hydra and the Evolution of Stem Cells'. *Bioessays* 31, no. 4: 478–86. DOI: 10.1002/bies.200800183.

Botkin, Daniel B. 2001. *No Man's Garden: Thoreau and a New Vision for Civilization and Nature.* Washington, DC: Island Press.

Bowes Museum. 2017. 'The Silver Swan'. http://thebowesmuseum.org.uk/Collections/Explore-The-Collection/The-Silver-Swan.

Brady, Heather. 2017. "'Faceless' Fish Seen for First Time in over a Century'. *National Geographic,* June 2. http://news.nationalgeographic.com/2017/06/faceless-fish-deep-sea-voyage-australia/.

Braidotti, Rosi. 2006. *Transpositions: On Nomadic Ethics.* Cambridge: Polity Press.

Braidotti, Rosi. 2013. *The Posthuman.* Cambridge: Polity Press.

Brain, Robert Michael. 2013. 'Materialising the Medium: Ectoplasm and the Quest for Supra-Normal Biology in Fin-de-Siècle Science and Art'. In *Vibratory Modernism,* edited by Anthony Enns and Shelley Trower, 115–44. New York: Palgrave Macmillan.

Braungart, Michael, and William McDonough. 2002. *Cradle to Cradle: Remaking the Way We Make Things.* New York: North Point Press.

Briggs, John, and F. David Peat. 1989. *Turbulent Mirror: An Illustrated Guide to Chaos Theory and the Science of Wholeness.* New York: HarperCollins.

British Glass. 2013. 'History of Glass'. https://www.britishglassfoundation.org.uk/a-history-of-glass/.

British Library. 2016. 'The Thinking Machine: W Ross Ashy and the Homeostat'. http://blogs.bl.uk/science/2016/04/the-thinking-machine.html.

Brockman, John. 1995. *The Third Culture.* New York: Simon & Schuster.

Brockman, John. 2011. 'Lynn Margulis 1938–2011 'Gaia Is a Tough Bitch."' *The Edge,* November 23. https://www.edge.org/conversation/lynn_margulis-lynn-margulis-1938-2011-gaia-is-a-tough-bitch.

Bronte, Emily. 2009. *Wuthering Heights.* Oxford: Oxford University Press.

Brooke, Anne P. 1994. 'Diet of the Fishing Bat, *Noctilio leporinus* (Chiroptera: Noctilionidae)'. *Journal of Mammalogy* 75, no. 1: 212–19. DOI: 10.2307/1382253.

Brooks, Michael. 1999. 'Quantum Foam'. *New Scientist* 28, no. 2191: 28.

Brouwers, Lucas. 2012. 'Did Life Evolve in a 'Warm Little Pond'?' *Scientific American,* February 16. https://blogs.scientificamerican.com/thoughtomics/did-life-evolve-in-a-warm-little-pond/.

Bucklin, Stephanie M. 2017. 'The Story of Dark Matter'. *Ars Technica,* February 3. https://arstechnica.com/science/2017/02/a-history-of-dark-matter/.

Bud, Robert. 1993. *The Uses of Life: A History of Biotechnology.* Cambridge: Cambridge University Press.

Buehler, Jake. 2017. 'Twisted Fishter: Mud Eels Do an Evolutionary About Face'. *Hakai Magazine,* September 11. https://www.hakaimagazine.com/article-short/twisted-fishter.

Buesseler, Ken O., John E. Andrews, Steven M. Pike, and Matthew A. Charette. 2004. 'The Effects of Iron Fertilization on Carbon Sequestration in the Southern Ocean'. *Science* 304, no. 5669: 414–17. DOI: 10.1126/science.1086895.

Bull, J.J. 2015. 'Evolutionary Reversion of Live Viral Vaccines: Can Genetic Engineering Subdue It?' *Virus Evolution* 1, no. 1, DOI: 10.1093/ve/vev005.

Burke, Michael P., and Stephen J. Klippenstein. 2017. 'Ephemeral Collision Complexes Mediate Chemically Termolecular Transformations That Affect System Chemistry'. *Nature Chemistry* 9: 1078–82. DOI: 10.1038/nchem.2842

Burnham, Antony D., and Andrew J. Berry. 2017. 'Formation of Hadean Granites by Melting of Igneous Crust'. *Nature Geoscience* 10, no. 6: 457–61. DOI: 10.1038/ngeo2942.

Butler, Samuel. 2008. *Evolution, Old and New.* London: Book Jungle.

Bütschli, Otto. 1892. *Untersuchungen über microskopische Schäume und das Protoplasma: Versuche und Beobachtungen zur Lösung der Frage nach den physikalischen Bedingungen der Lebenserscheinungen.* Leipzig: Engelmann.

Byrne, Peter. 2013. 'In Pursuit of Quantum Biology with Birgitta Whaley'. *Quanta Magazine,* July 30. https://www.quantamagazine.org/in-pursuit-of-quantum-biology-with-birgitta-whaley-20130730/.

Byrne, Peter. 2014. 'Early Life in Death Valley'. *Quanta Magazine,* April 24, 2014. https://www.quantamagazine.org/ancient-fossils-suggest-complex-life-evolved-on-land-20140424/.

Cairns-Smith, Alexander Graham. 1965. 'The Origin of Life and the Nature of the Primitive Gene'. *Journal of Theoretical Biology* 10, no. 1: 53–88. DOI: 10.1016/0022-5193(66)90178-0.

Cairns-Smith, Alexander Graham. 1985. *Seven Clues to the Origin of Life: A Scientific Detective Story*. Cambridge: Cambridge University Press.

Cairns-Smith, Alexander Graham. 1987. *Genetic Takeover: And the Mineral Origins of Life*. Cambridge: Cambridge University Press.

Calabrese, Edward J., Edward J. Stanek, Charles Edward Gilbert, and Ramon M. Barnes. 1990. 'Preliminary Adult Soil Ingestion Estimates: Results of a Pilot Study'. *Regulatory Toxicology and Pharmacology* 12, no. 1: 88–95. DOI: 10.1016/S0273-2300(05)80049-2.

Caltech Archives. 1988. 'Richard Feynman's Blackboard at the Time of His Death'. http://archives-dc.library.caltech.edu/islandora/object/ct1:483.

Calvino, Italo. 2002. *The Complete Cosmicomics*. New York: Penguin Modern Classics.

Caillois, Roger, and John Shepley. 1984. 'Mimicry and Legendary Psychasthenia'. *October* 31: 12–32. DOI: 10.2307/778354.

Canfield, Jack, and Mark Victor Hansen. 2012. *A 3rd Serving of Chicken Soup for the Soul: 101 More Stories to Open the Heart and Rekindle the Spirit*. Deerfield Beach: Backlist.

Cannon, Walter B. 1929. 'Organization for Physiological Homeostasis'. *Physiological Reviews* 9: 399–431. DOI: 10.1152/physrev.1929.9.3.399.

Caputo, Joseph. 2016. 'Creating Art with Genes and Bacteria'. *Elsevier Connect,* January 20, 2016. https://www.elsevier.com/connect/creating-art-with-genes-and-bacteria.

Carey, Bjorn. 2015. 'Just Add Water: Stanford Engineers Develop a Computer That Operates on Water Droplets'. *Stanford News,* June 8, 2015. http://news.stanford.edu/2015/06/08/computer-water-drops-060815/.

Carnall, Mark. 2017. 'Mysticism and Rudely-Shaped Rocks: Why 17th-Century Palaeontology Is Worth Revisiting'. *The Guardian,* September 7. https://www.theguardian.com/science/2017/sep/07/mysticism-and-rudely-shaped-rocks-why-17th-century-palaeontology-is-worth-revisiting.

Carrington, Damian. 2016. 'The Anthropocene Epoch: Scientists Declare Dawn of Human-Influenced Age'. *The Guardian,* August 29. https://www.theguardian.com/environment/2016/aug/29/declare-anthropocene-epoch-experts-urge-geological-congress-human-impact-earth.

Carrington, Leonora. 1989. 'Down Below'. In *The House of Fear: Notes from Down Below,* edited by Leonora Carrington, 27–36. London: Virago Press.

Carrington, Leonora. 2005. *The Hearing Trumpet.* London: Penguin Modern Classics.

Carroll, Lewis. 1946. *The Hunting of the Snark.* Oxford: Oxford University Press.

Carter, Angela. 2006. 'Wolf-Alice'. In *The Bloody Chamber and Other Stories.* London: Vintage Classics.

Carus, Paul. 1907. 'Goethe's Soul Conception'. *The Open Court* 12, no. 3: 745–51. https://opensiuc.lib.siu.edu/ocj/vol1907/iss12/3/.

Caschera, Filippo, Steen Rasmussen, and Martin M. Hanczyc. 2013. 'An Oil Droplet Division–Fusion Cycle'. *ChemPlusChem* 78, no. 1: 52–54. DOI: 10.1002/cplu.201200275.

Casselman, Anne. 2007. 'Strange but True: The Largest Organism on Earth Is a Fungus'. *Scientific American,* October 4. https://www.scientificamerican.com/article/strange-but-true-largest-organism-is-fungus/.

Castellano, Joseph M., Kira I. Mosher, Rachelle J. Abbey, Alisha A. McBride, Michelle L. James, Daniela Berdnik, Jadon C. Shen, et al. 2017. 'Human Umbilical Cord Plasma Proteins Revitalize Hippocampal Function in Aged Mice'. *Nature,* 544, no. 7651: 488–92. DOI: 10.1038/nature22067.

Caughill, Patrick. 2017. 'Researchers Have Officially Discovered a New Kind of Chemical Reaction'. *Futurism,* August 15. https://futurism.com/researchers-have-officially-discovered-a-new-kind-of-chemical-reaction/.

Ceballos, Gerardo, Paul R. Ehrlich, Anthony D. Barnosky, Andrés Garcia, Robert M. Pringle, and Todd M. Palmer. 2015. 'Accelerated Modern Human-Induced Species Losses: Entering the Sixth Mass Extinction'. *Science Advances* 1, no. 5: e1400253. DOI: 10.1126/sciadv.1400253.

Celsus. 1971. *De Medicina,* Volume 1. Cambridge: Harvard University Press.

Cepelewicz, Jordana. 2017. 'Beating the Odds for Lucky Mutations'. *Quanta Magazine,* August 16. https://www.quantamagazine.org/beating-the-odds-for-lucky-mutations-20170816/.

Cepelewicz, Jordana. 2018. "Traffic jams' of cells help to sculpt embryos'. *Quanta Magazine,* September 27. https://www.quantamagazine.org/traffic-jams-of-cells-help-to-sculpt-embryos-20180927/.

Chalmers, David. 1999. 'Facing Up to the Problem of Consciousness'. In *The Place of Mind,* edited by Brian Cooney, 382–400. Belmont: Wadsworth Cengage Learning.

Chandler, David L. 2015. 'How Some Beetles Produce a Scalding, Defensive Chemical Jet'. *MIT News,* April 30. http://news.mit.edu/2015/how-bombardier-beetles-produce-defensive-spray-0430.

Chase, Steven. 2002. *Angelic Spirituality: Medieval Perspectives on the Ways of Angels.* New York: Paulist Press.

Chatelin, Françoise. 2012. *Qualitative Computing: A Computational Journey into Nonlinearity.* Singapore: World Scientific.

Chavez, Carolina, Grisel Cruz-Becerra, Jia Feil, George A. Kassavetis, and James T. Kadonaga. 2019. 'Tardigrade Damage Suppressor Protein Binds to Nucleosomes and Protects DNA from Hydroxyl Radicals'. *eLife*, October 1. DOI: 10.7554/eLife.47682.

Chladni, Ernst Florens Friedrich. 1826. 'A New Catalogue of Meteoric Stones, Masses of Meteoric Iron, and Other Substances, the Fall of Which Has Been Made Known, Down to the Present Time'. *The Philosophical Magazine and Journal* 67, no. 333: 3–21. DOI: 10.1080/14786442608674005.

Chu, Jennifer. 2017. 'Transparent, Gel-Based Robots Can Catch and Release Live Fish'. *MIT News,* February 1. http://news.mit.edu/2017/transparent-gel-robots-catch-release-fish-0201.

Cira, Nate J., Adrien Benusiglio, and Manu Prakash. 2015. 'Vapour-Mediated Sensing and Motility in Two-Component Droplets'. *Nature* 519, no. 7544: 446–50. DOI: 10.1038/nature14272.

Clarke, Samuel and Gottfried Wilhelm Leibniz. 1998. *The Leibniz-Clarke Correspondence: Together with Extracts from Newton's Principia and Opticks,* edited by H.G. Alexander. Manchester: Manchester University Press.

Coelho, Paulo. 1993. *The Alchemist.* London: HarperCollins.

Coghlan, Andy. 2017a. 'Tardigrades Turn into Glass to Survive Complete Dehydration'. *New Scientist,* March 16. https://www.newscientist.com/article/2124893-tardigrades-turn-into-glass-to-survive-complete-dehydration/.

Coghlan, Andy. 2017b. 'Planet Earth Makes Its Own Water from Scratch Deep in the Mantle'. *New Scientist,* February 4. https://www.newscientist.com/article/2119475-planet-earth-makes-its-own-water-from-scratch-deep-in-the-mantle/.

Coleman, Sidney. 1975. 'Secret Symmetry: An Introduction to Spontaneous Symmetry Breakdown and Gauge Fields'. In *Laws of*

Hadronic Matter, edited by Antonino Zichichi, 138–215. New York: Academic Press.

Colín-García, María, Alejandro Heredia, Guadalupe Cordero, Antoni Camprubí, Alicia Negrón-Mendoza, Fernando Ortega-Gutiérrez, Hugo Beraldi, and Sergio Ramos-Bernal. 2016. 'Hydrothermal Vents and Prebiotic Chemistry: A Review'. *Boletín de la Sociedad Geológica Mexicana* 68, no. 3: 599–620. http://www.scielo.org.mx/scielo.php?script=sci_arttext&pid=S1405-33222016000300599.

Conti, Fiorenzo. 2001. 'Claude Bernard: Primer of the Second Biomedical Revolution'. *Nature Reviews Molecular Cell Biology* 2, no. 9: 703–7. DOI: 10.1038/35089594.

Coole, Diana and Samantha Frost, eds. 2010. *New Materialisms: Ontology, Agency, and Politics.* Durham: Duke University Press.

Coolidge, Frederick L. 2017. 'What Molecular Biology Has Neglected in Evolution: It's the Beginning of the World, and We Don't Know (About) It'. *Psychology Today,* January 14. https://www.psychologytoday.com/blog/how-think-neandertal/201701/what-molecular-biology-has-neglected-in-evolution.

Corsi, Giovanna, Maria Luisa dalla Chiara, and Giancarlo Ghirardi, eds. 1993. *Bridging the Gap: Philosophy, Mathematics, and Physics. Lectures on the Foundations of Science.* Dordrecht, Netherlands: Kluwer Academic.

Cowen, Ron. 2015. 'The Quantum Source of Space-Time'. *Nature* 527: 290–93. DOI: 10.1038/527290a.

Creighton, Jolene. 2015a. 'Amazing Video Shows Staggering Size of Black Holes (Video)'. *Futurism,* January 13. https://futurism.com/watch-amazing-video-shows-staggering-size-black-holes/.

Creighton, Jolene. 2015b. 'Gravity Isn't a Force, So How Does It Move Objects?' *Futurism,* August 19. https://futurism.com/gravity-isnt-a-force-so-how-does-it-move-objects/.

Crew, Bec. 2012. 'Pyura chilensis: The Closest Thing to Getting Blood from a Stone'. *Scientific American,* June 21, 2012. https://blogs.scientificamerican.com/running-ponies/pyura-chilensis-the-closest-thing-to-getting-blood-from-a-stone/.

Cronin, Leroy, Natalio Krasnogor, Benjamin G. Davis, Cameron Alexander, Neil Robertson, Joachim H.G. Steinke, Sven L.M. Schroeder, et al. 2006. 'The Imitation Game: A Computational Chemical Approach to Recognizing Life'. *Nature Biotechnology* 24, no. 10: 1203–6. DOI: 10.1038/nbt1006-1203.

Crouch, Blake. 2006. *Dark Matter.* London: Macmillan.

Crutzen, Paul J., and Eugene F. Stoermer. 2000. 'The 'Anthropocene''. *Global Change Newsletter* 41: 17–18.

Curie, Marie and Pierre Curie. 1923. *Autobiographical Notes*. New York: Macmillan.

Cuthberson, Anthony. 2018. 'Billionaire Trump Supporter Peter Thiel Denies Being a Vampire'. *The Independent,* November 8. https://www.independent.co.uk/life-style/gadgets-and-tech/news/peter-thiel-vampire-donald-trump-life-extension-blood-transfusion-ambrosia-palantir-a8614061.html.

Cuvier, Georges. 2006. *Cuvier's Animal Kingdom Arranged According to Its Organization*. Boston: Adamant Media Corporation.

Damisch, Hubert. 2002. *A Theory of Cloud: Toward a History of Painting*. Stanford: Stanford University Press.

Darwin, Charles. 2001. *On the Various Contrivances by which British and Foreign Orchids are Fertilized by Insects, and On the Good Effects of Intercrossing and on the Good Effect of Intercrossing*. Cambridge: Cambridge University Press.

Darwin, Charles. 2009. *The Power of Movement in Plants*. New York: Cornell University Library.

Darwin, Charles. 2010. *The Origin of the Species: By Means of Natural Selection*. Seattle: Senate.

Davisson, Clinton J. and Lester H. Germer. 1928. 'Reflection of Electrons by a Crystal of Nickel'. *Proceedings of the National Academy of Sciences of the United States of America* 14, no. 4: 317–322. DOI: 10.1073/pnas.14.4.317.

Dawkins, Richard. 2001. *A River Out of Eden: A Darwinian View of Life*. London: Phoenix.

Dawkins, Richard. 2006. *The Selfish Gene*. Oxford: Oxford University Press.

Dyson, Freeman. 1979. *Disturbing the Universe*. New York: Basic Books.

de Balzac, Honoré. 1977. *The Wild Ass's Skin*. London: Penguin Classics.

de Buffon, Georges-Louis Leclerc. 1783–1788. *Histoire naturelle des minéraux,* Volume 3. Paris: Imprimerie Royale.

de Jesus, Cecille. 2016. 'Understanding the Physics of Our Universe: What Is Quantum Mechanics?' *Futurism,* September 21. https://futurism.com/understanding-the-physics-of-our-universe-what-is-quantum-mechanics/.

de Lorenzo, Victor. 2014. 'From the Selfish Gene to Selfish Metabolism: Revisiting the Central Dogma'. *Bioessays* 36, no. 3: 226–35. DOI: 10.1002/bies.201300153.

de Lorenzo, Victor. 2015. 'It's the Metabolism, Stupid!' *Environmental Microbiology Reports* 7, no. 1: 18–19. DOI: 10.1111/1758-2229.12223.

de Lorenzo, Victor. 2018. 'Evolutionary Tinkering vs. Rational Engineering in the Times of Synthetic Biology'. *Life Sciences, Society and Policy* 14, no. 1: 18. DOI: 10.1186/s40504-018-0086-x.

de Marzio, M., Gaia Camiscasca, M.M. Conde, Mauro Rovere, and Paola Gallo. 2017. 'Structural Properties and Fragile to Strong Transition in Confined Water'. *Journal of Chemical Physics* 146. DOI: 10.1063/1.4975624.

Debré, Patrice. 1998. *Louis Pasteur*. Baltimore: Johns Hopkins University Press.

Deleuze, Gilles. 1995. *Negotiations 1972–1990*. Translated by Martin Joughin. New York: Columbia University Press.

Deleuze, Gilles. 2015. *The Logic of Sense*. Translated by Constantin V. Boundas, Mark Lester, and Charles J. Stivale. London: Bloomsbury Academic.

Deleuze, Gilles, and Félix Guattari. 1979. *A Thousand Plateaus: Capitalism and Schizophrenia*. Translated by Brian Massumi. London: Athlone Press.

Deleuze, Gilles, and Félix Guattari. 1983. *Anti-Oedipus: Capitalism and Schizophrenia*. Translated by Robert Hurley, Mark Seem, and Helen Lane. Minneapolis: University of Minnesota Press.

Denning, Peter J. 2007. 'Computing is a Natural Science'. *Communications of the ACM* 50, no. 7: 13–18. DOI: 10.1145/1272516.1272529.

Denton, Michael. 1986. *Evolution: A Theory in Crisis*. Chevy Chase: Adler & Adler.

Denton, Michael. 2016. *Evolution: Still a Theory in Crisis*. Seattle: Discovery Institute Press.

Deodhar, M.J. 2009. *Elementary Engineering Hydrology*. Delhi: Dorling Kindersley.

Descartes, René. 1985. *Philosophical Writings of Descartes*. Volume 1. Translated by John Cottingham, Robert Stoothoff and Dugald Murdoch. Cambridge: Cambridge University Press.

Dickinson, Goldsworthy Lowes. 1911. *The Greek View of Life*. New York: Doubleday, Page & Co.

Diderot, Denis. 1976. *Rameau's Nephew / D'Alembert's Dream*. London: Penguin Classics.

Dijkgraaf, Robbert. 2017. 'Quantum Questions Inspire New Math'. *Quanta Magazine,* March 30. https://www.quantamagazine.org/how-quantum-theory-is-inspiring-new-math-20170330.

Dirac, Paul A.M. 1927. 'The Quantum Theory of the Emission and Absorption of Radiation'. *Proceedings of the Royal Society A* 114, no. 767: 243–65. DOI: 10.1098/rspa.1927.0039.

Dirac, Paul A.M. 1933. 'Theory of Electrons and Positrons'. Nobel Lecture, December 12. https://www.nobelprize.org/prizes/physics/1933/dirac/lecture/.

Dirac, Paul A.M. 1951. 'Is There an Æther?' *Nature* 168: 906–7. DOI: 10.1038/168906a0.

Dizikes, Peter. 2011. 'When the Butterfly Effect Took Flight'. *MIT Technology Review,* February 22. https://www.technologyreview.com/s/422809/when-the-butterfly-effect-took-flight/.

Domazet-Lošo, Tomislav, Alexander Klimovich, Boris Anokhin, Friederike Anton-Erxleben, Mailin J. Hamm, Christina Lange, and Thomas C.G. Bosch. 2014. 'Naturally Occurring Tumours and the Basal Metazoan Hydra'. *Nature Communications* 5, art. 4222. DOI: 10.1038/ncomms5222.

Doyle, Arthur Conan. 1930. *The Edge of the Unknown.* New York: G.P. Putnam's Sons.

Driesch, Hans. 1928. 'Presidential Address'. *Proceedings of the Society for Psychical Research* 36: 97–103.

Driesch, Hans. 1929. *The Science and Philosophy of the Organism. Gifford Lectures, University of Aberdeen, 1907–1908.* Volume 2. London: A. & C. Black.

Du Maurier, Daphne. 2004. *The Glass Blowers.* London: Virago Press.

Dyson, Freeman. 2001. 'Is Life Analog Or Digital?' *Edge,* March 13. https://www.edge.org/conversation/freeman_dyson-is-life-analog-or-digital.

Eagleman, David. 2010. *Sum: Tales from the Afterlives.* Edinburgh: Canongate.

Earthbound 101. 2018. 'Who Are the Earthbound People?' *Institute for Earthbound Studies.* http://www.earthboundpeople.com/earthbound-101/.

Eck, Allison. 2016. 'How Do You Say 'Life' In Physics? A New Theory Sheds Light on the Emergence of Life's Complexity'. *Nautilus* 34. http://nautil.us/issue/34/adaptation/how-do-you-say-life-in-physics.

Edson, Mary C., Pamela Buckle Henning, and Shankar Sankaran. 2017. *A Guide to Systems Research: Philosophy, Processes and Practice*. Singapore: Springer.

Edwards, Lin. 2010. 'Maxwell's Demon Demonstration Turns Information into Energy'. *Phys.org,* November 15, 2010. https://phys.org/news/2010-11-maxwell-demon-energy.html#jCp.

Eigen, Manfred, and Peter Schuster. 1979. *The Hypercycle: A Principle of Natural Self-Organization*. Berlin: Springer-Verlag.

Einstein, Albert, Boris Podolsky, and Nathan Rosen. 1935. 'Can Quantum-Mechanical Description of Physical Reality Be Considered Complete?' *Physical Review* 47, no. 10: 777–80.

Eiseley, Loren. 1973. *The Immense Journey*. New York: Vintage Books.

Elettro, Hervé, Sébastien Neukirch, Fritz Vollrath, and Arnaud Antkowiak. 2016. 'In-Drop Capillary Spooling of Spider Capture Thread Inspires Hybrid Fibers with Mixed Solid-Liquid Mechanical Properties'. *Proceedings of the National Academy of Sciences of the United States of America* 113, no. 22: 6143–47. DOI: 10.1073/pnas.1602451113.

Ellington, Andrew D. 2012. 'Origins for Everyone'. *Evolution: Education and Outreach* 5, no. 3: 361–66. DOI: 10.1007/s12052-012-0440-z.

Encyclopedia of Life. 2017. 'CreatureCast: Siphonophores and Individuality'. *The Daily Catch,* February 10. http://theterramarproject.org/thedailycatch/creaturecast-siphonophores-and-individuality/.

Eng, Karen Frances. 2013. 'More to Life than DNA: Fellows Friday with Sheref Mansy'. *TED Blog,* October 11. http://blog.ted.com/more-to-life-than-dna-fellows-friday-with-sheref-mansy/.

Engels, Friedrich. 1947. *Anti-Dühring: Herr Eugen Dühring's Revolution in Science*. Moscow: Progress Publishers.

England, Jeremy L. 2015. 'Dissipative Adaptation in Driven Self-Assembly'. *Nature Nanotechnology* 10: 919–23. DOI: 10.1038/nnano.2015.250.

Epstein, Robert. 2016. 'The Empty Brain'. *Aeon,* May 18. https://aeon.co/essays/your-brain-does-not-process-information-and-it-is-not-a-computer.

Erickson, Millard J. 1983. *Christian Theology*. Grand Rapids: Baker Book House.

Eveleth, Rose. 2013. 'Guess What the Most Abundant Organism on Earth Is?' *Smithsonian.com,* February 15. http://www.smithsonianmag.com/smart-news/guess-what-the-most-abundant-organism-on-earth-is-19254662/.

Extance, Andy. 2018. 'How Atomic Imaging Is Being Pushed to Its Limits'. *Nature* 555: 545–47. DOI: 10.1038/d41586-018-03305-2.

Fänge, Ragnar. 1998. 'Introduction: Early Hagfish Research'. In *The Biology of Hagfishes*, edited by Jørgen Mørup Jørgensen, Jens Peter Lomholt, Roy E. Weber, and Hans Malte, xiii–xix. Dordrecht: Springer.

Farnes, J.S. 2018. 'A Unifying Theory of Dark Energy and Dark Matter: Negative Masses and Matter Creation within a Modified ACDM Framework'. *Astronomy & Astrophysics* 620. DOI: 10.1051/0004-6361/201832898.

Fernholm, Bo. 1998. 'Hagfish Systematics'. In *The Biology of Hagfishes*, edited by Jørgen Mørup Jørgensen, Jens Peter Lomholt, Roy E. Weber, and Hans Malte, 33–44. Dordrecht: Springer.

Flaubert, Gustave. 2002. *Temptation of St. Anthony*. New York: Random House.

Fleming, Nic. 2014. 'The Largest Living Thing on Earth Is a Humungous Fungus'. *BBC*, November 19. http://www.bbc.com/earth/story/20141114-the-biggest-organism-in-the-world.

Florijn, Bastiaan, Corentin Coulais, and Martin van Hecke. 2014. 'Programmable Mechanical Metamaterials'. *Physical Review Letters* 113, no. 17: 175503. DOI: 10.1103/PhysRevLett.113.175503.

Flusser, Vilém, and Louis Bec. 2012. *Vampyroteuthis Infernalis: A Treatise with a Report by the Institut Scientifique de Recherche Paranaturaliste*. Minneapolis: University of Minnesota Press.

Forsythe, William. 2014. 'Just Like That.: William Forsythe: Between Movement and Language'. In Erin Manning and Brian Massumi, *Thought in the Act: Passages in the Ecology of Experience*, 31–57. Minneapolis: University of Minnesota Press.

Foucault, Michel. 1998. *The Will to Knowledge: The History of Sexuality: 1*. Translated by Robert Hurley. London: Penguin Books.

Fox, Sidney W. 1988. "Clay Minerals and the Origin of Life', A.G. Cairns-Smith'. *The Quarterly Review of Biology* 63, no. 1: 66. https://www.jstor.org/stable/2827991.

Fox-Skelly, Jasmin. 2015. 'What Does It Take to Live at the Bottom of the Ocean?' Earth, *BBC*, January 29. http://www.bbc.co.uk/earth/story/20150129-life-at-the-bottom-of-the-ocean.

Füchslin, Rudolf M., Andrej Dzyakanchuk, Dandolo Flumini, Helmut Hauser, Kenneth J. Hunt, Rolf H. Luchsinger, Benedikt Reller, Stephan Scheidegger, and Richard Walker. 2013. 'Morphological Computation and Morphological Control: Steps toward a Formal

Theory and Applications'. *Artificial Life* 19, no. 1: 9–34. DOI: 10.1162/ARTL_a_00079.

Fudge, Douglas S., Nimrod Levy, Scott Chiu, and John M. Gosline. 2005. 'Composition, Morphology and Mechanics of Hagfish Slime'. *Journal of Experimental Biology* 208, no. 24: 4613–25. DOI: 10.1242/jeb.01963.

Fuller, Steve. 2011. *Humanity 2.0: What It Means to Be Human, Past, Present and Future.* Basingstoke: Palgrave Macmillan.

Fuller, Steve. 2016. 'Humanity's Lift-Off into Space: Prolegomena to a Cosmic Transhumanism'. In *Star Ark: A Living, Self-Sustaining Worldship,* edited by Rachel Armstrong, 383–93. Chichester: Springer/Praxis.

Fuller, Steve. 2018. Twitter feed @ProfSteveFuller.

Futera, Zdenek, Xue Yong, Yuanming Pan, John S. Tse, and Niall J. English. 2017. 'Formation and Properties of Water from Quartz and Hydrogen at High Pressure and Temperature'. *Earth and Planetary Science Letters* 461: 54–60. DOI: 10.1016/j.epsl.2016.12.031.

Gage, Mary. 1981. *Praise the Egg.* Colchester: The Book Service.

Gannon, Michael R., Alan Kurta, Armando Rodriguez-Durán, and Michael R. Willig. 2005. *Bats of Puerto Rico: An Island Focus and a Caribbean Perspective.* Lubbock: Texas Tech University Press.

Gánti, Tibor. 2003. *The Principles of Life.* New York: Oxford University Press.

Garm, Anders, Magnus Oskarsson, and Dan-Eric Nilsson. 2011. 'Box Jellyfish Use Terrestrial Cues for Navigation'. *Current Biology* 28, no. 9: 798–803. DOI: 10.1016/j.cub.2011.03.054.

Garman, S.W. 1877. 'Pseudis, 'The Paradoxical Frog''. *The American Naturalist* 11, no. 1: 587–91. DOI: 10.1086/271961.

Gat, Daniella, Yinon Mazar, Eddie Cytryn, and Yinon Rudich. 2017. 'Origin-Dependent Variations in the Atmospheric Microbiome Community in Eastern Mediterranean Dust Storms'. *Environmental Science & Technology* 51, no. 12: 6709–18. DOI: 10.1021/acs.est.7b00362.

Geddes, Patrick. 1920. *The Life and Work of Sir Jagadis C. Bose.* London: Longmans, Green and Co.

Gee, Henry. 1998. 'Pressure Brought to Bear'. *Nature,* November 5. DOI: 10.1038/news981105-1.

Giaimo, Cara. 2016. 'The Utopian Promise of Reprap, the 3D Printer That Can – Almost – Print Itself'. *Atlas Obscura,* February 21. http://www.atlasobscura.com/articles/the-utopian-promise-of-reprap-the-3d-printer-that-can-almost-print-itself.

Gibson, Daniel G., John I. Glass, Carole Lartigue, Vladimir N. Noskov, Ray-Yuan Chuang, Mikkel A. Algire, Gwynedd A. Benders, et al. 2010. 'Creation of a Bacterial Cell Controlled by a Chemically Synthesized Genome'. *Science* 329, no. 5987: 52–56. DOI: 10.1126/science.1190719.

Gilbert, Scott F. 1982. 'Intellectual Traditions in the Life Sciences: Molecular Biology and Biochemistry'. *Perspectives in Biology and Medicine* 26, no. 1: 151–62. DOI: 10.1353/pbm.1982.0009.

Glashow, Sheldon L. 1961. 'Partial-Symmetries of Weak Interactions'. *Nuclear Physics* 22, no. 4: 579–88. DOI: 10.1016/0029-5582(61)90469-2.

Gleick, James. 1997. *Chaos: Making a New Science.* London: Vintage.

Goethe, Johann Wolfgang von. 1999. *Faust: A Tragedy in Two Parts & The Urfaust.* Translated by John R. Williams. London: Wordsworth Classics of World Literature.

Golbin, A., Y. Golbin, L. Keith, and D. Keith. 1993. 'Mirror Imaging in Twins: Biological Polarization: An Evolving Hypothesis'. *Acta Geneticae Medicae et Gemellologiae* 42, no. 3–4: 237–43. DOI: 10.1017/S0001566000003238.

Gooth, Johannes, Anna C. Niemann, Tobias Meng, Adolfo G. Grushin, Karl Landsteiner, Bernd Gotsmann, Fabian Menges, et al. 2017. 'Experimental Signatures of the Mixed Axial-Gravitational Anomaly in the Weyl Semimetal NbP'. *Nature* 547, no. 7663: 324–27. DOI: 10.1038/nature23005.

Gordillo, Gastón. 2014. 'The Oceanic Void: The Eternal Becoming of Liquid Space'. *Space and Politics,* April 3. http://spaceandpolitics.blogspot.co.uk/2014/04/the-oceanic-void.html.

Gottlieb, Bruce, Lorraine E. Chalifour, Benjamin Mitmaker, Nathan Sheiner, Daniel Obrand, Cherrie Abraham, Melissa Meilleur, Tomoko Sugahara, Ghassan Bkaily, and Morris Schweitzer. 2009. 'BAK1 Gene Variation and Abdominal Aortic Aneurysms'. *Human Mutation* 30, no. 7: 1043–47. DOI: 10.1002/humu.21046.

Gould, Stephen Jay. 1979. 'A Quahog is a Quahog'. *Natural History* 88, no. 7: 18–26.

Gould, Stephen Jay. 1981. *The Mismeasure of Man.* New York: W.W. Norton and Company.

Gould, Stephen Jay. 1989. *Wonderful Life: The Burgess Shale and the Nature of History.* New York: W.W. Norton.

Gould, Stephen Jay. 1994. 'The Evolution of Life on Earth'. *Scientific American* 271, no. 4: 84.

Gould, Stephen Jay. 2007. *Punctuated Equilibrium.* Cambridge: Harvard University Press.

Gould, Stephen Jay and Richard C. Lewontin. 1979. 'The Spandrels of San Marco and the Panglossian Paradigm: A Critique of the Adaptationist Programme'. *Proceedings of the Royal Society of London B, Biological Sciences* 205, no. 1161: 581–98. DOI: 10.1098/rspb.1979.0086.

Gramsch, Alexander. 2013. 'Treating Bodies: Transformative and Communicative Practice'. In *The Oxford Handbook of the Archaeology of Death and Burial,* edited by Liv Nilsson Stutz and Sarah Tarlow, 459–74. Oxford: Oxford University Press.

Grannan, Katy. 2013. 'The Mermaids of Weeki Wachee Springs'. *New York Times Magazine,* July 5. https://www.nytimes.com/video/magazine/100000002313563/the-mermaids-of-weeki-wachee-springs.html.

Grass, Günter. 2008. *Peeling the Onion.* Translated by Michael Heim. London: Harvill Secker.

Grass, Günter. 2010. *The Tin Drum.* Translated by Ralph Manheim. London: Vintage Books.

Gunter, Chris and Ritu Dhand. 2002. 'Human Biology by Proxy'. *Nature* 420, no. 6915: 509. DOI: 10.1038/420509a.

Gymiah, David Dunkley. 2009. 'Preview to SCi Fi London – Rachel Armstrong @viewmagazine.tv'. *Vimeo,* May 3. https://vimeo.com/4455066.

Haeckel, Ernst. 1888. 'Report on the Siphonophora'. In *Report of the Scientific Results of the Voyage of H.M.S. Challenger. Zoology* 28: 234.

Haldane, John Scott. 1917. *Organism and Environment: As illustrated by the physiology of breathing.* New Haven: Yale University Press.

Haldane, John Burdon Sanderson. 1929. 'The Origin of Life'. *Rationalist Annual* 148: 3–10.

Haldane, John Burdon Sanderson. 1937. 'The Biochemistry of the Individual'. In *Perspectives in Biochemistry: Thirty-One Essays Presented to Sir Frederick Gowland Hopkins by Past and Present Members of His Laboratory,* edited by Joseph Needham and David E. Green, 1–10. Cambridge: Cambridge University Press.

Hamblyn, Richard. 2001. *The Invention of Clouds: How an Amateur Meteorologist Forged the Language of the Skies.* London: Picador.

Hameroff, Stuart, and Roger Penrose. 2014. 'Consciousness in the Universe: A Review of the 'Orch OR' Theory'. *Physics of Life Reviews* 11, no. 1: 39–78. DOI: 10.1016/j.plrev.2013.08.002.

Hanczyc, Martin M. 2008. 'The Early History of Protocells: The Search for the Recipe of Life'. In *Protocells: Bridging Nonliving and Living Matter,* edited by Steen Rasmussen, Mark A. Bedau, Liaohai Chen, David Deamer, David C. Krakauer, Norman H. Packard and Peter F. Stadler, 3–18. Cambridge: MIT Press.

Hanczyc, Martin M. 2011. 'Structure and the Synthesis of Life'. *Architectural Design* 81, no. 2: 26–33. DOI: 10.1002/ad.1209.

Hanczyc, Martin M., Shelly M. Fujikawa, and Jack W. Szostak. 2003. 'Experimental Models of Primitive Cellular Compartments: Encapsulation, Growth, and Division'. *Science* 302, no. 5645: 618–22. DOI: 10.1126/science.1089904.

Haraway, Donna. 1991. 'A Cyborg Manifesto: Science, Technology and Socialist-Feminism in the Late Twentieth Century'. In *Simians, Cyborgs, and Women: The Reinvention of Nature,* 149–81. New York: Routledge.

Haraway, Donna. 2015. 'Anthropocene, Capitalocene, Plantationocene, Chthulucene: Making Kin'. *Environmental Humanities* 6: 159–65. http://environmentalhumanities.org/arch/vol6/6.7.pdf.

Haraway, Donna. 2016. 'Tentacular Thinking: Anthropocene, Capitalocene, Chthulucene'. *e-flux* 75, September. https://www.e-flux.com/journal/75/67125/tentacular-thinking-anthropocene-capitalocene-chthulucene/.

Hardesty, Larry. 2010. 'Explained: Linear and Nonlinear Systems'. *MIT News,* February 26. http://news.mit.edu/2010/explained-linear-0226.

Harkness, Deborah E. 2008. *John Dee's Conversations with Angels: Cabala, Alchemy, and the End of Nature.* Cambridge: Cambridge University Press.

Harman, Graham. 2004. 'The Metaphysics of Objects: Latour and His Aftermath'. Lecture at Tolerancia/Toleration/Tolerância Conference, January 16, Lima, Peru.

Harman, Graham. 2012. *Weird Realism: Lovecraft and Philosophy.* Winchester: Zero Books.

Harris, Nicholas C., Gregory R. Steinbrecher, Mihika Prabhu, Yoav Lahini, Jacob Mower, Darius Bunandar, Changchen Chen, et al. 2017. 'Quantum Transport Simulations in a Programmable Nanophotonic Processor'. *Nature Photonics* 11, no. 7: 447–52. DOI: 10.1038/nphoton.2017.95.

Hawking, Stephen. 1995. *A Brief History of Time.* London: Bantam.

Hawking, Stephen. 2007. *The Theory of Everything: The Origin and Fate of the Universe.* Mumbai: Jaico.

Hawking, Stephen, Max Tegmark, Stuart Russell, and Frank Wilczek. 2014. 'Transcending Complacency on Superintelligent Machines'. *Huffington Post,* April 19. http://www.huffingtonpost.com/stephen-hawking/artificial-intelligence_b_5174265.html.

Haynes, Gavin. 2017. 'Ambrosia: The Startup Harvesting the Blood of the Young'. *The Guardian,* August 21. https://www.theguardian.com/society/shortcuts/2017/aug/21/ambrosia-the-startup-harvesting-the-blood-of-the-young.

Heaney, Seamus. 2002. 'Death of a Naturalist'. In *Opened Ground: Selected Poems 1966–1996,* 4. London: Faber and Faber.

Heller, Steven. 2015. 'Who Put the Play in Display'. *Print,* April 10. http://www.printmag.com/daily-heller/gardner-displays/.

Hildebrandt, Sabine. 2008. 'Capital Punishment and Anatomy: History and Ethics of an Ongoing Association'. *Clinical Anatomy* 21, no. 1: 5–14. DOI: 10.1002/ca.20571.

Hillman, James. 1991. 'Language'. In *A Blue Fire: Selected Writings by James Hillman,* edited by Thomas Moore, 28–30. New York: Harper Perennial.

Hochner, Binyamin. 2013. 'How Nervous Systems Evolve in Relation to Their Embodiment: What We Can Learn from Octopuses and Other Molluscs'. *Brain, Behavior and Evolution* 82, no. 1, 19–30. DOI: 10.1159/000353419.

Hodges, Nathaniel Dana Carlile. 1889. 'Protoplasm and Its History'. *Science* 14, no. 335: 352–55. https://www.jstor.org/stable/1763753.

Hoel, Erik P. 2017. 'When the Map Is Better Than the Territory'. *Entropy* 19, no. 5: 188. DOI: 10.3390/e19050188.

Homer. 1987. *The Iliad.* Translated by Martin Hammond. London: Penguin Classics.

Hooke, Robert. 2007. *Micrographia: Or Some Physiological Descriptions of Minute Bodies Made by Magnifying Glasses with Observations and Inquiries Thereupon.* New York: Cosimo Classics.

Hopkins, Ellen. 2008. *Identical.* New York: Margaret K. McElderry Books.

Hou, Zhipeng, Weijun Ren, Bei Ding, Guizhou Xu, Yue Wang, Bing Yang, Qiang Zhang, et al. 2017. 'Observation of Various and Spontaneous Magnetic Skyrmionic Bubbles at Room Temperate in a Frustrated Kagome Magnet with Uniaxial Magnetic Anisotropy'. *Advanced Materials* 29, no. 29: 1701144. DOI: 10.1002/adma.201701144.

Hoving, Hendrik J.T., and Bruce H. Robison. 2012. 'Vampire Squid: Detritivores in the Oxygen Minimum Zone'. *Proceedings of the Royal Society B* 279, no. 1747. DOI: 10.1098/rspb.2012.1357.

Howard, Luke. 1865. *Essay on the Modifications of Clouds.* Third Edition. London: John Churchill & Sons.

Hugill, Andrew. 2012. '*Pataphysics: A Useless Guide.* Cambridge: MIT Press.

Huneman, Philippe, and Denis M. Walsh, eds. 2017. *Challenging the Modern Synthesis: Adaptation, Development and Inheritance.* New York: Oxford University Press.

Hutton, James. 2010. *Theory of the Earth.* New York. Classic Books International.

Huxley, Julian. 1912. *The Individual in the Animal Kingdom.* New York: G.P. Putnam's Sons.

Huxley, Thomas Henry. 1880. *Lay Sermons, Addresses, and Reviews.* New York: Appleton and Company.

Huxley, Thomas Henry. 1884. 'Oysters and the Oyster Question'. *The English Illustrated Magazine* 1: 47–55.

Huxley, Thomas Henry. 1897. 'On the Educational Value of Natural History Sciences [1854]'. In *Science and Education,* edited by Thomas Henry Huxley, 38–64. New York: Appleton.

Hyde, Lewis, and Michael Chabon. 2010. *Trickster Makes This World: Mischief, Myth and Art.* New York: Farrar, Straus and Giroux.

Iida, Fumiya, and Cecilia Laschi. 2011. 'Soft Robotics: Challenges and Perspectives'. *Procedia Computer Science* 7: 99–102. DOI: 10.1016/j.procs.2011.12.030.

Irons, David. 1901. 'Natural Selection in Ethics'. *The Philosophical Review* 10, no. 3: 271–87. DOI: 10.2307/2176263.

Its Liquid Group. 2015. 'Opening: Liquid Cities New York City'. October 25. http://www.itsliquid.com/opening-liquid-cities-new-york-city.html.

Jabr, Ferris. 2014. 'The Improbable – But True – Evolutionary Tale of Flatfishes'. *Nova Next,* May 7. http://www.pbs.org/wgbh/nova/next/evolution/flatfish-evolution/.

James, William. 1890. *The Principles of Psychology.* New York: H. Holt and Company.

Japyassú, Hilton F., and Kevin N. Laland. 2017. 'Extended Spider Cognition'. *Animal Cognition* 20, no. 3: 375–95. DOI: 10.1007/s10071-017-1069-7.

Jarry, Alfred. 1997. *The Exploits and Opinions of Dr. Faustroll.* Cambridge: Exact Change.

Jenny, Hans. 2001. *Cymatics: A Study of Wave Phenomena and Vibration.* Edinburgh: B&W Publishing.

Johnson, Russell. n.d. 'The Last Flea Circus'. *Connected Traveler.* https://connectedtraveler.com/flea-circus-oktoberfest-munich/.

Jonas, Hans. 2001. *The Phenomenon of Life: Toward a Philosophical Biology.* Evanston: Northwestern University Press.

Jones, Rhys, Patrick Haufe, Edward Sells, Pejman Iravani, Vik Olliver, Chris Palmer, and Adrian Bowyer. 2011. 'RepRap: The Replicating Rapid Prototyper'. *Robotica* 29, no. 1: 177–91. DOI: 10.1017/S026357471000069X

Kaiser, Jocelyn. 2014. 'Young Blood Renews Old Mice'. *Science,* May 4. http://www.sciencemag.org/news/2014/05/young-blood-renews-old-mice.

Kaison, Natan-Haim, David Furman, and Yehuda Zeiri. 2017. 'Cavitation-Induced Synthesis of Biogenic Molecules on Primordial Earth'. *ACS Central Science* 3, no. 9: 1041–49. DOI: 10.1021/acscentsci.7b00325.

Katsikis, Georgios, James S. Cybulski, and Manu Prakash. 2015. 'Synchronous Universal Droplet Logic and Control'. *Nature Physics* 11, no. 7: 588–96. DOI: 10.1038/nphys3341.

Kauffman, Stuart A. 2003. 'The Adjacent Possible'. *Edge,* November 9. https://www.edge.org/conversation/stuart_a_kauffman-the-adjacent-possible.

Kauffman, Stuart A. 2008. *Reinventing the Sacred: A New View of Science, Reason, and Religion.* New York: Basic Books.

Kaufman, Marc. 2012. *First Contact: Scientific Breakthroughs in the Hunt for Life Beyond Earth.* New York: Simon & Schuster.

Keartes, Sarah. 2016. 'These Are Not the Russian Mutant Frogs You're Looking For'. *EarthTouch: NewsNetwork,* June 30. https://www.earthtouchnews.com/wtf/mutants-and-freaks/these-are-not-the-russian-mutant-frogs-youre-looking-for/.

Keck, David. 1998. *Angels and Angelology in the Middle Ages.* Oxford: Oxford University Press.

Keller, Evelyn Fox, and David Harel. 2007. 'Beyond the Gene'. *PLoS ONE* 2, no. 11: e1231. DOI: 10.1371/journal.pone.0001231.

Kelly, Kevin. 2006. 'Kevin Kelly'. In *Things We Believe but Cannot Prove,* edited by John Brockman, 207–9. New York: Pocket Books.

Kelvin, William Thomson, Lord. 1879. 'The Sorting Demon of Maxwell'. *Proceedings of the Royal Institution* 9: 113–14.

Kennedy, Maev. 2017. 'Mechanical Silver Swan That Entranced Mark Twain Lands at Science Museum'. *The Guardian,* February 2.

https://www.theguardian.com/artanddesign/2017/feb/02/mechanical-silver-swan-flies-nest-robots-exhibition-science-museum.

Kidspot. 2017. 'Making Mud Pies'. *NewsLifeMedia,* July 3. http://www.kidspot.com.au/things-to-do/activity-articles/making-mud-pies/news-story/a7de624576be1a600bc18f40fd7b28e1.

Kinzer, Stephen. 2002. 'Memory Persists in a Dalí Pavilion Revisited'. *The New York Times,* April 8. http://www.nytimes.com/2002/04/08/arts/memory-persists-in-a-dali-pavilion-revisited.html.

Kluger, Jeffrey. 2017. 'A Peek Inside the Transparent Frog'. *Time,* May 30. http://time.com/4798314/transparent-frog-new-species-amazon/.

Knight, Thomas. 2003. 'Idempotent Vector Design for Standard Assembly of Biobricks'. MIT Synthetic Biology Working Group. http://hdl.handle.net/1721.1/21168.

Kosoff, Maya. 2016. 'Peter Thiel Wants to Inject Himself with Young People's Blood'. *Vanity Fair,* August 1. http://www.vanityfair.com/news/2016/08/peter-thiel-wants-to-inject-himself-with-young-peoples-blood.

Koutsoyiannis, Demetris, and A.N. Angelakis. 2003. 'Hydrologic and Hydraulic Science and Technology in Ancient Greece'. In *Encyclopedia of Water Science,* edited by Bobby Alton Stewart and Terry A. Howell, 415–17. New York: Marcel Dekker.

Kožnjak, Boris. 2015. 'Who Let the Demon Out? Laplace and Boscovich on Determinism'. *Studies in History and Philosophy of Science* 51: 42–52. DOI: 10.1016/j.shpsa.2015.03.002.

Kragh, Helge. 2000. 'Max Planck: The Reluctant Revolutionary'. *Physics World* 13, no. 12: 31–36. DOI: 10.1088/2058-7058/13/12/34.

Kruszelnicki, Karl. 2004. *Great Mythconceptions: The Science Behind the Myths.* Sydney: HarperCollins.

Kuwamura, Kaiko, Takashi Minato, Shuichi Nishio, and Hiroshi Ishiguro. 2015. 'Inconsistency of Personality Evaluation Caused by Appearance Gap in Robotic Telecommunication'. *Interaction Studies* 16, no. 2: 249–71. DOI: 10.1075/is.16.2.10kuw.

Lachmann, Ludwig Maurits. 1977. 'Austrian Economics in the Present Crisis of Economic Thought'. In *Capital, Expectations and the Market Process: Essays on the Theory of the Market Economy,* 25–41. Kansas City: Sheed, Andrews and McMeel.

Lamb, Charles. 2011. *A Dissertation upon Roast Pig.* London: Penguin Books.

Landecker, Hannah. 2013. 'The Metabolism of Philosophy: In Three Parts'. *In Dialectic and Paradox: Configurations of the Third in Mo-*

dernity, edited by Ian Cooper and Bernhard P. Malkmus, 193–224. Bern: Peter Lang.

Langewiesche, William. 2008. 'Stealing Water'. *Vanity Fair,* May 1. http://www.vanityfair.com/news/2008/05/langewiesche200805.

Laplace, Pierre-Simon. 1902. *A Philosophical Essay on Probabilities.* London: John Wiley & Sons.

Laporte, Dominique. 2002. *History of Shit.* Cambridge: MIT Press.

Latour, Bruno. 1993. *We Have Never Been Modern.* Cambridge: Harvard University Press.

Latour, Bruno. 1996. 'On Actor-Network Theory: A Few Clarifications'. *Soziale Welt* 47, no. 4: 369–81. https://www.jstor.org/stable/40878163.

Latour, Bruno. 2013. 'Once Out of Nature: Natural Religion as a Pleonasm'. Gifford Lecture Series, University of Edinburgh. *Footnotes2Plato,* February 26. https://footnotes2plato.com/2013/02/26/bruno-latours-1st-gifford-lecture-once-out-of-nature-natural-religion-as-a-pleonasm/.

Laubichler, Manfred D. and Jane Maienschein, eds. 2007. *From Embryology to Evo–Devo: A History of Developmental Evolution.* Cambridge: MIT Press.

Le Guin, Ursula. 2001. *The Lathe of Heaven.* London: Gollancz.

Learoyd, Phil. 2006. 'A Short History of Blood Transfusion'. *National Blood Service, STT-042,* January. http://www.sld.cu/galerias/pdf/sitios/anestesiologia/history_of_transfusion.pdf.

Leary, Kyree. 2017. 'Silk Spun by Graphene-Fed Spiders Is One of the Strongest Materials on Earth'. *Futurism,* August 31, 2017. https://futurism.com/silk-spun-by-graphene-fed-spiders-is-one-of-the-strongest-materials-on-earth/.

Lederberg, Joshua, and A.T. McCray. 2001. ''Ome Sweet 'Omics: A Genealogical Treasury of Words'. *The Scientist* 15, no. 7: 8.

Ledford, Heidi. 2015. 'CRISPR, the Disruptor'. *Nature* 522, no. 7554, DOI: 10.1038/522020a.

Leduc, Stéphane. 1911. *The Mechanism of Life.* London: William Heinemann.

Lee, Matt. 2011. Oceanic *Ontology and Problematic Thought.* Self-published.

Lefevbre, Henri. 1991. *The Production of Space.* Translated by Donald Nicholson Smith. Oxford: Wiley-Blackwell.

Leggett, Hadley. 2009. '1 Million Spiders Make Golden Silk for Rare Cloth'. *Wired,* September 23. https://www.wired.com/2009/09/spider-silk/.

Lerario, Giovanni, Antonio Fieramosca, Fábio Barachati, Dario Ballarini, Konstantinos S. Daskalakis, Lorenzo Dominici, Milena De Giorgi, et al. 2017. 'Room-Temperature Superfluidity in a Polariton Condensate'. *Nature Physics* 13: 837–41. DOI: 10.1038/NPHYS4147.

Leroi, Armand Marie. 2005. *Mutants: On the Form, Varieties and Errors of the Human Body*. London: Harper Perennial.

Levi, Primo. 1986. 'Primo Levi's Heartbreaking, Heroic Answers to the Most Common Questions He Was Asked About "Survival in Auschwitz"'. *New Republic,* February 17. https://newrepublic.com/article/119959/interview-primo-levi-survival-auschwitz.

Levi, Primo. 2000. *The Periodic Table*. London: Penguin Modern Classics.

Lévi-Strauss, Claude. 1973. *Tristes Tropiques*. Translated by John and Doreen Weightman. London: Jonathan Cape.

Levy, David J. 2002. *Hans Jonas: The Integrity of Thinking*. Columbia: University of Missouri Press.

Lewes, George Henry. 1878. *Physical Basis of the Mind*. London: Trübner & Co.

Lincoln, Don. 2017. 'Huge Underground Lab Seeks to Explain 'Ghosts of the Universe''. *Live Science,* July 21. https://www.livescience.com/59891-underground-neutrino-lab-breaks-ground.html.

Linnaeus, Carl. 1735. *Systema Naturae. Sistens Regna Tria Natura in Classes et Ordines, Genera et Species redacta, Tabulisque Æneis Illustrata. Editio multo auctior & emendatior.* Leiden.

Linnaeus, Carl. 1746. *Fauna Svecica. Sistens Animalia Svecicæ Regni: Qvadrupedia, Aves, Amphibia, Pisces, Insecta, Vermes, Distributa per Classes & Ordines, Genera & Species. Cum Differentiis Specierum, Synonymis Autorum, Nominibus Incolarum, Locis Habitationum, Descriptionibus Insectorum.* Stockholm.

Linnaeus, Carl. 1758. *Systema Naturae*. Tenth Edition. Holmiae: Laurentii Salvii.

Living Architecture. 2016. 'Living Architecture LIAR – Transform Our Habitats from Inert Spaces into Programmable Sites'. http://livingarchitecture-h2020.eu.

Locke, John. 1976. *Political Writings*. Harmondsworth: Penguin.

Loerting, Thomas, Violeta Fuentes-Landete, Philip H. Handle, Markus Seidl, Katrin Amann-Winkel, Catalin Gainaru, and Roland Böhmer. 2015. 'The Glass Transition in High-Density Amorphous Ice'. *Journal of Non-Crystalline Solids* 407: 423–30. DOI: 10.1016/j.jnoncrysol.2014.09.003.

Loff, Sarah. 2017. 'Rains of Terror on Exoplanet HD 189733b'. *NASA*, August 7. https://www.nasa.gov/image-feature/rains-of-terror-on-exoplanet-hd-189733b.

Logan, William Bryant. 2007. *Dirt: The Ecstatic Skin of the Earth*. New York: W.W. Norton.

Logan, William Bryant. 2012. *Air: The Restless Shaper of the Earth*. New York: W.W. Norton.

Loke, Y.W. 2013. *Life's Vital Link*. Oxford: Oxford University Press.

Lokhorst, Gert-Jan. 2005. 'Descartes and the Pineal Gland'. *Stanford Encyclopedia of Philosophy*. https://plato.stanford.edu/entries/pineal-gland/.

Lorenz, Edward N. 1963. 'Deterministic Nonperiodic Flow'. *Journal of the Atmospheric Sciences* 20: 130–41. DOI: 10.1175/1520-0469(1963)020<0130:DNF>2.0.CO;2.

Loria, Kevin and Dave Mosher. 2017. 'NASA Has Photographed a Pearly White Storm on Jupiter That's Nearly as Big as Earth'. *Business Insider UK*, December 14. http://uk.businessinsider.com/jupiter-photo-pearls-nasa-juno-2016-12.

Louis, Godfey, and A. Santhosh Kumar. 2006. 'The Red Rain Phenomenon of Kerala and Its Possible Extraterrestrial Origin'. *Astrophysics* 302: 175–87. DOI: 10.1007/s10509-005-9025-4.

Love, Robert. 2013. 'Houdini's Greatest Trick: Debunking Medium Mina Crandon'. *Mental Floss*, October 31. http://mentalfloss.com/article/53424/houdinis-greatest-trick-debunking-medium-mina-crandon.

Lovecraft, H.P. 2002. *The Call of Cthulhu and Other Weird Stories*. London: Penguin Classics.

Lovelock, James E. 1979. *Gaia: A New Look at Life on Earth*. Oxford: Oxford University Press.

Lucretius. 2007. *On the Nature of Things*. Translated by Alicia Stallings. London: Penguin Classics.

Ludmir, Ethan B. and Lynn W. Enquist. 2009. 'Viral Genomes Are Part of the Phylogenetic Tree of Life'. *Nature Reviews Microbiology* 7, no. 8: 615. DOI: 10.1038/nrmicro2108-c4.

MacDorman, Karl F., and Debaleena Chattopadhyay. 2016. 'Reducing Consistency in Human Realism Increases the Uncanny Valley Effect; Increasing Category Uncertainty Does Not'. *Cognition* 146: 190–205. DOI: 10.1016/j.cognition.2015.09.019.

MacIsaac, Tara. 2014. 'Ectoplasm (Ghost Slime) Seriously Studied by a Nobel Prize Laureate and Other Scientists'. *The Epoch Times*, August 10. http://www.theepochtimes.com/n3/862611-ectoplasm-ghost-slime-seriously-studied-by-a-nobel-prize-laureate-and-other-scientists/.

Maeda, Shingo, Yusuke Hara, Ryo Yoshia, and Shuji Hashimoto. 2007. 'Chemical Robot – Design of Self-Walking Gel'. In *IEEE International Conference on Intelligent Robots and Systems*: 2150–55. DOI: 10.1109/IROS.2007.4399392.

Main, Douglas. 2013. 'Pufferfish Love Explains Mysterious Underwater Circles'. *Live Science,* October 2, 2013. https://www.livescience.com/40132-underwater-mystery-circles.html.

Margulis, Lynn, and Dorion Sagan. 1995. *What Is Life? The Eternal Enigma.* Berkeley: University of California Press.

Marine Biodiversity Hub. 2017. 'The Faceless Fish Looks Happier and Heartier Than It Did in 1887'. *Marine Biodiversity Hub,* May 31. https://www.nespmarine.edu.au/faceless-fish-looks-happier-and-heartier-it-did-1887.

Maritain, Jacques. 1944. *The Dream of Descartes.* New York: Philosophical Library.

Marshall, Michael. 2013. 'Bubbles of Fat Hint at Origin of Reproduction'. *New Scientist* 217, no. 2899: 6–7. DOI: doi.org/10.1016/S0262-4079(13)60074-3.

Martin, Glen. 2000. 'Vandals Slash Giant Redwood: Tree-Sitter Julia Butterfly Hill's Former Home Chain-Sawed'. *SFGate,* November 28. http://www.sfgate.com/green/article/Vandals-Slash-Giant-Redwood-Tree-sitter-Julia-3302945.php.

Martin, William, and Michael J. Russell. 2007. 'On the Origin of Biochemistry at an Alkaline Hydrothermal Vent'. *Philosophical Transactions of the Royal Society B* 362, no. 1486: 1887–926. DOI: 10.1098/rstb.2006.1881.

Martinez, C.M. and M.L.J. Stiassny. 2017. 'Can an Eel Be a Flatfish? Observations on Enigmatic Asymmetrical Heterenchelyids from the Guinea Coast of West Africa'. *Journal of Fish Biology* 91, no. 2: 673–78. DOI: 10.1111/jfb.13365.

Martinez, Daniel E. 1998. 'Mortality Patterns Suggest Lack of Senescence in Hydra'. *Experimental Gerontology* 33, no. 3: 217–25. DOI: 10.1016/S0531-5565(97)00113-7.

Markey, Sean. 2003. 'Monkeys Show Sense of Fairness, Study Says'. *National Geographic,* September 17. https://news.nationalgeographic.com/news/2003/09/0917_030917_monkeyfairness.html.

Maturana, Humberto R. and Francisco J. Varela. 1928. *Autopoiesis and Cognition.* Dordrecht: D. Reidel.

Maxwell, James Clerk. 1872. *Theory of Heat*. London: Longmans, Green & Co.

Maxwell, James Clerk. 1878. 'Ether'. *Encyclopædia Britannica,* Ninth Edition, Volume 8: 568–72.

Mayr, Ernst. 2004. *What Makes Biology Unique? Considerations on the Autonomy of a Scientific Discipline*. New York: Cambridge University Press.

McCammon, Robert R. 1992. *Boy's Life*. New York: Pocket Books.

McCay, Clive Maine, Frank Pope, Wanda Lunsford, Gladys Sperling, and P. Sambhavaphol. 1957. 'Parabiosis between Old and Young Rats'. *Gerontologica* 1: 7–17.

McGowan, Kat. 2014. 'How Life Made the Leap from Single Cells to Multicellular Animals'. *Wired,* August 1. https://www.wired.com/2014/08/where-animals-come-from/.

Medlock, Ben. 2017. 'The Body Is the Missing Link for Truly Intelligent Machines'. *Aeon,* March 14. https://aeon.co/ideas/the-body-is-the-missing-link-for-truly-intelligent-machines.

Meillassoux, Quentin. 2007. 'Subtraction and Contraction: Deleuze, Immanence, and Matter and Memory'. In *Collaps, Volume III: Unknown Deleuze*, edited by Robin Mackay, 63–107. Falmouth: Urbanomic.

Melville, Herman. 1992. *Moby Dick*. London: Wordsworth Classics.

Merz, Theo. 2013. 'Schrödinger's Cat Explained'. *The Telegraph,* August 12. http://www.telegraph.co.uk/technology/google/google-doodle/10237347/Schrodingers-Cat-explained.html.

Meyer, Marvin, and Harold Bloom. 1992. *The Gospel of Thomas: The Hidden Sayings of Jesus*. San Francisco: Harper Collins.

Meyers, Jason. 2015. 'War and the Weather: Why We Call Them Fronts'. *WCPO,* December 7. http://www.wcpo.com/storm-shield/storm-shield-featured/war-and-the-weather-why-we-call-them-fronts.

'Microsoft 'Deeply Sorry' for Racist and Sexist Tweets by AI Chatbot'. 2016. *The Guardian,* March 26. https://www.theguardian.com/technology/2016/mar/26/microsoft-deeply-sorry-for-offensive-tweets-by-ai-chatbot.

Mjoseth, Jeannine. 2012. 'Bioluminescent Comb Jellies Begin to Shed Light on the Evolution of Vision'. *National Human Genome Research Institute*. https://www.genome.gov/27551984/2012-news-feature-bioluminescent-comb-jellies-begin-to-shed-light-on-the-evolution-of-vision/.

Moelling, Karin. 2013. 'What Contemporary Viruses Tell Us About Evolution: A Personal View'. *Archives of Virology* 158, no. 9, 1833–48. DOI: 10.1007/s00705-013-1679-6.

Mohammed, Hisham, Irene Hernando-Herraez, Aurora Savino, Antonio Scialdone, Iain Macaulay, Carla Mulas, Tamir Chandra, et al. 2017. 'Single-Cell Landscape of Transcriptional Heterogeneity and Cell Fate Decisions During Mouse Early Gastrulation'. *Cell Reports* 20, no. 5: 1215–28. DOI: 10.1016/j.celrep.2017.07.009.

Montgomery, Sy. 2015. *Soul of an Octopus: A Surprising Exploration into the Wonder of Consciousness.* New York: Atria.

Mørch, Hedda Hassel. 2017. 'Is Matter Conscious? Why the Central Problem in Neuroscience Is Mirrored in Physics'. *Nautilus,* April 6. http://nautil.us/issue/47/consciousness/is-matter-conscious.

Moreno, Alvaro, and Matteo Mossio. 2015. *Biological Autonomy: A Philosophical and Theoretical Enquiry.* Dordrecht: Springer.

Morgan, Thomas Hunt. 1910. 'Chromosomes and Heredity'. *American Naturalist* 44, no. 524: 449–96. DOI: 10.1086/279163.

Morton, Timothy. 2010. *The Ecological Thought.* Cambridge: Harvard University Press.

Morton, Timothy. 2013. *Hyperobjects: Philosophy and Ecology After the End of the World.* Minneapolis: University of Minnesota Press.

Mottl, Michael J., Brian T. Glazer, Ralf I. Kaiser, and Karen J. Meech. 2007. 'Water and Astrobiology'. *Geochemistry* 67, no. 4: 253–82. DOI: 10.1016/j.chemer.2007.09.002.

Müller, Gerd B. 2007. 'Evo-Devo: Extending the Evolutionary Synthesis'. *Nature Reviews Genetics* 8: 943–49. DOI: 10.1038/nrg2219.

Museum of Awful Food. 2006. 'Hagfish-Slime Scones'. March 21. http://ewewgross.blogspot.co.uk/2006/03/hagfish-slime-scones.html.

Musser, George. 2017. 'A Defense of the Reality of Time'. *Quanta Magazine,* May 16. https://www.quantamagazine.org/a-defense-of-the-reality-of-time/.

National Geographic. 2011. 'Blue Whales and Communication'. *National Geographic,* March 26. http://www.nationalgeographic.com.au/science/blue-whales-and-communication.aspx.

Nature News. 1946. 'Heterogenesis and the Origin of Viruses'. *Nature,* 158: 406–7. DOI: 10.1038/158406a0.

Nature Reviews Microbiology. 2011. 'Microbiology by Numbers'. *Nature Reviews Microbiology* 9: 628. DOI: 10.1038/nrmicro2644.

Neal, David T., and Tanya L. Chartrand. 2011. 'Embodied Emotion Perception: Amplifying and Dampening Facial Feedback Modulates Emotion Perception Accuracy'. *Social Psychological and Personality Science* 2, no. 6: 673–78. DOI: 10.1177/1948550611406138.

Nealson, Kenneth H., Terry Platt, and J. Woodland Hastings. 1970. 'Cellular Control of the Synthesis and Activity of the Bacterial Luminescence System'. *Journal of Bacteriology* 104, no. 1: 313–22.

Negarestani, Reza. 2008. *Cyclonopedia: Complicity with Anonymous Materials.* Melbourne: re.press.

Negarestani, Reza. 2014. *Torture Concrete: Jean-Luc Moulène and the Protocol of Abstraction.* New York: Sequence Press.

Negroponte, Nicholas. 1996. *Being Digital.* New York: Knopf Double-day.

Neugroschel, Joachim. 2006. *The Golem: A New Translation of the Classic Play and Selected Short Stories.* New York: W.W. Norton & Company.

Neveu, Marc, Hyo-Joong Kim, and Steven A. Benner. 2013. 'The 'Strong' RNA World Hypothesis: Fifty Years Old'. *Astrobiology* 13, no. 4, 391–403. DOI: 10.1089/ast.2012.0868.

New York Times. 1907. 'Soul Has Weight, Physician Thinks'. March 11. https://timesmachine.nytimes.com/timesmachine/1907/03/11/106743221.pdf.

Newman, Lex. 2001. 'Unmasking Descartes's Case for the Bête Machine Doctrine'. *Canadian Journal of Philosophy* 31, no. 3: 369–426.

Newton, Isaac. 2007. 'Original Letter from Isaac Newton to Richard Bentley'. *The Newton Project.* http://www.newtonproject.ox.ac.uk/view/texts/normalized/THEM00258.

Nicholson, Daniel J. 2013. 'Organisms ≠ Machines'. *Studies in History and Philosophy of Biological and Biomedical Sciences* 44: 669–78. DOI: 10.1016/j.shpsc.2013.05.014.

Nicholson, Daniel J. 2018. 'Reconceptualizing the Organism: From Complex Machine to Flowing Stream'. In *Everything Flows: Towards a Processual Philosophy of Biology,* edited by Daniel J. Nicholson and John Dupré, 139–166. Oxford: Oxford University Press.

Nitschke, Wolfgang, and Michael J. Russell. 2013. 'Beating the Acetyl Coenzyme A-Pathway to the Origin of Life'. *Philososophical Transactions of the Royal Socciety B* 368, no. 1622: 20120258. DOI: 10.1098/rstb.2012.0258.

Norman, Jeremy. 2017. 'Georgius Agricola Issues De Re Metallica, the Most Famous Classic on Mining and Metallurgy (1556)'. *HistoryofInformation.com.* http://www.historyofinformation.com/expanded.php.

Novak, Marcos. 1992. 'Liquid Architectures in Cyberspace'. In *Cyberspace: First Steps,* edited by Michael Benedikt, 272–85. Cambridge: MIT Press.

Novak, Matt. 2011. 'Weather Control as a Cold War Weapon'. *Smithsonian.com,* December 5. http://www.smithsonianmag.com/history/weather-control-as-a-cold-war-weapon-1777409/.

Nowak, Ronald M. 1999. *Walker's Mammals of the World,* Volume I. Baltimore: Johns Hopkins University Press.

NurrieStearns, Mary. 2017. 'The Soul's Code: An Interview with James Hillman'. *Personal Transformation.* http://www.personaltransformation.com/james_hillman.html.

Nuwer, Rachel. 2015. 'The Seven Ways to Have a Near-Death Experience'. *BBC News,* March 3. http://www.bbc.com/future/story/20150303-what-its-really-like-to-die.

Odum, Eugene P. 1993. 'Biosphere 2: A New Kind of Science'. *Science* 260, no. 5110: 878–79.

Oparin, Alexander Ivanovich. 1953. *The Origin of Life.* New York: Dover Publications.

Oppenheimer, Mark. 2014. 'Austin's Moon Towers, beyond 'Dazed and Confused''. *New York Times,* February 13. https://www.nytimes.com/2014/02/16/travel/austins-moon-towers-beyond-dazed-and-confused.html.

Oransky, Ivan. 2011. 'A Flying What? Symbiosis Retracts Paper Claiming New Species Arise from Accidental Mating'. *Retraction Watch,* November 2. https://retractionwatch.com/2011/11/02/a-flying-what-symbiosis-retracts-paper-claiming-new-species-arise-from-accidental-mating/.

Ouellette, Jennifer. 2012. 'Why Did Life Move to the Land? For the View'. *Quanta Magazine,* March 7. https://www.quantamagazine.org/why-did-life-move-to-land-for-the-view-20170307/.

Ouellette, Jennifer. 2017. 'Dark Matter Recipe Calls for One Part Superfluid'. *Quanta Magazine,* June 13. https://www.quantamagazine.org/dark-matter-recipe-calls-for-one-part-superfluid-20170613/.

Ovid. 2004. *Metamorphoses: A New Verse Translation.* Translated by D.A. Raeburn. London: Penguin Books.

PACE Report. 2008. 'Programmable Artificial Cell Evolution. From Chemotaxis towards Soft Robots'. http://www.istpace.org/Web_Final_Report/Applications/Appl_potent_future_cells/descr_app_fut_cells/chemotaxis_soft_robots/index.html.

Paley, William. 2008. *Natural Theology.* Oxford: Oxford University Press.

Palmer, Tom. 1975. *The Famous Flea Act.* Chicago: Magic.

Paradis, James G. 2007. *Samuel Butler, Victorian Against the Grain: A Critical Overview.* Toronto: University of Toronto Press.

Parker, Najja. 2017. 'When You Die, You Can Tell You're Dead, New Study Says'. *AJC,* October 19. https://www.ajc.com/news/world/when-you-die-you-can-tell-you-dead-study-says/Upf8WJo4UjKtAh8UGG3lkM/.

Patton, Kimberley. C. 2006. *The Sea Can Wash Away All Evils: Modern Marine Pollution and the Ancient Cathartic Ocean.* New York: Columbia University Press.

Paulson, Steve. 2017. 'Roger Penrose on Why Consciousness Does Not Compute'. *Nautilus,* May 4, 2017. http://nautil.us//issue/47/consciousness/roger-penrose-on-why-consciousness-does-not-compute.

Pennisi, Elizabeth. 2003. 'DNA's Cast of Thousands'. *Science* 300, no. 5617: 282–85. DOI: 10.1126/science.300.5617.282.

Pennsylvania State University. 2017. 'New Scientist 6: Nicholas Steno'. Department of Geosciences, PennState College of Earth and Mineral Sciences. https://www.e-education.psu.edu/earth520/node/1803.

Pepys, Samuel. 2010. *The Diaries of Samuel Pepys: Volume VII – 1666.* Teddington: The Echo Library.

Peterson, Ivars. 1993. *Newton's Clock: Chaos in the Solar System.* New York: W.H. Freeman and Company.

Petridou, Nicoletta I., Silvia Grigolon, Guillaume Salbreux, Edouard Hannezo, and Carl-Philipp Heisenberg. 2018. 'Fluidization-Mediated Tissue Spreading by Mitotic Cell Rounding and Non-Canonical Wnt Signalling'. *Nature Cell Biology* 21: 169–78. DOI: 10.1038/s41556-018-0247-4.

Phys.org. 2008. 'Scientists Solve Mystery of Glassy Water'. *Phys.org,* January 31. https://phys.org/news/2008-01-scientists-mystery-glassy.html.

Pinker, Steven. 2015. '2015: What Do You Think About Machines That Think? Thinking Does Not Imply Subjugating'. *Edge,* January 21. https://www.edge.org/response-detail/26243.

Plato. 1961. *The Collected Dialogues of Plato Including the Letters.* Princeton: Princeton University Press.

Platt, John. 2012. 'Amazing Underwater 'Crop Circles' Spun by Japanese Puffer Fish'. *MNN,* September 25,. https://www.mnn.com/earth-matters/animals/stories/amazing-underwater-crop-circles-spun-by-japanese-puffer-fish.

Pliny the Elder. 1991. *Natural History.* London: Penguin Classics.

Plot, Robert. 1677. *The Natural History of Oxfordshire, Being an Essay toward the Natural History of England.* Oxford: Theater; London Mr. S. Millers.

Pollan, Michael. 2013. 'The Intelligent Plant: Scientists Debate a New Way of Understanding Flora'. *The New Yorker,* December 23. http://www.newyorker.com/magazine/2013/12/23/the-intelligent-plant.

Pongracz, Jodie D., David Paetkau, Marsha Branigan, and Evan Richardson. 2017. 'Recent Hybridization between a Polar Bear and Grizzly Bears in the Canadian Arctic'. *Arctic* 70, no. 2: 151–60. DOI: 10.14430/arctic4643.

Poppenhaeger, K., J.H.M.M. Schmitt, and S.J. Wolk. 2013. 'Transit Observations of the Hot Jupiter HD 189733b at X-Ray Wavelengths'. *The Astrophysical Journal* 773, no. 1, art. 62. DOI: 10.1088/0004-637X/773/1/62.

Popular Miscellany. 1878. 'Spider-Architecture'. *The Popular Science Monthly* 14: 247.

Prigogine, Ilya. 1997. *The End of Certainty: Time, Chaos and the New Laws of Nature.* New York: Free Press.

Prigogine, Ilya. n.d. 'The Arrow of Time'. Inaugural lecture, 'The Chaotic Universe' workshop, Pescara, Italy. *IcraNetwork.* http://www.icra.it/publications/books/prigogine/motivation.htm.

Priye, Aashish, Yungcheng Yu, Yassin A. Hassan, and Victor M. Ugaz. 2016. 'Synchronized Chaotic Targeting and Acceleration of Surface Chemistry in Prebiotic Hydrothermal Microenvironments'. *Proceedings of the National Academy of Sciences of the United States of America* 114, no. 6: 1275–80. DOI: 10.1073/pnas.1612924114.

Prodhan, Georgina. 2016. 'Europe's Robots to Become 'Electronic Persons' under Draft Plan'. *Reuters,* June 21. http://www.reuters.com/article/us-europe-robotics-lawmaking-idUSKCN0Z72AY.

Proust, Marcel. 2003. *In Search of Lost Time: Sodom and Gomorrah.* London: Penguin Modern Classics.

Pruned. 2012. 'Gardens as Crypto-Water Computers'. *Pruned,* January 23. http://pruned.blogspot.co.uk/2012/01/gardens-as-crypto-water-computers.html.

Radford, Benjamin. 2014. 'Raining Frogs & Fish: A Whirlwind of Theories'. *Live Science,* April 10. https://www.livescience.com/44760-raining-frogs.html.

Rajgopal, K.S. 2015. 'Unravelling the 'Blood Rain' Mystery'. *The Hindu,* April 1. http://www.thehindu.com/sci-tech/science/unravelling-the-blood-rain-mystery/article7057859.ece.

Ray, Matthew B. 1934. 'The Hippocratic Tradition: The Hippocratic Writings – Continued'. *Postgraduate Medical Journal* 10, no. 101: 116–22. DOI: 10.1136/pgmj.10.101.116.

Rayleigh, John William Strutt, Lord. 1916. 'On the Convective Currents in a Horizontal Layer of Fluid When the Higher Temperature Is on the Under Side'. *Philosophical Magazine and Journal of Science* 32, no. 192: 529–46.

Razavy, Mohsen. 2003. *Quantum Theory of Tunneling*. Singapore: World Scientific.

Reid, Robert G.B. 2007. *Biological Emergences: Evolution by Natural Experiment*. Cambridge: MIT Press.

Reigner, Michael. 2016. 'The Man Who Gave Himself Away'. *Mosaic,* September 12. https://mosaicscience.com/story/George-Price-altruism-equation/.

Revkin, Andrew C. 2013. 'When Is a Person Not a Human? When It's a Dolphin, or Chimp, or…'. *New York Times,* April 10. https://dotearth.blogs.nytimes.com/2013/04/10/when-is-a-person-not-a-human-when-its-a-dolphin-or-chimp-or/.

Reynolds, Pamela L. 2018. 'Seagrass and Seagrass Beds'. *Ocean Portal.* http://ocean.si.edu/seagrass-and-seagrass-beds.

Richet, Charles. 2003. 'Various Reflections on the Sixth Sense: A Few Phenomena That May Be Connected to a Sixth Sense'. *SurvivalAfterDeath.info.* http://www.survivalafterdeath.info/articles/richet/reflections.htm.

Richet, Charles. 2010. *Thirty Years of Psychical Research*. Whitefish: Kessinger Publishing.

Rimbaud, Arthur. 2004a. *Selected Poems and Letters*. Translated by Jeremy Harding and John Sturrock. London: Penguin Classics.

Rimbaud, Arthur. 2004b. *I Promise to Be Good: The Letters of Arthur Rimbaud: II*. Translated by Wyatt Alexander Mason. New York: Modern Library.

Rimbaud, Arthur. 2005. 'Farewell'. In *Rimbaud: Complete Works, Selected Letters: A Bilingual Edition,* translated by Wallace Fowlie. Chicago: University of Chicago Press.

Ritzer, George, and Barry Smart. 2001. *Handbook of Social Theory*. London: Sage Publications.

Roach, John. 2006. 'Grizzly-Polar Bear Hybrid Found – But What Does It Mean?' *National Geographic,* May 16. https://www.nationalgeographic.com/animals/2006/05/grizzly-polar-bear-hybrid-animals/.

Rose, Michael R. and Todd H. Oakley. 2007. 'The New Biology: Beyond the Modern Synthesis'. *Biology Direct* 2, no. 30. DOI: 10.1186/1745-6150-2-30.

Rose, Nikolas. 2006. *The Politics of Life Itself: Biomedicine, Power, and Subjectivity in the Twenty-First Century*. Princeton: Princeton University Press.

Rosen, Robert. 1991. *Life Itself: A Comprehensive Inquiry into the Nature, Origin, and Fabrication of Life*. New York: Columbia University Press.

Rosenthal, Bernice Glatzer. 2002. *New Myth, New World: From Nietzsche to Stalinism*. University Park: Pennsylvania State University Press.

Rousseau, Bryant. 2016. 'In New Zealand, Lands and Rivers Can Be People (Legally Speaking)'. *New York Times,* July 13. https://www.nytimes.com/2016/07/14/world/what-in-the-world/in-new-zealand-lands-and-rivers-can-be-people-legally-speaking.html.

Rukeyser, Muriel. 1968. *The Speed of Darkness*. New York: Random House.

Ruse, Michael. 2013. *The Gaia Hypothesis: Science on a Pagan Planet*. Chicago: University of Chicago Press.

Ruskin, John. 1900. *Fors Clavigera: Letters to the Workmen and Labourers of Great Britain (1894),* Vol 1. Boston: Jefferson Press.

Russell, Bertrand. 1920. *Introduction to Mathematical Philosophy*. New York: Macmillan Co.

Russell, Edward Stuart. 1924. *The Study of Living Things: Prolegomena to a Functional Biology*. London: Methuen.

Salter, James. 1975. *Light Years*. New York: Vintage International.

Sample, Ian. 2015. 'Can We Reverse the Ageing Process by Putting Young Blood into Older People?' *The Guardian,* August 4. https://www.theguardian.com/science/2015/aug/04/can-we-reverse-ageing-process-young-blood-older-people.

Sandburg, Carl. 1970. *The Complete Poems of Carl Sandburg*. Orlando: Harcourt Brace International.

Sapp, Jan. 1983. 'The Struggle for Authority in the Field of Heredity, 1900-1932: New Perspectives on the Rise of Genetics'. *Journal of the History of Biology* 16, no. 3: 311–42. https://www.jstor.org/stable/4330861.

Sataline, Suzanne, and Ian Sample. 2018. 'Scientist in China Defends Human Embryo Gene Editing'. *The Guardian,* November 28. https://www.theguardian.com/science/2018/nov/28/scientist-in-china-defends-human-embryo-gene-editing.

Scanlan, John. 2005. *On Garbage*. London: Reaktion.

Schoenheimer, Rudolf. 1942. *The Dynamic State of Body Constituents*. Cambridge: Harvard University Press.

Schopf, Thomas J.M. 1984. 'Rates of Evolution and the Notion of 'Living Fossils''. *Annual Review of Earth and Planetary Sciences* 12: 245–92. DOI: 10.1146/annurev.ea.12.050184.001333.

Schrödinger, Erwin. 1995. *The Interpretation of Quantum Mechanics: Dublin Seminars (1949–1955) and Other Unpublished Essays*. Woodbridge: Ox Bow Press.

Schrödinger, Erwin. 2012. *What Is Life? With Mind and Matter And Autobiographical Sketches*. Cambridge: Cambridge University Press.

Schultz, Stanley G. 2003. 'The Internal Environment'. In *Essential Medical Physiology*, edited by Leonard R. Johnson, 3–10. San Diego: Elsevier Academic Press.

Scoles, Sarah. 2016. 'How Vera Rubin Confirmed Dark Matter'. *Astronomy Magazine*, October 4. http://www.astronomy.com/news/2016/10/vera-rubin.

Scudellari, Megan. 2015. 'Ageing Research: Blood to Blood'. *Nature* 517, no. 7535: 426–29. DOI: 10.1038/517426a.

Sebé-Pedrós, Arnau, Manuel Irimia, Javier del Campo, Helena Parra-Acero, Carsten Russ, Chad Nusbaum, Benjamin J. Blencowe, and Iñaki Ruiz-Trillo. 2013. 'Regulated Aggregative Multicellularity in a Close Unicellular Relative of Metazoan'. *eLife*: e01287. DOI: 10.7554/eLife.01287.

Senter, Phil, Uta Mattox, and Eid E. Haddad. 2016. 'Snake to Monster: Conrad Gessner's *Schlangenbuch* and the Evolution of the Dragon in the Literature of Natural History'. *Journal of Folklore Research* 53, no. 1: 67–124. DOI: 10.2979/jfolkrese.53.1-4.67.

Serres, Michel. 1996. *Genesis*. Ann Arbor: University of Michigan Press.

Serres, Michel. 2010. *Malfeasance: Appropriation through Pollution?* Translated by Anne-Marie Feenberg-Dibon. Stanford: Stanford University Press.

Serres, Michel. 2016. *The Five Senses: A Philosophy of Mingled Bodies*. London: Bloomsbury Academic.

Service, Robert F. 2016. 'Synthetic Microbe Lives with Fewer Than 500 Genes'. *Science*, March 24. http://www.sciencemag.org/news/2016/03/synthetic-microbe-lives-less-500-genes.

Serwane, Friedhelm, Alessandro Mongera, Payam Rowghanian, David A. Kealhofer, Adam A. Lucio, Zachary M. Hockenberry, and

Otger Campàs. 2016. 'In Vivo Quantification of Spatially Varying Mechanical Properties in Developing Tissues'. *Nature Methods* 14, no. 2: 181–86. DOI: 10.1038/nmeth.4101.

Shannon, Claude E., and Warren Weaver. 1949. *The Mathematical Theory of Information*. Urbana: University of Illinois Press.

Shanta, Bhakti Niskama. 2015. 'Life and Consciousness – The Vedāntic View'. *Communicative and Integrative Biology* 8, no. 5: e1085138. DOI: 10.1080/19420889.2015.1085138.

Shapiro, Robert. 1987. *Origins: A Skeptic's Guide to the Creation of Life on Earth*. Toronto: Bantam Books.

Shear, William A., and Alexander J. Werth. 2014. 'The Evolutionary Truth About Living Fossils'. *American Scientist* 102, no. 6: 434–43. DOI: 10.1511/2014.111.434.

Shelley, Mary. 2014. *Frankenstein*. Richmond: Alma Classics.

Shepherd, Robert F., Adam A. Stokes, Jacob Freake, Jabulani Barber, Phillip W. Snyder, Aaron D. Mazzeo, Ludovico Cademartiri, Stephen A. Morin, and George M. Whitesides. 2013. 'Using Explosions to Power a Soft Robot'. *Angewandte Chemie* 52, no. 10: 2892–96. DOI: 10.1002/anie.201209540.

Simon, Matt. 2014a. 'Absurd Creature of the Week: This Beetle Fires Boiling Chemicals Out of Its Bum'. *Wired*, May 16. https://www.wired.com/2014/05/absurd-creature-of-the-week-bombardier-beetle/.

Simon, Matt. 2014b. 'Absurd Creature of the Week: The Beautiful but Deadly Undersea Raver That Digests Its Victims Alive'. *Wired*, October 19. https://www.wired.com/2014/10/absurd-creature-week-comb-jelly-puts-one-hell-laser-show-man/.

Simonite, Tom. 2009. 'Chemical 'Caterpillar' Points to Electronics-Free Robots'. *New Scientist,* April 28. https://www.newscientist.com/article/dn16910-chemical-caterpillar-points-to-electronics-free-robots/.

Singer, Emily. 2015. 'Did Neurons Evolve Twice?' *Quanta Magazine,* March 25. https://www.quantamagazine.org/comb-jelly-neurons-spark-evolution-debate-20150325/.

Sinnott, Edmund W. 1955. *The Biology of the Spirit*. New York: Viking Press.

Sirucek, Stefan. 2014. 'What's That Weird Purple Sea Creature? Explaining Viral Video'. *National Geographic*, September 23. http://voices.nationalgeographic.org/2014/09/23/jellyfish-siphonophore-gulf-of-mexico-science-animals-deep-sea-discovery/.

Sloterdijk, Peter. 2011. *Spheres I: Bubbles*. Translated by Wieland Hoban. Los Angeles: Semiotext(e).

Sloterdijk, Peter. 2014. *Spheres II: Globes*. Translated by Wieland Hoban. Los Angeles: Semiotext(e).

Sloterdijk, Peter. 2016. *Spheres III: Foams*. Translated by Wieland Hoban. Los Angeles: Semiotext(e).

Small, Meredith F. 2008. 'The Human Soul: An Ancient Idea'. *Live Science,* November 28. http://www.livescience.com/7631-human-soul-ancient-idea.html.

Smith, Drew. 2015. *Oyster: A Gastronomic History*. New York: Abrams Books.

Smolin, Lee. 2008. *The Trouble with Physics: The Rise of String Theory, the Fall of a Science and What Comes Next*. London: Penguin.

Snopes.com. 2013. 'Weight of the Soul: Did A Physician Once Attempt to Measure the Weight of the Soul?' *Snopes.com,* April 24. http://www.snopes.com/religion/soulweight.asp.

Sokol, Joshua. 2017a. 'How Nature Solves Problems through Computation'. *Quanta Magazine,* July 6. https://www.quantamagazine.org/how-nature-solves-problems-through-computation-20170706/.

Sokol, Joshua. 2017b. 'The Thoughts of a Spider Web'. *Quanta Magazine,* May 23. https://www.quantamagazine.org/the-thoughts-of-a-spiderweb-20170523/.

Sole-Smith, Virginia. 2013. 'The Last Mermaid Show'. *New York Times Magazine,* July 5. http://www.nytimes.com/2013/07/07/magazine/the-last-mermaid-show.html.

Sowerby, Richard. 2016. *Angels in Early Medieval England*. Oxford: Oxford University Press.

St. John of Damascus. 2017. *The Sacred Writings of St. John of Damascus*. Translated by Stewart Dingwall Fordyce Salmond. Altenmünster: Jazzybee Verlag.

Stalpaert, Christel. 2012. 'Salvador Dalí's Dream of Venus at the 1939 New York World's Fair: Capitalist Funhouse or Surrealist Landmark?' In *Drunk on Capitalism. An Interdisciplinary Reflection on Market Economy, Art and Science,* edited by Robrecht Vanderbeeken, Frederik Le Roy, Christel Stalpaert, and Diederik Aerts, 101–15. New York: Springer.

Stano, Pasquale, and Fabio Mavelli. 2015. 'Protocells Models in Origin of Life and Synthetic Biology'. *Life* 5, no. 4: 1700–1702. DOI: 10.3390/life5041700.

Stapledon, Olaf. 1999. *Star Maker*. London: Gollancz.

Steadman, Ian. 2013. 'Hamburg Unveils World's First Algae-Powered Building'. *Wired*, April 16. http://www.wired.com/design/2013/04/algae-powered-building/.

Steed, Jonathan W, and Jerry L. Atwood. 2009. *Supramolecular Chemistry*. Chichester: J. Wiley & Sons.

Steele, Robert E., Charles N. David, and Ulrich Technau. 2012. 'A Genomic View of 500 Million Years of Cnidarian Evolution'. *Trends in Genetics* 27, no. 1: 7–13. DOI: 10.1016/j.tig.2010.10.002.

Steinberg, Philip, and Kimberley Peters. 2015. 'Wet Ontologies, Fluid Spaces: Giving Depth to Volume through Oceanic Thinking'. *Environment & Planning D: Society & Space* 33, no. 2: 247–64. DOI: 10.1068/d14148p.

Stengers, Isabelle. 2000. 'God's Heart and the Stuff of Life'. *Pli* 9: 86–118. https://plijournal.com/files/stengers_pli_9.pdf.

Stengers, Isabelle, and Michael Lissack. 2004. 'The Challenge of Complexity: Unfolding the Ethics of Science. In Memoriam Ilya Prigogine'. *Emergence: Complexity and Organization* 6, no. 1–2: 92–99.

Stiles, Eugene. 1996. *A Small Book of Angels*. San Francisco: Pomegranate Artbooks.

Stromberg, Joseph. 2012. 'How Does the Tiny Waterbear Survive Outer Space?' *Smithsonian.com*, September 11. http://www.smithsonianmag.com/science-nature/how-does-the-tiny-waterbear-survive-in-outer-space-30891298/.

Subcommission on Quaternary Stratigraphy. 2016. 'Working Group on the 'Anthropocene''. *International Commission on Stratigraphy.* http://quaternary.stratigraphy.org/working-groups/anthropocene/.

Suthers, Roderick A. 1965. 'Acoustic Orientation by Fish-Catching Bats'. *Journal of Experimental Zoology* 158, no. 3: 319–48. DOI: 10.1002/jez.1401580307.

Szostak, Jack W. 2012. 'Attempts to Define Life Do Not Help to Understand the Origin of Life'. *Journal of Biomolecular Structure and Dynamics* 29, no. 4: 599–600. DOI: 10.1080/073911012010524998.

Tatlock, John S.P. 1914. 'Some Mediaeval Cases of Blood-Rain'. *Classical Philology* 9, no. 4: 442–47. https://www.jstor.org/stable/261454.

Taut, Bruno. 1919. *Une couronne pour la ville: Die Stadtkrone*. Village Le Perrey: Editions du Linteau.

Taylor, Tim, Mark Bedau, Alastair Channon, David Ackley, Wolfgang Banzhaf, Guillaume Belson, Emily Dolson, et al. 2016. 'Open-Ended Evolution: Perspectives from the OEE Workshop in York'. *Artificial Life* 22, no. 3: 408–23. DOI: 10.1162/ARTL_a_00210.

Tegmark, Max. 2014. *Our Mathematical Universe: My Quest for the Ultimate Nature of Reality.* London: Allen Lane.

Temperton, James. 2015. 'We Can Now 3D-Print Glass: And It Looks Amazing'. *Wired,* August 21. http://www.wired.co.uk/article/3d-printed-glass-mit-additive-manufacturing.

Teramobile. 2008. 'The First Mobile Terawatt Laser in the World for Atmospheric Studies'. *Teramobile,* March 18. http://www.teramobile.org/teramobile.html.

Thewissen, J.G.M. 2014. *The Walking Whales: From Land to Water in Eight Million Years.* Oakland: University of California Press.

Thewissen, J.G.M., Lisa Noelle Cooper, Mark T. Clementz, Sunil Bajpai, and B.N. Tiwari. 2007. 'Whales Originate from Aquatic Artiodactyls in the Eocene Epoch of India'. *Nature* 450: 1190–94. DOI: 10.1038/nature06343.

Thompson, William Irwin, ed. 1991. *Gaia 2 – Emergence: The New Science of Becoming.* New York: Lindisfarne Press.

Thomson, Helen. 2014. 'Young Blood to Be Used in Ultimate Rejuvenation Trial'. *New Scientist,* August 20. https://www.newscientist.com/article/mg22329831-400-young-blood-to-be-used-in-ultimate-rejuvenation-trial/.

Thomson, J. Arthur. 1925. *Science and Religion.* New York: Scribner's.

Tirard, Stéphane. 2011. 'Haldane's Conception of Origins of Life'. In *Encyclopedia of Astrobiology,* edited by Muriel Gargaud, Ricardo Amils, José Cernicharo Quintanilla, H. James Cleaves II, William M. Irvine, Daniele.L. Pinti, Michel Viso, 724. Berlin: Springer-Verlag.

Tissot, Bernard P. and Dietrich H. Welte. 1978. 'Coal and Its Relation to Oil and Gas'. In *Petroleum Formation and Occurrence,* edited by Bernard P. Tissot and Dietrich H. Welte, 202–24. Berlin: Springer.

Tokarczuk, Olga. 2003. *House of Day, House of Night.* Evanston: Northwestern University Press.

Tokarczuk, Olga. 2010. *Primeval and Other Times.* Prague: Twisted Spoon Press.

Tollefsen, Olav. 2017. 'Learning Computers to Recognize the Differences between Cats and Dogs Using Convolutional Neural Networks'. *Linkedin,* March 13. https://www.linkedin.com/pulse/learning-computers-recognize-differences-between-cats-olav-tollefsen.

Trifonov, Edward N. 2011. 'Vocabulary of Definitions of Life Suggests a Definition'. *Journal of Biomolecular Structure and Dynamics* 29, no. 2: 259–266. DOI: 10.1080/073911011010524992.

Trotter, J.K. 2017. 'Someone Is Trying to Discredit the Story of Peter Thiel's Interest in Young Blood'. *Gizmodo,* June 16. https://gizmodo.com/someone-is-trying-to-discredit-the-story-of-peter-thiel-1796135794.

Tschumi, Bernard. 2012. *Architecture Concepts: Red is Not a Colour.* New York: Rizzoli.

Tsing, Anna Lowenhaupt. 2015. 'A Feminist Approach to the Anthropocene: Earth Stalked by Man'. *YouTube,* November 10. https://www.youtube.com/watch?v=ps8J6a7g_BA.

Tucker, Holly. 2011. 'Blood Lust: The Early History of Transfusion'. *Scientific American,* July 12. https://blogs.scientificamerican.com/guest-blog/blood-lust-the-early-history-of-transfusion/.

Turing, Alan M. 1950. 'Computing Machinery and Intelligence'. *Mind* 59, no. 236: 433–60. DOI: 10.1093/mind/LIX.236.433.

Turing, Alan M. 1952. 'The Chemical Basis of Morphogenesis'. *Philosophical Transactions of the Royal Society B* 237, no. 641: 37–72. DOI: 10.1098/rstb.1952.0012.

Turney, Jon. 2015. *I, Superorganism: Learning to Love Your Inner Ecosystem.* London: Faber and Faber.

United Nations Office for Disaster Risk Reduction. 2012. 'US $6.7 Billion Floodgates to Protect Venice in 2014'. *UNISDR,* December 21. https://www.unisdr.org/archive/30174.

University of Reading. 2014. 'Turing Test Success Marks Milestone in Computing History'. *University of Reading,* June 8. http://www.reading.ac.uk/news-and-events/releases/PR583836.aspx.

Van Gulick, Robert. 2014. 'Consciousness'. *Stanford Encyclopedia of Philosophy.* https://plato.stanford.edu/entries/consciousness/.

Van Kranendonk, Martin J., David W. Deamer, and Tara Djokic. 2017. 'Life on Earth Came from a Hot Volcanic Pool, Not the Sea, New Evidence Suggests'. *Scientific American,* August 1. https://www.scientificamerican.com/article/life-on-earth-came-from-a-hot-volcanic-pool-not-the-sea-new-evidence-suggests/.

van Strien, Marij. 2014. 'On the Origins and Foundations of Laplacian Determinism'. *Studies in History and Philosophy of Science Part A* 45: 24–31. DOI: 10.1016/j.shpsa.2013.12.003.

Varley, John. 1828. *A Treatise on Zodiacal Physiognomy.* London: Printed for the author.

Vedral, Vlatko. 2015. 'Living in a Quantum World'. *Scientific American* 24: 98–103.

Venter, J. Craig. 2007. 'Craig Venter – Life: What a Concept! An Edge Special Event at Eastover Farm'. *Edge,* August 27. https://www.

edge.org/conversation/j_craig_venter-craig-venter—life-what-a-concept.

Vidal, John. 2011. 'Bolivia Enshrines Natural World's Rights with Equal Status For Mother Earth'. *The Guardian,* April 10. https://www.theguardian.com/environment/2011/apr/10/bolivia-enshrines-natural-worlds-rights.

Villarreal, Luis P. 2008. 'Are Viruses Alive?' *Scientific American,* August 8. https://www.scientificamerican.com/article/are-viruses-alive-2004/.

Vivenza, Gloria. 2005. 'The Agent, the Actor and the Spectator: Adam Smith's Metaphors in Recent Literature'. *History of Economic Ideas* 13, no. 1: 37–56. https://www.jstor.org/stable/23723200.

von Bertalanffy, Ludwig. 1933. *Modern Theories of Development: An Introduction to Theoretical Biology.* London: Humphrey Milford: Oxford University Press.

von Bertalanffy, Ludwig. 1950. 'The Theory of Open Systems in Physics and Biology'. *Science* 111, no. 2872: 23–29. DOI: 10.1126/science.111.2872.23.

von Bertalanaffy, Ludwig. 1968. *General System Theory: Foundations, Development, Applications.* New York: Braziller.

Vonnegut, Kurt. 2008. *Cat's Cradle.* London: Penguin Modern Classics.

von Reichenbach, Karl. 2003. *Odic Force: Letters on Od and Magnetism.* Whitefish: Kessinger Publishing Co.

Wachter, Sandra. 2018. 'OII London Lecture: Show Me Your Data and I'll Tell You Who You Are'. *Oxford Internet Institute,* October 30. https://www.oii.ox.ac.uk/videos/oii-london-lecture-show-me-your-data-and-ill-tell-you-who-you-are/.

Wächtershäuser, Günter. 2000. 'Origin of Life: Life as We Don't Know It'. *Science* 289, no. 5483: 1307–8. DOI: 10.1126/science.289.5483.1307.

Waddington, Conrad Hal. 1940. *Organizers and Genes.* Cambridge: Cambridge University Press.

Waddington, Conrad Hal. 1957. *The Strategy of the Genes.* London: George Allen & Unwin.

Wang, Kevin. 2014. 'Origins of Life: A Means to a Thermodynamically Favourable End'. *Yale Scientific,* July 1. http://www.yalescientific.org/2014/07/origins-of-life-a-means-to-a-thermodynamically-favorable-end/.

Watts, Alan. 2014. *The Weather Handbook: An Essential Guide to How Weather Is Formed and Develops.* London: Adlard Coles.

Wells, H.G. 2012. *The Invisible Man.* London: Penguin Classics.

Wheeler, Michael. 2011. 'Martin Heidegger. 2.2.3, Being-in-the-World'. *Stanford Encyclopedia of Philosophy*. https://plato.stanford.edu/entries/heidegger/.

Whewell, William. 1840. *The Philosophy of the Inductive Sciences, Volume Two*. London: John W. Parker.

White, Joshua R., Randall S. Cerveny, and Robert C. Balling. 2012. 'Seasonality in European Red Dust/'Blood' Rain Events'. *American Meteorological Society* 93, no. 4: 471–76. DOI: 10.1175/BAMS-D-11-00142.1.

Whitehead, Alfred North. 1925. *Science and the Modern World*. Cambridge: Cambridge University Press.

Whitehead, Alfred North. 1979. *Process and Reality*. Second Revised Edition. New York: Free Press.

Wickramasinghe, Chandra. 2015. *The Search for our Cosmic Ancestry*. Singapore: World Scientific.

Wigner, Eugene P. 1960. 'The Unreasonable Effectiveness of Mathematics in the Natural Sciences'. *Communications in Pure and Applied Mathematics* 13, no. 1: 1–14. DOI: 10.1002/cpa.3160130102.

Wilczek, Frank. 2017. 'Inside the Knotty World of 'Anyon' Particles'. *Quanta Magazine,* February 28. https://www.quantamagazine.org/how-anyon-particles-emerge-from-quantum-knots-20170228.

Williams, Anna. 2016. 'Hundreds of Genes Seen Sparking to Life Two Days after Death'. *New Scientist,* June 21. https://www.newscientist.com/article/2094644-hundreds-of-genes-seen-sparking-to-life-two-days-after-death/.

Williams, Tom A., and T. Martin Embley. 2014. 'Archaeal 'Dark Matter' and the Origin of Eukaryotes'. *Genome Biology and Evolution* 6: no. 3: 474–81. DOI: 10.1093/gbe/evu031.

Williams, Wendy. 2011. 'So You Think You're Smarter Than a Cephalopod?' *Smithsonian,* May 11. https://ocean.si.edu/ocean-life/invertebrates/so-you-think-youre-smarter-cephalopod.

Williamson, Donald I. 2006a. 'Hybridization in the Evolution of Animal Form and Life-Cycle'. *Zoological Journal of the Linnean Society* 148, no. 4: 585–602. DOI: 10.1111/j.1096-3642.2006.00236.x.

Williamson, Donald I. 2006b. 'Donald Williamson'. In *What We Believe but Cannot Prove,* edited by John Brockman, 187–88. New York: Pocket Books.

Wilson, Edward O. 1990. *Biophilia*. Cambridge: Harvard University Press.

Winegard, T.M. and D.S. Fudge. 2010. 'Deployment of Hagfish Slime Thread Skeins Requires the Transmission of Mixing Forces via

Mucin Strands'. *Journal of Experimental Biology* 213: 1235–40. DOI: 10.1242/jeb.038075.

Wiseman, Richard. 2011. *Paranormality: Why We See What Isn't There.* London: Macmillan.

Wissner-Gross, A.D., and C.E. Freer. 2013. 'Causal Entropic Forces'. *Physical Review Letters* 110, no. 16: 168702. DOI: 10.1103/PhysRevLett.110.168702.

Woese, Carl R. 2004. 'A New Biology for a New Century'. *Microbiology and Molecular Biology Reviews* 68, no. 2: 173–86. DOI: 10.1128/MMBR.68.2.173-186.2004.

Wohlleben, Peter. 2016. *The Hidden Life of Trees: What They Feel, How They Communicate.* Vancouver: Greystone Books.

Wolchover, Natalie. 2014. 'A New Physics Theory of Life'. *Quanta Magazine,* January 22. https://www.quantamagazine.org/20140122-a-new-physics-theory-of-life/.

Wolchover, Natalie. 2016. 'The Case against Dark Matter'. *Quanta Magazine,* November 29. https://www.quantamagazine.org/erik-verlindes-gravity-minus-dark-matter-20161129/.

Wolchover, Natalie. 2017a. 'Physicists Uncover Geometric 'Theory Space''. *Quanta Magazine,* February 23. https://www.quantamagazine.org/using-the-bootstrap-physicists-uncover-geometry-of-theory-space-20170223/.

Wolchover, Natalie. 2017b. 'A Theory of Reality as More Than the Sum of Its Parts'. *Quanta Magazine,* June 1. https://www.quantamagazine.org/a-theory-of-reality-as-more-than-the-sum-of-its-parts-20170601/.

Wolchover, Natalie. 2017c. 'Droplets That 'Come to Life''. *Quanta Magazine,* January 20. https://www.quantamagazine.org/droplets-that-act-like-cells-20170120/.

Woywodt, Alexander, and Akos Kiss. 2002. 'Geophagia: The History of Earth-Eating'. *Journal of the Royal Society of Medicine* 95, no. 2: 143–46. DOI: 10.1177/014107680209500313.

Wyndham, John. 2002. THE DAY OF THE TRIFFIDS. London: Penguin Classics.

Yang, Dayong, Songming Peng, Mark R. Hartman, Tiffany Gupton-Campolongo, Edward J. Rice, Anna Kathryn Chang, Zi Gu, G.Q. Lu, and Dan Luo. 2013. 'Enhanced Transcription and Translation in Clay Hydrogel and Implications for Early Life Evolution'. *Scientific Reports* 3, art. 3165. DOI: 10.1038/srep03165.

Yao, N.Y., A.C. Potter, I.-D. Potirniche, and A. Vishwanath. 2017. 'Discrete Time Crystals: Rigidity, Criticality and Realizations'. *Physical Review Letters* 118, 030401. DOI: 10.1103/PhysRevLett.118.030401.

Yeager, Ashley. 2017. 'Discoveries Fuels Flight over Universe's First Light'. *Quanta Magazine,* May 19. https://www.quantamagazine.org/discoveries-fuel-fight-over-universes-first-light-20170519/.

Yirka, Bob. 2012. 'Researchers Create Gel That Displays Spontaneous Motion (w/Video)'. *Phys.org,* November 12. https://phys.org/news/2012-11-gel-spontaneous-motion-video.html.

Yong, Ed. 2016. 'The Mysterious Thing about a Marvellous New Synthetic Cell'. *The Atlantic,* March 24. https://www.theatlantic.com/science/archive/2016/03/the-quest-to-make-synthetic-cells-shows-how-little-we-know-about-life/475053/.

Young. Sera L., Paul W. Sherman, Julius B. Lucks, and Gretel H. Pelto. 2011. 'Why on Earth? Evaluating Hypotheses about the Physiological Functions of Human Geophagy'. *The Quarterly Review of Biology* 86, no. 2: 97–120. DOI: 10.1086/659884.

Zajonc, Arthur. 1984. 'The Wearer of Shapes: Goethe's Study of Clouds and Weather'. *Orion Nature Quarterly* 3, no. 1: 35–46.

Zenil, Hector. 2013. 'A Behavioural Foundation for Natural Computing and a Programmability Test'. *arXiv.* doi: 10.1007/s13347-012-0095-2

Zhabotinsky, Anatol Markovich. 1964. 'Periodic Processes of Malonic Acid Oxidation in a Liquid Phase'. *Biofizika* 9: 306–11.

Zimmer, Carl. 2007. 'Aliens among Us: Do We Share Earth with Alternative Life Forms?' *Discover Magazine,* June 27. http://discovermagazine.com/2007/jul/aliens-among-us.

Zimmer, Carl. 2012. 'Mammals Made by Viruses'. *Discover Magazine,* February 14. http://blogs.discovermagazine.com/loom/2012/02/14/mammals-made-by-viruses/.

Zimmer, Carl. 2014. 'Strange Findings on Comb Jellies Uproot Animal Family Tree'. *National Geographic,* May 21. http://news.nationalgeographic.com/news/2014/05/140521-comb-jelly-ctenophores-oldest-animal-family-tree-science/.

Zirkle, Conway. 1935. 'The Inheritance of Acquired Characters and the Provisional Hypothesis of Pangenesis'. *The American Naturalist* 69, no. 724: 417–45. https://www.jstor.org/stable/2457042.

Zyga, Lisa. 2017. 'Magnetic Nanoknots Evoke Lord Kelvin's Vortex Theory of Atoms'. *Phys.org,* June 23. https://phys.org/news/2017-06-magnetic-nanoknots-evoke-lord-kelvin.html.